I0034534

REDEFINING STRATEGIC ROUTES TO FINANCIAL RESILIENCE IN ASEAN+3

Edited by Diwa Guinigundo, Masahiro Kawai,
Cyn-Young Park, and Ramkishen S. Rajan

DECEMBER 2021

ASIAN DEVELOPMENT BANK

ADB

Contents

Tables, Figures, and Boxes	vi
Foreword	xii
Preface	xiv
Acknowledgments	xviii
Editors	xx
Authors	xxii

1. Overview of Financial Development and Cooperation in ASEAN+3 — 1

1.1 Introduction — 1
1.2 Financial Openness and Growth: Theory and Evidence — 3
1.3 Evolution of Financial Systems in ASEAN+3 — 7
1.4 The Impact of COVID-19 on Financial Systems — 20
1.5 An Unfinished Agenda: Lessons Learned and the Way Forward — 24
1.6 Conclusion — 32
References — 36

2. Sailing the Same Stormy Seas: Slow-Burn Contagion Risk in ASEAN+3 — 49

2.1 Introduction — 49
2.2 Review of Literature — 52
2.3 Sudden-Stop Contagion Risk in ASEAN+3 Economies — 54
2.4 Concentration Risk of Slow-Burn Contagion in ASEAN+3 Economies — 59
2.5 Global Banking Networks and Shapley Values — 65
2.6 Conclusion: Suggested Policy Measures — 73
References — 79
Appendix — 84

3. **The Global Monetary System and Use of Regional Currencies**   **86**
   in ASEAN+3
   3.1 Introduction   86
   3.2 United States Dollar Dominance and Resilience   87
       in the Global Monetary System
   3.3 ASEAN+3 Economies from the Trilemma Perspective   97
   3.4 Use of Regional Currencies in ASEAN+3 Economies   105
   3.5 ASEAN+3 Policy Initiatives   118
   3.6 Conclusion   139
   References   143

4. **Fintech in ASEAN+3 and Implications for Financial Inclusion**   **160**
   and Financial Stability
   4.1 Introduction   160
   4.2 Development and Current Status of Fintech in Asia   162
   4.3 Current Status of Financial Inclusion in Asia   179
       and Role of Fintech
   4.4 COVID-19 and Fintech Adoption   188
   4.5 Implications of Fintech for Financial Stability   191
   4.6 Administrative and Regulatory Frameworks   198
       for Ensuring Financial Stability   198
   4.7 Implications for Design of Monetary Policy   207
   4.8 Role of Regional Cooperation   209
   4.9 Conclusion   214
   References   217

5. **Financing Sustainable Infrastructure Investment in ASEAN+3**   **227**
   5.1 Introduction   227
   5.2 Role of Public Finance   232
   5.3 Expanding Involvement of the Private Sector   237
   5.4 Crosscutting Issue: Green Finance   255
   5.5 Crosscutting Issue: COVID-19 Pandemic   265
   5.6 Regional Financial Cooperation in Support of Sustainable   272
       Infrastructure Investment
   5.7 Conclusion   274
   References   276

6. **Pension Challenges in Aging Asia**   **281**
   6.1 Introduction   281
   6.2 Aging and the Macroeconomy   282
   6.3 Aging Asia's Challenging Pensions Environment   289

	6.4 Pensions and Regional Cooperation	313
	6.5 Conclusion	353
	References	355
7.	**Regional Financial Cooperation in ASEAN+3: Taking Stock**	**361**
	and Moving Forward	**361**
	7.1 Introduction	361
	7.2 Key Insights and Policy Priorities	362
	7.3 Financial Integration and Regional Safety Nets:	371
	Asia and Europe Compared	371
	7.4 Conclusion	378
	References	379
Index		**382**

Tables, Figures, and Boxes

Tables

1.1	Sovereign Bonds Issuance to Address the Pandemic	21
1.2	Classification of Exchange Rate Arrangements for Selected Asia and Pacific Economies, 2020	26
2.1	International Bank Claims on ASEAN ex-Singapore by Jurisdiction of Lending Banks, 2009 and 2019	62
2.2	International Bank Claims on the People's Republic of China and the Republic of Korea by Jurisdiction of Lending Banks, 2009 and 2019	63
2.3	Cross-Border Bank Loan and Deposit Claims on Residents of Singapore and Hong Kong, China by Location of Banking Office, 2009 and 2019	64
2.4	The Global Network of the Major Creditor Jurisdictions of ASEAN ex-Singapore, the People's Republic of China, and the Republic of Korea	71
2.5	Shapley Values That Account for the Global Banking Network	71
3.1	State of Preparation for Central Bank Digital Currencies in ASEAN+3 Economies	133
4.1	Comparison of Fintech and Conventional Payments in Asia	165
4.2	Value of Digital Payments Transactions, 2020 Estimated	166
4.3	Research and Development in ASEAN+3 Related to Central Bank Digital Currency	175
4.4	Online Alternative Finance Market Value and Development of ASEAN+3	177
4.5	Total Transaction Value of Major Alternative Finance Segments in Asia and the Pacific, 2020	178

4.6   Comparison of Alternative Finance Lending   179
      and Conventional Lending, 2019
4.7   Share of SME Loans in Total Bank Loans, ASEAN   185
4.8   Digital Finance Outstanding, Share of GDP   187
4.9   Fintech-Related Macrofinancial and Microfinancial Risks   192
4.10 Bali Fintech Agenda Elements: Balancing Opportunities and Risks 200
5.1   Estimated Infrastructure Investments and Gaps,   228
      25 Developing Asian Economies, 2016–2020
5.2   Public and Private Infrastructure Investment in Asia, 2010–2014   232
5.3   General Government Gross Fixed Capital Formation in ASEAN+3 233
5.4   General Government Revenue in ASEAN+3   235
5.5   Sources of Private Sector Credit in ASEAN+3   238
5.6   Development of Local Currency Bond Markets, 2001–2011   241
5.7   UNEP Framework and Tools for Mobilizing Private   259
      Finance for Green Projects
5.8   Tools Specific to Upgrading Governance Architecture   260
6.1   Selected Indicators of Pension Systems in ASEAN+3   293
6.2   Pension Systems in Selected ASEAN+3 Economies   294
6.3   Summary of Pension Reforms   307
6.4   Factors That Affect the Adequacy of Pension Benefits   311
6.5   Factors That Affect Sustainability of Pension Benefits   313
6.6   Investment Allocation of the Largest 300 Pension Funds, 2017   321
6.7   Asian Pension Funds' Allocation of Assets, 2017   322
6.8   Pension Assets Returns, 2008 to 2018   322
6.9   Pension Investment Restrictions   329
6.10 Examples of Technology's Social Security Applications   336
6.11 Social Protection for Asian Migrant Workers   352
7.1   Comparing the Main Elements of CMIM and ESM   374

Figures

1.2   Foreign Bank Participation Rates   6
1.1   Foreign Bank Presence in ASEAN+3   6
1.3   Financial Structure in ASEAN+3   11
1.4   Size of Local Currency Bond Markets in ASEAN+3   12
1.5   Outstanding Domestic Public Debt Securities, 1980s to 2010s   13
1.6   Outstanding Domestic Private Debt Securities, 1980s to 2010s   13
1.7   Outstanding International Private Debt Securities, 1980s to 2010s   14
1.8   ASEAN+3 Local Currency Bond Markets, 2007–2020   15
1.9   Investor Profile of Local Currency Government Bonds in ASEAN+3   15
1.10 Average Maturity of ASEAN+3 Local Currency Bonds, 2008–2020   16

1.11 Sector Breakdown of ASEAN+3 Corporate Bond Issuance,   16
     2005–2020
1.12 Degree of Internationalization of Bond Markets in ASEAN+3   17
1.13 US-Dollar-Denominated Nonfinancial Corporate Debt   18
     in ASEAN+3
1.14 Debt Composition of Nonfinancial Corporations   20
     in Emerging Markets
1.15 Export Invoicing Currencies for ASEAN+3   27
1.16 Exchange Rate Movements in ASEAN+3, January–May 2021   28
1.17 Foreign Exchange Reserves in ASEAN+3   29
1.18 Foreign Exchange Reserves in ASEAN+3   30
2.1   How Much Can the Principal Components Explain?   56
2.2   Loadings on the First Principal Component   57
2.3   Current Account Balance, 2017–2019 Average   58
2.4   Credit-to-GDP Gaps, 2015–2019   59
2.5   Calculating the Characteristic Function with Two Banking Systems   69
2.6   Shapley Values for ASEAN ex-Singapore, 2019   71
2.7   Shapley Values for the People's Republic of China   72
     and the Republic of Korea, 2019
3.1   Shares of Major Currencies in International Trade   89
     and Overall International Settlements
3.2   Shares of Major Currencies in Foreign Exchange   90
     Market Turnover and Reserves
3.3   Shares of Major Currencies in Cross-Border Bank   91
     Liabilities and International Debt Securities Issued
3.4   Estimated Currency Blocs with or without   93
     the PRC Yuan, 2011–2015
3.5   GDP and Trade Shares of ASEAN+3 Economies,   97
     United States, and Europe
3.6   Trilemma Triangle   98
3.7   Trilemma Indexes for Japan, the PRC, ASEAN,   100
     and Global Economy Groups, 1970–2018
3.8a Trilemma Triangles for ASEAN+3 Economies   103
     and Global Economy Groups, 1986–2017
3.8b Trilemma Triangles for Selected ASEAN+3 Economies,   104
     1970–2017
3.9   Shares of ASEAN+3 Currencies in Foreign Exchange Market   106
     Turnover and Overall International Settlements
3.10 Shares of US, Home, and ASEAN+3 Currencies   107
     in Trade for Selected ASEAN+3 Economies

3.11 Shares of the US, Home and Other Currencies in Japan,   109
     the Republic of Korea, and Thailand's Trade with Partners, 2020
3.12 Shares of Major Currencies in Cross-Border Bank Liabilities   112
     of the PRC, Japan, the Republic of Korea, and ASEAN
3.13 Shares of Major Currencies in Cross-Border Bank Liabilities   113
     of ASEAN+3 Economies
3.14 Shares of Major and Home Currencies in International Debt   114
     Securities Issued by the PRC, Japan, the Republic of Korea,
     and ASEAN
3.15 Shares of Major and Home Currencies in International Debt   116
     Securities Issued by ASEAN+3 Economies, 2020
3.16 Weights of the US Dollar, Yen, and Yuan   118
     as Anchor Currencies for Selected ASEAN+3 Economies
3.17 Japanese Yen Shares in Trade Invoicing or Settlement   121
     for Indonesia, the Republic of Korea, and Thailand
3.18 US Dollar and Baht Shares in Thai Trade with ASEAN,   123
     Cambodia, the Lao PDR, Myanmar, and Viet Nam, 2020
3.19 Yuan Cross-Border Settlements for International Transactions   124
3.20 Yuan Shares in Trade Invoicing and/or Settlement   125
     for Selected ASEAN+3 Economies
Appendix Figure 3.1   Shares of US Dollar, Home,   149
     and Other Currencies in Trade with Partners
Appendix Figure 3.2   Currency Compositions of Cross-Border   154
     Bank Liabilities, ASEAN+3 Economies
Appendix Figure 3.3   Currency Compositions of International Debt   156
     Securities Issued by ASEAN+3 Economies, 1980–2020
4.1   Growth of Digital Payments Transaction Value in Asia   167
4.2   Penetration Rate of Users of Digital Payments in Asia   168
4.3   Share of Consumers Using Mobile Payments, 2019   168
4.4   Penetration of Users of Digital Payments   169
       in the People's Republic of China
4.5   Share of Adult Population with a Financial Institution Account,   181
       2014 and 2017
4.6   Share of Adult Population Using Digital Payments   181
4.7   Share of Adult Population with a Mobile Money Account   182
4.8   Gaps in Usage and Awareness of Fintech Products   183
       in the PRC and Viet Nam
4.9   Commercial Bank Loans to SMEs   185
4.10 Banked Status of Fintech Customers in ASEAN, 2019   186
4.11 Impact of COVID-19 on Adoption of Fintech Mobile Apps   189

5.1   Sources of Public and Private Sector   229
      Infrastructure Finance
5.2   Expected Rate of Return and Risk Profile   230
      of Project Bonds versus Benchmark Yield
5.3   Challenges in Promoting Green Infrastructure   231
5.4   Debt Service in Selected Developing Asian Economies,   234
      2019 and 2020
5.5   Local Currency Marketable Government Debt   242
      in Emerging Markets
5.6   Conflict of Interest between Users and Investors   243
5.7   Structure of Proposed Floating-Rate Infrastructure Bonds   245
5.8   Land Trust Structure and the Three Bodies of Trust   250
5.9   Land Trust for Infrastructure Investment   251
5.10 Comparing Public Debt in 2019 and 2021   266
5.11 Progress of Environmental, Social, and Governance Bonds in Asia   270
5.12 Green, Social, and Sustainability Bond Issuance   270
      of Selected ASEAN+3 Economies by Issuer
6.1   Fertility Rate in Selected East and Southeast Asian Economies,   283
      1950–2020
6.2   Life Expectancy at Age 60 in Selected East   284
      and Southeast Asian Economies, 1950–2020
6.3   Median Age in Selected East and Southeast Asian Economies,   285
      1950–2020
6.4   Old-Age Dependency Ratio in Selected East and Southeast   285
      Asian Economies, 1950–2020
6.5   Pension Landscape General Typology   291
6.6   Pension Expenditures in Selected ASEAN+3 Economies, 2015   300
6.7   Social Insurance and Social Assistance Expenditures   301
      in Selected ASEAN+3 Economies, 2015
6.8   Financing Elderly Consumption in Selected ASEAN+3 Economies,   302
      Latest Data from 1998 to 2015
6.9   Retirement Savings Gap in Selected Economies, 2015 and 2050   303
6.10 Global Pension Overall Index, 2020   309
6.11 Migrants from Selected ASEAN+3 Economies and Their Share   345
      in the Population Living Outside of Home Country, 2019
6.12 Destination of Migrants from Selected ASEAN+3 Economies   346
      by Origin, 2019
6.13 Migrants from ASEAN+3 Economies by Destination,   347
      1990–2019
7.1   Intraregional Shares, 2020—ASEAN+3 versus Euro Area   372
7.2   The Trilemma of Financial Stability   376

Boxes

1.1 Policy Timeline for Local Currency Bond Markets in ASEAN+3   8
2.1 The Mathematical Properties of the Shapley Value   68
3.1 Costs and Benefits of Currency Internationalization   127
5.1 Calculating the Spillover Tax Revenue   246
5.2 Applying the UNEP Framework to Selected ASEAN+3 Economies   261
5.3 Role of Debt Capital Market in Green Finance   263
6.1 Pension Systems in Cambodia, the Lao People's Democratic   298
     Republic, and Viet Nam   298
6.2 Why Women Have Less Retirement Savings?   306
6.3 The Pension Funds Industry: A Quick Survey   316
6.4 Prudent Person Rule, Green Finance, and Investment Policies   326
6.5 Singapore's Annuity Scheme   331
6.6 Uber and Lyft: Are Platform Drivers Employees?   339
6.7 Facilitating Tax Payments   343
6.8 The People's Republic of China's Hukou System   348
     and Pension Portability

Foreword

Nearly a quarter century ago, the risks and challenges of increased financial globalization, combined with insufficient regulatory oversight, resulted in the Asian financial crisis. The lack of strategic regional cooperation helped fuel the speculative attacks, loss of investor confidence, and contagion across the region. It led to massive capital outflows, large currency devaluations, as well as bankruptcies, job losses, and recession. The crisis made clear that financial cooperation is essential for managing extreme financial events. One result was the creation of a regional financial safety net—the Chiang Mai Initiative Multilateralization—and the ASEAN+3 Macroeconomic Research Office (AMRO).

The COVID-19 pandemic has placed the region's financial systems under considerable strain. Stimulus has increased outstanding debt. There is now added pressure to find sufficient financing for a sustained and more inclusive recovery. As the Association of Southeast Asian Nations (ASEAN)+3 economies work to move forward and rebuild smartly, it is imperative that they take stock of the lessons learned to strengthen financial cooperation and resilience. To support this process, the Asian Development Bank and AMRO—which celebrates its 10th anniversary this year—joined forces to assess the major economic and financial developments since the Asian financial crisis and identify valuable policy lessons in two publications.

The first is *Trauma to Triumph—Rising from the Ashes of the Asian Financial Crisis*. It weaves together the recollections of key decision-makers on how they tackled critical issues during the crisis, and 10 years later, during the 2007–2008 global financial crisis.

This second volume, *Redefining Strategic Routes to Financial Resilience in ASEAN+3,* examines the short- and medium-term challenges facing policy makers. Forward looking, it begins the discussion on how best to continue pursuing the regional financial cooperation agenda and resolve pressing issues. Topics range from capital market development and capital flows to cross-border banking concentration, digitalization, United States dollar dominance, green infrastructure finance, and the development of pension systems.

The importance of deepening capital markets while keeping macroprudential risks at bay cannot be overemphasized. Strengthening safeguards against regional "slow-burn" contagion and the risks of fintech and bigtech involvement in financial services is also crucial for financial stability.

Further, building an integrated policy framework for macrofinancial stabilization, expanding green infrastructure finance, and broadening dialogue on the stability and flexibility of pension systems are vital for future development.

In addition, given the increasing use of technology in financial services, this volume explores the reforms needed to elevate financial market development and enhance regulatory cooperation.

This compilation of studies aims to help strengthen financial stability and inclusion while reducing vulnerability to crises. I believe it provides an important and timely contribution to ASEAN+3 policy dialogue and financial cooperation.

Bambang Susantono
Vice-President for Knowledge Management
and Sustainable Development
Asian Development Bank

Preface

This volume, *Redefining Strategic Routes to Financial Resilience in ASEAN+3*, is a sequel to *Trauma to Triumph—Rising from the Ashes of the Asian Financial Crisis* prepared by the ASEAN+3 Macroeconomic Research Office (AMRO). The enormous endeavor of documenting the peaks and troughs of the past quarter century had its genesis in the Association of Southeast Asian Nations (ASEAN)+3 finance ministers and central bank governors reaching an informal consensus in 2018 on the need to identify and learn the most important lessons from the Asian financial crisis. Their special focus on financial cooperation recognized that economies can best overcome crises by working together closely, exchanging data and experiences through policy dialogue at both turbulent and calm times, developing and deepening financial markets in a concerted way, and coordinating policies within a regional context.

The experience of a severe financial crisis more than two decades ago was nothing short of traumatic for Asia. Yet, dramatic changes have emerged from the crisis experience. It taught ASEAN+3 economies the importance of strengthening their macroeconomic policies and fundamentals, reforming their financial systems through well-designed supervision and regulation, and building effective financial safety nets to protect against external shocks. The region learned that a system of checks, balances, and close financial monitoring is critical to avoiding surprises.

Without doubt, the ASEAN+3 region is now wiser as a result. The Chiang Mai Initiative, which was later upgraded to the Chiang Mai Initiative Multilateralization (CMIM), deserves singular mention here as it formed the first regional financial safety net arrangement and capped regional recovery efforts. The region quickly regained its footing through the global financial crisis of 2007–2009 and the debt crisis in Europe that nipped at the heels of financial stability. Indeed, it can be said with some confidence that ASEAN+3 economies—now building on a foundation of closer financial ties—handled these challenges well. Cooperation initiatives helped to apply lessons learned to coping with the effects of the COVID-19 pandemic on the financial system, which began in March 2020.

In the context of the health crisis, this volume provides a timely reframing of challenges, opportunities, and appropriate strategies for strengthening the region's resilience to future economic and financial shocks. The volume also presents a comprehensive exploration of progress and hurdles across various facets of financial cooperation and integration since the global financial crisis.

The deepening of local currency corporate bond markets as an alternative source of funding is an important part of the agenda to reduce dependence on short-term bank loans and mitigate capital flow volatility. To address the concentration of sovereign bonds among Asian debt instruments, central banks may wish to establish a regional repo market to lower credit and liquidity risks in cross-border financial transactions. The name of the game is to broaden the investor base including foreign investors, strengthen risk management capacities, and improve financial resilience.

This volume argues that recognizing and managing concentration risks in the region's bank-dominated financial systems is crucial. Past crises show vulnerabilities are often quick to emerge when cross-border borrowing is focused within a small network of big global banks. As a few large banks extend their dominance across global banking networks, the risk of a regionwide slow-burn contagion has also increased. Macroprudential policies may be especially valuable in the context of regional cooperation that treats some banks as systemically important when managing the risk of contagion.

The volume also addresses the issue of the United States Dollar dominance given the region's heavy reliance on the greenback for international trade, investment, and financial transactions. Access to adequate US dollar liquidity is critical for sustaining economic growth and financial stability in the region while a majority of foreign exchange reserves are denominated in the US currency. In addition to exchange rate flexibility to help cushion the impact of external shocks, effective options include the internationalization of regional currencies and their increased use for commercial settlements. In this context, further liberalization and coordination of foreign exchange rules and regulations relating to cross-border settlements will be important. The pandemic and its consequences for social mobility and business activity have made digital transactions and fintech almost indispensable. In this context, the volume looks at maximizing fintech applications for greater financial inclusion and stability in ASEAN+3. However, the flipside is fintech's potential to amplify inequities across social groupings. Risks to financial stability could also emerge from fintech players eating into the market of banks and other financial institutions by offering peer-to-peer lending, crowdfunding, and even cryptoassets.

Moreover, formidable challenges remain, especially in closing infrastructure investment gaps and promoting sustainable investment. The large infrastructure development gap widens further when climate change is considered. Encouraging private-sector investment in infrastructure projects, including public–private partnerships, is vital given the limited sources of public-sector financing. One way to obtain private funding might be through land value capture, calibrating taxes with rising land values that result from public infrastructure upgrades. Incentives could be provided and credit enhancements considered so as to reduce the risks that have hampered infrastructure funding for many years. There exists ample room for stepping up efforts to emphasize environmental and social sustainability in financing investment within the ASEAN+3 region.

Another challenge is to develop pension and insurance sectors to manage the effects of an aging population. Pension systems are a vital conduit for increasing financial resilience across the region, yet are underdeveloped in many middle-income ASEAN+3 economies. Amid the growing market for pensions products comes a responsibility for pension systems to ensure their financial sustainability and the opportunity to direct large and long-term investments to the region's expanding bond markets. As regional integration increases the mobility of labor, bilateral social security agreements to improve portability of pensions may be necessary given that multilateral negotiations are harder to shape. This volume offers strategic perspectives on possible future actions on pension systems for improved financing for long-term investments while enhancing their sustainability.

Finally, this volume concludes with how ASEAN+3 economies can support each other with regional financial safety nets. Financial interconnectedness in the region has deepened. Since interconnectedness comes at the price of increased spillovers, the clear and future challenge is to be prepared for them. One good marker in operationalizing financial cooperation is to bolster the role of international financial institutions, including AMRO and the CMIM in addressing liquidity shortages in the region with the International Monetary Fund and by providing macroeconomic surveillance.

Without sharp focus on the steps needed to redefine financial cooperation in the region, there remains the risk of reforms losing steam. Measures may succeed in buffering the impact of external shocks, but short-term complacency may soften resolve, cloud long-term vision, and serve to delay much-needed reforms until another crisis. Unwavering attention to lessons learned through financial cooperation over the past two decades— bookended at one end by the Asian financial crisis and by the COVID-19 pandemic's reshaping of economies at the other—is timely. We hope this volume helps guide continuing efforts of ASEAN+3 economies to improve the region's roadmap to a more resilient financial future.

Diwa Guinigundo
Former Deputy Governor
Monetary and Economics Sector
Bangko Sentral ng Pilipinas

Masahiro Kawai
Representative Director and Director General
Economic Research Institute for Northeast Asia

Cyn-Young Park
Director, Regional Cooperation and Integration Division
Economic Research and Regional Cooperation Department
Asian Development Bank

Ramkishen S. Rajan
Yong Pung How Professor
Lee Kuan Yew School of Public Policy
National University of Singapore

Acknowledgments

This publication was prepared by the Regional Cooperation and Integration Division (ERCI) of the Economic Research and Regional Cooperation Department (ERCD) of the Asian Development Bank (ADB). It received support from technical assistance project 6592: Building Financial Resilience and Stability to Reinvigorate Growth. This project is financed by the Investment Climate Facilitation Fund, the People's Republic of China Poverty Reduction and Regional Cooperation Fund, the Republic of Korea e-Asia and Knowledge Partnership Fund, and ADB's technical assistance special fund.

The editorial team is also grateful for the helpful comments and suggestions provided by participants of the ADB online chapter review sessions, ADB-ASEAN+3 Macroeconomic Research Office (AMRO) joint review session, and ADB ERCD discussion meeting. The team appreciates the input of Joseph Ernest Zveglich Jr., Satoru Yamadera, Hoe Ee Khor, Jae Young Lee, and Jinho Choi, as well as the collaboration and support of Kazuo Kobayashi and Masato Matsutani of AMRO. Contributions and excellent research support from Ryan Jacildo are gratefully acknowledged. The team also appreciates the assistance of Maria Josephine Duque-Comia (senior economics officer, ADB); Mara Claire Tayag (senior economics officer, ADB); Pilar Dayag; Ana Kristel Lapid; Clemence Fatima Cruz; and Dominique Hannah Sy.

Rogelio Mercado, Jr. (economist, ERCI/ERCD); Sanchita Basu Das (economist, ERCI/ERCD); and James Villafuerte (senior economist, Southeast Asia Department, ADB) led the coordination of all contributors to this publication, under the guidance and supervision of Cyn-Young Park, director of ERCI/ERCD. Paulo Rodelio Halili (senior economics officer, ERCI/ERCD) and Marilyn Aure Parra (senior operations assistant, ERCI/ERCD) provided support. The editorial team is also grateful to all those who helped in the production of this edited book volume, including James Unwin and Eric Van Zant for editing the book chapters; Jan Carlo dela Cruz for creating the cover design; Michael Cortes for typesetting and layout; Lawrence Casiraya for proofreading, Jess Macasaet for page proof checking, with assistance from Paulo Rodelio Halili, Ryan Jacildo, and Carol Ongchangco; and Indexing Partners for indexing services. The editors also acknowledge the printing and publishing support by the Printing Services Unit of ADB's Corporate Services Department, and the Publishing team of the Department of Communications.

Editors

Diwa Guinigundo is former deputy governor for the Monetary and Economics Sector at the Bangko Sentral ng Pilipinas (BSP). He served the BSP for more than 40 years. He was previously designated as alternate executive director at the International Monetary Fund and the head of Research at The South East Asian Central Banks (SEACEN) Research and Training Centre. He chaired the SEACEN Task Force on SEACEN membership and the Executive Meeting of East Asia and the Pacific (EMEAP) Monetary and Financial Stability Committee. He also co-chaired the SEACEN Experts Group on Capital Flows and the ASEAN Senior Level Committee on Financial Integration. He holds a bachelor of arts (BA) degree in economics from the University of the Philippines and master of science (MSc) degree in economics from the London School of Economics.

Masahiro Kawai is representative director and director general of the Economic Research Institute for Northeast Asia. He previously served as the dean and chief executive officer of the Asian Development Bank Institute and the head of the Office of Regional Economic Integration, Asian Development Bank (ADB). He was the chief economist for the World Bank's East Asia and the Pacific Region and the deputy vice-minister for International Affairs at the Ministry of Finance in Japan. He has also taught economics at Johns Hopkins University and at the University of Tokyo. He has published extensively on open-economy macroeconomics, economic and financial globalization, regional economic integration and cooperation in Asia, and the international monetary system. He holds a BA in economics from the University of Tokyo and a doctor of philosophy (PhD) degree in economics from Stanford University.

Cyn-Young Park is director of the Regional Cooperation and Integration Division in the Economic Research and Regional Cooperation Department of ADB. In her current capacity, she manages a team of economists who examine economic and policy issues related to regional cooperation and integration (RCI) and develop strategies and approaches to support RCI. She has been a main author of and contributor to ADB's major publications; and has published extensively in peer-reviewed academic journals. She has also conducted lectures about the Asian economy and financial markets and participated in various global and regional forums. Prior to joining ADB, she served as economist at the Organisation for Economic Co-operation and Development. She received her PhD in economics from Columbia University. She holds a BA in international economics from Seoul National University.

Ramkishen S. Rajan is Yong Pung How Professor at the Lee Kuan Yew School of Public Policy, National University of Singapore (NUS). He has previously been on the faculty at ESSEC Business School–Asia-Pacific, George Mason University, and University of Adelaide, and has held visiting teaching appointments at Claremont McKenna College, Claremont Graduate University, and Singapore Management University. He is also currently a research affiliate at the Global Research Unit, City University of Hong Kong; an adjunct fellow at the Research and Information System for Developing Countries; and a senior research fellow and a member of the Advisory Council at Claremont Institute for Economic Policy Studies. He has held visiting fellowships and consulting positions at various research institutes in Asia and international organizations. He holds a BA in social sciences (honors) from NUS, a master of arts (MA) degree from University of Michigan–Ann Arbor, and MA and PhD from Claremont Graduate University.

Authors

Bihong Huang is economist, International Monetary Fund.

Hiro Ito is professor of economics and Department of Economics chair, Portland State University.

Masahiro Kawai is representative director and director general, the Economic Research Institute for Northeast Asia and Professor Emeritus, University of Tokyo.

Saloni Lakhia is an MA candidate in public policy and social research, International Christian University, and a former research associate, Asian Development Bank Institute (ADBI).

Peter Morgan is senior consulting economist and vice-chair of Research, ADBI.

Cyn-Young Park is director, Regional Cooperation and Integration Division, Economic Research and Regional Cooperation Department, Asian Development Bank (ADB).

Gloria Pasadilla is partner and director, Leadership Design Pte, Ltd, Singapore. Singapore, and former senior analyst, APEC Policy Support Unit, APEC Secretariat, Singapore.

Ramkishen S. Rajan is Yong Pung How Professor, Lee Kuan Yew School of Public Policy, National University of Singapore.

Eli Remolona is professor of finance and director of Central Banking, Asia School of Business.

Josef T. Yap is consultant, ADB Economic Research and Regional Cooperation Department, and former president of the Philippine Institute for Development Studies.

Naoyuki Yoshino is professor emeritus, Keio University, and former dean and chief executive officer, ADBI.

1 Overview of Financial Development and Cooperation in ASEAN+3

Cyn-Young Park and Ramkishen S. Rajan

1.1 Introduction

Asian financial systems have achieved significant development and integration over the past decades. From mostly state-funded and bank-dominated during the period of industrialization in the 1970s and 1980s, the region's financial systems have become more diversified and market-based. While most Asian financial systems remain bank-dominated, the scope of financial products and services has broadened and new corporate financing sources are proliferating.

Fundamental changes and reforms are often triggered by large shocks or episodes of financial crisis. The Asian finance sector's experience is no different. Indeed, it was not until the Asian financial crisis that the region's economies embarked on major reforms to restructure, strengthen, and diversify their financial systems. For the ASEAN+3 economies—the 10 members of the Association of Southeast Asian Nations (ASEAN), plus its main trading partners, the People's Republic of China (PRC), Japan, and the Republic of Korea—reforms went hand-in-hand with a conscious effort to promote financial cooperation and hence reduce the risks of repeating a crisis.

Highlights of financial cooperation include the introduction in 2010 of a multilateral currency swap arrangement, the Chiang Mai Initiative Multilateralization (CMIM), and the creation of the ASEAN+3 Macroeconomic Research Office (AMRO) which was accorded legal status as an international organization in 2016. These have given a fillip to financial cooperation among ASEAN+3 economies. Rather than retreat from global financial markets, the economies recognized the need to become more connected with them, while trying to do so in a manner that minimizes disruption. The region's financial systems held up relatively well during the United States (US) taper tantrum in 2013, and again in the turmoil of March 2020 at the height of panic over the coronavirus disease (COVID-19) pandemic, thanks in part to the post-Asian financial crisis reforms and policy lessons that led to improved macrofinancial surveillance, strengthened financial regulations, and enhanced regional financial safety net arrangements and institutions.

This volume explores the present state of affairs of financial cooperation and development in the region since the global financial crisis. It takes the story forward from the first volume, which offered useful historical context to financial development since the Asian financial crisis struck in 1997.[1] Much has been achieved in the past 25 years, yet a great deal still needs to be done to make the region's finance sectors more inclusive and safer for society. This includes developing market structure to expand and build a more liquid financial system and finding innovative ways to finance the real sectors and reach people excluded from the formal financial system. It also means continuous strengthening of financial resilience and safeguarding stability amid the rapid economic and financial development driven by advances in technology.

This first chapter sets the scene for how regional efforts can continue to improve financial systems in Asia. It starts by offering some theory about and evidence of financial integration and its opportunities and challenges, and goes on to review the evolution of ASEAN+3 financial systems with a focus on the growing internationalization of the ASEAN+3 banking system and the development of local currency bond markets over the past 2 decades. A comprehensive picture of challenges ahead cannot ignore the shock of COVID-19 on regional financial systems, nor the looming risks to debt sustainability and the revolutionary impact of digital transformation on financial services. To gauge the region's resilience to financial contagion, the chapter examines sides to the debate around the capacity of flexible exchange rates to insulate from global shocks, especially in the context of growing US dollar borrowing and its dominance in pricing for international trade. It also touches upon the role of international reserves as a self-help mechanism and revisits actions being taken to improve regional monetary cooperation. While aiming to put issues facing ASEAN+3 policy makers into sharp focus, the chapter concludes with suggestions of steps that can be taken as a region to build more resilient financial systems.

---

[1] Published by ASEAN+3 Macroeconomic Research Office, the first volume, *Trauma to Triumph—Rising from the Ashes of the Asian Financial Crisis,* weaves together the recollections of key decision-makers on how they tackled critical issues during the Asian financial crisis and the 2007–2008 global financial crisis.

1.2 Financial Openness and Growth: Theory and Evidence

Financial openness and integration is a complex concept with many dimensions, including *de jure* capital account openness, how financial institutions can better operate across jurisdictions, and the extent to capital can flow across borders (i.e., *de facto* openness). Several studies, beginning with the influential works of McKinnon (1973) and Shaw (1973), have argued that a movement away from "financially repressive" policies can bring growth benefits by eliminating credit controls, deregulating interest rates, and allowing banks to compete with each other. While the initial McKinnon-Shaw analysis focused on domestic financial liberalization, a burgeoning literature has since extended the discussion to external aspects. The general conclusion is that financial development combined with proper sequencing of liberalization could spur economic growth through efficient allocation of capital across borders and transfer of best practices in technological know-how and management, complemented by increased production specialization and better risk management (Bekaert, Harvey, and Lundblad 2005, Williamson and Mahar 1998).[2]

However, a large body of literature building on Stiglitz (2004) has cautioned that information asymmetries stemming from a lack of transparency in financial institutions could lead to inefficient allocation of capital, generating maturity mismatches that contribute to costly financial crises (Stiglitz and Weiss 1981). The empirical literature does not establish conclusively that financial openness has had any discernible positive impact on growth (Eichengreen 2001, Contessi and Weinberger 2009, Kose et al. 2009). While the growth effects of financial openness are contested, it can be said with certainty that where liberalization fails to take place in a well-sequenced and timed manner—such as development of the domestic financial market and regulatory system before financial openness, and openness to long-term capital before short-term capital—episodes of severe financial instability and distress may result (Bird and Rajan 2001, Cobham 2002, Prasad and Rajan 2008).[3] Similarly, Kose, Prasad, and Taylor (2011) find the indirect benefits of international financial integration on growth, such as developing domestic financial markets and improving corporate and public governance, may be more important than direct benefits. They also note that for countries to reap some of these benefits, they require a certain "threshold" of domestic financial and institutional development, without

---

[2] Jafarov, Maino, and Pani (2019) include recent empirical evidence on how financial repression negatively affects economic growth.

[3] For a discussion on the consequences of ill-sequenced or perverse financial liberalization, see Auerbach and Willett (2003).

which financial liberalization may be accompanied by unintended risks, including financial crises.[4]

In summary, financial integration offers potential benefits but also poses risks and costs. Past literature points to a broad set of indirect "collateral benefits" of financial openness. However, in some cases the benefits, such as of local financial sector development, institutional development, better governance, and macroeconomic discipline, may be enjoyed only if "threshold conditions" related to financial market development, institutional quality, governance, macroeconomic policies, and the like are met. This suggests that there may be bidirectional causality. For instance, although enhanced financial openness encourages efficient financial markets, whenever existing financial markets are underdeveloped, the gains from openness may be limited and it may fail to attract capital or the "right" form of capital. Countries below the threshold may fall into a 'financial globalization trap' (Prasad et al. 2003), something that the low- and middle-income members of ASEAN+3 have to pay attention to.[5]

Experiences with the Asian financial crisis and subsequent crises have underscored the importance of sequencing market-oriented reforms with financial liberalization (McKinnon 1991), focusing on improvements in regulation and supervision, transparency, and contract enforcement (Beck, Demirgüç-Kunt, and Levine 2003; La Porta et al. 1997). The global financial crisis further highlighted the risk from deeply entwined financial networks that allow fast and wide transmission of shocks across markets and borders. It also cast doubt on the ability of financial regulators to properly monitor overly complex financial products and transactions amid rapid globalization or innovation.

Viewing financial globalization through the narrow prism of global capital flows, cross-border capital surged remarkably in the years prior to the global financial crisis, with overall gross capital inflows peaking at $12.0 trillion in 2007, or about 19% of global gross domestic product (GDP). Following a sharp decline in gross capital inflows to ASEAN+3 in 2008 and 2009, the region attracted significant capital in bouts between 2010 and 2013, with gross capital inflows touching $1.0 trillion in 2013, surpassing levels in 2007

---

[4] Also see Aizenman, Jinjarak, and Park (2015) for a discussion on the possible nonlinear relationship between financial development and output growth.

[5] Financial globalization trap refers to a low-level stable equilibrium (Cassimon and Van Campenhout 2006). Higher-income countries that avoid this trap could still experience sharp reversals in capital flows and accompanying adverse effects from time to time and may need to safeguard against such capital account shocks.

(IMF, Balance of Payments Statistics). Such record capital inflows consisted mostly of relatively short-term bank-related and other private flows (Balakrishnan et al. 2012).

Another important dimension of financial integration is foreign bank presence and cross-border banking activities. Foreign banks could contribute to overall financial sector development by helping reduce cost structures; improving operational efficiency; and by introducing new technologies and banking products, marketing skills and management, and corporate governance structures. They could also make financial services more accessible for households and firms.[6] Based on available data for ASEAN+3, as Figure 1.1 captures, the average share of foreign banking institutions in the total number of banks has steadily risen from 2010 to 2013, but has declined since to about 42% in 2020. In comparison, the average share of banking assets owned by foreign banks appears to have not changed much in the last 10 years.[7] The foreign bank participation rate in the ASEAN+3 economies is also lower than other regions such as sub-Saharan Africa and Latin America and the Caribbean (Figure 1.2).

---

[6] See Levine (1996) for an early discussion of these issues. Also, see Rajan and Gopalan (2015) for a discussion on the macroeconomic and financial implications of foreign bank presence in emerging markets.

[7] A country-wise breakdown within the ASEAN+3 region reveals a very uneven picture in terms of foreign bank penetration across the region. For instance, while the average foreign bank share in banking sector's assets in Indonesia is less than 7% between 2010 and 2020, the corresponding figure is 56% in Cambodia (2014-2020) and over 21% in Malaysia (2010-2020).

Figure 1.1: Foreign Bank Presence in ASEAN+3

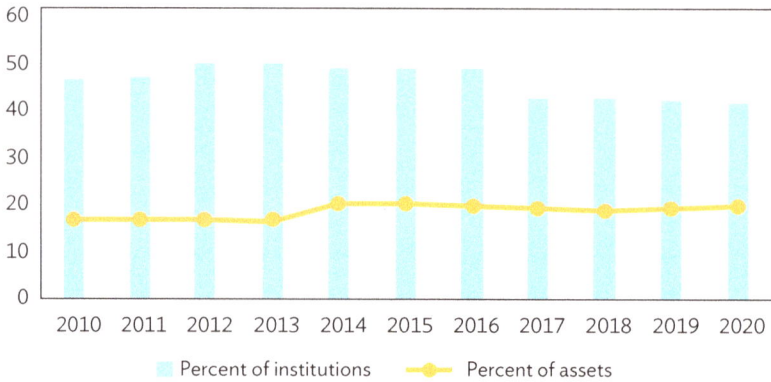

Percent of institutions   Percent of assets

Note: The data pertain to simple averages of economy-level ratios covering economies with data. The definitions and coverage may vary across economies. The economy composition of each variable also differs. For assets, all ASEAN+3 economies are covered except those whose data are not publicly available. The data series of Cambodia and Viet Nam start in 2014 and 2012, respectively. For institutions, the data set includes Cambodia, the People's Republic of China, Indonesia, the Republic of Korea, the Lao People's Democratic Republic, the Philippines, Singapore, and Thailand. The data series for Cambodia and Indonesia start in 2012 and 2017, respectively. Source: Authors, based on CEIC and national sources.

Figure 1.2: Foreign Bank Participation Rates
(average of the median rates by region, 2006-2020)

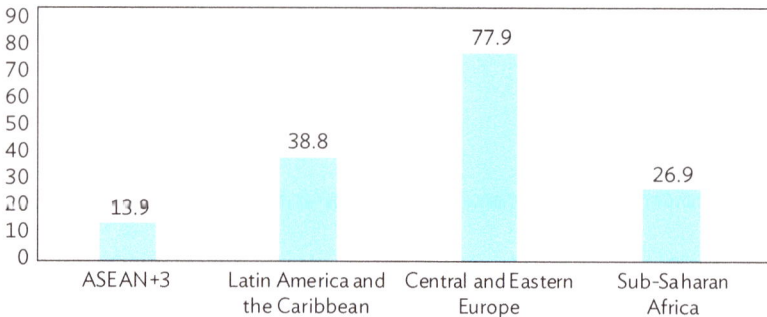

Note: The calculations follow the methodology of Ehlers and McGuire (2017). ASEAN+3 sample excludes the Lao People's Democratic Republic. Latin America includes Argentina, Brazil, Chile, Colombia, Mexico, and Peru based on Ehlers and McGuire (2017). Central and Eastern Europe includes Bulgaria, the Czech Republic, Estonia, Hungary, Lithuania, Poland, Slovenia, Slovakia, Romania, and Turkey based on Ehlers and McGuire (2017). Sub-Saharan Africa includes Angola, Benin, Botswana, Cote d'Ivoire, Kenya, Nigeria, Senegal, Seychelles, South Africa, and Uganda. For Argentina, due to data limitations, the participation rate from 2018 to 2020 is assumed to be equal to the rate in 2017. For Lithuania, the domestic credit data from 2006 to 2008 are based on the old compilation, data for 2009 is missing, and data from 2010 onward are based on the new compilation. Due to data limitations, the participation rate in 2009 is assumed to be equal to the participation rate in 2010. Source: Authors, based on BIS consolidated and locational banking statistics and the IMF International Financial Statistics Database (accessed September 2021).

1.3 Evolution of Financial Systems in ASEAN+3

Financial systems in Asia have transformed from largely state-directed and predominantly bank-based systems during the industrialization period, to be more liberalized and market-based since the late 1980s and early 1990s. Through the experiences of the Asian and global financial crises, the region's financial systems now also have more robust regulatory frameworks, sound macrofinancial policies, and regional safety net arrangements, and are more resilient to shocks. While bank-based finance is still dominant in ASEAN+3, over the past several decades, equity and bond markets have grown markedly. Yet, capital market development varies greatly across ASEAN+3 economies—particularly with the large gap between Cambodia, the Lao People's Democratic Republic (Lao PDR), and Myanmar, and the rest of ASEAN. Cambodia, the Lao PDR, and Myanmar are the region's youngest markets, with smallest capitalization and fewer than 10 companies on their stock exchanges (OECD 2019). The domestic bond markets in these three countries are either underdeveloped or inactive. Given this, they are not covered in detail in the following sections.[8]

Post-Asian Financial Crisis Reforms: Improved Regulation, Diversification, and Resilience

The Asian financial crisis prompted a wave of reforms in financial systems across the region, with decisive steps in affected economies (e.g., Indonesia, the Republic of Korea, Malaysia, the Philippines, and Thailand) to improve bank supervision and regulation and corporate governance. Bank-based financial systems combined with fixed exchange rates were seen as posing systemic risk, as banks took a major role in corporate finance by channeling foreign-currency-denominated short-term borrowing from overseas to domestic-currency-denominated long-term loans. This in turn caused currency and maturity mismatches. A strong push followed the crisis to lessen dependence on banks and the implicit guarantees that governments offered those financial institutions, particularly through the development of local currency bond markets.

Strong regional efforts emerged to build more efficient and liquid domestic debt markets (Box 1.1). In 2003, regional central banks together launched the first Asian Bond Fund (ABF1), which invested pooled savings into sovereign and quasi-sovereign bond markets to improve market liquidity.

---

[8]   Yaguchi (2018) discusses some of the challenges faced by these countries in bond market development.

While under ABF1, part of central bank reserves was invested in US-dollar-denominated bonds issued by the Executive Meeting of East Asia and the Pacific (EMEAP) member governments[9] with the aim of increasing demand for regional sovereign bonds; ABF2 in 2005 saw part of reserves invested in sovereign and quasi-sovereign bonds denominated in local currency. Simultaneously, ASEAN+3 economies introduced the Asian Bond Markets Initiative (ABMI) to identify and address critical issues hindering local bond market development (Park 2016). ABMI has been fostering local currency bond market development and integration in the region (Akamatsu and Puongsophol 2018).

Box 1.1: Policy Timeline for Local Currency Bond Markets in ASEAN+3

2002   Asian Bond Markets Initiative (ABMI) is launched under ASEAN+3 to develop a liquid and well-functioning local currency bond market.

2003   Asian Bond Fund 1 (ABF1) is launched by central banks of the Executives' Meeting of East Asia and the Pacific (EMEAP) members to invest pooled savings in the US-dollar sovereign and quasi-sovereign debt issued by eight member economies (the People's Republic of China; Hong Kong, China; Indonesia; the Republic Korea; Malaysia; the Philippines; Singapore; and Thailand). ABF1 pooled $1 billion of international reserves from the participating eight central banks.

2004   ABMI launches Asian Bonds Online as a one-stop data and information portal for institutional investors, policy makers, and researchers participating in local currency debt markets.

2005   Asian Bond Fund 2 (ABF2) extends the ABF1 concept with $2 billion invested in sovereign and quasi-sovereign issues denominated in local currencies in the same eight markets.

2008   ASEAN+3 ministers sign the New ABMI Road Map to set up task forces to address specific issues in local bond market development.

2010   ASEAN+3 establishes the Asian Bond Market Forum (ABMF) as a platform to foster standardization of market practices and harmonization of regulations relating to cross-border bond transactions in the region, including for corporate bonds.

continued on next page

---

[9]   EMEAP comprises the central banks of 11 economies: Australia; the People's Republic of China (PRC); Hong Kong, China; Indonesia; Japan; the Republic of Korea; Malaysia; New Zealand; the Philippines; Singapore; and Thailand.

Box1.1 (continued)

2010   The Credit Guarantee and Investment Facility (CGIF) is launched as a trust fund within the Asian Development Bank (ADB) to provide credit enhancement to promote larger and cross-border corporate bond issues. CGIF starts operations in 2012, with authorized capital of $700 million.

2012   ABMF releases the ASEAN+3 Bond Market Guide, the first officially recognized publication of bond market regulations and settlement procedures in ASEAN+3 economies.

2013   ASEAN+3 establishes the Cross-Border Settlement Infrastructure Forum (CSIF) to help prepare a road map and implementation plan for the improvement of regional cross border settlement infrastructure.
ABMF publishes the Sub-Forum 1 (SF1) Phase 2 Report: Proposal on ASEAN+3 Multi- Currency Bond Issuance Framework as a regionally standardized bond issuance framework, and the Sub-Forum 2 (SF2) Phase 2 Report: ASEAN+3 Information on Transaction Flows and Settlement Infrastructures.

2014   CSIF publishes the Basic Principles on Establishing a Regional Settlement Intermediary and Next Steps Forward: Cross-Border Settlement Infrastructure Forum.

2015   ABMF releases implementation guidelines for the ASEAN+3 Multi-Currency Bond Issuance Framework (AMBIF), which helps facilitate intraregional transactions through standardized bond and note issuance, and investment processes.
ABMF releases two Phase 3 reports: Implementation of the AMBIF and Harmonization and Standardization of Bond Market Infrastructures in ASEAN+3.

2018   CSIF publishes the Common Understanding on Cross-Border Business Continuity Planning and Cybersecurity to support the development of Central Securities Depository (CSD) and Real-Time Gross Settlement (RTGS) linkages.

Source: Levinger and Li (2014), Park (2016), and ADB (2008, 2012, 2015, 2019).

Figure 1.3 reveals that the share of bank assets to GDP in ASEAN+3 has been rising gradually from 235% in 2007 to reach almost 300% of ASEAN+3 GDP in 2017. It tapered a little thereafter before surging to over 334% of GDP in 2020. Similarly, assets of nonbank financial institutions as a share of the region's GDP has been rising gradually since 2011, and was about 138% in 2019. While banks still dominate ASEAN+3 financial systems, both market capitalization and the size of the local currency bond markets as a share of the region's GDP have increased markedly.[10] The market capitalization of listed domestic companies rose from a little over 49% of GDP in 2008 to about 97% in 2020, while the share of local currency bond markets increased markedly from around 98% in 2007 to over 125% in 2020.[11]

Developing a sophisticated and liquid corporate bond market is particularly important for the region in light of its massive long-term financing needs. Considering that bond markets provide long-term financing, they not only can facilitate infrastructure development but also offer a way to efficiently manage and channel excess savings (Shimizu 2018). A well-developed corporate bond market can also support financial stability by offering a viable alternative to bank loans.

Improvements in the bank regulation and supervision framework and financial diversification likely contributed to the resilience of Asian economies during the global financial crisis and the sovereign debt crisis in the euro area that followed a few years later. Most Asian economies recovered rather quickly afterward. But some consider that such resilience also partly reflected the continued segmentation and underdevelopment of the region's capital markets from global financial markets and networks.[12]

---

[10] While arguably most efforts have been placed on development of regional bond markets considered here, some policy efforts have supported the development of equity markets in the region, including the ASEAN Capital Market Forum (ACMF) created in April 2004 to improve regional market infrastructure and connectivity. For details on ACMF and Asian equity market development and integration in general, see OECD (2019).

[11] For market capitalization, all ASEAN+3 economies have data in 2020 except Brunei Darussalam, which does not have an equity market, and the Lao People's Democratic Republic (Lao PDR) whose data are only until 2019 as of this writing. The sources and calculations are indicated in the note of the Figure 1.3.

[12] This was also the observation for ASEAN countries made by Lee and Park (2008), Park (2011), and Gochoco-Bautista and Remolona (2012).

Figure 1.3: Financial Structure in ASEAN+3
(% GDP)

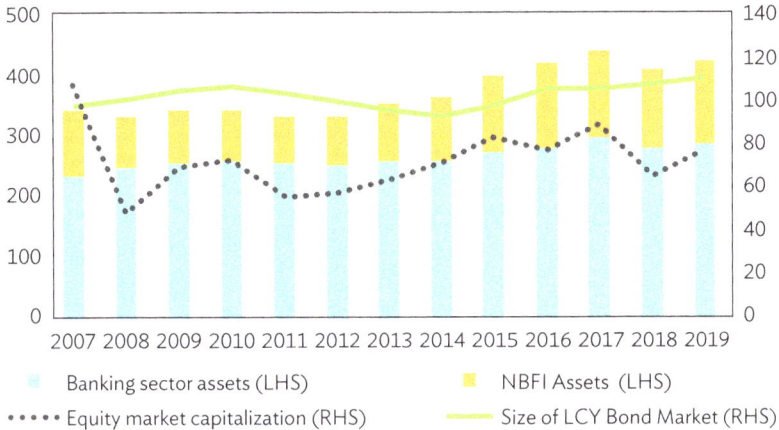

GDP = gross domestic product, LCY = local currency, LHS = left-hand scale, NBFI = nonbank financial institutions, RHS = right-hand scale.
Note: The Association of Southeast Asian Nations (ASEAN)+3 aggregated data per variable pertain to the ratio of the sum of the assets and GDP covering ASEAN+3 economies with available data. The banking sector assets data are from the CEIC, the IMF International Financial Statistics Database, and national sources (accessed August 2021). The data refer to the assets of *other depository corporations*, *domestic money banks*, or domestic banking sector. For Singapore, the data refer to the sum of assets under domestic banking units and Asian currency units. For Viet Nam, the data series starts in 2008. The NBFI asset data are from the Financial Stability Board 2020 Global Monitoring Report on Non-bank Financial Intermediation Monitoring Dataset and the IMF International Financial Statistics Database (accessed August 2021). These data refer to NBFI assets or other financial corporation assets. The data series starts in 2013 for Cambodia and 2017 for the Philippines. The outstanding local currency bonds data are from AsianBondsOnline (accessed August 2021). The equity market capitalization refers to the capitalization of listed domestic companies. The data are from the World Bank, *World Development Indicators* (WDI) and national sources (accessed August 2021). Brunei Darussalam is not included in the calculation since it does not have a stock exchange as of this writing. The stock exchanges of Cambodia, the Lao PDR, and Myanmar were respectively established in 2012, 2010, and 2015. For Viet Nam, the data series starts in 2008. The GDP levels data used to calculate the ratios are from the IMF World Economic Outlook April 2020 Database and AsianBondsOnline for the outstanding local currency bond ratio (accessed August 2021). In 2020, the banking sector assets in ASEAN+3 is more than 334% of GDP, the market capitalization of domestic companies is about 97% of GDP (excluding the Lao PDR whose data are only until 2019), and the size of the local currency bond market is more than 125% of GDP. The data for NBFI assets, as a proportion of GDP, are only until 2019.
Source: Authors, based on AsianBondsOnline; CEIC; Financial Stability Board 2020 Global Monitoring Report on Non-bank Financial Intermediation Monitoring Dataset; IMF International Financial Statistics Database; the IMF World Economic Outlook April 2020 Database; national sources; and World Bank, *World Development Indicators* (accessed August 2021).

Global Financial Crisis: Rapid Credit Growth, Dollar Dominance, Potential Risks

Deep and liquid domestic capital markets should offer the corporate sector more diversified financing solutions and improve the availability of long-maturity and local currency options. Capital markets also help mitigate foreign exchange exposure and contribute to financial stability. Studies suggest local currency bond issuance may not be as strongly procyclical as bank lending, at least based on evidence from advanced economies (Adrian, Colla, and Shin 2012; Becker and Ivashina 2014; Kashyap, Stein, and Wilcox 1993).

Local currency bond markets in ASEAN+3 have grown considerably in size over the past few decades. In absolute terms, aggregate local currency bonds outstanding were close to $32 trillion in 2020, surpassing the $21 trillion US Treasury market, though still less than the aggregate US local currency market, which was worth about $51 trillion (Figure 1.4). The expansion has been driven by remarkable growth in the market for yuan-denominated bonds in the PRC. The PRC's bond market has surpassed Japan's in 2017, where volumes declined between 2011 and 2015 before recovering in recent years.

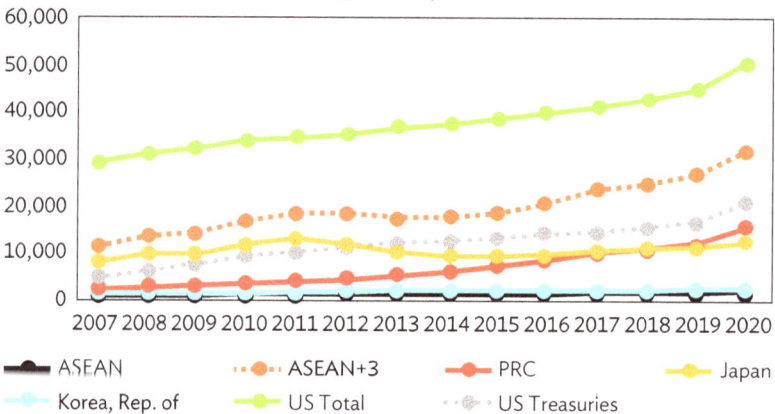

Figure 1.4: Size of Local Currency Bond Markets in ASEAN+3 ($ billion)

PRC = People's Republic of China, US = United States.
Note: Data for ASEAN include Indonesia, Malaysia, the Philippines, Singapore, Thailand, and Viet Nam.
Source: AsianBondsOnline and SIFMA US Fixed Income Securities Statistics August 2021 (accessed August 2021).

The region also witnessed strong increases in domestic public and private debt issuance in the last few years, notwithstanding some episodes of financial market downturns (Figures 1.5 and 1.6). The ASEAN economies, however, pulled back somewhat in their issuance of offshore private debt since 2010, in contrast to the trend in East Asia and high-income Asian economies (Figure 1.7).

Figure 1.5: Outstanding Domestic Public Debt Securities, 1980s to 2010s
(% GDP)

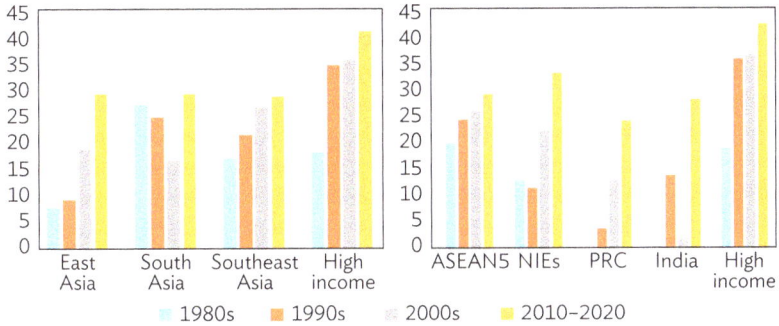

ASEAN5 = Indonesia, Malaysia, the Philippines, Thailand, and Viet Nam; GDP = gross domestic product; NIEs (newly industrialized economies) = Hong Kong, China; the Republic of Korea; Singapore; and Taipei,China; PRC = People's Republic of China.
Note: The data refer to decade averages. The subregional groupings follow ADB definition though not all economies have data. The global high-income economy aggregation is based on World Bank definition.
Source: ADB, based on BIS Debt Securities Statistics; CEIC; International Monetary Fund (IMF) International Financial Statistics; IMF World Economic Outlook April 2021 Database; World Bank Global Financial Development Database; and World Bank, *World Development Indicators* (all accessed September 2021).

Figure 1.6: Outstanding Domestic Private Debt Securities, 1980s to 2010s
(% GDP)

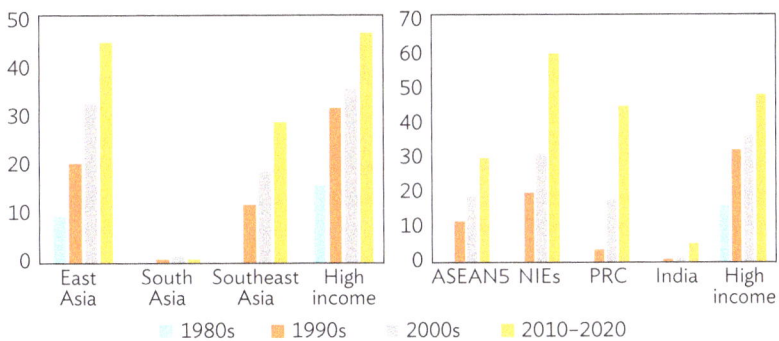

ASEAN5 = Indonesia, Malaysia, the Philippines, Thailand, and Viet Nam; GDP = gross domestic product; NIEs (newly industrialized economies) = Hong Kong, China; the Republic of Korea; Singapore; and Taipei,China; PRC = People's Republic of China.
Note: The data refer to decade averages. The subregional groupings follow ADB definitions though not all economies have data. The high-income economy aggregation is based on World Bank definition.
Source: ADB, based on BIS Debt Securities Statistics; CEIC; International Monetary Fund (IMF) International Financial Statistics; IMF World Economic Outlook April 2021 Database; World Bank Global Financial Development Database; and World Bank, *World Development Indicators* (all accessed September 2021).

**Figure 1.7: Outstanding International Private Debt Securities,
1980s to 2010s**
(% GDP)

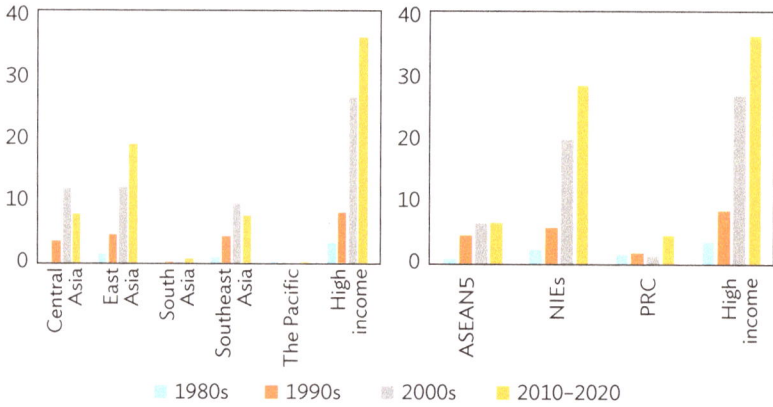

1980s   1990s   2000s   2010–2020

ASEAN5 = Indonesia, Malaysia, the Philippines, Thailand, and Viet Nam; GDP = gross domestic product; NIEs (newly industrialized economies) = Hong Kong, China; the Republic of Korea; Singapore; and Taipei,China; PRC = People's Republic of China.
Note: The data refer to decade averages. The subregional groupings follow ADB definitions though not all economies have data. High-income economy aggregation is based on World Bank definition.
Source: ADB, based on BIS Debt Securities Statistics; CEIC; International Monetary Fund (IMF), *International Financial Statistics*; IMF World Economic Outlook April 2021 Database; World Bank Global Financial Development Database; and World Bank, *World Development Indicators* (all accessed September 2021).

As corporate bond markets have grown at a healthy pace since the global financial crisis, the share of corporate bonds outstanding to GDP in ASEAN+3 more than doubled from 14% in 2007 to 33% in 2020, while the corresponding share of government bonds to GDP in ASEAN+3 rose from 66% to 91%. Nevertheless, local currency corporate bond markets must deal with structural development issues, such as narrow investor profiles, the relatively short maturity profile of local currency corporate bonds, the low trading volume in secondary markets, and limited issuer participation with significant concentration of corporate bond issuers (Figures 1.8 to 1.11).

The years of local currency bond market expansion in ASEAN+3 attracted growing foreign investment although its share has declined in the last few years, presumably exacerbated by the pandemic in 2020. Figure 1.12 shows the share of foreign holdings in local currency government bonds in 2019 was nearly 40% in Indonesia, around 25% in Malaysia, about 17% in Thailand, and more than 10% in the Republic of Korea. However, while the foreign share continued to rise in the +3 (the PRC, Japan, and the Republic of Korea) economies in 2020, it fell in all ASEAN economies where data are available.

Figure 1.8: ASEAN+3 Local Currency Bond Markets, 2007–2020
(% of GDP)

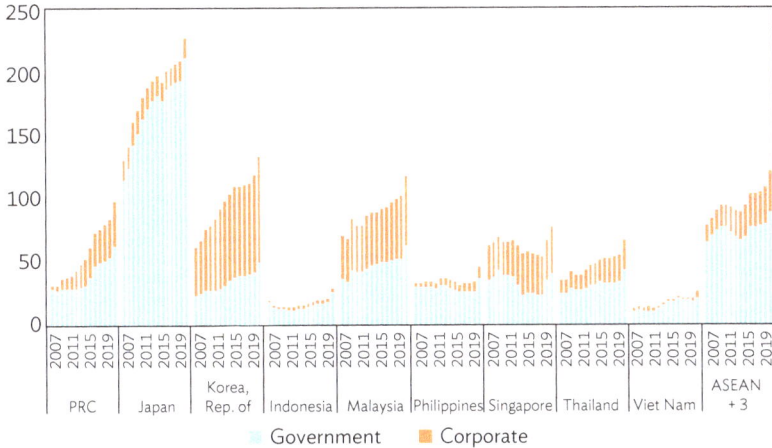

GDP = gross domestic product, PRC = People's Republic of China.
Note: Government bonds exclude central bank bonds. The ASEAN+3 aggregated values pertain to the ratio of the sum of the local currency bonds and GDP covering countries with available data.
Source: AsianBondsOnline (accessed August 2021).

Figure 1.9: Investor Profile of Local Currency Government Bonds in ASEAN+3
(%)

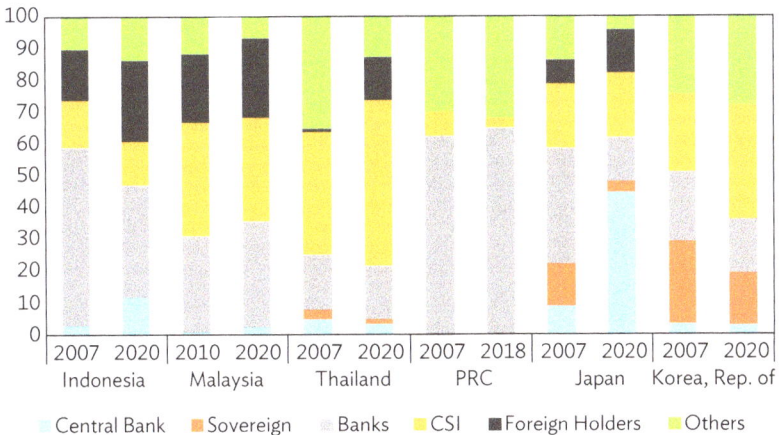

CSI = contractual savings institutions, LCY = local currency, PRC = People's Republic of China.
Note: CSIs include contractual savings funds and insurance companies. The disaggregation of the data for PRC and the Republic of Korea does not include foreign holders. For Thailand, foreign holders refer to nonresidents.
Source: Authors, based on AsianBondsOnline (accessed August 2021).

Figure 1.10: Average Maturity of ASEAN+3 Local Currency Bonds, 2008–2020
(%)

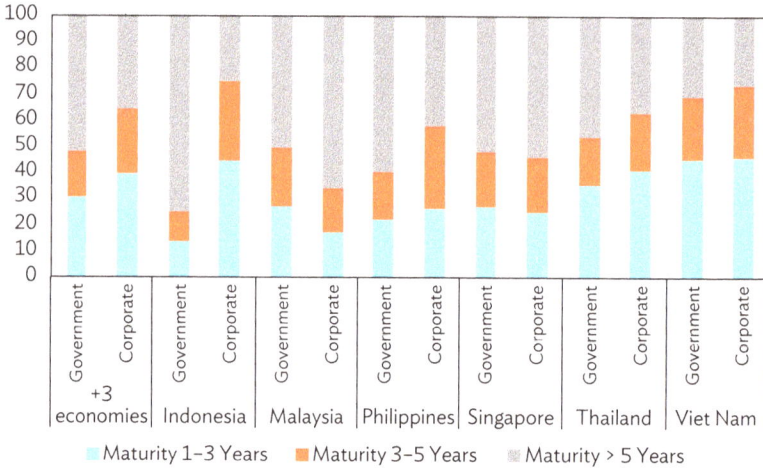

Maturity 1–3 Years   Maturity 3–5 Years   Maturity > 5 Years

LCY = local currency.
Note: +3 economies = Japan, the People's Republic of China, and the Republic of Korea. As for Japan's data, the breakdown is available for government securities, but not for corporate securities. The available corporate bonds data series starts in 2009 for Indonesia and 2010 for Malaysia. For the Republic of Korea, the available data series is from 2010 to 2018.
Source: Authors, based on AsianBondsOnline (accessed August 2021).

Figure 1.11: Sector Breakdown of ASEAN+3 Corporate Bond Issuance, 2005–2020

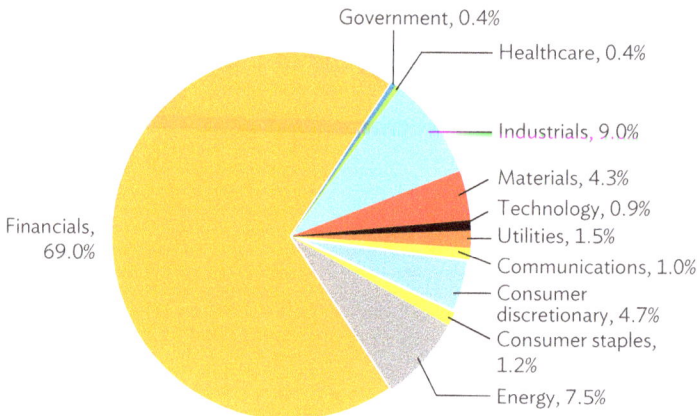

Government, 0.4%
Healthcare, 0.4%
Industrials, 9.0%
Materials, 4.3%
Technology, 0.9%
Utilities, 1.5%
Communications, 1.0%
Consumer discretionary, 4.7%
Consumer staples, 1.2%
Energy, 7.5%
Financials, 69.0%

Note: The data are based on Bloomberg Industry Classification Standard Level 1. Financials include real estate. The economies included in the calculations are Indonesia, Malaysia, the People's Republic of China, the Philippines, the Republic of Korea, Singapore, Thailand, and Viet Nam.
Source: Authors, based on data compiled by Bloomberg L.P. (accessed August 2021).

The average foreign holdings of local currency government bonds in ASEAN+3 was about 15% in 2019 and 13% in 2020, up notably from less than 9% in 2008. While keeping the costs of funding low, foreign exposure may leave countries in the region vulnerable to sharp capital flow reversals. As IMF (2020) notes, higher foreign participation in local currency bond markets could increase the volatility of bond yields in emerging market economies with limited depth.[13]

Figure 1.12: Degree of Internationalization of Bond Markets in ASEAN+3

(%)

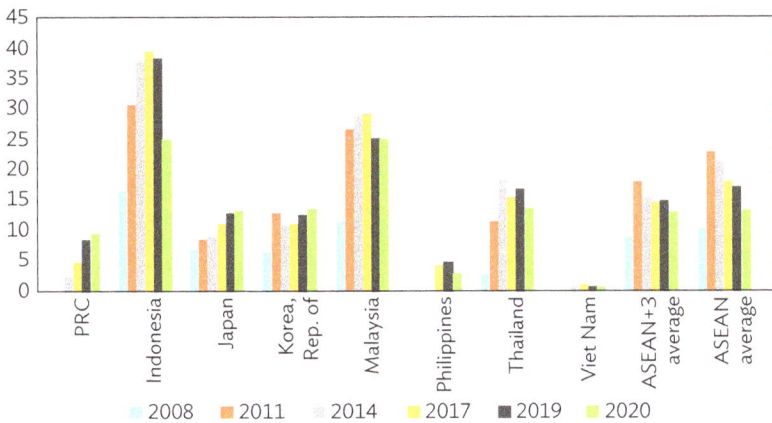

PRC = People's Republic of China.
Note: The data capture the proportion of local currency government bonds held by foreign investors relative to the amount of local currency government bonds outstanding in a specific market. The ASEAN and ASEAN+3 aggregated values pertain to simple averages of economy-level ratios covering economies with data for the period. The Philippines does not have data in 2008, 2011, and 2014. The PRC and Viet Nam do not have data in 2008 and 2011.
Source: Authors, based on AsianBondsOnline data (accessed August 2021).

The gradual transition from bank to capital market financing has also corresponded to a sharp increase in international bond issuance by nonfinancial corporations in emerging markets, including in Asia. Dollar-denominated corporate bond issuance increased sharply in ASEAN+3 economies after the global financial crisis, owing to their good growth, favorable yields, and expected currency appreciations. Figure 1.13 shows that, in absolute terms, nonfinancial corporate debt denominated in US dollars doubled from the global financial crisis, from less than $553 billion in 2007 to more than $1.3 trillion in 2020.

[13] In particular, conditional on domestic factors, when the size of foreign investor bond holdings exceeds about 40% of the country's international reserves, the volatility of yields is found to increase by about 15% (IMF 2020).

Figure 1.13: US-Dollar-Denominated Nonfinancial Corporate Debt in ASEAN+3

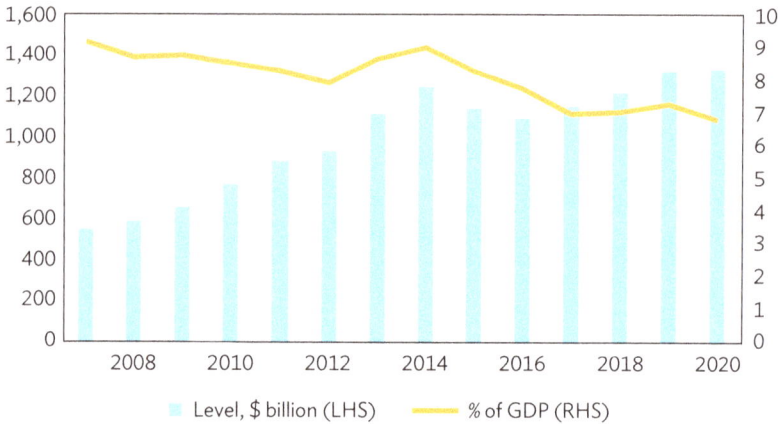

LHS = left-hand scale, RHS = right-hand scale, US = United States.
Note: Data available only for the People's Republic of China, Indonesia, Malaysia, the Republic of Korea, Singapore, and Thailand. For ASEAN+3, values as a percentage of gross domestic product (GDP) pertain to the ratio of the sum of nonfinancial corporate debt and GDP of economies with data.
Source: Authors, based on Institute of International Finance Global Debt Monitor Database (accessed August 2021).

The strong rise in foreign currency bond issuances of some Asian firms, however, raises concerns about currency mismatches, especially for firms that lack natural hedges against exchange rate exposure (such as in real estate and construction).[14] The seeming inability of firms to borrow onshore in local currencies suggests that the "original sin redux" featured in Eichengreen and Hausmann (1999, 2005), and Eichengreen, Hausmann, and Panizza (2007) is still relevant for regional corporate bond markets, if not government bond markets. Examining 5,500 firms in seven Asian emerging economies (Hong Kong, China; Indonesia; Malaysia, the Philippines; Singapore; Taipei,China; and Thailand) between 2002 and 2013, Mizen et al. (2018) find that less seasoned firms may start issuing bonds overseas before moving onshore as markets develop. However, they also note that as capital accounts open up further and hedging instruments start developing, more seasoned firms may again start to issue bonds overseas in foreign currency, motivated by opportunities for gains from cost/interest differentials.

---

[14] Additionally, foreign currency corporate bonds issued by emerging markets are more likely to be driven by global factors rather than domestic macro fundamentals and are therefore vulnerable to global cycle turns and sudden capital outflows (Ayala, Nedeljkovic, and Saborowski 2017).

Carstens and Shin (2019) note that the development of local currency bond markets may not fully protect emerging market economies from exchange rate shocks. This is the hypothesis of the original sin redux: borrowing in local currency from foreign lenders does not remove the currency mismatch, it simply shifts the problem from the balance sheets of borrowers to lenders. The lenders to emerging market economies tend not to hedge their local currency exposure. For those with obligations to beneficiaries or policyholders in their home countries, an emerging market currency depreciation would lower the value of their assets in emerging market economies in their own currency, tightening balance sheet constraints. This may trigger massive selloffs or hedging and widen bond spreads due to the exit of foreign investors.[15] One possible solution is to broaden the domestic investor base to make bond markets less sensitive to currency valuation changes (Hofmann, Patel, and Wu 2021; Hofmann, Shim, and Shin 2019).[16]

The different forms and channels of international debt issuance reflect their financial systems' development and integration with global markets (Figure 1.14). But increased sophistication of international financing activities also suggests hidden sources of external vulnerability (McCauley, McGuire, and Sushko 2015). For example, 93% of the PRC's dollar (nonfinancial) corporate bonds are offshore issuances by affiliates and may not be visible in the country's external debt statistics. Similarly, borrowing in dollars by Korean manufacturers through forward sales (in exchange for won) is an exposure not easily tracked. Growth in indirect dollar credit has been adequately managed by Korean regulators mainly through macroprudential measures. These examples imply that while the region has managed to emerge from the global financial crisis relatively unscathed, anchoring financial stability amid rapid financial innovation and strong capital flows remains a serious challenge.

---

[15] Hofmann, Shim, and Shin (2019) elaborate on the links between exchange rates and bond market risk premia in emerging economies.

[16] Other solutions include sterilized foreign exchange intervention to reduce exchange rate volatility and establishing prudential measures to curtail foreign bond inflows (Hofmann, Patel, and Wu 2021; Hofmann, Shim, and Shin 2019). Chapter 2 of this volume includes a brief discussion on the corporate bond market.

Figure 1.14: Debt Composition of Nonfinancial Corporations in Emerging Markets

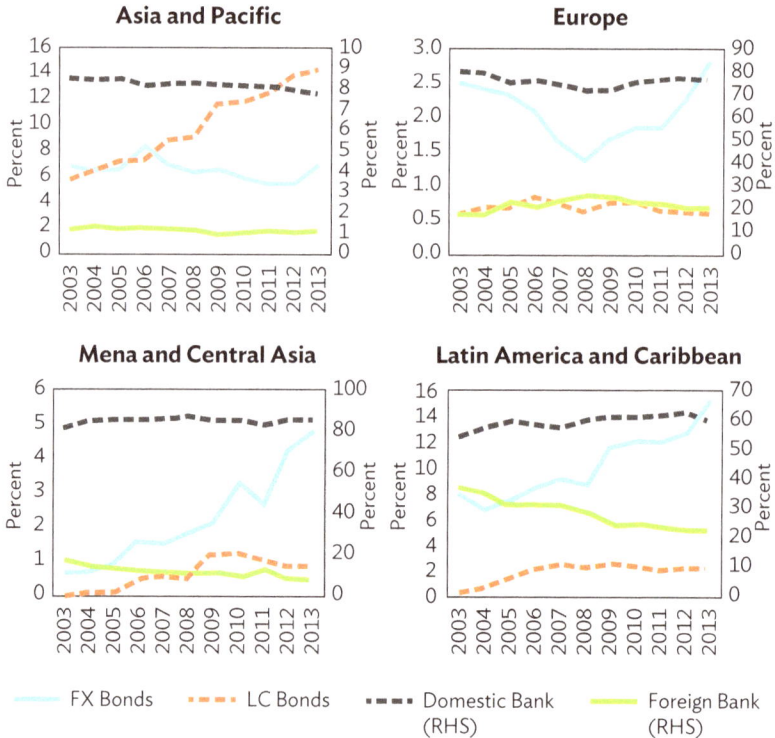

Asia and Pacific

Europe

Mena and Central Asia

Latin America and Caribbean

—— FX Bonds   ▪▪▪▪ LC Bonds   ▪▪▪▪ Domestic Bank (RHS)   —— Foreign Bank (RHS)

FX = foreign exchange, LC = local currency, RHS = right-hand scale.
Note: The charts show the averages by region. Regional groupings follow International Monetary Fund definitions.
Source: Ayala, Nedeljkovic, and Saborowski (2017).

1.4 The Impact of COVID-19 on Financial Systems

COVID-19 and its associated economic downturns again tested ASEAN+3 economies' financial resilience during the pandemic-induced crisis period. Given underlying structural weaknesses such as limited diversification in corporate financing sources and heavy reliance on the US dollar for increasingly internationalized business and financial activities, ASEAN+3 financial systems continue to be vulnerable to the sudden reversal of capital flows and exchange rate volatility. The pandemic also added financial challenges from sharp increases in fiscal spending, possible deterioration in bank asset quality, and the acceleration of digital transformation.

A Surge in Debt and Risks of Debt Sustainability

Immediate challenges brought by the pandemic relate to a surge in debt and risks of debt sustainability. The depth of the COVID-19 shock necessitates that countries undertake massive fiscal stimulus packages. Only a few countries in the region with strong fiscal positions like Singapore may be able to draw on their past reserve holdings to fund multiple fiscal packages close to 20% of GDP.[17] Many other countries in the region have had to raise funding through the sovereign bond market. Indonesia was among early movers, raising $4.2 billion from dollar-denominated "pandemic bonds" in April 2020. This was followed by the Philippines, which issued $2.4 billion in pandemic bonds in May 2020 (Table 1.1). As the fiscal needs of regional governments rise, one can expect more of these sovereign issuances.

Table 1.1: Sovereign Bonds Issuance to Address the Pandemic

Issuer	Coupon (%)	Issue Date	Tenor (Years)	Principal Currency	Amount Issued ($ billion)	Offered Yield to Maturity (%)	S&P Rating
Indonesia	4.45	4/15/2020	50	USD	1.0	4.50	BBB
Indonesia	4.20	4/15/2020	30	USD	1.6	4.25	BBB
Indonesia	3.85	4/15/2020	10.5	USD	1.6	3.90	BBB
Philippines	2.95	5/5/2020	25	USD	1.4	2.95	BBB+
Philippines	2.46	5/5/2020	10	USD	1.0	2.46	BBB+

USD = United States dollar.
Source: Lopez (2020), based on Refinitiv data.

The development of regional bond markets has been important in facilitating the aggressive fiscal responses to the pandemic in many ASEAN+3 economies. However, once the pandemic is contained, the unwinding of COVID-19-related debt has to be managed carefully. The ASEAN+3 community needs strong leadership to avoid a debt debacle. Otherwise, this risk could unfold as soon as the US Federal Reserve (Federal Reserve) starts normalizing its ultra-easy monetary policy, which may lead to tighter global credit conditions, and an unwinding of large-scale stimulus packages in the region begins without proper planning and management. The focus of financial markets could easily turn to the issue of size of fiscal debt and deficits. If this happens, borrowing costs could climb and cause financial upheaval (AMRO 2020a).

---

[17] However, the acute fiscal shock due to COVID-19 along with structural fiscal pressures due to aging demographics has led the Singapore government to recently pass easing of legislation that would allow the government to issue long-term bonds in the future to finance large-scale infrastructure projects (Yuen-C 2021).

Another concern is a potential surge in nonperforming loans due to sharp economic slowdowns and a deteriorating business environment. The massive rise in debt and bankruptcies among firms and households could destabilize the banking and financial system, if not properly managed during the recovery phase. And such financial stress could also spill over to other economies through cross-border banking networks.

AMRO (2020a) highlights concerns about financial distress among the region's highly interconnected banks reverberating through the region's financial systems causing significant credit losses and collateral damage. Park and Shin (2020) investigate the impact on banking flows of a rise in bank nonperforming loan ratios in both lender and emerging market borrower countries and find that a rise in the nonperforming loan ratios of both lender and borrower countries is positively associated with increased banking capital outflows from emerging market economies. An emerging market economy with higher nonperforming loans may be particularly vulnerable to such portfolio rebalancing and deleveraging of globally active banks in advanced economies. For example, major global lenders may account for souring loans by adjusting their international portfolio assets and reducing lending to emerging markets.

The scale of interdependencies means that regional financial cooperation should not be overlooked. The most salient development on regulatory cooperation is Basel 3, which was introduced after the global financial crisis to strengthen global regulatory standards on bank capital adequacy (which now requires a larger countercyclical capital buffer), stress testing, and market liquidity. To address more fundamental issues of nonperforming loans in increasingly interconnected financial systems, countries should focus on international stabilization and reform efforts, particularly in developing national and regional resolution mechanisms and a well-functioning secondary market for nonperforming loans.

Rapid Digital Transformation and the Changing Financial Landscape

COVID-19 has given a big impetus to e-payments and digital banking and financial services (lending, remittances, insurance, trade finance, and so on) combined with new technologies such as artificial intelligence, blockchains, and cloud computing.[18] On a positive note, an increase in digital financial services could enhance financial efficiency and inclusion. However,

---

[18] See ADB (2021) for a more general discussion of rise of digitalization in Asia.

concerns have been raised that the rapid rise in fintech adoption in the post-pandemic era may unsettle financial stability.

As Aizenman (2020) notes, an increase in the supply of fintech credit could result in the emergence of 'shadow intermediaries' and redirect financial intermediation from the regulated banking sector, creating unintended consequences. While the fintech revolution pressures traditional banks to offer faster, cheaper, and more effective financial services, it could also complicate monetary transmission. Further, as Boot et al. (2020) show, the disintermediation of financial supply chains could generate concerns about regulatory arbitrage as the risks are subsumed into complex network structures. Accelerated digital transformation could have a significant bearing on the financial landscape and regional cooperation for financial efficiency and stability.

Moving forward, it is important to strike a balance between managing financial innovation and change (including fintech and emerging trends such as digital currency) to boost financial efficiency while still maintaining financial stability. The region needs to find ways to further deregulate and promote digitalization of financial services industries without unduly exposing them to excessive risk.

Narrowing the Gap in Financial Inclusion

A growing consensus among global policy makers suggests that developing economies should place financial inclusion at the top of the agenda given its significant benefits for people and firms. A study by Ayyagari and Beck (2015) presents a list of benefits, but finds that although developing Asia has more banking sector depth than other developing regions, the picture on access to financial services is bleak as fewer than 27% of adults have an account in a formal financial institution and only 33% of enterprises report having a credit line or loan from a financial institution. Biggest barriers identified by the authors include cost and geographical access, which policy makers in the region could attempt to resolve.

Fintech or the use of digital technology to broaden access to finance could also play an essential role in expanding financial inclusion. According to some estimates, digital financial solutions can fill about 40% of unmet demand for payment services and 20% of the credit requirements of poor households and small businesses in Asia.[19] While helpful in closing the financial inclusion gap, fintech entails both risks to financial stability and regulatory challenges, with consumers of digital finance needing protection against a plethora of issues about data governance (related to how data are accessed, used, and stored), which mostly concern data privacy and safety and consumer protection (ADB 2018).

1.5 An Unfinished Agenda: Lessons Learned and the Way Forward

Booms and busts in capital flows remain a significant source of financial risk in ASEAN+3 economies. During the COVID-19 pandemic, a sharp reversal in portfolio flows was again primarily related to the bond market and consequent impacts on currency. It would therefore be important to reassess where regional economies stand with regard to the use of exchange rate flexibility as a shock absorber. At a time of increased financial uncertainty raising credit risks, global and local banks alike can experience liquidity shortfalls in international credit markets. Emerging market economies with sizable external liabilities are vulnerable to sudden shifts in investor sentiment. That these liabilities are denominated in local currency terms does not shield them from the flight to safety, as reflected in the "original sin redux" hypothesis.

Exchange Flexibility and US Dollar Dominance

Data from the exchange rate arrangements for the broader Asian region as reported in the IMF's Annual Report on Exchange Arrangements and Restrictions (AREAR) for 2020 are shown in Table 1.2.[20] While most emerging markets have transitioned to floating exchange rate regimes (Cavoli, Gopalan, and Rajan 2019), countries that have adopted inflation targeting continue to use foreign exchange intervention as a prominent policy instrument. This can be partly explained by their ongoing concern that excessive exchange-rate volatility may amplify rather than absorb shocks (Hofmann, Shim, and Shin 2020; Patel and Cavallino 2019).

---

[19] This is based on a study commissioned by ADB on accelerating financial inclusion in Southeast Asia through digital finance (Oliver Wyman and MicroSave 2017).

[20] This discussion partially draws on and updates the discussion in Cavoli, Gopalan, and Rajan (2019).

More generally, there is a growing recognition that the insulating powers of exchange rates (as shock absorbers) may be waning (Rey 2013, 2016).[21] This is especially true in countries where the US dollar is dominant as the invoicing currency for trade—the so-called Dominant Currency Pricing (DCP) paradigm. With nearly 80% of ASEAN+3's exports over the past 2 decades being invoiced (and settled) in US dollars (Figure 1.15),[22] studies have shown that the DCP weakens the ability of countries to benefit from currency depreciation spurring economic recovery in the short-term, thereby limiting the role of exchange rates in cushioning external shocks (Adler et al. 2020, Gopinath 2016, Gopinath et al. 2020).[23] While some regional surveys suggest a gradual move toward invoicing in local and regional currencies, US dollar dominance remains firmly entrenched (Shimizu et al. 2019).[24]

Adler et al. (2020) further point out that DCP may also be closely related to the paradigm of Dominant Currency Financing (DCF), which broadly refers to firms relying on US-dollar funding through both the banking system and the bond market, as discussed previously (also see Bruno and Shin 2015; Hofmann, Shim, and Shin 2020). The nexus between DCP and DCF remains under-researched. More to the point, is the use of US dollar as a DCP because of its ready and cheap financing given its established role as a DCF? Or is the US dollar's role as DCP (for historical reasons, having been the largest export market for the region's final goods after World War II; commodities invoiced in exports, historical fixed exchange rates, high transaction costs of regional currency exchange, and so on) the reason behind firms choosing US dollars as a natural hedge and central banks holding on to US dollars as a safe asset?

---

[21] We are alluding here to the so-called Trilemma versus Dilemma debate in international finance. There have been a number of critiques and nuances to the dilemma hypothesis, including Obstfeld, Ostry, and Qureshi (2018, 2019), Klein and Shambaugh (2015), and Eichengreen et al. (2020), who argue that the conventional wisdom regarding Impossible Monetary Trilemma remains relevant especially for emerging economies (i.e., exchange rate flexibility does have insulation powers). Also see Cheng and Rajan (2020) and Han and Wei (2018) who suggest that there may exist a 2.5 lemma between the Dilemma and Trilemma. This remains an area of ongoing debate.

[22] Countries for which data are available include Cambodia, Indonesia, Japan, Malaysia, the Republic of Korea, and Thailand. Among the +3 countries, it is pertinent to note that the corresponding average share of exports from Japan invoiced in US dollars was only 50% between 1990 and 2020, while it was quite high for the Republic Korea at 85%. Chapter 3 of this volume includes more on this.

[23] Participation in regional and global value chains also makes trade less exchange rate elastic in general, even with local currency pricing (de Soyres et al. 2018).

[24] For the specific case of growing share of local currency use for Japanese exports to Asia, see Ito et al. (2018).

Table 1.2: Classification of Exchange Rate Arrangements for Selected Asia and Pacific Economies, 2020

Exchange rate arrangement (number of countries)	Monetary Policy Framework						
	Exchange rate anchor				Monetary aggregate target	Inflation targeting framework	Other
	US dollar	Euro	Composite	Other			
No separate legal tender	Timor-Leste; Marshall Islands; Federated States of Micronesia; Palau			Kiribati; Tuvalu			
Currency board	Hong Kong, China			Brunei Darussalam			
Conventional peg			Fiji	Bhutan; Nepal			
Stabilized arrangement	Maldives		Viet Nam			Sri Lanka (4/19)	Solomon Islands
Crawl-like arrangement	Cambodia (3/19)		Singapore		Bangladesh; Papua New Guinea		Mongolia (1/19)
Other managed arrangement					PRC		
Floating						Indonesia; Korea, Rep. of; Philippines; Thailand; New Zealand	Tonga (1/19); Vanuatu; Pakistan; Malaysia
Free floating						Australia; Japan	

PRC = People's Republic of China.

Note: If a country's *de facto* exchange rate arrangement was reclassified by the IMF during the reporting period, the date of change is indicated in parentheses (month, year). The de facto classification is based on IMF's assessment in its AREAR. https://www.elibrary.areaer.imf.org/Documents/Exchange%20Rate%20Classification%20Methodology/ExchangeRateClassificationSystemDefinitions_2008.pdf

Source: IMF AREAER (2020).

Figure 1.15: Export Invoicing Currencies for ASEAN+3
(% total exports)

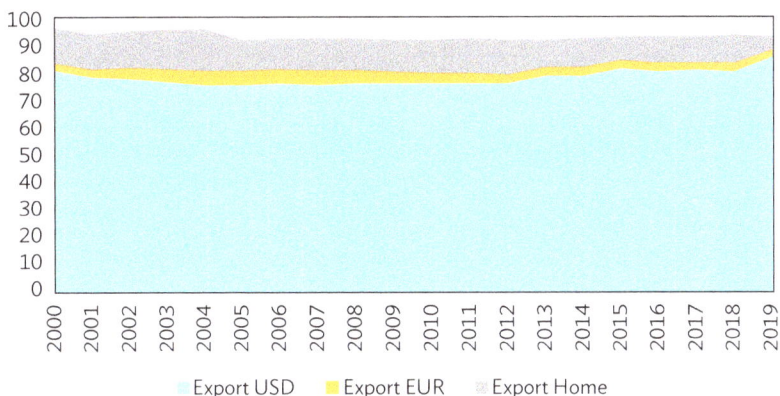

EUR = euro, USD = United States dollar.
Note: Data for ASEAN+3 is the simple average of percentage shares of export invoices in US dollars, euro, and the home currency. Countries for which data are available include Cambodia, Indonesia, Japan, Malaysia, the Republic of Korea, and Thailand.
Source: Boz et al. (2020).

While this is an open area of research, from a policy perspective,[25] the combination of DCP and DCF aggravates the negative impact of exchange-rate depreciations on such firms and more generally blunts the insulating effects of exchange-rate flexibility.[26] These concerns are particularly relevant in the context of the pandemic, which led to significant exchange rate and reserves pressures in many emerging markets, including in ASEAN+3 (Figure 1.16).[27]

---

[25] The work by Gopinath and Stein (2020) is one of the few papers that has looked at the US dollar's role jointly as a DCF and DCP from a theoretical perspective and they conclude the following: (T)here is a fundamental connection between the dollar's role as the currency in which non-US exporters predominantly invoice their sales, and its prominence in global banking and finance. Moreover, these two roles feedback on and reinforce each other. Going in one direction, a large volume of dollar invoicing in international trade creates an increased demand for safe dollar deposits, thereby conferring an exorbitant privilege on the dollar in terms of reduced borrowing costs. Going in the other direction, these low dollar-denominated borrowing costs make it attractive for non-US exporters to invoice their sales in dollars, so that they can more easily tap the cheap dollar funding. The end result of this two-way feedback can be an asymmetric entrenchment of the dollar as the global currency of choice, even when other countries are roughly similar to the US in terms of economic fundamentals such as their share of overall world-wide imports.

[26] While DCP has been about trade and DCF about capital flows, Bruno and Shin (2018), and Bruno, Kim, and Shin (2018) link the two by considering the case where bank-intermediated trade financing is denominated primarily in US dollars.

[27] See ADB (2021) for a discussion on policy responses to the pandemic among regional economies.

Figure 1.16: Exchange Rate Movements in ASEAN+3, January–May 2021

(Index, 15 Jan 2020 = 100)

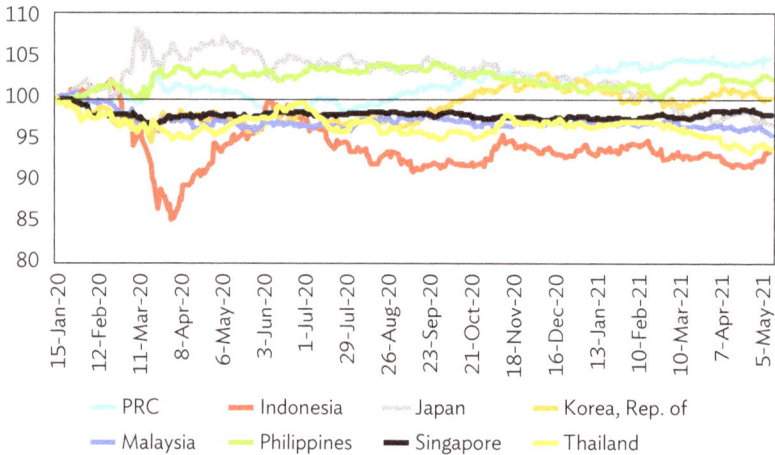

PRC = People's Republic of China.
Note: Nominal effective exchange rate (broad index), rebased at 15 Jan 2020 = 100. An increase indicates an appreciation of the economy's currency against a broad basket of currencies.
Source: Authors, based on BIS *Effective Exchange Rate Indices* (accessed May 2021).

The persistent and widespread use of the US dollar as an invoicing and financing currency remains a significant source of financial vulnerability and points to the need to reinvigorate the debate on reform of the international reserve system to include multiple international currencies (Park, Rosenkranz, and Tayag 2020).[28] For their part, regional economies must continue to support the development of a local currency settlement framework among themselves to reduce the extent of US dollar invoicing.[29] While these are medium- and longer-term structural policies, many regional economies have developed a practical and eclectic toolkit to manage exchange rate and balance of payments pressures through a combination of sterilized foreign exchange intervention and active use of macroprudential and capital flow management measures (Carstens 2019, Cheng and Rajan 2020, Ghosh, Ostry, and Qureshi 2017, Hofmann, Patel, and Wu 2021).[30] A clear conceptual framework is lacking for policy makers to understand

---

[28] It remains an open question whether the rise of the PRC central bank digital currency, private digital currencies especially stable coins such as the Diem could challenge the US position as the DCF (Rajan and Cheng 2020).

[29] Important steps in this regard among regional economies are explained in Chapter 3.

[30] Carstens (2019) describes emerging economy central banks' policy reaction function "as a multi-instrument reaction function responding to multiple-indicator variables, including the exchange rate."

how to use multiple tools in a manner that improves policy tradeoffs. That said, the IMF's Integrated Framework (Basu et al. 2020, Adrian et al. 2020) is an important first step, though scope exists for further discussion about making the framework more relevant to ASEAN+3, if necessary by incorporating region-specific considerations.

Reserve Accumulation and Regional Monetary Cooperation

Without a reliable lender of last resort, countries in the region have resorted to accumulating foreign exchange reserves, and continued to do so even in the aftermath of the global financial crisis, at least up until 2013. Foreign exchange reserves in ASEAN+3 as a whole have more than doubled from $3 trillion in 2007 to over $6 trillion in 2013. The level marginally declined from 2013 to 2016, which coincided with the taper tantrum episode as countries tried to defend their currencies from sharp depreciations, capital flight and the PRC's decline in reserves between mid-2014 and mid-2016.[31] Reserve accumulation in the region resumed after, and reserves stood at over $6 trillion in 2020 (Figure 1.17).

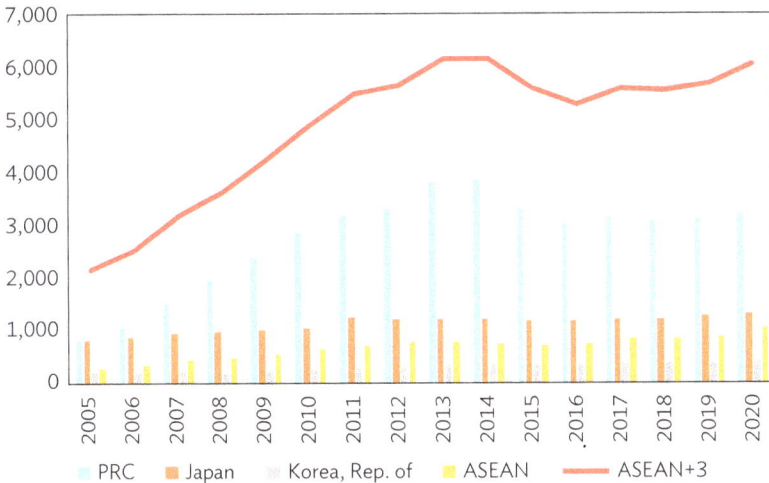

Figure 1.17: Foreign Exchange Reserves in ASEAN+3
($ billion)

PRC = People's Republic of China.
Note: The measure excludes gold.
Source: Authors, based on World Bank, *World Development Indicators* (accessed August 2021).

---

[31] There was also likely a currency valuation effect from US-dollar appreciation against other reserve currencies. See Ito and McCauley (2019) for a discussion on the currency composition of reserves.

The size of reserves held by the countries in the ASEAN+3 region appears to be broadly adequate for precautionary purposes, based on the conservative estimates of the IMF's Assessing Reserve Adequacy Emerging Markets (ARA EM) metric which considers trade, short-term debt, size of the monetary base, and portfolio liabilities (IMF 2013). Countries that have reserves within the 100% to 150% of this composite metric were considered broadly adequate as of 2019. Most ASEAN+3 countries are within this range, with the PRC the sole exception in the last few years (Figure 1.18).

Figure 1.18: Foreign Exchange Reserves in ASEAN+3
(% of IMF's ARA EM Metric)

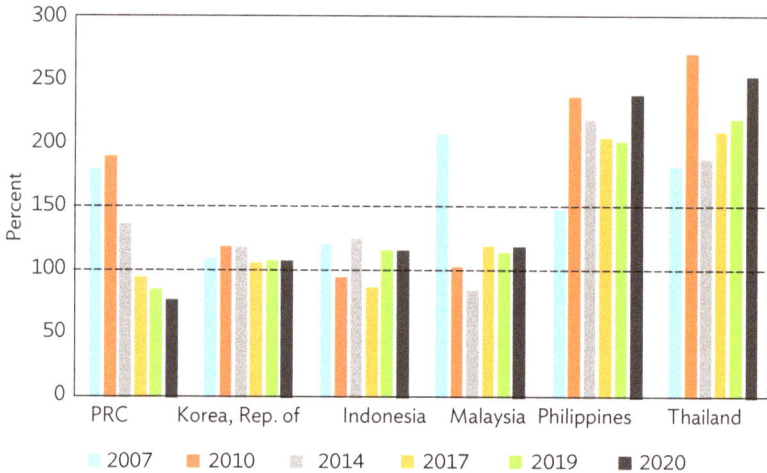

ARA EM = Assessing Reserve Adequacy Emerging Markets, IMF = International Monetary Fund, PRC = People's Republic of China.
Source: IMF, Assessing Reserve Adequacy Database (accessed May 2021).

Although countries in the region continue to hold the largest buffers of reserves in the world, this self-insurance mechanism has been recognized for some time as costly and in need of being complemented by a credible regional reserve pooling arrangement (Bird and Rajan 2003).[32] Following the global financial crisis, ASEAN+3 made some significant institutional advancements with regard to regional financing arrangements built on the Chiang Mai Initiative Multilateralization (CMIM) and the ASEAN+3 Macroeconomic Research Office (AMRO).

---

[32] See Arslan and Cantú (2019) for a wider-ranging discussion of motives for reserve accumulation and measures of reserve adequacy in emerging economies more generally.

While CMIM is expected to play an important role in the global financial safety net, doubt remains about its operability because it has yet to be drawn upon in times of crisis.[33] To improve market confidence, ASEAN+3 members have improved flexibility and operational readiness, including amending the CMIM Agreement and CMIM Operational Guidelines from June 2020 (AMRO 2020b). ASEAN+3 members have also adopted an information-sharing mechanism between the CMIM and its partner the IMF, and conducted test runs to better understand operational risks and enhance readiness. Test runs highlighted issues emanating from assistance provisions, such as incompatibility between CMIM's shorter repayment periods and program length and the IMF's longer-term financing arrangements, and the need for the two institutions to take a shared view on the policy adjustment path, financing needs, and policy conditionality for a recipient country (IMF 2017).

At the 23rd ASEAN+3 Finance Ministers and Central Bank Governors' Meetingon 18 September 2020, finance ministers and central bank governors announced a plan to "institutionalize voluntary and demand-driven, for both requesting and providing parties, local currency contributions in the CMIM." This reflected suggestions that allowing for local currency contributions to the CMIM may spur local/regional currency invoicing, settlement, and financing to reduce the region's excessive dependence on the US dollar (Kim 2019, Lu 2019, and Sussangkarn 2019).

While the motivation for the proposed plan is apparent given the region's US dollar vulnerabilities, the suggestion is not without concerns. The main aim of CMIM is to manage liquidity concerns in the region which in turn are often due to dislocations and shortages in US dollar funding markets. Requiring the CMIM to use local currencies may in some ways hinder its effectiveness as a regional financing facility, while also leading to mission creep. This should be of particular concern given that the CMIM itself remains unutilized even as ASEAN+3 economies have had to deal with sudden changes in market conditions for US dollar funding. Instead, some economies (the Republic Korea and Singapore) have been able to access temporary bilateral swap lines with the Federal Reserve. However, most economies in the region remain excluded from Fed swaps, leaving them vulnerable to supply shocks in the US dollar market.[34]

---

[33] Some would counter that the region has not needed to draw on the CMIM as of now as the economies have been by and large fundamentally sound.

[34] On 31 March 2020, the Federal Reserve also announced the establishment of a temporary repurchase agreement facility for foreign and international monetary authorities (FIMA Repo Facility), whereby FIMA account holders—central banks and other international monetary authorities with accounts at the Federal Reserve Bank of New York—could enter into repurchase agreements with the Federal Reserve. (Government of the United States, Board of Governors of the Federal Reserve System 2020).

As a consequence, many regional economies have begun to pursue bilateral swaps and local currency settlements to reduce the US dollar's structural dominance while also employing their ability to act as liquidity backstops to help promote financial stability. Bilateral swap agreements may be better placed than the CMIM to develop the use of local currency and support development of local currency settlement frameworks among regional economies.[35] As the network continues to grow, concerns may emerge about how to better integrate these bilateral swaps with the CMIM. Greater attention is needed on the collaborative use of bilateral swaps and multicurrency swap mechanisms offered by the CMIM (see Han 2021 and Chapter 7 of this volume).

1.6 Conclusion

In a post-pandemic world, as Asia starts to focus on the recovery and rebuilding for greater economic resilience and sustainability, it is critical that ASEAN+3 economies formulate collective responses to handle global shocks. While invariably some will call for regional cooperation to be envisioned on a much grander scale, it is important to keep in mind that financial and monetary cooperation in Asia does not have a long history and only started to take shape after the Asian financial crisis. As was highlighted in the ASEAN+3 vision document *Strategic Directions of Finance Process:* "The year 2019 mark[ed] the 20th anniversary of ASEAN+3 Financial Cooperation. Along with the tides of regional economic integration, the ASEAN+3 Finance Process has been making great progress in enhancing regional economic and financial stability during the past two decades" (AMRO 2019).

Overall, financial cooperation is essential for safeguarding financial stability by increasing financial interconnectedness, promoting borderless digital finance, and rebalancing the region's continued dependence on the US dollar and international financial networks. Cooperation has been strengthened in the areas of monitoring (and surveillance) of macroeconomic conditions, capital flows and financial systems, information and expertise sharing, and development of financial safety nets. A clearer understanding of countries' motivations for regional cooperation would further improve the design of institutions providing financial safety nets (such as AMRO and CMIM) and the structure of emergency arrangements (CMIM, bilateral currency swaps,

---

[35] The PRC is using the Belt and Road Initiative to further promote the regional and global use of the yuan. Japan has also been promoting the yen for international transactions and the development of direct exchange markets between the yen and other ASEAN+3 currencies.

and the relationship with the IMF). This would be a step closer to achieving long-lasting financial stability in the region.

In the past few decades, the ASEAN+3 region has seen a host of regional initiatives to support growing intraregional interdependencies and to help buffer the region against currency and financial market volatility. On the financial cooperation side, as discussed in this chapter, the policy focus has been on building financial stability and resilience by reinforcing regional financial safety nets and developing markets for local currency bonds and long-term capital. As noted, financial openness (broadly encompassing cross-border banking and financial activities with all types of capital flows) has driven domestic financial market development. Yet, growing internationalization of banking and the emergence of local currency bond markets (attracting foreign investors and participation) has also brought additional risks, notably with regard to global shocks and vulnerability to fluctuations in the US dollar.

The COVID-19 pandemic has reset the spotlight on the vulnerability of emerging markets to sudden stops in volatile capital flows and acute exchange-rate and balance-of-payments pressures. This is also down to deeply entrenched structural weakness in the region's financial systems, such as dollar dominance, and the need to further diversify corporate financing sources and reform the banking system, especially given the rise in shadow funding, including nonbank financial institutions. In addition, the dominant role of the US dollar for international invoicing and financing casts doubt on the current capacity of the region's foreign exchange and reserve management to absorb external shocks.

While bond markets these days spur far greater regional financial intermediation compared to 2 decades ago, the region's financial systems remain heavily bank-based. In the context of the rise of regional systemically important banks, this is one facet of a complex picture that this volume explores in detail. Chapter 2 explores the issue of regional bank flows using data from the BIS Consolidated Banking Statistics. Its focus is on the concentration risks from cross-border lending activities by large, interconnected global and regional banks, which being few in number make the region susceptible to systemic risks through a "common lender" effect that could be a source of financial contagion and related domestic credit supply disruptions.

Chapter 3 explores the dominance of the US dollar as an international currency in general and takes stock of the usage of regional currencies for trade, investment, financial transactions, and exchange rate management among ASEAN+3 economies. With growing trade, investment, and financial integration, extensive use of the US dollar in intraregional transactions has caused concern as the economies have been especially susceptible to sudden squeeze in US dollar liquidity or sharp appreciations in the greenback, as happened in the early stages of the COVID-19 pandemic in 2020 and during the global financial crisis in 2007–2009 and the taper tantrum episode of 2013. The chapter contrasts the US dollar's preeminence with the limited roles played by regional currencies, including the Japanese yen and the PRC yuan, and highlights factors that impede regional currencies' use in cross-border transactions—even as some ASEAN+3 economies have taken significant steps to internationalize their currencies. It also presents some policy suggestions for enhancing the regional use of local currencies in the ASEAN+3 region.

Chapter 4 reviews the main developments of digital finance and fintech in the region and discusses their implications for financial inclusion and financial stability at the microfinancial and macrofinancial levels as well as in the design of monetary policy. The safe distancing and lockdown measures imposed by countries due to COVID-19 have provided a fillip to the ongoing move toward digitalization in finance and other areas within and among the ASEAN+3 economies. Digital finance and fintech have the ability to lower costs of financial intermediation and accelerate access to finance and will likely become an important driver of regional financial cooperation going forward. Since fintech service providers pose regulatory challenges not always adequately captured by bank-centered regulatory frameworks, the chapter also discusses how regional cooperation can realize fintech's potential while mitigating its risks.

The medium- and longer-term growth prospects of ASEAN+3 will be hindered unless the region plugs massive infrastructure gaps highlighted by ADB (ADB 2017). To date, infrastructure investments have been mostly funded from public sector budgets rather than the private sector.[36] However, it will be crucial to increase private sector participation in development finance given the vast financing gap and limited public sector financing since aggressive responses to the COVID-19 pandemic and rising debts are further reducing the fiscal space for action. While infrastructure

---

[36] According to ADB (2017), around 81% of investments in ASEAN (Southeast Asia) are public sector investments, while 19% are private investment.

financing to support rapid urbanization, regional growth, and poverty reduction in ASEAN+3 is crucial, it is equally important to proceed in an environmentally sound manner. The issue of innovative approaches to sustainable infrastructure financing, including utilizing regional capital markets to engage private financing more effectively, is the broad focus of Chapter 5. The chapter also explores how spillover effects of infrastructure investments might generate positive effects on tax revenues and improve the bankability of infrastructure projects, which in turn could attract private investors.

While demography is not destiny, it is well known that ASEAN+3 economies (especially in the +3 economies, along with Singapore, Thailand, and even Viet Nam) are rapidly aging because of a combination of low and declining fertility rates and rising life expectancies. Chapter 6 examines the impact of aging on the macroeconomy, with specific focus on labor force participation, savings, growth and productivity. It also offers a discussion on the diverse regional pension landscape and looks at the pension challenges that spring from population aging and the advent of the digital revolution. It also explores areas of regional cooperation, including the scope for investing in "alternative" assets such as infrastructure, and the portability of pensions across regional economies to match the mobility of workers.

The final chapter of this volume on ASEAN+3 regional financial cooperation summarizes key policy challenges, priorities, and recommendations. It draws attention to policy initiatives pertaining to financial and monetary cooperation and pulls together the main messages from preceding chapters. This provides important context and support for the priorities that ASEAN+3 finance and central bank officials identified in their Strategic Directions of Finance Process vision document.

References

Adler, G., C. Casas, L.M. Cubeddu, G. Gopinath, N. Li, S. Meleshchuk, C. Osorio Buitron, D. Puy, and Y. Timmer. 2020. Dominant Currencies and External Adjustment. *IMF Staff Discussion Note*. No. 20/05. Washington, DC: International Monetary Fund. https://www.imf.org/-/media/Files/Publications/SDN/2020/English/SDNEA2020005.ashx.

Adrian, T., C.J. Erceg, J. Lindé, P. Zabczyk, and J. Zhou. 2020. A Quantitative Model for the Integrated Policy Framework. *IMF Working Paper*. WP/20/122. Washington, DC: International Monetary Fund. https://www.imf.org/-/media/Files/Publications/WP/2020/English/wpiea2020122-print-pdf.ashx.

Adrian, T., P. Colla, and H.S. Shin. 2012. Which Financial Frictions? Parsing the Evidence from the Financial Crisis of 2007 to 2009. *NBER Working Paper Series*. No. 18335. Cambridge, MA: National Bureau of Economic Research. https://www.nber.org/system/files/working_papers/w18335/w18335.pdf.

Aizenman, J. 2020. Macroeconomic Challenges and the Resilience of Emerging Market Economies in the 21st Century. *ADBI Working Paper Series*. No. 1131. Tokyo: Asian Development Bank Institute. https://www.adb.org/sites/default/files/publication/606501/adbi-wp1131.pdf.

Aizenman, J., Y. Jinjarak, and D. Park. 2015. Financial Development and Output Growth in Developing Asia and Latin America: A Comparative Sectoral Analysis. *NBER Working Paper Series*. No. 20917. Cambridge, MA: National Bureau of Economic Research. https://www.nber.org/system/files/working_papers/w20917/w20917.pdf.

Akamatsu, N. and K. Puongsophol. 2018. *Good Practices in Developing Bond Market: Association of Southeast Asian Nations Plus Three*. Manila: Asian Development Bank. https://asianbondsonline.adb.org/documents/abmi_good_practices_developing_bond_market.pdf.

Arslan, Y. and C. Cantú. 2019. The Size of Foreign Exchange Reserves. *BIS Papers*. No. 104. Basel: Bank for International Settlements. https://www.bis.org/publ/bppdf/bispap104a_rh.pdf.

ASEAN+3 Macroeconomic Research Office (AMRO). 2019. *Strategic Directions of ASEAN+3 Finance Process*. Singapore. https://amro-asia.org/wp-content/uploads/2019/05/Strategic-Directions-of-ASEAN3-Finance-Process_for-circulation_after-Asian financial crisisDM3-clean.pdf.

————. 2020a. US Dollar Funding Stress in the ASEAN+3 Region. Analytical Note. Singapore. https://www.amro-asia.org/wp-content/uploads/2020/04/AMRO-Analytical-Note_US-Dollar-Funding-Stress-in-the-ASEAN3-Region_27-Apr-2020.pdf.

————. 2020b. The Amended Chiang Mai Initiative Multilateralization (CMIM) Comes Into Effect on 23 June 2020. *Press Release*. 23 June. https://www.amro-asia.org/the-amended-chiang-mai-initiative-multilateralisation-cmim-comes-into-effect-on-june-23-2020/.

Asian Development Bank (ADB). 2008. *ASEAN+3 New ABMI Roadmap*. Manila. https://asianbondsonline.adb.org/publications/adb/2008/abmi_roadmap.pdf.

————. 2012. *ASEAN+3 Bond Market Guide*. Manila. https://www.adb.org/sites/default/files/publication/29702/asean3-bond-market-guide.pdf.

————. 2015. *Implementation of the ASEAN+3 Multi-Currency Bond Issuance Framework: ASEAN+3 Bond Market Forum Sub-Forum 1 Phase 3 Report*. Manila. https://www.adb.org/sites/default/files/publication/173257/implementation-ambif-sf1-p3.pdf.

————. 2017. *Meeting Asia's Infrastructure Needs*. Manila. http://dx.doi.org/10.22617/FLS168388-2.

————. 2018. *Harnessing Technology for More Inclusive and Sustainable Finance in Asia and the Pacific*. Manila. https://www.adb.org/sites/default/files/publication/456936/technology-finance-asia-pacific.pdf.

————. 2019. *Good Practices for Developing a Local Currency Bond Market: Lessons from the ASEAN+3 Asian Bond Markets Initiative*. Manila. https://www.adb.org/sites/default/files/publication/499671/developing-lcy-bond-market.pdf.

————. 2021. *Asian Economic Integration Report 2021: Making Digital Platforms Work for Asia and the Pacific*. Manila. http://dx.doi.org/10.22617/TCS210048-2.

————. AsianBondsOnline. https://asianbondsonline.adb.org/data-portal/ (accessed August 2021).

Auerbach, N. N. and T. D. Willett. 2003. The Political Economy of Perverse Financial Liberalization: Examples from the Asian Crisis. *Working Papers*, Claremont Colleges. Los Angeles. https://scholarship. claremont.edu/cgi/viewcontent.cgi?article=1149&context=scripp s_fac_pub.

Ayala, D., M. Nedeljkovic, and C. Saborowski. 2017. What Slice of the Pie? The Corporate Bond Market Boom in Emerging Economies. *CESifo Working Paper*. No. 6376. Munich: Center for Economic Studies and ifo Institute (CESifo). http://hdl.handle.net/10419/155618.

Ayyagari, M. and T. Beck. 2015. Financial Inclusion in Asia: An Overview. *ADB Economics Working Paper Series*. No. 449. Manila: Asian Development Bank. https://www.adb.org/sites/default/files/ publication/173377/ewp-449.pdf.

Balakrishnan, R., S. Nowak, S. Panth, and Y. Wu. 2012. Surging Capital Flows to Emerging Asia: Facts, Impacts and Responses. *IMF Working Paper*. No. 12/130. Washington, DC: International Monetary Fund. https://www.imf.org/external/pubs/ft/wp/2012/wp12130.pdf.

Bank for International Settlements (BIS). Consolidated Banking Statistics. https://www.bis.org/statistics/consstats.htm?m=6%7C31%7C70 (accessed September 2021).

_____. Debt Securities Statistics. https://www.bis.org/statistics/secstats. htm (accessed September 2021).

_____. Effective Exchange Rate Indices. https://www.bis.org/statistics/eer. htm (accessed May 2021).

_____. Locational Banking Statistics. https://www.bis.org/statistics/ bankstats.htm?m=6%7C31%7C69 (accessed September 2021).

Basu, S. S., E. Boz, G. Gopinath, F. Roch, and F. D. Unsal. 2020. A Conceptual Model for the Integrated Policy Framework. *IMF Working Paper*. WP/20/121. Washington, DC: International Monetary Fund. https://www.imf.org/-/media/Files/Publications/WP/2020/ English/wpiea2020121-print-pdf.ashx.

Beck, T., A. Demirgüç-Kunt, and R. Levine. 2003. Law, Endowments and Finance. *Journal of Financial Economics*. 70 (2). pp. 137–81. https://doi.org/10.1016/S0304-405X(03)00144-2.

Becker, B. and V. Ivashina. 2014. Cyclicality of Credit Supply: Firm Level Evidence. *Journal of Monetary Economics*. 62. pp. 76–93. https://doi.org/10.1016/j.jmoneco.2013.10.002.

Bekaert G., C. R. Harvey, and C. T. Lundblad. 2005. Does Financial Liberalization Spur Growth? *Journal of Financial Economics*. 77 (1). pp. 3–55. https://www0.gsb.columbia.edu/faculty/gbekaert/papers/financial_liberalization.pdf.

Bird, G. and R. Rajan. 2001. Banks, Financial Liberalisation and Financial Crises in Emerging Markets. *The World Economy*. 24 (7). pp. 889–910. Wiley Blackwell. https://doi.org/10.1111/1467-9701.00388.

_____. 2003. Too Much of a Good Thing? The Adequacy of International Reserves in the Aftermath of Crises. *The World Economy*. 26 (6). pp. 873–91. https://doi.org/10.1111/1467-9701.00552.

Boot, A. W. A., P. Hoffmann, L. Laeven, and L. Ratnovski. 2020. Financial Intermediation and Technology: What's Old, What's New? *IMF Working Paper*. No. 20/161. Washington, DC: International Monetary Fund. https://www.imf.org/-/media/Files/Publications/WP/2020/English/wpiea2020161-print-pdf.ashx.

Boz, E., C. Casas, G. Georgiadis, G. Gopinath, H. Le Mezo, A. Mehl, and T. Nguyen. 2020. Patterns in Invoicing Currency in Global Trade. *IMF Working Paper*. WP/20/126. Washington, DC: International Monetary Fund. https://www.imf.org/en/Publications/WP/Issues/2020/07/17/Patterns-in-Invoicing-Currency-in-Global-Trade-49574.

Bruno, V. and I. Shin. 2015. Global Dollar Credit and Carry Trades: A Firm-Level Analysis. *BIS Working Papers*. No 510. Basel: Bank for International Settlements. https://www.bis.org/publ/work510.pdf.

_____. 2018. Currency Depreciation and Emerging Market Corporate Distress. *BIS Working Papers*. No 753. Basel: Bank for International Settlements. https://www.bis.org/publ/work753.pdf.

Bruno, V., I. Kim, and H. S. Shin. 2018. Exchange Rates and the Working Capital Channel of Trade Fluctuations. *BIS Working Papers*. No 694. Basel: Bank for International Settlements. https://www.bis.org/publ/work694.pdf.

Carstens, A. 2019. Exchange Rates and Monetary Policy Frameworks in Emerging Market Economies. *Speech*. Lecture at the London School of Economics, London. https://www.bis.org/speeches/sp190502.htm.

Carstens, A. and H. S. Shin. 2019. Emerging Markets Aren't Out of the Woods Yet. *Foreign Affairs*. 15 March. https://www.foreignaffairs.com/articles/2019-03-15/emerging-markets-arent-out-woods-yet?

Cassimon, D. and B. Van Campenhout. 2016. In Search of Financial Globalization Traps, Working Paper No. 2006.06. Institute of Development Policy and Management, University of Antwerp.

Cavoli, T., S. Gopalan, and R. S. Rajan. 2019. Exchange Rate Policies in Asia in an Era of Financial Globalisation: An Empirical Assessment. *The World Economy.* 42 (6). pp.1774–95. https://doi.org/10.1111/twec.12767.

Cheng, R. and R. S. Rajan. 2020. Monetary Trilemma, Dilemma, or Something in Between? *International Finance.* 23 (2). pp. 257–276. https://doi.org/10.1111/infi.12363.

Cobham, A. 2002. Capital Account Liberalization and Poverty. *Global Social Policy.* 2 (2). pp. 163–88. https://doi.org/10.1177/1468018102002002740.

Contessi, S. and A. Weinberger. 2009. Foreign Direct Investment, Productivity, and Country Growth: An Overview. *Federal Reserve Bank of St. Louis Review.* 91 (2), March/April. pp. 61–78. https://doi.org/10.20955/r.91.61-78.

de Soyres, F., E. Frohm, V. Gunnella, and E. Pavlova. 2018. Bought, Sold and Bought Again: The Impact of Complex Value Chains on Export Elasticities. *Policy Research Working Paper.* No. WPS8535. Washington, DC: World Bank. http://documents1.worldbank.org/curated/en/816441531511812643/pdf/WPS8535.pdf.

Ehlers, T. and P. McGuire. 2017. Foreign Banks and Credit Conditions in EMEs. *BIS Papers.* No. 91. Basel: Bank for International Settlements. https://www.bis.org/publ/bppdf/bispap91g_rh.pdf.

Eichengreen, B. 2001. Capital Account Liberalization: What Do Cross-Country Studies Tell Us? *World Bank Economic Review.* 15 (3) pp. 341–65. Washington, DC: World Bank. https://openknowledge.worldbank.org/handle/10986/17435.

Eichengreen, B. and R. Hausmann. 1999. Exchange Rates and Financial Fragility. *NBER Working Papers.* No. 7418. Cambridge, MA: National Bureau of Economic Research. https://www.nber.org/system/files/working_papers/w7418/w7418.pdf.

_____. 2005. Original Sin. In *Other People's Money: Debt Denomination and Financial Instability,* edited by B. Eichengreen and Ricardo Hausmann. Chicago: University of Chicago Press. https://doi.org/10.7208/chicago/9780226194578.001.0001.

Eichengreen, B., R. Hausman, and U. Panizza. 2007. Currency Mismatches, Debt Intolerance, and Original Sin: Why They Are Not the Same and Why it Matters. In *Capital Controls and Capital Flows in Emerging Economies: Policies, Practices and Consequences*, edited by S. Edwards. Chicago: University of Chicago Press. https://www.nber.org/system/files/chapters/c0150/c0150.pdf.

Eichengreen, B., D. Park, A. Ramayandi, and K. Shin. 2020. Exchange Rates and Insulation in Emerging Markets. *Open Economies Review.* 31(3). pp. 565–618. https://doi.org/10.1007/s11079-020-09587-2.

Financial Stability Board. 2020. *Global Monitoring Report on Non-Bank Financial Intermediation 2020*. Monitoring Dataset. https://www.fsb.org/2020/12/global-monitoring-report-on-non-bank-financial-intermediation-2020/ (accessed August 2021).

Ghosh, A. R., J. D. Ostry, and M. S. Qureshi. 2017. Managing the Tide: How do Emerging Markets Respond to Capital Flows? *IMF Working Paper.* WP/17/69. Washington, DC: International Monetary Fund. https://www.imf.org/-/media/Files/Publications/WP/2017/wp1769.ashx.

Gochoco-Bautista, M. S. and E. Remolona. 2012. Going Regional: How to Deepen ASEAN's Financial Markets. *ADB Economics Working Paper Series.* No. 300. Manila: Asian Development Bank. https://www.adb.org/sites/default/files/publication/29689/economics-wp-300.pdf.

Gopinath, G. 2016. The International Price System. *Jackson Hole Symposium Proceedings.* https://scholar.harvard.edu/gopinath/publications/international-price-system.

Gopinath, G., E. Boz, C. Casas, F. J. Díez, P-O. Gourinchas, and M. Plagborg-Møller. 2020. Dominant Currency Paradigm. *American Economic Review.* 110 (3). pp. 677–719. https://doi.org/10.1257/aer.20171201.

Gopinath, G. and J. Stein. 2020. Banking, Trade and the Making of a Dominant Currency. *Quarterly Journal of Economics.* 136 (2), May 2021. pp. 783–830. https://doi.org/10.1093/qje/qjaa036.

Government of the United States, Board of Governors of the Federal Reserve System. 2020. Federal Reserve Announces Establishment of a Temporary FIMA Repo Facility to Help Support the Smooth Functioning of Financial Markets. *Press Release.* 31 March. https://www.federalreserve.gov/newsevents/pressreleases/monetary20200331a.htm.

Han, B. 2021. Synergizing ASEAN+3's Regional and Bilateral Swap Arrangements for Greater Emergency Financing. *AMRO Blog*. Singapore: The ASEAN+3 Macroeconomic Research Office. https://www.amro-asia.org/synergizing-asean3s-regional-and-bilateral-swap-arrangements-for-greater-emergency-financing/?utm_source=rss&utm_medium=rss&utm_campaign=synergizing-asean3s-regional-and-bilateral-swap-arrangements-for-greater-emergency-financing.

Han, X. and S. J. Wei. 2018. International Transmissions of Monetary Shocks: Between a Trilemma and a Dilemma. *Journal of International Economics*. 110. pp. 205–19. https://doi.org/10.1016/j.jinteco.2017.11.005.

Hofmann, B., N. Patel, and S. P. Y. Wu. 2021. The Original Sin Redux: A Model Based Evaluation. Unpublished. https://www.dropbox.com/s/c54l4toezljd5uc/hpw_draft_latest.pdf?dl=0.

Hofmann, B., I. Shim, and H. S. Shin. 2019. Bond Risk Premia and the Exchange Rate. *BIS Working Paper*. No. 775. Basel: Bank for International Settlements. https://www.bis.org/publ/work775.pdf.

———. 2020. Emerging Market Economy Exchange Rates and Local Currency Bond Markets Amid the Covid-19 Pandemic. *BIS Bulletin* 5. Basel: Bank for International Settlements. https://www.bis.org/publ/bisbull05.pdf.

International Monetary Fund (IMF). 2013. Assessing Reserve Adequacy—Further Considerations. *IMF Policy Paper*. Washington, DC. https://www.imf.org/external/np/pp/eng/2013/111313d.pdf.

———. 2017. *Collaboration Between Regional Financing Arrangements and the IMF*. Washington, DC. https://www.imf.org/-/media/Files/Publications/PP/2017/pp073117-collaboration-between-regional-financing-arrangements-and-the-imf.ashx.

———. 2020. Chapter 3: Emerging and Frontier Markets: Managing Volatile Portfolio Flows. *Global Financial Stability Report: Markets in the Time of COVID-19*. Washington, DC. https://www.imf.org/-/media/Files/Publications/GFSR/2020/April/English/ch3.ashx.

———. 2021. *Annual Report on Exchange Arrangements and Restrictions (AREAR) 2020*. Washington, DC. https://www.elibrary-areaer.imf.org/Pages/Home.aspx.

———. International Financial Statistics. https://data.imf.org/?sk=4C514D48-B6BA-49ED-8AB9-52B0C1A0179B (accessed August and September 2021).

_____. IMF Assessing Reserve Adequacy Database. https://www.imf.org/external/datamapper/datasets/ARA (accessed May 2021).

_____. World Economic Outlook Database. April 2021. https://www.imf.org/en/Publications/WEO/weo-database/2021/April (accessed August 2021 and September 2021).

Institute of International Finance. Global Debt Monitor Database. https://www.iif.com/Research/Capital-Flows-and-Debt/Global-Debt-Monitor (accessed August 2021).

Ito, T., S. Koibuchi, K. Sato, and J. Shimizu. 2018. *Managing Currency Risk: How Japanese Firms Choose Invoicing Currency*. Research Institute of Economy, Trade and Industry. London: Edward Elgar. https://www.e-elgar.com/shop/gbp/managing-currency-risk-9781785360121.html.

Ito, H. and R. N. McCauley. 2019. The Currency Composition of Foreign Exchange Reserves. *BIS Working Papers*. No. 828. Basel: Bank for International Settlements. https://www.bis.org/publ/work828.pdf.

Jafarov, E., R. Maino, and M. Pani. 2019. Financial Repression is Knocking at the Door, Again: Should we be Concerned? *IMF Working Paper*. WP/19/211. Washington, DC: International Monetary Fund. https://www.imf.org/en/Publications/WP/Issues/2019/09/30/Financial-Repression-is-Knocking-at-the-Door-Again-48641.

Kashyap, A. K., J. C. Stein, and D. W. Wilcox. 1993. Monetary Policy and Credit Conditions: Evidence from the Composition of External Finance. *American Economic Review*. 83 (1). pp. 78–98. https://scholar.harvard.edu/files/stein/files/aer-1993.pdf.

Kim, S. 2019. Plausibility of Local Currency Contribution to the CMIM. In *Local Currency Contribution to the CMIM*. AMRO Research Collaboration Program RCP/19-01. Singapore: The ASEAN+3 Macroeconomic Research Office. https://www.amro-asia.org/wp-content/uploads/2019/01/Chapter-4-plausiblity-of-local-currency-contribution-to-the-CMIM_final.pdf.

Klein, M. W. and J. C. Shambaugh. 2015. Rounding the Corners of the Policy Trilemma: Sources of Monetary Policy Autonomy. *American Economic Journal: Macroeconomics*. 7 (4). pp. 33–66. http://dx.doi.org/10.1257/mac.20130237.

Kose, M. A., E. S. Prasad, and A. D. Taylor. 2011. Threshold in the Process of International Financial Integration. *Journal of International Money and Finance.* 30 (1). pp. 147–79. http://hdl.handle.net/10986/4801.

Kose, M. A., E. S. Prasad, K. Rogoff, and S. J. Wei. 2009. Financial Globalization: A Reappraisal. *IMF Staff Papers.* 56 (1). pp. 8–62. Washington, DC: International Monetary Fund. http://prasad.dyson. cornell.edu/doc/research/imfsp200836a.pdf.

La Porta, R., F. Lopez-De-Silanes, A. Shleifer, and R. W. Vishny. 1997. Legal Determinants of External Finance. *The Journal of Finance.* 52 (3). pp. 1131–150. https://doi.org/10.2307/2329518.

Lee, J. W. and C. Y. Park. 2008. Global Financial Turmoil: Impact and Challenges for Asia. *Working Paper Series on Regional Economic Integration.* No. 18. Manila: Asian Development Bank. https://www.adb.org/sites/default/files/publication/28475/wp18-impact-challenges-asia-financial-systems.pdf.

Levine, R. 1996. Foreign Banks, Financial Development, and Economic Growth. In *International Financial Markets: Harmonization versus Competition,* edited by C.E. Barfield. Washington, DC: The AEI Press. http://faculty.haas.berkeley.edu/ross_levine/papers/1996_book_barfield_foreignbank%20&%20growth.pdf .

Levinger, H. and C. Li. 2014. What's Behind Recent Trends in Asian Corporate Bond Markets? *Current Issues: Emerging Markets.* 31 January. Frankfurt am Main: Deutsche Bank Research. https://www.dbresearch.com/PROD/RPS_EN-PROD/ PROD0000000000451971/What%E2%80%99s_behind_ recent_trends_in_Asian_corporate_bon.pdf?undefined &realload=GH~so6L8sljMxYrrMHxxvf/3sFX5ajvZSzOd/ St5I8Mq9hM4Z'XHAG9TayJYNN5IDsnIKszinQ2oJAlivqSaF0g==

Lopez, A. O. 2020. The Wave of Covid Bonds. *AIIB Blog.* Beijing: Asian Infrastructure Investment Bank. 23 June. https://www.aiib.org/en/ news-events/media-center/blog/2020/The-Wave-of-Covid-Bonds. html.

Lu, F. 2019. Modality of Local Currency Contribution to the CMIM. In *Local Currency Contribution to the CMIM.* AMRO Research Collaboration Program RCP/19-01. Singapore: The ASEAN+3 Macroeconomic Research Office. https://amro-asia.org/wp-content/uploads/2019/01/Chapter-5-Modality-of-local-currency-contribution-to-the-CMIM_final.pdf.

McCauley, R., P. McGuire, and V. Sushko. 2015. Global Dollar Credit: Links to US Monetary Policy and Leverage. *BIS Working Papers*. No 483. Basel: Bank for the International Settlements. https://www.bis.org/publ/work483.pdf.

McKinnon, R. 1973. *Money and Capital in Economic Development.* Washington, DC: Brookings Institution.

_____. 1991. *The Order of Economic Liberalization. Financial Control in the Transition to a Market Economy.* Baltimore: Johns Hopkins University Press.

Mizen, P., F. Packer, E. Remolona, and S. Tsoukas. 2018. Original Sin in Corporate Finance: New Evidence from Asian Bond Issuers in Onshore and Offshore Markets. *Working Paper.* 18/04. Nottingham: Centre for Finance, Credit and Macroeconomics, University of Nottingham School of Economics, UK. http://awww.ukdctn.org/cfcm/documents/papers/cfcm-2018-04.pdf.

Obstfeld, M., J. D. Ostry, and M. S. Qureshi. 2018. Global Financial Cycles and the Exchange Rate Regime. *American Economic Review.* 108 (2). pp. 499–504. https://doi.org/10.1257/pandp.20181057.

_____. 2019. A Tie That Binds: Revisiting the Trilemma in Emerging Market Economies. *The Review of Economics and Statistics.* 101 (2). 279–93. http://dx.doi.org/10.1162/rest_a_00740.

Oliver Wyman and MicroSave. 2017. *Accelerating Financial Inclusion in South-East Asia with Digital Finance.* Commissioned by the Asian Development Bank. http://dx.doi.org/10.22617/RPT178622-2.

Organisation for Economic Co-operation and Development (OECD). 2019. Equity Market Review of Asia 2019. *OECD Capital Market Series.* Paris. http://www.oecd.org/daf/ca/oecd-equity-market-review-asia.htm.

Park, C. Y. 2011. Asian Financial System: Development and Challenges. *ADB Economics Working Paper Series.* No. 285. Manila: Asian Development Bank. https://www.adb.org/sites/default/files/publication/30442/economics-wp285.pdf.

_____. 2016. Developing Local Currency Bond Markets in Asia. *ADB Economics Working Paper Series.* No. 495. Manila: Asian Development Bank. https://www.adb.org/sites/default/files/publication/190289/ewp-495.pdf.

Park C. Y., P. Rosenkranz, and M. C. Tayag. 2020. COVID-19 Exposes Asian Banks' Vulnerability to US Dollar Funding. *ADB Briefs*. No. 146. Manila: Asian Development Bank. https://www.adb.org/sites/default/files/publication/616091/covid-19-asian-banks-vulnerability-us-dollar-funding.pdf.

Park, C. Y. and K. Shin. 2020. The Impact of Nonperforming Loans on Cross-Border Bank Lending: Implications for Emerging Market Economies. *ADB Briefs*. No. 136. Manila: Asian Development Bank. https://www.adb.org/sites/default/files/publication/609481/adb-brief-136-nonperforming-loans-cross-border-lending.pdf.

Patel, N. and P. Cavallino. 2019. FX Intervention: Goals, Strategies and Tactics. *BIS Papers*. No. 104b. Basel: Bank for the International Settlements. https://www.bis.org/publ/bppdf/bispap104b_rh.pdf.

Prasad, E. S. and R. Rajan. 2008. A Pragmatic Approach to Capital Account Liberalization. *NBER Working Paper Series*. No. 14051. Cambridge, MA: National Bureau of Economic Research. https://www.nber.org/system/files/working_papers/w14051/w14051.pdf.

Prasad, E. S., K. Rogoff, S. J. Wei, and M. A. Kose. 2003. Effects of Financial Globalization on Developing Countries: Some Empirical Evidence. *IMF Occasional Papers*. No. 220. Washington, DC: International Monetary Fund.

Rajan, R. S. and R. Cheng. 2020. Rise of Sovereign Digital Currencies: Domestic and Global Implications. *The Business Times*. 18 November. https://www.businesstimes.com.sg/opinion/rise-of-sovereign-digital-currencies-domestic-and-global-implications.

Rajan, R. S. and S. Gopalan. 2015. *Economic Management in a Volatile Environment: Monetary and Financial Issues*. Chapters 7–10. London: Palgrave-Macmillan.

Rey, H. 2013. Dilemma not Trilemma: The Global Cycle and Monetary Policy Independence. *Global Dimensions of Unconventional Monetary Policy*. Proceedings, Economic Policy Symposium, Jackson Hole, Federal Reserve Bank of Kansas City Economic Policy Symposium. http://www.helenerey.eu/AjaxRequestHandler.ashx?Function=GetSecuredDOC&DOCUrl=App_Data/helenerey_eu/Published-Papers_en-GB/_Documents_2015-16/147802013_67186463733_jacksonholedraftweb.pdf.

_____. 2016. International Channels of Transmission of Monetary Policy and the Mundellian Trilemma. *IMF Economic Review*. 64. pp. 6–35. https://doi.org/10.1057/imfer.2016.4.

Securities Industry and Financial Markets Association (SIFMA) 2021. US Fixed Income Securities Statistics August 2021. https://www.sifma.org/resources/research/us-fixed-income-securities-statistics/ (accessed August 2021).

Shaw, E. 1973. *Financial Deepening in Economic Development*. New York: Oxford University Press.

Shimizu, S. 2018. Development of Asian Bond Markets and Challenges: Keys to Market Expansion. *Public Policy Review*. 14 (5). pp. 955–1000. Tokyo: Policy Research Institute, Ministry of Finance Japan. https://www.mof.go.jp/english/pri/publication/pp_review/ppr14_05_06.pdf.

Shimizu, J., J. Y. Lee, and J. Choi. 2019. Chapter 2. Regional Integration and Use of Local Currencies in the Region. *Local Currency Contribution to the CMIM*. Singapore. https://www.amro-asia.org/wp-content/uploads/2019/01/Chapter-2-Regional-integration-and-use-of-local-currencies-in-the-region.pdf.

Stiglitz, J. 2004. Information and the Change in the Paradigm in Economics, Part 2. *The American Economist*. 48 (1). pp. 17–49. https://doi.org/10.1177/056943450404800103.

Stiglitz, J. and A. Weiss. 1981. Credit Rationing in Markets with Imperfect Information. *American Economic Review*. 71 (3). pp. 393–410. https://pages.ucsd.edu/~aronatas/project/academic/Stiglitz%20credit.pdf.

Sussangkarn, C. 2019. Promoting Local Currency Usage in the Region In *Local Currency Contribution to the CMIM*. AMRO Research Collaboration Program RCP/19-01. Singapore: The ASEAN+3 Macroeconomic Research Office. https://amro-asia.org/wp-content/uploads/2019/01/Chapter-3-Promoting-local-currency-usage-in-the-region_final.pdf.

Williamson, J. and M. Mahar. 1998. A Survey of Financial Liberalization. *Essays in International Finance*. No. 211. Princeton, NJ: Princeton University. https://ies.princeton.edu/pdf/E211.pdf.

World Bank. Global Financial Development Database. https://www.worldbank.org/en/publication/gfdr/data/global-financial-development-database (accessed September 2021).

_____. *World Development Indicators*. https://datacatalog.worldbank.org/dataset/world-development-indicators (accessed August 2021 and September 2021).

Yaguchi, M. 2018. Urgent Need for Developing Bond Markets in the ASEAN Late Comers: Efforts in Cambodia, Lao PDR and Myanmar. Newsletter, Institute for International Monetary Affairs. https://www.iima.or.jp/en/docs/newsletter/2018/NL2018No_20_e.pdf.

Yuen-C, T. 2021. Parliament Passes Law on Borrowing to Fund National Infrastructure. *The Straits Times*. 11 May. Singapore. https://www.straitstimes.com/singapore/politics/parliament-passes-law-on-borrowing-to-fund-significant-national-infrastructure.

Eli Remolona[1]

2.1 Introduction

ASEAN+3 economies have drawn important lessons from past crises which point to two sources of systemic risk: sudden stops and slow-burn contagion. A sudden stop happens when a financial crisis comes thick and fast: the country sees massive capital outflows, a sharp currency depreciation, a stock market collapse, and an economy sliding quickly into recession.[2] A slow-burn contagion is about a prolonged tightening of international credit conditions and economies that struggle from a persistent lack of credit. The two events need not occur in the same place. The sudden stop may happen in a particular region but cause global banks exposed to that region to stop lending elsewhere, in what is called the common lender channel of contagion.

When sudden stops turn into contagion, it can be assumed that something connects the affected countries to one another. Wyplosz, Eichengreen, and Rose (1996) find evidence of contagion that spreads more easily to countries closely tied by trade linkages. This interconnectedness could also involve what Aizenman, Hutchison, and Jinjarak (2013) describe as correlated investor sentiment. Indeed, Masson (1998) characterizes contagion as a situation in which a crisis in one country leads foreign investors to change their minds or their risk tolerances with regard to other countries. Consistent with a change in risk tolerances, Kim, Loretan, and Remolona (2010)

---

[1] The author thanks Diwa Guinigundo, Masahiro Kawai, Khor Hoe Ee, Rogelio Mercado Jr., Ramkishen S. Rajan, Johnny Ravalo, Yasuyuki Sawada, Ilhyock Shim, Kwanho Shin, James Villafuerte, and Philip Wooldridge for helpful comments.

[2] Mendoza (2010, p. 1941) defines sudden stops as "reversals of international capital flows, reflected in sudden increases in net exports and the current account."

present evidence from the credit-default swap (CDS) market showing that the contagion in the global financial crisis happened because risk was repriced worldwide. Indeed, Wu et al. (2016) find that while economic fundamentals tend to drive regional contagion, a collapse in investor appetite for risk tends to drive global contagion.

This change in investors' minds or in prices of risk may be a function of the extent to which the countries are connected to the same financial cycle. Rey (2015) has identified a global financial cycle that is related to the United States (US) monetary policy. Possibly of more concern to ASEAN+3 economies is a common regional factor. Cheung, Qian, and Remolona (2019) find a common factor in the movements of current-account balances in Asia, and this helps explain the accumulation of international reserves in the region. In the taxonomy of Kara, Tian, and Yellen (2015), identifying such a common factor would be a non-network way of measuring interconnectedness.

Before the Asian financial crisis of 1997, the common factor may have reflected what Park and Rajan (2021) describe as "premature and perverse financial liberalization, with inadequate attention paid to prudential regulations, as well as the fact that the ASEAN+3 region had a severely underdeveloped financial system that was predominantly bank-based." Another common factor would be the "original sin," which has been characterized by Hausmann and Panizza (2003) as the inability of countries to borrow in their own currencies. When they borrow in foreign currencies, the resulting mismatch makes them vulnerable to crisis. Such conditions evidently led Asia into financial crisis in 1997, given that three of the five countries had accumulated deep current-account deficits while tolerating excessive growth in domestic credit.[3]

The risk of a region-wide slow-burn contagion would depend in part on the common funding concentration risk of the various economies to the same set of banks, especially when these banks are tightly interconnected. Koch and Remolona (2018) show that in the Asian financial crisis, the common lender channel was a source of slow-burn contagion, in which international lending to the five crisis-hit countries did not recover for at least 5 years.

More recently, for the ASEAN+3 economies, common lenders that could fuel slow-burn contagion seem to have changed places since the global financial crisis. In terms of direct cross-border borrowing from global banks,

---

[3] Indonesia and the Republic of Korea had somewhat more modest deficits.

the concentration in euro area banks has evidently declined while concentration in Japanese and United Kingdom (UK) banks has increased.

In measuring concentration risk, however, it is important to account for links among global banks. In this chapter, the Shapley value is proposed as a direct network measure of interconnectedness. Its unique analytical advantage is in taking account of the contributions to systemic risk from different combinations of major lending jurisdictions—just as these have always been a factor in historical episodes of regional and global crises.

This chapter finds that shifts in interconnectedness have not been even across ASEAN+3 countries. The concentration risk faced by ASEAN economies excluding Singapore has risen, especially in their loans from banks in Japan and the United States.[4] At the same time, the concentration risks of the People's Republic of China (PRC) and the Republic of Korea are very similar and have risen, especially with regard to common exposures to UK and euro area banks. In the end, the "ASEAN 9" economies (ASEAN member countries excluding Singapore) have the highest concentration risk in loans from Japanese banks, while the PRC and the Republic of Korea are exposed to a similar magnitude of concentration risk in loans from banks in the UK, the US, and the euro area.[5]

Nonetheless, at least for now, ASEAN+3 financial systems can deal with these risks from a position of strength. Current accounts are largely in surplus. The region's banks hold capital buffers that exceed international regulatory standards. Even while central banks are sitting on large piles of international reserves, a regional commitment under the Chiang Mai Initiative Multilateralization (CMIM) makes funding from members available should any in the group need balance-of-payments support.[6] Even so, further development of corporate bond markets is still needed so that they can take a role as an alternative source of funding, or—as former chair of the US Federal Reserve Board Alan Greenspan famously put it—as a "spare tire" (Greenspan 1999). More broadly, even as banking integration proceeds in the region, a regional framework for dealing with the risk of a region-wide slow-burn contagion is still needed.

---

[4] As explained in Section 2.4, Singapore is excluded from this group of borrowers, because as an offshore banking center, it plays the role of an intermediary rather than a borrower.

[5] This order of banking jurisdictions reflects their importance in concentration risk. This ordering rule will be followed in the rest of the paper.

[6] The author owes this point to Diwa Guinigundo.

In what follows, the discussion starts with a review of the literature on sudden stops and slow-burn contagion, then examines the risk of sudden stops in the ASEAN+3 economies. Concentration risk of slow-burn contagion is further considered in terms of direct exposures. Thereafter, the chapter takes account of the global banking network and measure concentration risk in the form of Shapley values. A discussion of policy options concludes the chapter.

2.2 Review of Literature

The literature distinguishes between two types of cross-border propagation of financial crises. To adopt the terms used by Kaminsky, Reinhart, and Vegh (2003), such contagion may be "fast and furious" as in sudden stops, or it may be "slow-burn" as in a prolonged period of tight credit. Wu, Erdem, Kalotychou, and Remolona (2016) find sudden-stop contagion primarily a regional phenomenon, while slow-burn spillover effects can often be global. While sudden stop tends to operate through asset prices and capital flows, slow burn tends to operate through bank lending.

The large literature on financial crises has established that financial crises originate from lending booms. With data from 1870 to 2008, for example, Schularick and Taylor (2012) show that crises are simply "credit booms gone bust." The credit boom is typically driven by a period of unwarranted optimism. In the case of the boom leading to the Asian financial crisis, optimism seems to have been generated by economic reforms, largely in the form of financial liberalization in the various countries. As Park and Rajan (2021) point out, these turned out to have paid inadequate attention to prudential regulation.

In emerging markets, credit booms are often enabled by cross-border credit flows. Avdjiev, McCauley, and McGuire (2012) find that it is specifically international bank credit that tends to matter, rather than positions in local currency. Such international credit also often is a mechanism for the transmission of slow-burn contagion across countries.

When contagion arises as credit booms go bust, some sort of interconnectedness among the economies involved must exist. There are many ways to measure interconnectedness. Kara, Tian, and Yellen (2015) distinguish between network and non-network measures. Network measures may be direct or indirect. Direct measures explicitly map pairwise relationships between institutions.

An indirect way for interconnectedness to manifest is the presence of a financial cycle that affects different economies. Rey (2015), for example, identifies a global financial cycle in capital flows, asset prices, and credit growth. She finds that the cycle is correlated with VIX, an indicator of risk aversion in financial markets. Forbes and Warnock (2012) find that the timing of surges and stops in capital flows are related to VIX. Rey's analysis suggests that a determinant of the global financial cycle is monetary policy in the US. Bruno and Shin (2015) provide evidence that US monetary policy affects the leverage of global banks and credit growth in the international financial system. There is a regional version of Rey's financial cycle. In looking at the accumulation of reserves in Asia, Cheung, Qian, and Remolona (2019) find a common regional factor related to current-account balances.

While historically, the source of regional crises and contagion in the Asian region has been cross-border bank lending, corporate bond flows can also cause problems. Mizen et al. (2018) looked at 5,668 financing decisions by firms in seven Asian emerging markets over 1995 to 2012. These markets include five ASEAN countries: Indonesia, Malaysia, the Philippines, Singapore, and Thailand. They find that even in countries with onshore markets, it is often easier for unseasoned firms to issue corporate bonds offshore in a foreign currency than to issue onshore in the local currency. Indeed, Coppola et al. (2020) find large corporations in ASEAN+3 have been issuing corporate bonds in US dollars through their affiliates abroad. The largest such issuance has been by companies from the PRC.

Park and Shin (2018), using bilateral data from the Bank for International Settlements (BIS) international banking statistics, find that direct exposures of the country's own and the overall region's banking sectors to crisis-affected countries are systematically related to capital outflows during the global financial crisis. They also find that when lenders and borrowers belong to the same region, the lenders are less likely to retreat from those same borrowers at the time of financial stress. Koch and Remolona (2018) document the bank lending channel of contagion, in which international banks that suffer heavy losses in one country tend to reduce lending to other countries. They document such slow-burn contagion in the Asian financial crisis, and the same in the global financial crisis through 2008 and 2009, and the European sovereign debt crisis from 2010 to 2012.

Underlying such slow-burn contagion is the interconnectedness of the global banking system. Measuring the systemic risk of this often focuses on downside tail risks. Acharya et al. (2012), for example, have proposed the systemic expected shortfall to reflect an institution's propensity to be undercapitalized when the system as a whole is undercapitalized. Adrian and Brunnermeier (2016) have proposed "CoVar," which is a systemic risk version of the value-at-risk measure used by individual commercial banks.

In these situations, the development of local currency corporate bond markets may mitigate the risks of regional contagion. Gyntelberg, Ma, and Remolona (2005) find that such markets are often illiquid due to narrow investor bases, inadequate microstructures, and a lack of timely information about issuers. Amstad et al. (2016) discuss ways these conditions can be turned around in Asian emerging markets.

2.3 Sudden-Stop Contagion Risk in ASEAN+3 Economies

A balance-of-payments crisis is also known as a sudden stop. It is a situation in which the external financing of a current-account deficit comes to an abrupt halt. As pointed out by Cecchetti and Schoenholtz (2018), a sudden stop forces a country to adjust sharply so as to close its current-account deficit. The adjustment often means a contraction of credit in the financial system and a reduction in investment that are so drastic they plunge an economy into a recession. Moreover, as shown by the Asian financial crisis, a sudden stop in one country can easily lead to sudden stops in neighboring countries. The risk of such a sudden-stop contagion depends partly on how closely precrisis current-account balances in the region move together.

The risk of sudden stops is often transmitted through asset prices. To measure systemic risks in general, Diebold and Yilmaz (2014) propose variance decompositions of stock returns and volatilities. This is an indirect way of measuring interconnectedness. Variance decompositions of volatilities are particularly interesting. This is because volatilities can be seen as indicators of fear in the market. Focusing on systemic risk in financial markets, Dungey, Luciani, and Veredas (2013) propose a methodology based on the Google PageRank algorithm to rank systemically important financial institutions (SIFIs). They take account of the interconnections between the finance sector and the real economy.

In an interesting example of measuring interconnectedness indirectly, Fry-McKibbin, Hsiao, and Tang (2014) identify nine crisis episodes using a regime-switching model. To analyze the nature of a sudden-stop contagion, they focus on the dependence structures of equity markets through correlation, co-skewness, and co-volatility. They find that the Great Recession of 2008–2010 was a true global financial crisis, and financial interconnectedness was the source of crisis transmission.

A Common Regional Factor

Cheung, Qian, and Remolona (2019) seek to identify a common regional financial factor that can lead to a contagion in sudden stops. Identifying such a factor is a non-network way of measuring interconnectedness. The motivation is to explain the build-up of international reserves in Asia since the Asian financial crisis. There are three possible common factors: (i) an economic growth variable, (ii) a current-account balance variable, and (iii) a financial-account balance variable. Cheung, Qian, and Remolona find that the current-account balance variable is the only statistically significant common economic factor.

Hence, in this chapter the risk of a sudden-stop contagion is assessed by analyzing the covariation in the current-account balances of the ASEAN+3 countries. This covariation will reflect the whole network of trade links and financing links between these countries and also the network of links between them and third countries. The question is: Can just a small number of factors explain these links?

To answer that, the principal components are extracted from current-account movements. Principal components are a long-established way of reducing the dimensionality of a data set. They do so by means of orthogonal linear transformations of the data. In the analysis here, they are a parsimonious way of modeling the covariance structure of current-account movements. The resulting country loadings on the principal components are indirect measures of centrality in the network.

In assessing the risk of sudden-stop contagion in ASEAN+3, only the countries for which quarterly current-account data are available from Q1 2010 to Q4 2018 are considered. We exclude Japan, because of its special role as a creditor country. Singapore and Hong Kong, China are also excluded because of their role as offshore banking centers. This leaves seven of the larger countries: the PRC, Indonesia, the Republic of Korea, Malaysia, the Philippines, Thailand, and Viet Nam. The principal components are then extracted from the quarterly change in the ratio of the current-account balance to GDP for each of the seven countries from Q1 2010 to Q4 2018.

How much can the principal components explain? In Figure 2.1, the pie chart shows how much each of three principal components can explain current-account movements during the sample period. As shown in the pie chart, the first principal component explains 32% of the variation in the current-account movements of the seven ASEAN+3 countries in the sample. The second principal component explains 19% of that variation and the third principal component 15%.

Figure 2.1: How Much Can the Principal Components Explain?

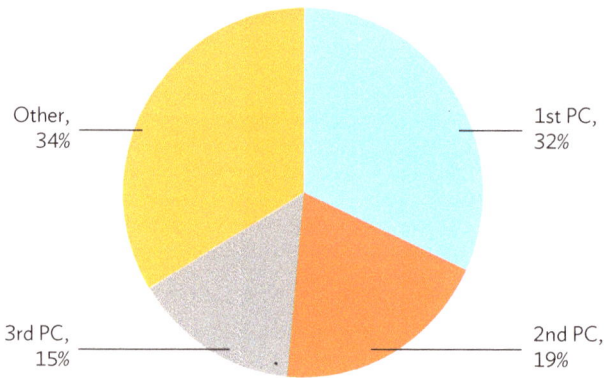

Other,
34%

1st PC,
32%

3rd PC,
15%

2nd PC,
19%

PC = principal component.
Note: The data refer to the principal components of the quarter-on-quarter changes in the current account balance-to-GDP ratios of Indonesia, Malaysia, the People's Republic of China, the Philippines, the Republic of Korea, Thailand, and Viet Nam. The period covered is from Q1 2010 to Q4 2019.
Source: Author, based on CEIC, IMF International Financial Statistics Database, and national sources (accessed May 2021).

Country loadings on these principal components provide a convenient indirect measure of network interconnectedness. Figure 2.2 focuses only on the loadings on the first principal component. The current accounts of Indonesia, Malaysia, and Thailand load most heavily on this principal component, with each exceeding 50%. This means if one of these countries were to experience a sudden stop, network links would lead the other two into a sudden stop. The PRC and the Republic of Korea both load negatively on the first principal component, with both loadings exceeding 50% in absolute value. This suggests that if either the Republic of Korea or the PRC experienced a sudden stop, the other economy is likely to find itself in the same boat. Loadings for the Philippines and Viet Nam are both relatively small, suggesting that they are not likely to be part of a sudden-stop contagion involving the others.

Figure 2.2: Loadings on the First Principal Component

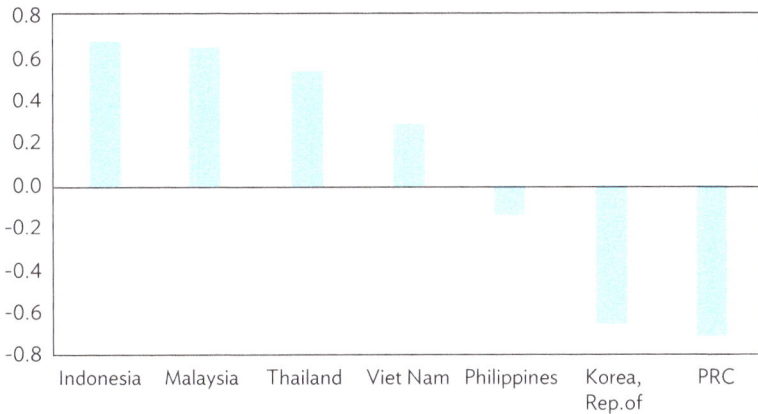

PRC = People's Republic of China.
Note: The data refer to the principal components of the quarter-on-quarter changes in the current
account balance-to-GDP ratios of Indonesia, Malaysia, the PRC, the Philippines, the Republic of Korea,
Thailand, and Viet Nam. The period covered is from Q1 2010 to Q4 2019.
Source: Author, based on CEIC, IMF International Financial Statistics Database, and national sources
(accessed May 2021).

For the ASEAN+3 economies, the risk of sudden-stop contagion is clearly different from what it was before the Asian financial crisis. At that time, the crisis engulfed five of the sample countries. This time, Indonesia, Malaysia, and Thailand are still closely interconnected, while the PRC and the Republic of Korea are more closely interconnected. At the same time, contagion risks are now mitigated by these countries' large international reserves.

Today's Risk of Sudden-Stop Contagion

As of 2019, the risk of a sudden-stop contagion among the ASEAN+3 economics is less than it was just before the Asian financial crisis. Among the 13 economies (including Hong Kong, China), as shown in Figure 2.3, only Cambodia and the Lao People's Democratic Republic are running current-account deficits in excess of 7% of GDP. As small economies, they are unlikely to be a source of sudden-stop contagion. Indonesia and the Philippines are also running current-account deficits but they are under 3% of GDP. By contrast, the eight other economies are running significant current-account surpluses.

Figure 2.3: Current Account Balance, 2017–2019 Average
(% of GDP)

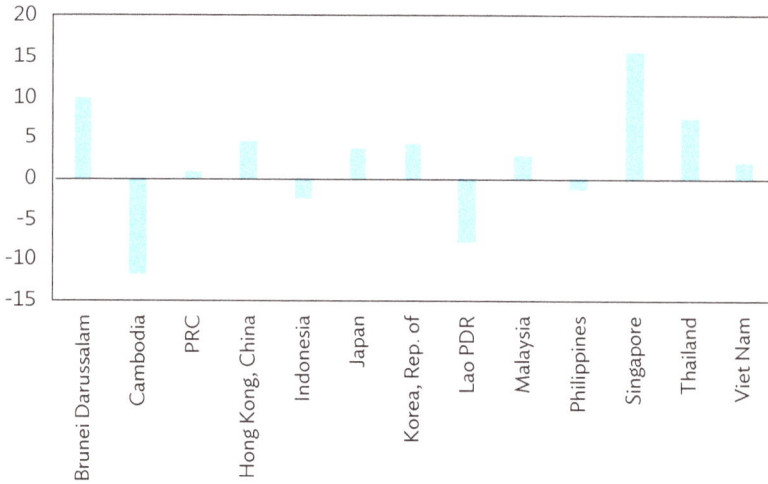

GDP = gross domestic product, Lao PDR = Lao People's Democratic Republic, PRC = People's Republic of China.
Source: Author, based on CEIC, IMF International Financial Statistics Database, and official sources (accessed May 2021).

Moreover, the domestic front is not showing credit growth at concerning levels. The credit-to-GDP gap is the early-warning indicator favored by the BIS. Aldasoro, Borio, and Drehmann (2018) argue this indicator is as good as any in predicting a financial crisis. As shown in Figure 2.4, the six largest countries among the ASEAN+3, which are the only ones for which BIS provides estimates of the credit-to-GDP gap, do not show excessive credit growth.

If there is something to worry about at this time, it is not sudden-stop contagion, but rather slow-burn contagion.

Figure 2.4: Credit-to-GDP Gaps, 2015–2019
(%)

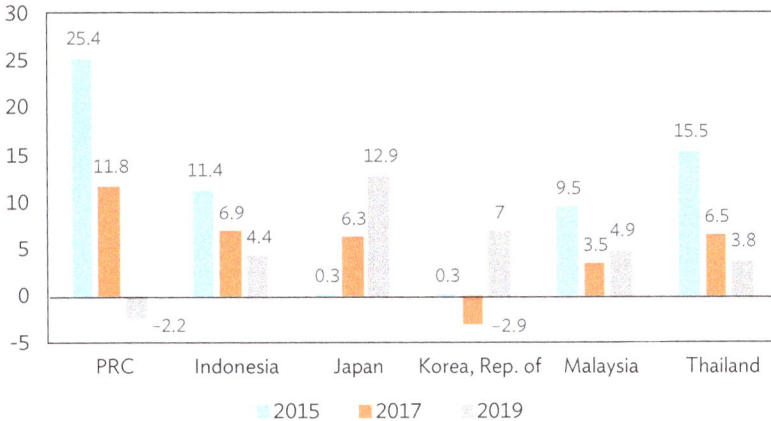

GDP = gross domestic product, PRC = People's Republic of China.
Note: Credit-to-GDP gaps is defined as the difference between the credit-to-GDP ratio and its long-term trend, in percentage points. Long-term trend is calculated using a one-sided Hodrick-Prescott filter with a lambda of 400,000.
Source: BIS Credit-to-GDP Gaps Database (accessed July 2020).

2.4 Concentration Risk of Slow-Burn Contagion in ASEAN+3 Economies

Shifts in banking interconnectedness among the ASEAN+3 countries in the decade since the global financial crisis are important to understand. That is because they indicate the fundamental nature of the slow-burn contagion operating through the common lender channel. This channel is discussed in detail by Koch and Remolona (2018) for the Asian financial crisis, the global financial crisis, and the European sovereign debt crisis. Where ASEAN+3 financial systems end up in their interconnections in 2019 would then be indicative of funding concentration risk and future channels of slow-burn contagion.

Grouping the Borrowing Countries

The analysis in this section relies on data from the BIS Consolidated Banking Statistics. These data properly assign credit risk exposures to creditors' home jurisdiction—unlike locational statistics, which assign exposures to where the claims are booked. In the consolidated data set, 23 of the largest creditor countries report such data by bank nationality. Among them, the euro area countries are lumped together because they share the same currency. Among the 19 jurisdictions in the euro area, 11 of the largest report international bank claims data to the BIS.

The borrowing countries are divided into two groups: (i) the ASEAN 9 (ASEAN economies excluding Singapore); and (ii) the PRC and the Republic of Korea (two of the "plus 3" of the ASEAN+3 economies, with Japan the third). This is not an arbitrary division. From the point of view of funding concentration risk, the interconnectedness of the various ASEAN 9 countries involves largely the same lending banks, just as the interconnectedness of the PRC and the Republic of Korea involves largely the same banks. In other words, when it comes to contagion, the ASEAN 9 countries are in the same common lender channel as each other, while the PRC and the Republic of Korea would similarly find themselves together in another common lender channel. In the BIS data set, total claims on the ASEAN 9 countries as of end-2019 were $358 billion and amounted to $669 billion on the PRC and the Republic of Korea together.[7]

Among the ASEAN 9, three of the large borrowers—Indonesia, Malaysia, and the Philippines—have very similar concentration risks. The three have Japanese banks as their most important source of cross-border loans and rely heavily for those loans on banks in the UK; the US; and Taipei,China. A fourth large borrower, Thailand, is somewhat different in that it relies on "outside area" banks, in which PRC banks seem likely to play significant roles. A fifth large borrower, Viet Nam, is different in that it does not borrow from US banks. The main difference between the PRC and the Republic of Korea is that the former relies most heavily on UK banks, while the latter relies more on US and Japanese banks.

When it comes to Singapore and Hong Kong, China, both are offshore banking centers that are intermediaries rather than direct lending or borrowing jurisdictions. They were considered separately and their intermediary roles were analyzed with the help of a different data set, the BIS Locational Banking Statistics. Unlike the Consolidated Banking Statistics, as mentioned before, the locational data estimate claims based on where they are booked rather than the nationality of the lender that bears the credit risk.

---

[7] Unfortunately, the PRC has yet to report consolidated banking statistics to the BIS. However, it is suspected that Chinese banks account for a large part of "outside area" lending to the region (Koch and Remolona 2018).

Japan is also considered separately. While it is one of the +3 countries, its significance is as a creditor country rather than a borrowing country, and it is an important part of the global network of major creditor jurisdictions.

Lending Jurisdictions Play Musical Chairs

In the decade since 2009, our two groups of borrowing countries showed somewhat divergent trends in their reliance on cross-border bank credit. International bank claims on the five largest ASEAN 9 economies as a group increased from 2.5% of their combined GDP in 2009 to 4.6% of their GDP in 2019. In contrast, on the part of the PRC and the Republic of Korea, such claims declined slightly from 4.4% of their combined GDP in 2009 to 4.0% in 2019.

Over the past decade, the most remarkable shift in banking interconnections with the ASEAN+3 as a whole was the ascendancy of UK banks and the decline of euro area banks. The start of the decade saw US banks dominating cross-border lending to the PRC and the Republic of Korea, and Japanese banks dominating such lending to the ASEAN 9 countries. By the end, UK banks had gained the most ground, especially in the PRC and the Republic of Korea. Japanese banks also gained some, strengthening their already dominant position in the ASEAN 9 countries. In the meantime, euro area banks lost much of their market share, especially in the ASEAN 9 countries.

Japanese banks as lenders to ASEAN ex-Singapore

The euro area banks suffered heavy losses in the European sovereign debt crisis of 2010–2013. Consistent with the common lender channel of contagion, these banks drastically reduced their lending activity in Asia. As reported in Table 2.1, they went from a 13% share of international claims on the ASEAN 9 countries in 2009 to just 5% in 2019. UK banks also lost ground, although not nearly to the same extent as the euro area banks. The share of claims from UK banks fell from 12% in 2009 to 9% in 2019.

Table 2.1: International Bank Claims on ASEAN ex-Singapore by Jurisdiction of Lending Banks, 2009 and 2019

Lending Jurisdiction	Q4 2009		Q4 2019	
	Amount Outstanding ($ billion)	Proportion (% share)	Amount Outstanding ($ billion)	Proportion (% share)
Japan	28.1	18.3%	93.3	26.1%
Outside area	8.5	5.5%	40.9	11.4%
United Kingdom	17.7	11.5%	32.1	9.0%
Taipei,China	4.2	2.7%	26.4	7.4%
United States	14.0	9.1%	26.3	7.4%
Euro area	20.1	13.1%	18.4	5.1%
Switzerland	–	–	14.0	3.9%
Republic of Korea	–	–	8.4	2.3%
Australia	2.7	1.7%	7.5	2.1%
Canada	0.9	0.6%	1.0	0.3%
Sweden	–	–	0.3	0.1%
Others	57.5	37.4%	89.2	24.9%
Total	153.6	100.0%	357.6	100.0%

Note: "Outside area" refers to jurisdictions that do not provide consolidate bank claims data to the Bank for International Settlements (BIS). As explained in Koch and Remolona (2018), "outside area" lending likely includes lending by banks in the People's Republic of China.
Source: Author, based on BIS Consolidated Banking Statistics Database (accessed July 2020)

Japanese banks entered the breach left by euro area and UK banks. In 2009, Japanese banks already held the dominant share of international claims on the ASEAN 9 countries as a group, accounting for 18%. In the course of the decade that followed, these banks became even more dominant, so that by 2019 they held 26% of those claims in the region. "Outside area" banks also gained market share, and it is possible that Chinese banks account for a large part of such gains.

UK banks as lenders to the PRC and the Republic of Korea

In the meantime, on the side of the PRC and the Republic of Korea, the decade saw lending activity by UK banks displacing US banks. In 2009, US banks were the dominant lenders to the PRC and the Republic of Korea, accounting for 21% of international claims to the two countries (Table 2.2). Like euro area banks, however, the large US banks also suffered heavy losses in the global crisis, and like euro area banks they found themselves withdrawing from Asia. In the course of the decade, they more than half of their market share (or over 12 percentage points) in the two borrowing countries, so that by 2019 they accounted for only 8.4% of international claims. Japanese banks also lost market share, almost to the same extent

|enough|as US banks. It was the outside area banks who took over. In the course of the decade, they expanded their market share by 31 percentage points, and accounted for 46% of international claims by 2019.

Table 2.2: International Bank Claims on the People's Republic of China and the Republic of Korea by Jurisdiction of Lending Banks, 2009 and 2019

Lending Jurisdiction	Q4 2009		Q4 2019	
	Amount Outstanding ($ billion)	Proportion (% share)	Amount Outstanding ($ billion)	Proportion (% share)
Outside area	66.2	15.6%	490.0	46.3%
United Kingdom	48.9	11.5%	122.7	11.6%
United States	87.9	20.7%	89.0	8.4%
Japan	53.9	12.7%	64.5	6.1%
Euro area	41.8	9.8%	55.9	5.3%
Switzerland	–	–	35.7	3.4%
Taipei,China	7.1	1.7%	26.3	2.5%
Australia	5.4	1.3%	20.9	2.0%
Canada	7.2	1.7%	15.9	1.5%
Republic of Korea	–	–	14.7	1.4%
Sweden	1.6	0.4%	1.1	0.1%
Other	104.1	24.5%	122.2	11.5%
Total	424.2	100.0%	1,058.8	100.0%

PRC = People's Republic of China.
Note: "Outside area" refers to jurisdictions that do not provide consolidate bank claims data to the Bank for International Settlements (BIS). As explained in Koch and Remolona (2018), "outside area" lending likely includes lending by banks in the PRC.
Source: Author, based on BIS Consolidated Banking Statistics Database (accessed July 2020).

The role of the Singapore and Hong Kong, China banking centers

To understand the role of Singapore and Hong Kong, China as banking centers in the region, the chapter examines how these two centers intermediate funds. It is presumed that funds originating from bank jurisdictions outside the region often first find their way to banks in Hong Kong, China; the PRC; or Singapore before they are lent to borrowers in other ASEAN+3 economies. Hence, data from the BIS Locational Banking Statistics, which report cross-border bank claims on residents of Singapore and Hong Kong, China, are used. These claims are typically loans or deposits and are broken down by the location of the banking offices that hold these claims.

Before the global crisis of 2008–2009, Singapore and Hong Kong, China played somewhat different roles in intermediating savings from different parts of the world. At that time, as documented by Remolona and Shim

(2015), banks in Hong Kong, China tended to take savings from outside the region and lend them to borrowers within the region. Banks in Singapore, by contrast, tended to take savings from the region and lend them outside the region. Since the crisis, however, the two banking centers have increasingly played similar roles, taking savings from outside the region and lending them within the region.

In 2009, both banking centers were tied closely to UK and euro area banks. As shown in Table 2.3, banking offices in the UK and euro area held loan and deposit claims amounting to 21% of such cross-border claims on residents of Singapore and Hong Kong, China. By 2019, however, banking offices in the euro area had become the leading holders of these claims, with 18% of the total. Banking offices in the UK and the US together held another 19%. Locational data do not tell us how the funds eventually find their way to the ultimate borrowers in the rest of the ASEAN+3 economies.

Table 2.3: Cross-Border Bank Loan and Deposit Claims on Residents of Singapore and Hong Kong, China by Location of Banking Office, 2009 and 2019

Location of Banks	Q4 2009		Q4 2019	
	Amount Outstanding ($ billion)	Proportion (% share)	Amount Outstanding ($ billion)	Proportion (% share)
Euro area	56.1	10.2%	173.7	17.6%
United States	32.8	6.0%	93.9	9.5%
United Kingdom	58.7	10.7%	90.1	9.1%
Hong Kong, China[1]	–	–	80.8	8.2%
Australia	6.3	1.1%	33.8	3.4%
Taipei,China	19.5	3.5%	29.4	3.0%
Macau, China	–	–	16.4	1.7%
Switzerland	23.0	4.2%	15.5	1.6%
Luxembourg	28.0	5.1%	7.1	0.7%
Republic of Korea	5.4	1.0%	4.6	0.5%
Others	320.3	58.2%	442.5	44.8%
Total	550.1	100.0%	987.8	100.0%

[1] Banking offices in Hong Kong, China are reported to hold claims on Singapore residents. It is likely that banking offices in Singapore hold also hold claims on residents of Hong Kong, China. However, Singapore does not report such data to the Bank for International Settlements (BIS).
Source: Author, based on BIS Locational Banking Statistics Database (accessed July 2020).

It is significant that Japanese banks are nowhere to be seen in these locational data on loans and deposits to residents of Singapore and Hong Kong, China, and yet the consolidated statistics show them to be playing a dominant role as ultimate lenders. One way to reconcile the two sets of data is to see the interbank markets in Singapore and Hong Kong, China as facilitating a process by which banks in the euro area, the UK, and the US lend to Japanese banks, which in turn lend the funds to borrowers in the rest of ASEAN+3. Indeed, locational data for Q4 2019 show that banks in Japan have loan and deposit liabilities to banks in Hong Kong, China amounting to $101 billion, second only to loan and deposit liabilities to banks in the US.

Much of this intermediation is evidently conducted in US dollars. The BIS locational data also provide a breakdown of cross-border loans and deposits by currency. The US dollar accounts for 66% of these claims in Hong Kong, China as of Q4 2019 and 68% of these claims in Singapore. In Hong Kong, China, the euro is the second most important currency, accounting for 11% of these claims. In Singapore, however, the Japanese yen is the second most important currency, accounting for 10% of these claims. Indeed, Gourinchas (2019) has shown the dominance of the US dollar has increased over time, partly because of complementarities in the use of this currency for both trade and finance.

2.5 Global Banking Networks and Shapley Values

In assessing concentration risk, there is need to go beyond the direct exposures and take account of the indirect exposures through the global banking network. In this network, global banks lend actively to one another. Such global interbank lending can be quite significant, as shown in Table 2.4. Allen and Gale (2000) explain how global banks insure themselves against regional liquidity shocks by holding claims against each other. However, this arrangement is vulnerable. A small liquidity shock in one region can spill over to others. There is also a currency dimension. When Japanese banks lend abroad, they tend to lend in US dollars and evidently get those by swapping yen with dollars from US banks.

Hence, a banking jurisdiction's role within the network is important. To Alves et al. (2013), the simplest measure of connectivity is a "bank's degree," which is the number of links from that bank to other banks. Those links could be given weights in various ways, such as by their relative importance. The Shapley value is used as a measure of network centrality. This measure is more appealing than just counting the links between banks. Not only does it account for the size of those links, it also accounts for all possible episodes of financial stress. In some episodes, certain links will matter and others will not, while in other episodes all links may matter. In the Asian financial crisis, for example, the links that mattered most involved the Japanese banks.

In the European sovereign debt crisis, the links that mattered most were with euro area banks.

The Global Banking Network

In measuring links among global banks, the focus of this chapter is on the five jurisdictions—Japan; the UK; the US; the euro area; and Taipei,China — from whom ASEAN+3 economies borrow the most. The BIS Consolidated Statistics report lending and borrowing between bank counterparties in the different jurisdictions. Relying on those statistics, Table 2.4 shows the proportion of what banks in a given jurisdiction borrow from banks in the other jurisdictions. The strongest global interconnections are between US and Japanese banks, and between euro area and UK banks. The table shows that Japanese banks account for 37% of what US banks borrow from banks abroad. At the same time, US banks account for 27% of what Japanese banks borrow from banks abroad. At the same time, euro area banks account for 52% of what UK banks borrow from other banks. UK banks account for 12% of euro area bank borrowing from banks outside the currency area. By contrast, global interconnections involving Taipei,China banks are relatively weak, although they do rely significantly on funds from US banks.

Table 2.4: The Global Network of the Major Creditor Jurisdictions of ASEAN ex-Singapore, the People's Republic of China, and the Republic of Korea
Proportion of interbank lending to total claims
on borrowing jurisdictions, 2019 (% share)

Lending Jurisdictions	Borrowing Jurisdictions				
	Japan	United Kingdom	United States	Euro area	Taipei,China
Japan		12.6%	37.1%	16.2%	18.5%
United Kingdom	15.4%		17.8%	11.7%	19.7%
United States	26.8%	10.4%		13.6%	31.9%
Euro area	30.2%	51.8%	20.7%		--
Taipei,China	2.8%	1.1%	1.4%	--	

PRC = People's Republic of China.
Source: Author, based on BIS Consolidated Banking Statistics Database (accessed July 2020).

This calculation uses only the creditor jurisdictions that account for the top four direct exposures to each of our two borrowing groups within ASEAN+3, as of 2019. For the ASEAN 9, these jurisdictions are Japan; the UK; Taipei,China; and the US. For the PRC and the Republic of Korea, these are the UK, the US, Japan, and the euro area. For both groups of borrowers, "outside area" creditors figure significantly. Unfortunately, there are no data on who exactly these creditors are and there is no data on their links with the global banking network.[8] Fortunately, it is likely that these creditor banks have weak links to the global network, and leaving them out of the analysis will not provide misleading results.

Why Shapley Values?

In the taxonomy of Kara, Tian, and Yellen (2015), the Shapley value is a direct network measure of interconnectedness. Instead of explicitly mapping pairwise relationships between institutions, however, the data available allow us to carry out this mapping only at the level of banking jurisdictions. The Shapley value offers the analytical advantage that, unlike other network measures, it recognizes the empirical reality that not all important contagion episodes encompass the whole network. Some important contagions are regional, others global. For example, in looking at nine recent episodes of equity-price contagion, Fry-McKibbin, Hsiao, and Tang (2014) find that only the Great Recession of 2008–2009 was truly global in scope. The analysis below considers 15 possible combinations of lending jurisdictions that lead to systemic risk. In addition, the Shapley value offers appealing analytical properties, such as additivity, symmetry, and uniqueness of the solution.

To calculate Shapley values, each lending jurisdiction is treated as a player in a cooperative game. In specifying characteristic functions for different coalitions of players, different combinations of major jurisdictions that could be involved in a contagion through the common lender channel are considered (Box 2.1). In the language of game theory, the "payoff" to the coalition corresponds to the contribution to the concentration risk of the corresponding jurisdictions. It is assumed that concentration risk is proportional to the size of the claims on the borrowing countries. This is consistent with Koch and Remolona (2018), who find that when Japanese banks had the largest proportion of claims on the crisis-hit countries of 1997, they were also the banks that reduced lending the most, reducing their exposure to the region by 80% over 5 years in the wake of the crisis. Although Japanese banks at that time were struggling with their own domestic crisis, the onset of their withdrawal from crisis countries corresponded closely to the Asian financial crisis.

---

[8] As noted by Koch and Remolona (2018), "Chinese banks have become an increasingly important provider of international bank credit, to borrowers both within and outside Asia. At the moment, [however] the PRC does not report consolidated banking claims."

Box 2.1: The Mathematical Properties of the Shapley Value

The Shapley value is a concept introduced by Shapley (1953) for cooperative games. In such a game, a coalition of players generates a payoff that is shared by the coalition as a whole. The Shapley value divides up that payoff to allocate it to individual players based on their marginal contributions. For our purposes, the payoff is the amount of concentration risk.

Tarashev, Borio, and Tsatsaronis (2010) have applied the concept to measuring systemic risk in a network of banks. As they point out, the concept has appealing mathematical properties for measuring network centrality:

Additivity: The sum of Shapley values equals the aggregate measure of concentration risk.

Symmetry: It does not matter in which order each banking jurisdiction is considered.

Dummy axiom: If the banking jurisdiction is not a source of concentration risk, its Shapley value is zero.

Linearity: The linear combination that relates characteristic functions is the same as the linear combination that relates Shapley values.

As shown by Mas-Colell, Whinston, and Green (1995), these properties lead to a unique division of the payoff.

Calculating the Shapley value involves specifying a characteristic function, which maps every possible coalition of players to a payoff. Given the specified the characteristic functions, the Shapley value for player i is calculated as:

$$\emptyset_i(N) = \frac{1}{|N|!} \sum_G [\gamma(B_i^G \cup \{i\}) - \gamma(B_i^G)]$$

where N is the number of players, $\gamma(B_i^G \cup \{i\})$ is the payoff to the coalition that includes player i and $\gamma(B_i^G)$ is the payoff to the coalition that does not include player i. The formula assigns the same probability to every possible coalition.

To illustrate the calculation, consider for now only Japan and the UK, two ASEAN 9 creditor jurisdictions. By itself, Japan's exposure is 26% of all claims on the ASEAN 9 economies. However, UK interbank exposure to Japan is 13%. As shown in Figure 2.5, taking this into account results in an additional exposure of Japanese banks to ASEAN 9 of 4% and an additional exposure of UK banks of 1%. The two jurisdictions together would then represent a concentration risk of 40%.[9] In our calculation of Shapley values, interbank exposures are assumed to have the effect of heightening concentration risk, consistent with analysis by Allen and Gale (2000) of the vulnerability of the interbank market to liquidity shocks. The appendix provides a step-by-step calculation of the Shapley values.

Figure 2.5: Calculating the Characteristic Function with Two Banking Systems

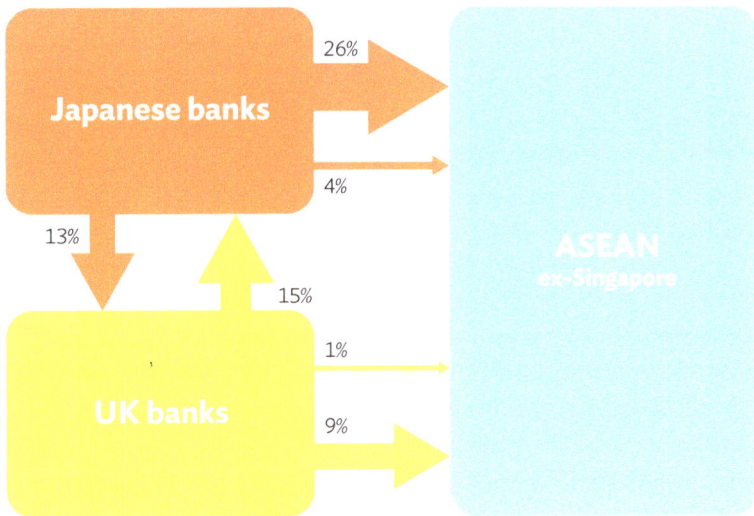

UK = United Kingdom.
Source: Author.

As mentioned above, the calculations only include the four most important lending jurisdictions for ASEAN ex-Singapore and for the PRC and the Republic of Korea. Historically, at most three lending jurisdictions have been involved in regional or global financial crises: Moreover, to go beyond four lending jurisdictions would be an exercise in false precision, given

---

[9] This is the sum of the following four components: (i) 0.26 (direct exposure of Japanese banks; (ii) 0.01 (indirect exposure of UK banks through Japanese banks) or 0.15 times 0.26; (iii) 0.09 (direct exposure of UK banks); and (iv) 0.01 (indirect exposure of Japanese banks through UK banks) or 0.13 times 0.09.

that available data do not allow the exposures to "outside area" lending jurisdictions to be accounted. Even with only four lending jurisdictions, the number of all possible coalitions N is 15, where each coalition represents a possible episode of slow-burn systemic risk involving the common lender channel. There are four possible coalitions that include only a single lending jurisdiction, six possible coalitions that include two, four possible coalitions that include three jurisdictions, and one possible coalition that includes all four.

The Difference Made by the Global Banking Network

To highlight the amplification effects of the global banking network, concentration risk is calculated by assuming that financing in the interbank market leads to additional exposure to borrowing countries that is proportional to the amount of interbank lending. This will be reflected in the calculation of payoffs to various coalitions of players when deriving Shapley values. For ASEAN ex-Singapore, the calculation is carried out for the banking network that includes banks from Japan; the UK; Taipei,China; and the US, which have the four largest direct credit exposures to the nine countries. For the PRC and Republic of Korea, the calculation includes the UK, the US, Japan, and euro area banks, which have the four largest direct credit exposures to the two countries. In each case, as mentioned above, the four different global lending jurisdictions lead to 15 possible coalitions.

The Shapley value calculations show that for ASEAN ex-Singapore, the network effects make the most difference in the concentration risk of US banks. Without the network effects, the nine countries together face a concentration risk in these banks of 7.4%. As reported in Table 2.5 and Figure 2.6, once the network effects are taken into account, the Shapley value shows a concentration risk that rises to 14.6%, which is an amplification of 97%. Nonetheless, the highest concentration risk remains with Japanese banks, with a Shapley value of 34%. As expected, network effects make the least difference in the concentration risk of Taipei,China banks, which are the banks with the weakest links in the global interbank network.

Table 2.5: Shapley Values That Account for the Global Banking Network

Top Four Creditor Jurisdictions	Claims in 2019 ($ billions)	Proportion of Total Claims (%)	Shapley Values (%)	Amplification (%)
Borrowers: ASEAN ex-Singapore (ASEAN 9)				
Japan	93.3	26.1	34.0	30.3
United Kingdom	32.1	9.0	12.8	42.2
Taipei,China	26.4	7.4	9.2	24.3
United States	26.3	7.4	14.6	97.3
Total		49.9	71.6	43.5
Borrowers: PRC and the Republic of Korea				
United Kingdom	122.7	11.6	17.5	50.4
United States	89.0	8.4	13.5	60.1
Japan	64.5	6.1	11.1	81.1
Euro area	55.9	5.3	11.3	112.3
Total		31.4	53.4.0	69.5

PRC = People's Republic of China.
Note: Contagion and Shapley values take account of lending links between creditor jurisdictions. ASEAN 9 is comprised of ASEAN economies excluding Singapore. Since the Shapley values are measured relative to the proportion of total claims, the sum of these values may exceed 100%.
Source: Author, based on BIS Consolidated Banking Statistics Database (accessed July 2020).

Figure 2.6: Shapley Values for ASEAN ex-Singapore, 2019 (%)

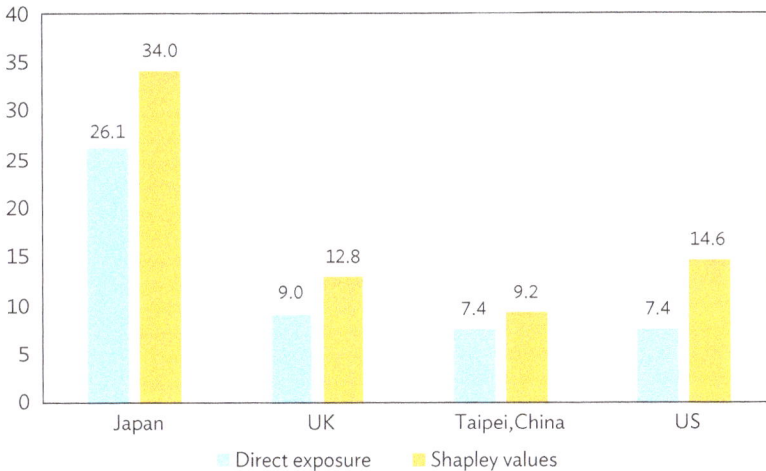

UK = United Kingdom, US = United States.
Source: Author's, based on BIS Consolidated Banking Statistics Database (accessed July 2020).

For the PRC and the Republic of Korea, the network effects make the most difference for the concentration risk of euro area banks. As shown in Table 2.5 and Figure 2.7, this risk rises from 5.3% to 11.3%, a network amplification of 112%. Nonetheless, the highest source of concentration risk remains the UK banks, with a Shapley value of 17.5%.

In general, the PRC and the Republic of Korea have lower concentration risk than the ASEAN 9 financial systems. This is in part because ASEAN 9 economies are somewhat more diversified in their international borrowing, although the lending jurisdictions tend to have strong interbank links between one another. While the Shapley values for the ASEAN 9 economies exceed 20% for loans from Japanese banks, none of these values for the PRC and the Republic of Korea come close to 20% for any lending jurisdiction. Nonetheless, a concern for both countries is the rather large sum of unidentified claims as reflected in "outside area" claims. This concern may be mitigated soon as the PRC and others begin to report consolidated banking statistics to the BIS.

Figure 2.7: Shapley Values for the People's Republic of China and the Republic of Korea, 2019
(%)

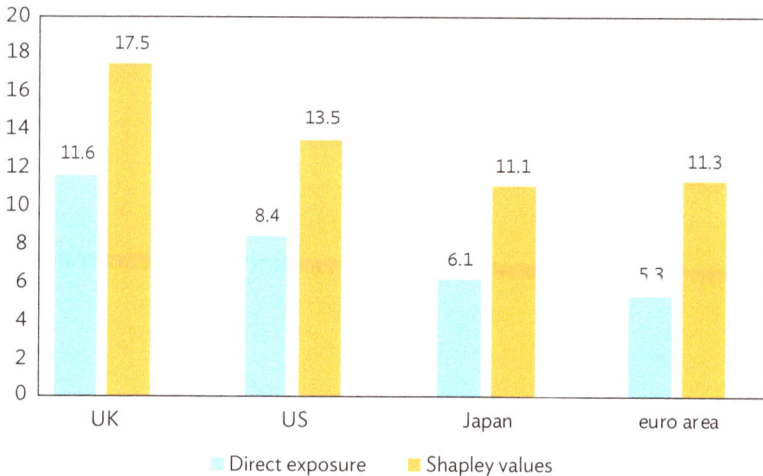

PRC = People's Republic of China, UK = United Kingdom, US = United States.
Source: Author, based on BIS Consolidated Banking Statistics Database (accessed July 2020).

2.6 Conclusion: Suggested Policy Measures

This chapter distinguishes between two sources of systemic risk: sudden stops and slow-burn contagion. The chapter shows that since the Asian financial crisis, economies of the region have addressed their vulnerability to sudden stops. When it comes to the vulnerability to slow-burn contagion, however, policy makers have work to do.

As the financial systems of the ASEAN+3 countries look to the rest of the 2020s, they do so from a position of resilience. The current accounts of most of the larger economies are in surplus. Banks are well capitalized and evidence from credit-to-GDP gaps suggests that domestic borrowers are not over leveraged. Their central banks have accumulated massive international reserves, while the Chiang Mai Initiative Multilateralization (CMIM) stands ready to provide some backup liquidity.

Moreover, as Park and Rajan (2021) have pointed out, "many of the ASEAN+3 economies initiated major finance sector reforms as a means of restructuring, strengthening and diversifying their financial systems." They add that "the fast-growing and highly intricate networks of trade, investment and cross-border financial flows within ASEAN+3, along with the fact that individually the economies are vulnerable to global shocks that might need a coordinated response, has led the region to consciously promote greater financial cooperation over the last two decades."

Turning to the remaining area of concern, the chapter explains how slow-burn contagion operates through the common lender channel. This vulnerability is exacerbated when the common lenders are themselves highly interconnected in a global banking network. Proposing the Shapley value as a measure of interconnectedness, this chapter finds that the ASEAN 9 economies face the highest levels of concentration risk in loans from Japanese banks, while for the PRC and the Republic of Korea the risk to some degree is largest in loans from banks in the UK, the UK, and the euro area.

To tackle the issue of concentration risk in foreign borrowing, one area that could use regional cooperation is in the development of local currency bond markets. Regulatory challenges also remain. Even as financial integration proceeds in the region, a regional framework is still needed for dealing with the risk of a region wide slow-burn contagion.

To further mitigate the concentration risk of slow-burn contagion, policy makers of the ASEAN+3 economies have at least two policy options. At the domestic level, they may consider macroprudential measures that restrict borrowing abroad. At the regional level, they may consider working within the ASEAN Banking Integration Framework (ABIF) to use Shapley values as measures of the concentration risk associated with slow-burn contagion and perhaps use these measures as a criterion in identifying R-SIBs.

Developing Local Currency Corporate Bond Markets

While local currency corporate bond markets in the ASEAN+3 economies have seen remarkable development in the past decade, these markets are still not able to play the role of Greenspan's spare tire in the event of a financial crisis. Indeed, Gochoco-Bautista and Remolona (2012) find that in the larger ASEAN+3 economies, banking systems are already reasonably well-developed, and markets for equities and government bonds have achieved critical mass even while remaining purely domestic. The corporate bond markets have lagged behind. Gochoco-Bautista and Remolona conclude that "the tug-of-war between the geography of information in the direction of more localized markets versus the critical mass required by network externalities makes the case for regional integration stronger for corporate bond markets than for other financial markets."

Indeed, among the fruits of regional cooperation has been an important regional initiative to foster local currency bond markets. That initiative is the Asian Bond Fund 2 (ABF2), a fund that invests in eight local currency bond markets in the region. As explained by Ma and Remolona (2005) and Chan et al. (2012), the fund has been part of a process of learning by doing, in which the central banks involved in the fund were able to identify significant impediments to market development. With those removed, ABF2 has become the largest index fund for local currency bond markets in the region.

In this context, it is useful to reiterate one of the proposals of Gochoco-Bautista and Remolona: that the ASEAN+3 central banks cooperate in establishing a regional repo market to provide cross-border liquidity to dealers in local currency corporate bonds. A few central banks in the region already have in place bilateral agreements that provide for the local currency settlement of swaps, repo transactions, and other cross-border transactions. For repo transactions, the agreements allow local currency government bonds to be accepted as collateral. The central banks that are party to these agreements include the Reserve Bank of Australia, Bank Indonesia, the Bank of Korea,

Bank Negara Malaysia, the Monetary Authority of Singapore, and the Bank of Thailand. Bilateral agreements could serve as the basis for an ASEAN-wide master agreement that would allow local currency corporate bonds from the region to be accepted as collateral in cross-border repo transactions.

Under this proposal, the regional master repo agreement might best be one that specifies tri-party contracts. These contracts would require a few clearing central banks. This clearing role could be played by the People's Bank of China (PBOC), the Bank of Japan, the Hong Kong Monetary Authority, and the Monetary Authority of Singapore. The People's Bank of China already plays a similar role for offshore yuan. If corporate bonds were included as eligible repo collateral, the clearing banks could prequalify these bonds and assess the appropriate repo haircuts for them.

A possible challenge in the use of local currency corporate bonds as collateral is their credit quality. Collateral that is internationally rated below double-A would seem unlikely to be acceptable even when subjected to haircuts. Amstad et al. (2016) do find that when it comes to local credit ratings, by far most corporate bonds issued in Indonesia, the PRC, the Republic of Korea, Malaysia, and the Philippines are highly rated, enjoying either triple-A or double-A ratings. In equivalent international credit ratings, however, these bonds would be rated close to that of the sovereign, which in this case could be as low as triple-B.[10] Nonetheless, the bilateral agreements already mentioned do accept government bonds with such low ratings as collateral in repo transactions, and so should arguably allow similarly rated corporate bonds to serve as collateral.

If all that the proposed regional repo market did was to provide liquidity to existing corporate bonds, the proposal would not be that helpful. Earnest development of the region's corporate bond markets must include making them more accessible to lower-rated issuers. Hence, it is important that the proposed regional repo market accepts lower-rated issues as collateral.

To resolve the conflict between what is acceptable as repo collateral and what is required for the market to develop, ASEAN governments may wish to turn to the Credit Guarantee and Investment Facility (CGIF). This is a trust fund of the Asian Development Bank (ADB) which was established precisely to promote the development of deep and liquid local currency

---

[10] As of the writing of this report, the S&P sovereign ratings are double-A for the Republic of Korea; single-A for the PRC, Malaysia, and the Philippines; and triple-B for Indonesia.

bond markets in ASEAN+3 countries.[11] Here, the CGIF could provide enough of a credit guarantee to lower-rated corporate bond issues so that they would be acceptable as collateral in a regional repo market. Such a repo market would in turn serve to enhance the liquidity of these corporate bonds.

Macroprudential Measures

Macroprudential measures have become fairly common in Asia. Kim's (2019) study of macroprudential policy in 11 Asian countries finds that the most frequently used tools are the loan-to-value ratio and the reserve requirement. Some countries also use various forms of bank capital buffers. Bank Indonesia has implemented a capital conservation buffer, while the Bank of Korea has implemented one based on countercyclical capital.

Among the less common tools is the macroprudential stability levy. This is imposed by the Bank of Korea on banks' noncore foreign currency liabilities. Since the levy was introduced in 2011, it seems to have succeeded in its intention of lengthening the maturity structure of foreign borrowing.

Something like the Republic of Korea's macroprudential stability levy could be deployed against concentration risk. In this case, the imposition of the levy should be transparent. For example, it could be imposed on foreign loans from banks that come from a jurisdiction for which the computed Shapley value exceeds 10%. For the average ASEAN 9 country, based on the Shapley values reported in Table 2.5, this would mean applying the levy to Japanese, UK, and US bank loans. For the PRC and the Republic of Korea, this would mean applying the levy to UK, US, euro area, and Japanese bank loans.

Macroprudential measures in general should be carried out in coordination with monetary policy. Using panel vector autoregression, Kim (2019) concludes that contractionary macroprudential policy affects credit and output in much the same way that monetary tightening does. If this is the case, macroprudential measures might focus more on credit and monetary policy more on output.

---

[11]   For more on the CGIF, see: https://www.cgif-abmi.org/.

Global and Regional Systemically Important Banks

The effects of macroprudential policy in one country often spill over into other countries. Patel (2017), for example, draws on a survey of emerging market central banks to identify channels through which the influence of macroprudential measures extends across national borders. These channels point to the need for international cooperation of macroprudential measures.

One of the mechanisms for cooperation is the Financial Stability Board (FSB), which includes the previous Financial Stability Forum's members and Group of 20 members that were not part of the forum, including the PRC; Hong Kong, China; Indonesia; Japan; the Republic of Korea; and Singapore. As part of its work, the FSB has been designating global systemically important banks (G-SIBs). The G-SIBs are identified through a transparent methodology. Domestic authorities then subject them to four sets of requirements: (i) higher capital buffers; (ii) standards of total loss-absorbing capacity; (iii) resolvability; and (iv) higher supervisory expectations.

When it comes to the higher capital buffers, the G-SIBs are placed in five different buckets, requiring different levels of additional capital. The assignment to buckets is based on a simple assessment methodology that relies on five "denominators" carrying the same weights:

- Size: Total exposures as defined in the Basel III leverage ratio.

- Cross-jurisdictional activity: Cross-jurisdictional claims and liabilities.

- Interconnectedness: Intra-financial system assets and liabilities, and securities outstanding.

- Substitutability/financial infrastructure: Assets under custody, payments infrastructure, and capital market underwriting activity.

- Complexity: Notional amounts of over-the-counter derivatives and other indicators.

While the denominators for cross-jurisdictional activity and interconnectedness are related to Shapley values, they are quite different. The Shapley values are more focused on the concentration risk of slow-burn contagion as faced by specific groups of borrowing countries, for which some lending jurisdictions are more important than others. The Shapley values also account for possible systemic risk scenarios in which the different lending jurisdictions could be involved. In this respect, the calculated Shapley values highlight the more important interconnections among the banking jurisdictions that are likely to drive the common lender channel of contagion.

For purposes of the resilience of the ASEAN+3 financial systems, the supervisory authorities could designate R-SIBs rather than rely entirely on the G-SIB framework. The objective of designating R-SIBs would be to impose additional capital buffers on their bank subsidiaries in the region, following the FSB practice with regard to G-SIBs. These buffers would be calibrated to discourage slow-burn contagion concentration risk, preferably using Shapley values as a denominator in the assessment methodology.

Relying on BIS Consolidated Banking Statistics to compute Shapley values means the identification of R-SIBs would be about their home jurisdictions rather than about individual banks. A caveat in using the current calculations of Shapley values is that the possibly large claims of banks in the PRC are not yet reported in the underlying consolidated statistics. Fortunately, this shortcoming will be remedied soon, because the PBOC has now committed to reporting such data to the BIS.

A possible mechanism for regional cooperation is the Executives' Meeting of East Asia-Pacific (EMEAP) central banks, a group that guides regional bank regulation through its Working Group on Banking Supervision. The members of EMEAP include nine of the ASEAN+3 central banks, the PBOC, Hong Kong Monetary Authority, Bank Indonesia, Bank of Japan, Bank of Korea, Bank Negara Malaysia, Bangko Sentral ng Pilipinas, Monetary Authority of Singapore, and Bank of Thailand. The Working Group on Banking Supervision also includes as members banking supervisory authorities such as the China Banking Regulatory Commission, Indonesia's Otoritas Jasa Keuangan, Japan's Financial Services Agency, and the Republic of Korea's Financial Supervisory Service.

References

Acharya, V., L.H. Pedersen, T. Philippon, and M. Richardson. 2017. Measuring Systemic Risk. *Review of Financial Studies.*30 (1). pp. 2–47. https://doi.org/10.1093/rfs/hhw088.

Adrian, T. and M. Brunnermeier. 2016. CoVar. *American Economic Review.* 106 (7). pp. 1705–41. https://doi.org/10.1257/aer.20120555.

Aizenman, J., M. Hutchison, and Y. Jinjarak. 2013. What is the Risk of European Sovereign Debt Defaults? Fiscal Space, CDS Spreads and Market Pricing of Risk. *Journal of International Money and Finance.* 34. pp. 37–59. https://doi.org/10.1016/j.jimonfin.2012.11.011.

Aldasoro, I., C. Borio, and M. Drehmann. 2018. Early Warning Indicators of Banking Crises: Expanding the Family. *BIS Quarterly Review*. March. pp. 29–45. Basel: Bank for International Settlements. https://www.bis.org/publ/qtrpdf/r_qt1803e.htm.

Allen, F. and D. Gale. 2000. Financial Contagion. *Journal of Political Economy.* 108 (1). pp. 1–33. https://doi.org/10.1086/262109.

Alves, I., S. Ferrari, P. Franchini, J-C. Heam, P. Jurca, S. Langfield, S. Laviola, F. Liedorp, A. Sánchez, S. Tavolaro, and G. Vuillemey. 2013. The Structure and Resilience of the European Interbank Market. *Occasional Paper Series*. No 3. September. Frankfurt am Main: European Systemic Risk Board. https://www.esrb.europa.eu/pub/pdf/occasional/20130916_occasional_paper_3.pdf.

Amstad, M., S. Kong, F. Packer, and E. Remolona. 2016. A Spare Tire for Capital Markets: Fostering Corporate Bond Markets in Asia. *BIS Papers*. No. 85. June. Basel: Bank for International Settlements. https://www.bis.org/publ/bppdf/bispap85.pdf.

Avdjiev, S., R. McCauley, and P. McGuire. 2012. Rapid Credit Growth and International Credit: Challenges for Asia. In *Exchange Rate Appreciation, Capital Flows and Excess Liquidity: Adjustment and Effectiveness of Policy Responses*, edited by V. Pontines and R Siregar. Kuala Lumpur: The SEACEN Centre. https://www.seacen.org/publications/RePEc/702001-100297-PDF.pdf.

Bank for International Settlements (BIS). Consolidated Banking Statistics Database. https://www.bis.org/statistics/consstats.htm (accessed July 2020).

_____. Credit-to-GDP Gaps Database. https://www.bis.org/statistics/c_gaps.htm (accessed July 2020).

Bruno, V. and H.S. Shin. 2015. Capital Flows and the Risk-taking Channel of Monetary Policy. *Journal of Monetary Economics.* 71. pp. 119–32. https://doi.org/10.1016/j.jmoneco.2014.11.011.

Cecchetti, S. and K. Schoenholtz. 2018. Sudden Stops: A Primer on Balance-of-Payments Crises. *Money and Banking.* 25 June. https://www.moneyandbanking.com/commentary/2018/6/24/sudden-stops-a-primer-on-balance-of-payments-crises.

Chan, E., M. Chui, F. Packer, and E Remolona. 2012. Local Currency Bond Markets and the Asian Bond Fund 2 Initiative. *Weathering Financial Crises: Bond Markets in Asia and the Pacific. BIS Papers.* No. 63. January. Basel: Bank for International Settlements. https://www.bis.org/publ/bppdf/bispap63.pdf.

Cheung, Y.W., X. Qian, and E. Remolona. 2019. The Hoarding of International Reserves: It's a Neighborly Day in Asia. *Pacific Economic Review.* 24 (2). pp. 208–40. https://doi.org/10.1111/1468-0106.12297.

Coppola, A., M. Maggiori, B. Neiman, and J. Schreger. 2020. Redrawing the Map of Global Capital Flows: The Role of Financing and Tax Havens. *NBER Paper.* No. 26855. March. Cambridge, MA: National Bureau of Economics Research. https://doi.org/10.3386/w26855.

Diebold, F.X. and K. Yilmaz. 2014. On the Network Topology of Variance Decompositions: Measuring the Connectedness of Financial Firms. *Journal of Econometrics.* 182 (1). pp. 119–34. https://doi.org/10.1016/j.jeconom.2014.04.012.

Dungey, M., M. Luciani, and D. Veredas. 2014. Googling SIFIs. *Systemic Risk: Liquidity Risk, Governance and Financial Stability* http://dx.doi.org/10.2139/ssrn.2166504.

Forbes, K.J. and F. Warnock. 2012. Capital Flow Waves: Surges, Stops, Flight and Retrenchment. *Journal of International Economics.* 88 (2). pp. 235–51. https://doi.org/10.1016/j.jinteco.2012.03.006.

Fry-McKibbin, R., C. Y-L. Hsiao, and C. Tang. 2013. Contagion and Global Financial Crises: Lessons from Nine Crisis Episodes. *Open Economies Review.* 25. pp. 521–70. https://doi.org/10.1007/s11079-013-9289-1.

Gochoco-Bautista, M.S. and E. Remolona. 2012. Going Regional: How to Deepen ASEAN's Financial Markets. *ADB Economics Working Paper Series.* No. 300. Manila: Asian Development Bank. https://www.adb.org/sites/default/files/publication/29689/economics-wp-300.pdf.

Gourinchas, P.O. 2019. The Dollar Hegemon? Evidence and Implications for Policy Makers. Paper Prepared for the 6th Asian Monetary Policy Forum. May 2019. Singapore. https://doi.org/10.1142/9789811238628_0007.

Greenspan, A. 1999. Do Efficient Financial Markets Mitigate Financial Crises? *Remarks*. Financial Markets Conference of the Federal Reserve Bank of Atlanta. Sea Island, Georgia. 19 October. https://www.federalreserve.gov/boarddocs/speeches/1999/19991019.htm.

Gyntelberg, J., G. Ma, and E. Remolona. 2005. Corporate Bond Markets in Asia. *BIS Quarterly Review*. December. Basel: Bank for International Settlements. https://www.bis.org/publ/qtrpdf/r_qt0512g.pdf.

Hausmann, R. and U. Panizza. 2003. On the Determinants of Original Sin: An Empirical Investigation. *Journal of International Money and Finance*. 22 (7). pp. 957–90. https://doi.org/10.1016/j.jimonfin.2003.09.006.

International Monetary Fund (IMF). International Financial Statistics Database. https://data.imf.org/?sk=4C514D48-B6BA-49ED-8AB9-52B0C1A0179B (accessed May 2021).

Kaminsky, G., C. Reinhart, and C.A. Vegh. 2003. The Unholy Trinity of Financial Contagion. *Journal of Economic Perspective*. 17 (4). pp. 51–74. https://doi.org/10.1257/089533003772034899.

Kara, G., M. Tian, and M. Yellen. 2015. Taxonomy of Studies on Interconnectedness. *FEDS Notes*. 31 July. Washington, DC: Board of Governors of the Federal Reserve System. https://doi.org/10.17016/2380-7172.1569.

Kim, D.H., M. Loretan, and E. Remolona. 2010. Contagion and Risk Premia in the Amplification of Crisis: Evidence from Asian Names in the Global CDS Market. *Journal of Asian Economics*. 21 (3). pp. 314–26. https://doi.org/10.1016/j.asieco.2009.07.010.

Kim, S. 2019. Macroprudential Policy in Asian Economies. *ADB Economics Working Paper Series*. No 577. Manila: Asian Development Bank. http://dx.doi.org/10.22617/WPS190114-2.

Koch, C. and E. Remolona. 2018. Common Lenders in Emerging Asia: Their Changing Roles in Three Crises. *BIS Quarterly Review*. March. pp. 17–28. Basel: Bank for International Settlements. https://www.bis.org/publ/qtrpdf/r_qt1803b.pdf.

Ma, G. and E. Remolona. 2005. Opening Markets Through a Regional Bond Fund: Lessons from ABF2. *BIS Quarterly Review*. June. pp. 81–92. Basel: Bank for International Settlements. https://www.bis.org/publ/qtrpdf/r_qt0506g.pdf.

Mas-Colell, A., M.D. Whinston, and J.R. Green. 1995. *Microeconomic Theory*. Oxford: Oxford University Press.

Masson, P. 1998. Contagion: Monsoonal Effect, Spillovers and Jumps Between Multiple Equilibria. *IMF Working Papers*. No. 98/142. Washington, DC: International Monetary Fund. https://www.imf.org/-/media/Websites/IMF/imported-full-text-pdf/external/pubs/ft/wp/_wp98142.ashx.

Mendoza, E.G. 2010. Sudden Stops, Financial Crises, and Leverage. *American Economic Review*. 100 (5). pp. 1941–66.

Mizen, P., F. Packer, E. Remolona, and S. Tsoukas. 2018. Original Sin in Corporate Finance: New Evidence from Asian Bond Issuers in Onshore and Offshore Markets. *CFCM Working Paper*. No. 18/04. Nottingham: Centre for Finance, Credit and Macroeconomics, University of Nottingham. https://www.nottingham.ac.uk/cfcm/documents/papers/cfcm-2018-04.pdf.

Park, C.Y. and R.S. Rajan. 2021. Overview of Financial Development and Cooperation in ASEAN+3. *In Redefining Strategic Routes to Financial Resilience in ASEAN+3*, edited by D. Guinigundo, M. Kawai, C. Y. Park, and R. S. Rajan. Manila: Asian Development Bank.

Park, C.Y. and K. Shin. 2018. Global Banking Network and Regional Financial Contagion. *ADB Economics Working Papers*. No. 546. Manila: Asian Development Bank. http://dx.doi.org/10.22617/WPS189353-2.

Patel, N. 2017. Macroprudential Frameworks: Cross-border Issues BIS Papers. No. 94. Basel: Bank for International Settlements. https://www.bis.org/publ/bppdf/bispap94d_rh.pdf.

Remolona, E. and I. Shim. 2015. The Rise of Regional Banking in Asia and the Pacific. *BIS Quarterly Review*. September. pp. 119–34. Basel: Bank for International Settlements. https://www.bis.org/publ/qtrpdf/r_qt1509j.pdf.

Rey, H. 2015. Dilemma Not Trilemma: The Global Financial Cycle and Monetary Policy Independence. *NBER Working Paper*. No. 21162. Revised February 2018. Cambridge, MA: National Bureau of Economics Research. http://dx.doi.org/10.3386/w21162.

Schularick, M. and A.M. Taylor. 2012. Credit Booms Gone Bust: Monetary Policy, Leverage Cycles and Financial Crises: 1870–2008. *American Economic Review*. 102 (2). pp. 1029–61. http://dx.doi.org/10.1257/aer.102.2.1029.

Shapley, L. S. 1953. A Value for n-Person Games. In *Contributions to the Theory of Games (AM-28), Volume II*, edited by H.W. Kuhn and A.W. Tucker. *Annals of Mathematics Studies* 28. https://doi.org/10.1515/9781400881970-018.

Tarashev, N., C. Borio, and K. Tsatsaronis. 2010. Attributing Systemic Risk to Individual Institutions. *BIS Working Papers*. No. 308. Basel: Bank for International Settlements. https://www.bis.org/publ/work308.pdf.

Wu, E., M. Erdem, E. Kalotychou, and E. Remolona. 2016. The Anatomy of Sovereign Risk Contagion. *Journal of International Money and Finance*. 69. pp. 264–86. https://doi.org/10.1016/j.jimonfin.2016.07.002.

Wyplosz, C., B. Eichengreen, and A.K. Rose. 1996. Contagious Currency Crises. *NBER Working Paper*. No. 5681. Cambridge, MA: National Bureau of Economics Research. https://doi.org/10.3386/w5681.

Appendix

A Step-by-Step Calculation of Shapley Values as Measures of Funding Concentration Risk with Two Banking Jurisdictions

To illustrate how the Shapley value is calculated as a way of measuring the funding concentration risk, the example of two banking jurisdictions lending heavily to ASEAN economies except Singapore are used, namely Japan and the UK. The calculation involves specifying a characteristic function and payoff for each possible coalition of lending jurisdictions.

Step 1: Specify the characteristic functions and payoffs.

Two possible coalitions involve one banking jurisdiction each. The characteristic functions and corresponding payoffs are given by the direct shares of Japanese and UK banks in international claims on ASEAN ex-Singapore (Table 2.1):

$$\gamma(JP) = 26.1\% \qquad \gamma(UK) = 9.0\%$$

where JP represents Japanese banking jurisdiction and UK represents the UK jurisdiction.

There is only one other possible coalition: the one that involves the two banking jurisdictions together. The payoff for this coalition is given by:

$$\gamma(JP,UK) = [26.1\% + 9.0\%] + (26.1\%)(15.4\%) + (9.0\%)(12.6\%) = 40.3\%$$

where the first term (in brackets) is the sum of the direct shares $\gamma(JP)$ and $\gamma(UK)$; the second term is the part of the Japanese banking share that is accounted by interbank lending from UK banks, as reported in Table 2.4; and the third term is the part of the UK banking share accounted for by interbank lending from Japanese banks, also reported in Table 2.4.

Step 2: Calculate Shapley values.

Once the characteristic functions and payoffs have been specified, the Shapley value for player JP is calculated as:

$$\varnothing_{JP}(2) = \tfrac{1}{2}\,\gamma(JP) + \tfrac{1}{2}\left[\gamma(JP,UK) - \gamma(UK)\right] = 28.7\%$$

while for player *UK*, it is calculated as:

$$\varnothing_{UK}(2) = \frac{1}{2}\,\gamma(UK) + \frac{1}{2}[\gamma(JP,UK) - \gamma(JP)] = 11.6\%$$

One can check that the sum of the Shapley values is 40.3%, which gives us back the payoff to the coalition $\gamma(JP,UK)$.

3

The Global Monetary System and Use of Regional Currencies in ASEAN+3

Hiro Ito and Masahiro Kawai[1]

3.1 Introduction

The United States (US) dollar is unquestionably the most dominant international currency and functions as the foundation of the current international monetary system. While US shares in global GDP and trade have fallen in the last few decades, dollar shares in global foreign currency trading, foreign exchange reserves, and cross-border bank loans and international debt issues have remained stable.

The dollar's effective exchange rate appreciated when the COVID-19 pandemic triggered a global economic crisis in March 2020, and many other financial asset prices plunged.[2] That the Japanese yen appreciated more than the dollar at the beginning of the economic crisis reflected investors' tendency to go "risk-off" and park short-term investments in safe currencies such as the yen and the Swiss franc, and was a result of the limited spread of the coronavirus at that time. Once the infection spread globally, especially in the US, and many countries resorted to lockdowns to contain it, their economic situations worsened and financial instability loomed. These developments drew investors to safe dollar assets such as US Treasuries, contributing further to dollar appreciation.[3]

---

[1] The authors are grateful to Diwa Guinigundo, Haruhiko Kuroda, Cyn-Young Park, Sanchita Basu Das, Rogelio Mercado Jr., and other ADB colleagues and workshop participants for their constructive comments.

[2] From 21 January 2020 (when COVID-19 cases emerged in Wuhan, People's Republic of China) to 19 March (when pandemic-driven financial turmoil hit the US), the US dollar strengthened by 8.6% against major trading partners. However, in the week to 20 March, the Dow Jones Industrial Average fell by 17.3%.

[3] In late March 2020, the panicky situation in the US and global markets worsened to the point where dollar liquidity was preferred over other assets. This was reflected in an increase in the US 10-year government bond yields as the market panicked and investors tried to cash in government bonds for dollar bills, pushing down bond prices.

US dollar appreciation during a global crisis is not unprecedented. When Lehman Brothers collapsed in September 2008, the currency immediately rose even though the underlying subprime loan crisis in the US was the source of the global financial crisis. Dollar appreciation surprised many economists who were expecting persistent deficits in the US current account to cause dollar depreciation in the event of a crisis (Krugman 2007). Essentially, the liquidity crunch forced US financial institutions to repatriate dollar assets to strengthen their cash positions at home.

Though more than a decade apart, the pandemic and the financial crisis signify how the US dollar's part as an international currency has endured, and that the current international monetary system is built on the dollar as the dominant global currency. The flipside of its wide use globally is that other national currencies have minor or little roles to play in international transactions. This is particularly so with ASEAN+3 economies, i.e., the 10 Association of Southeast Asian Nations (ASEAN) member countries, plus the People's Republic of China (PRC), Japan, and the Republic of Korea. This suggests that investigation into how and why the dollar is dominant globally and in the ASEAN+3 region can shed light on how the use of regional currencies can be promoted.

This chapter explores the prevalence of US dollars for international trade, investment, finance, foreign exchange reserve holdings, and exchange-rate management. How ASEAN+3 economies have balanced different degrees of exchange rate stability, capital account openness, and monetary policy independence over the last 50 years is a topic ripe for discussion, especially when viewed through the lens of the "trilemma" hypothesis in international finance. How regional currencies are making headway for use in international transactions and increasingly seen as alternatives to the dollar in the settlement of trade, foreign direct investment (FDI) and financial transactions, and as official assets in national reserves also features in this chapter.

3.2 United States Dollar Dominance and Resilience in the Global Monetary System

The current global monetary system is characterized by the dominance of the US dollar, as shown by data such as its high shares across an exhaustive list: invoicing or cross-border settlement of trade and overall international transactions, global foreign exchange market turnovers, foreign exchange reserve holdings, cross-border bank liabilities, and international debt securities. While the euro is the dominant currency in Europe though not globally, Asian currencies such as the yen and the PRC yuan are not even dominant in Asia.

The Dollar as the Dominant International Currency

Trade invoicing or settlement

The most prominent role of the US dollar is for trade invoicing or settlement. Gopinath (2015) points out the dollar's outsized role in invoicing half or more of international trade. Figure 3.1a illustrates the shares of the dollar in export invoicing or settlement for individual countries compared to the shares of their total exports that are destined for the US. The figure demonstrates that economies rely more on the dollar for international trade than their trade relationships with the US might suggest. If the dollar did not play a dominant role, one would expect its invoicing or settlement share in export transactions of economies to be proportional to the share of the US as a destination for an economy's exports.[4] The figure clearly indicates that economies invoice or settle their exports in the dollar much more than proportionally in line with the share of their exports to the US.

Figure 3.1b shows the currency composition of all international settlements reported by Society for Worldwide Interbank Financial Telecommunication SC (SWIFT). It is clear that the dollar has the biggest use for international settlements, followed by the euro, while other major currencies, such as the UK's pound sterling and the Japanese yen, are far less important. Although the dollar is the most important international settlement currency, it is not so dominant and was actually less important than the euro in the early 2010s. Since then, the euro has been a strong second most important international settlement currency

---

[4] A comparable figure for the euro, which presents the euro shares in export invoicing against the shares of countries' exports to the euro area, would show that many observation points are scattered around the 45-degree line. This suggests that countries tend to use the euro for export invoicing in a way proportional to their exports to the euro area (Ito and Kawai 2016).

Figure 3.1: Shares of Major Currencies in International Trade and Overall International Settlements
(%)

a. Trade invoicing or settlement

b. Overall international settlements

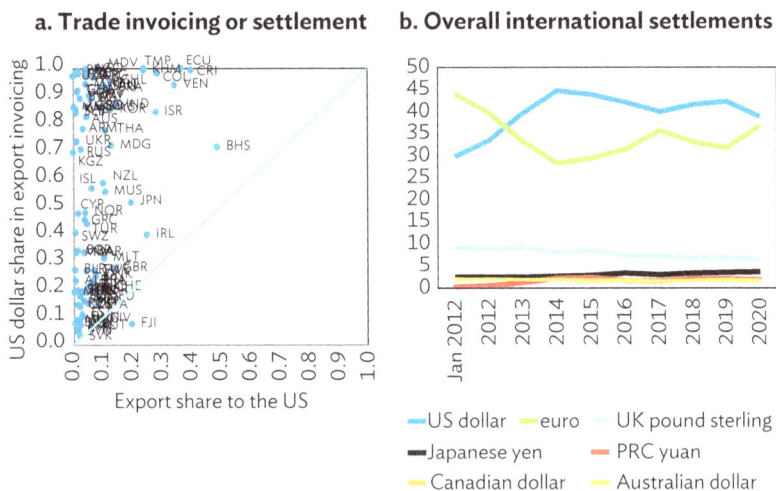

PRC = People's Republic of China, UK = United Kingdom, US = United States.
Note: In panel a, the horizontal axis is each economy's average share of export to the US in total export, and the vertical axis is the economy's average share of US dollar invoicing/settlement in total export, both in 2014–2018. Panel b reports currency shares in customer initiated and institutional payments, based on values at the end of each year except the first observation in the figure..
Source: Authors, based on Boz et al. (2020) and from SWIFT, *RMB Tracker*, various issues (all accessed July 2021).

Foreign exchange trading and official foreign reserves

Figure 3.2a summarizes the currency composition of foreign exchange trading in the world's major markets from 1989 to 2019, based on the triennial survey of the Bank for International Settlements (BIS). The figure indicates the US dollar is used in 80%–90% of foreign exchange trading over the past 30 years, recording 88% in 2019. The euro share has slipped from 38% in 2001 to 32% in 2019, perhaps due to the euro area debt and banking crisis in 2011–2015. The share of the yen also fell from 27% in 1989 to 17% in 2019, a level below the previous trough in 2007. That share is still higher than for pound sterling, which was 13% in 2019. The share of the yuan in the global currency markets has risen since the mid-2000s, and recorded 4% in 2019.

Figure 3.2: Shares of Major Currencies in Foreign Exchange Market Turnover and Reserves
(%)

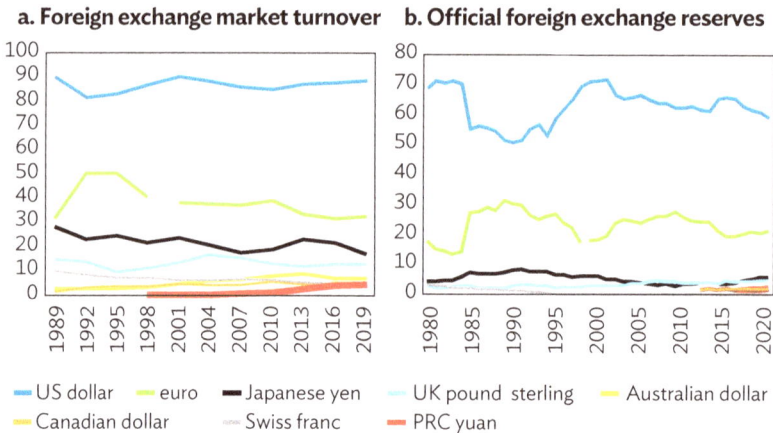

a. Foreign exchange market turnover   **b. Official foreign exchange reserves**

Legend: US dollar — euro — Japanese yen — UK pound sterling — Australian dollar — Canadian dollar — Swiss franc — PRC yuan

PRC = People's Republic of China, UK = United Kingdom, US = United States.
Note: The sum of the percentage shares of individual currencies totals 200% instead of 100% in panel a, because two currencies are involved in a single transaction. Data for the euro before its introduction are obtained as the sum of Euro Currency Unit and legacy currencies that are now the euro.
Source: Authors, based on BIS, *Triennial Central Bank Survey: Foreign Exchange Turnover* (accessed September 2019), and IMF, Currency Composition of Official Foreign Exchange Reserves (COFFER) (accessed August 2021).

Figure 3.2b reports the currency composition of foreign exchange reserves held by all International Monetary Fund (IMF) reporting member countries. It shows that the share of the US dollar has been relatively high at 50%–70% as the dominant reserve currency and was 59% in 2020. The share of the euro has been in the range of 20%–30% and was 21% in 2020. The shares of other reserve currencies have been very low in comparison to those of the dollar and the euro. The share of the yen has been at the 4%–9% range and recorded 6% in 2020, but it still occupies third position. The pound sterling continues to play a role as a reserve currency, accounting for 5% in 2020. The yuan was recognized as a reserve currency from 2016 after its inclusion in the IMF's special drawing rights basket. Having accounted for 1% of global foreign exchange reserves in 2016, the yuan share rose to 2% in 2020. Therefore, it is not yet one of the most heavily held global reserve currencies, although its share is now higher than those of the Canadian dollar, Australian dollar, and Swiss franc.

Cross-border bank loans and international debt securities issued

Figure 3.3a presents the currency composition of cross-border bank liabilities based on BIS Locational Banking Statistics. It shows that the share of the US dollar was in excess of 60% in the early 1980s, and while this began to decline in the latter half of the 1980s, it has still maintained a 45%–55% share over the last 30 years, recording 49% in 2020. The euro share is the second highest and has risen over time, registering 29% in 2020. The yen's share was low in the early 1980s, began to rise in the second half of that decade, maintained moderately high use at more than 10% in the 1990s, and has declined since then, falling to 4% in 2020, which was slightly less than the pound sterling share. No data are reported for the yuan.

Figure 3.3: Shares of Major Currencies in Cross-Border Bank Liabilities and International Debt Securities Issued
(%)

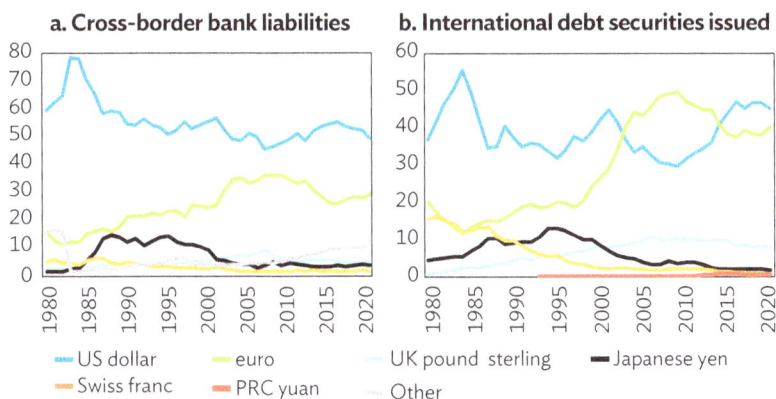

a. Cross-border bank liabilities

b. International debt securities issued

US dollar — euro — UK pound sterling — Japanese yen — Swiss franc — PRC yuan — Other

PRC = People's Republic of China, UK = United Kingdom, US = United States.
Note: Data for the euro refer to legacy currencies now included in the euro before euro data appear. In the case of international debt securities, data for the euro refer to EU1, i.e., the sum of European Currency Unit, euro, and legacy currencies now included in the euro, up to 2015, and EUR from 2016.
Source: Authors, based on BIS, *Locational Banking Statistics* and BIS, *Debt Securities Statistics* (all accessed August 2021).

Figure 3.3b presents the currency composition of the stock of international debt securities issued. It shows that the share of debt issued in euros was higher than for dollars between the early 2000s and the early 2010s and was overtaken by the dollar in the mid-2010s. In recent years, the dollar share recorded as high, but not so dominant, at 45% while the euro share was 40% in 2020. The share of the yen was moderately high in the mid-1990s, at close to 15%, but declined to a mere 2% in 2020. The pound sterling share has been higher than the yen share since the early 2000s, registering 8% in 2020. The yuan share has remained low at less than 1%, recording 0.4% in 2020.

Dominance of the US Dollar Zone

Researchers have attempted to identify the size of a currency bloc. A study by Tovar and Nor (2018) has tried this by estimating major currencies' weights for each economy's implicit currency basket in its exchange-rate management. The calculations use both the Frankel and Wei (1994) method to estimate the weights of the dollar, euro, pound sterling, and yen without considering the role played by the yuan as a major international currency and the Kawai and Pontines (2016) method to estimate the weights of major currencies, including for the yuan.

Tovar and Nor calculate the sizes of major currency zones by using estimated weights on major currencies and GDP for each economy. They find the US dollar zone (with the US as its core) dominant over the last 50 years, followed by the euro zone (with the euro area comprising 19 members in 2020 as its core), the pound sterling zone, the yen zone, and the yuan zone.

Figure 3.4, adapted from Tovar and Nor, identifies the countries of major currency blocs, with or without the yuan included in the analysis.[5] For example, a country is classified as belonging to the dollar (or yuan) zone if the estimated weight of the dollar (or yuan) is the highest among all weights for the country. The figure demonstrates that without including the yuan, the sizes of the zones for the dollar and euro look large, but are smaller when the PRC currency is included. The yuan zone (with the PRC as its core) emerges in the analysis as a relatively large currency bloc. This suggests that in recent years, the yuan zone has expanded fast. However, as discussed in Section 3.4, the yuan's rise as an anchor currency—a major international currency with a positive weight in an economy's implicit currency basket, which influences the economy's exchange-rate management policy—has not been matched by a concomitant increase in yuan use for international transactions.

---

[5] With both the yuan and US dollar included on the right-hand side of the estimating equation, the traditional Frankel–Wei method faces the problem of severe multicollinearity as the yuan is managed heavily in relation to the dollar, and thus cannot provide stable and robust estimates for these currencies. In such a case, the Kawai-Pontines method is more appropriate as it addresses the multicollinearity problem and yields estimates that are superior to, and more robust than, those obtained by the Frankel–Wei method.

Figure 3.4: Estimated Currency Blocs with or without the PRC Yuan, 2011–2015

a. Without the CNY   **b. With the CNY**

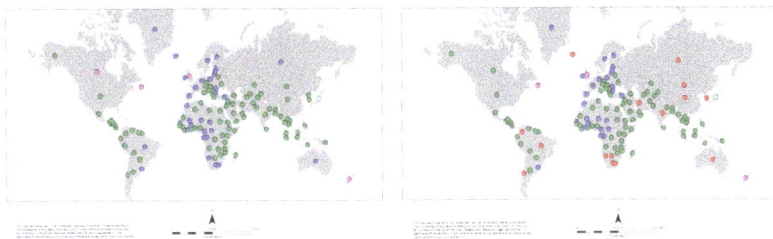

Most Influential Reserve ● EUR   ● GBP   JPY   ● USD   ● CNY

CNY = PRC yuan, EUR = euro, GBP = United Kingdom pound sterling, JPY = Japanese yen, USD = United States dollar.
Note: Analysis of reserve currency blocs without the CNY is based on the Frankel–Wei method, and analysis of reserve currency blocs with the CNY is based on the Kawai–Pontines method. The results in both panels are averages for 2011–2015. Maps are redrawn by using data made available by Camilo E. Tovar and Tania Mohd Nor.
Source: Tovar and Nor (2018).

One of the problems in Figure 3.4 is the lack of distinction between countries that stabilize or manage their exchange rates in relation to a single anchor currency (or a basket of major currencies) and those that do not manage their exchange rates under pure floats. For example, countries like Australia, Canada, and New Zealand have adopted freely flexible exchange rates, but Tovar and Nor consider them as either pound sterling, US dollar, euro, or yuan zone countries. Countries under pure floats should not be judged as part of any currency zone.[6] Thus, a distinction is needed between two types of country: those under a pure floating regime and those under pegged or managed regimes, after which only those countries that stabilize or manage exchange rates should be classified into particular currency zones.

Implications and Issues of US Dollar Dominance

This analysis shows the US dollar has had a significant and mostly dominant role except in a few cases, such as overall international settlements and international debt securities issued. It has been remarkably stable and resilient without showing either a persistent decline or rising trend over the last 30 to 40 years.

---

[6] A judgment must be made on the degree of exchange rate stability for each economy. In the case of Australia, Canada, New Zealand, and a few other countries, as the exchange rate stability of their currencies is low in recent years, they should not be judged as belonging to major currency zones.

Implications of dollar dominance

Dollar dominance has several important implications. First, the US can enjoy "exorbitant privilege" (Eichengreen 2011), including the ability to run persistent current account deficits without encountering the crisis situations that many emerging economies would face, to dismiss external pressure on macroeconomic policy disciplines, and to avoid the constraints of the "trilemma" of international finance. In the trilemma, policy makers face a trade-off in choosing two out of three policy goals: exchange rate stability, capital account openness, and monetary policy independence. Second, dollar dominance means the US Federal Reserve's monetary policy actions have significant spillover effects on the rest of the world and often create credit cycles affecting many emerging economies. Third, the limited international role of other currencies raises the issue of how other economies can obtain international liquidity when they need it, such as during times of global financial turbulence and crisis.

The importance of the US dollar as a source of international liquidity is illustrated by the impact of the Federal Reserve's actions during the global financial crisis and the recent COVID-19 crisis. At the start of the subprime crisis in the US, the global economy faced a dollar liquidity shortage and the Federal Reserve extended temporary dollar liquidity swap arrangements to 14 foreign central banks from 12 December 2007 to 29 October 2008.[7] Following the outbreak of COVID-19, the Federal Reserve reopened dollar liquidity swaps with the same 14 central banks and created a new facility to allow other central banks with which it did not have swap agreements to exchange their US Treasury bills for dollar liquidity through repurchase agreements.[8]

---

[7] The temporary currency swap arrangements expired on 1 February 2010. The 14 central banks included 5 major central banks (Canada, the euro area, Japan, Switzerland, and the UK) with which the Federal Reserve decided to hold standing arrangements in October 2010 and 9 others (Australia, Brazil, Denmark, the Republic of Korea, Mexico, New Zealand, Norway, Singapore, and Sweden) (Board of Governors of the Federal Reserve System n.d.).

[8] Aizenman and Pasricha (2010) and Aizenman, Ito, and Pasricha (2021) find that those emerging economies with large financial and trade exposures to the US got the swap lines. Also, by having a repurchase agreement that involved US Treasuries, the facility was designed to favor economies that already had large amounts of dollar assets. Thus, while the US acted in a seemingly altruistic manner by providing swap lines and repo facilities to other economies, the decision was driven by national economic interest.

Factors Behind Dollar Dominance

Several factors behind US dollar dominance are apparent. First, the US is still the largest and most dynamic economic power as the global source of innovation, ideas, and technologies. The force of the real side of the economy is a strong supporting factor for dollar dominance (Eichengreen 2011, Prasad 2014, Rogoff and Tashiro 2015). Second, the dollar-based financial market is the most open, deepest, broadest, and most liquid in the world (Gopinath and Stein 2018a,b; Ito and Chinn 2015; Ito and Kawai 2016; Maggiori et al. 2019). This is an important source of resilience of its value even during the Lehman collapse in 2008 and the COVID-19 pandemic and economic crisis in 2020–2021. Third, the status of the Federal Reserve as one of the most responsible central banks in the world has contributed to the dollar being the dominant and most resilient international currency. Despite the US running persistent current account deficits and becoming the largest net liability country, confidence in the dollar remains strong. Finally, "network externalities" and incumbency "inertia" continue to support the dollar as an unparalleled international currency (Krugman 1980, Ito and Chinn 2015).[9]

However, this does not mean that the dollar will remain the dominant international currency indefinitely. The euro area, which is close to the US economy in size and has a larger population, has the potential to propel the euro into an international currency comparable to the dollar if it can form a truly integrated fiscal and banking (and possibly political) union and develop a deep, broad, and liquid financial market. For the PRC, given that its economy is expected to surpass the US in nominal GDP at market exchange rates in around 2030, the country is in a position to create an international currency capable of challenging the US dollar if it can undertake deep structural reforms and achieve a fully open capital account.

Risks and Challenges

There are several risks and challenges to the dollar's position as the dominant international currency. First, this status creates tension between US national interests and global monetary and financial stability. As the US

---

[9] Rey (2001) argues that if one particular currency is dominant in trade invoicing, the currency's transaction cost tends to decline as market size grows. Such a "thick market externality" tends to favor currencies of countries with large trade volumes and openness for trade invoicing. Chinn and Frankel (2007, 2008) point out the inertia effect for the choice of reserve currencies and that there is a "tipping point" or threshold above which the share of a currency in official foreign reserves can rise rapidly due to externalities.

central bank, the Federal Reserve sets monetary policy to stabilize the US economy and achieve target domestic inflation, not for the entire world economy. In contrast, the world economy needs a sufficient supply of dollars as international liquidity to support global finance. If such international liquidity is not provided smoothly or in a reliable way, the world economy can be affected negatively. As long as the Federal Reserve sets monetary policy in a stable, predicable manner, negative implications for the rest of the world are limited.[10] But large swings in US monetary policy can create major capital flow volatility for the rest of the world. This was observed during the global financial crisis and its aftermath in events such as quantitative easing and the taper tantrum. As long as the Federal Reserve provides adequate international liquidity to the rest of the world in a predictable manner and acts responsibly, particularly during acute liquidity shortage or financial crisis, the global economy would function relatively smoothly. But there is no guarantee that the Federal Reserve would always act predictably and responsibly in times of global financial difficulties.

The most fundamental issue is the relative decline of the US economy and the rise of emerging economies, particularly those in Asia. The fact that the world relies on the dollar—the currency of a country whose economy will continue to shrink relative to the world economy—poses significant challenges. ASEAN+3 economies have together already surpassed the size of the US economy (Figure 3.5).[11] The challenge for ASEAN+3 as the largest economic group globally, in terms of nominal GDP, is to develop its own regional currency for trade, investment, and financial transactions as well as for reserve holdings and exchange rate anchoring. The emergence of such a regional currency would also benefit global finance by providing a safe asset to the rest of the world.

---

[10] If the Federal Reserve changes its monetary policy in an unpredictable way, such as during the global financial crisis and the taper tantrum, this can hurt emerging economies. Increased predictability of US monetary policy, through good communication with markets and other authorities (using, say, Group of 20 processes), is highly desirable for economies including those in ASEAN+3.

[11] The figure shows that the US share of global GDP has declined from 30% in the 1980s to 28% in the 2000s and 23% in the 2010s, while the share of ASEAN+3 economies as a group has risen from 18% to 20% and 26% in the same time frames. Trade takes a similar—and more notable—trend, that is, the global trade share of ASEAN+3 has risen rapidly over time from around 15% in the 1980s to more than 25% in the 2010s, far exceeding the share of the US which recorded just above 10% in the 2010s, although ASEAN+3's global trade share remains smaller than that of the European Union.

**Figure 3.5: GDP and Trade Shares of ASEAN+3 Economies,
United States, and Europe**

(% in world total)

**a. Nominal GDP
at market exchange rates**

b. Trade in goods and services

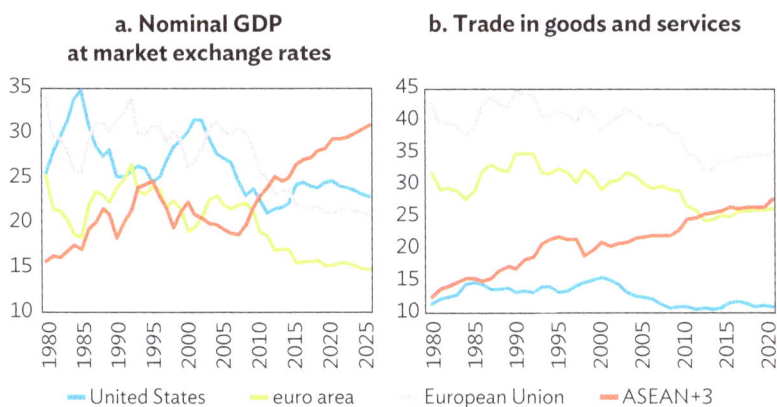

━ United States   ━ euro area   European Union   ━ ASEAN+3

ASEAN+3 = Association of Southeast Asian Nations plus the People's Republic of China, Japan, and
the Republic of Korea; GDP = gross domestic product.
Note: ASEAN+3 data include Hong Kong, China. European Union data include the United Kingdom.
Data in panel a, for 2020–2025, are based on estimates and projections from the International
Monetary Fund.
Source: Authors, based on IMF, *World Economic Outlook database*, April 2021 (accessed June 2021)
and UNCTAD, *Data Centre* (accessed August 2021).

3.3 ASEAN+3 Economies from the Trilemma Perspective

The ASEAN+3 region is characterized by diverse exchange rate arrangements
with most economies shifting away from fixed exchange rate arrangements
toward greater exchange rate flexibility particularly since the Asian financial
crisis. Given the different degrees of financial market development and
the different preferences toward monetary policy independence
(or autonomy), ASEAN+3 economies have chosen their preferred
combinations of exchange rate stability, capital account openness, and
monetary policy independence.

This section discusses how ASEAN+3 economies have balanced exchange
rate stability, capital account openness, and monetary policy independence
over the last 50 years from the "trilemma" perspective.

The Trilemma in International Finance

Different economies have pursued different open macroeconomic policy choices. Configuring policy choices is never easy. However, complicated policy combinations can be captured through the trilemma in international finance of trade-offs between different attributes (Figure 3.6).

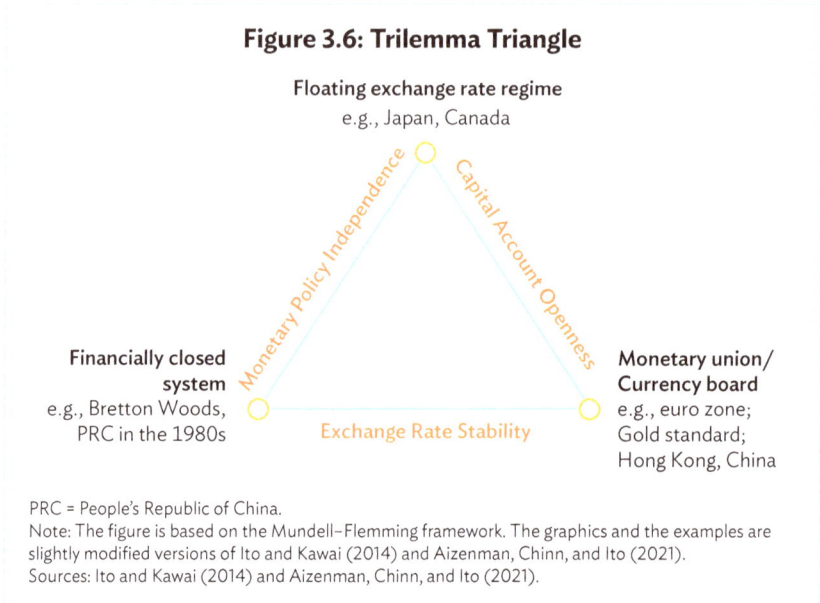

Figure 3.6: Trilemma Triangle

Floating exchange rate regime
e.g., Japan, Canada

Monetary Policy Independence

Capital Account Openness

Financially closed system
e.g., Bretton Woods, PRC in the 1980s

Exchange Rate Stability

Monetary union/ Currency board
e.g., euro zone; Gold standard; Hong Kong, China

PRC = People's Republic of China.
Note: The figure is based on the Mundell–Flemming framework. The graphics and the examples are slightly modified versions of Ito and Kawai (2014) and Aizenman, Chinn, and Ito (2021).
Sources: Ito and Kawai (2014) and Aizenman, Chinn, and Ito (2021).

Exchange rate stability is measured by how tightly monetary authorities stabilize or manage exchange rates against a single major anchor currency or a basket of major currencies. Economies under a fixed exchange rate regime can have stable currencies, while a freely flexible exchange rate regime does not provide stability. Capital account openness refers to the degree to which an economy has liberalized capital account transactions and allows capital to move across borders without restriction. Economies with capital account openness naturally hold significant external assets and liabilities, while restricted ones do not. Monetary policy independence gives monetary authorities freedom to set policy in pursuit of macroeconomic objectives without being tethered by external constraints. Economies that can freely set monetary policy instruments (such as the short-term interest rate) to pursue stable economic growth at low and stable inflation achieve a high degree of monetary policy independence, while others cannot if they fix exchange rates under free mobility of capital.

Since the US abandoned the dollar-gold link half a century ago, monetary authorities in the world have attempted to achieve different combinations of three policy choices, particularly the three corners. In other words, history is full of "corner solutions." The Bretton Woods system sacrificed international capital mobility for exchange rate stability and monetary policy independence. Economic and Monetary Union in Europe is built on the intra-area fixed exchange rate arrangement (with extra-area exchange rate flexibility on the flipside) and free capital mobility, but essentially has abandoned monetary policy independence in the euro area's small member countries.[12]

To comprehend the development of international monetary arrangements of individual economies, Aizenman, Chinn, and Ito (2013) and Ito and Kawai (2014) have developed the metrics of "trilemma" indexes. Here, the updated version of the index introduced by Ito and Kawai (2014) is used to cover 99 countries over 1970–2018.[13]

Observations on Trilemma Indexes

Figure 3.7 illustrates the average values of the three trilemma indexes for different income and regional groups of economies. It shows that high-income economies have achieved significant capital account openness over the last 40 years, starting from a low level in the 1970s comparable to those of the present middle- and low-income and emerging economies. These economies have likely changed policy priorities from the combination of relatively strong exchange rate stability and monetary policy independence (with limited capital account openness) during the 1970s to that of lesser exchange rate stability and lower monetary policy independence.[14]

Middle- and low-income countries generally have seen capital account openness increase from a low to an intermediate level. They have also pursued exchange rate stability and monetary policy independence, with

---

[12] Policy makers do not always have to adopt "corner solutions." They can, using the trilemma triangle example, implement a combination to attain one particular side without fully achieving any of the remaining two, in which case one of the choices is fully achieved and the other two are achieved only partially. Or they can implement a combination represented by a "dot" inside the trilemma triangle.

[13] The details of how the three indexes of exchange rate stability, capital account openness, and monetary policy independence are constructed as explained in Ito and Kawai (2014), which covered 90 economies for 1970–2010.

[14] High-income economies' trend toward low monetary policy independence may seem surprising, but this is largely because euro area countries are included. Essentially, most euro area countries chose to abandon monetary policy independence in favor of maintaining exchange rate stability and capital account openness.

Figure 3.7: Trilemma Indexes for Japan, the PRC, ASEAN, and Global Economy Groups, 1970–2018

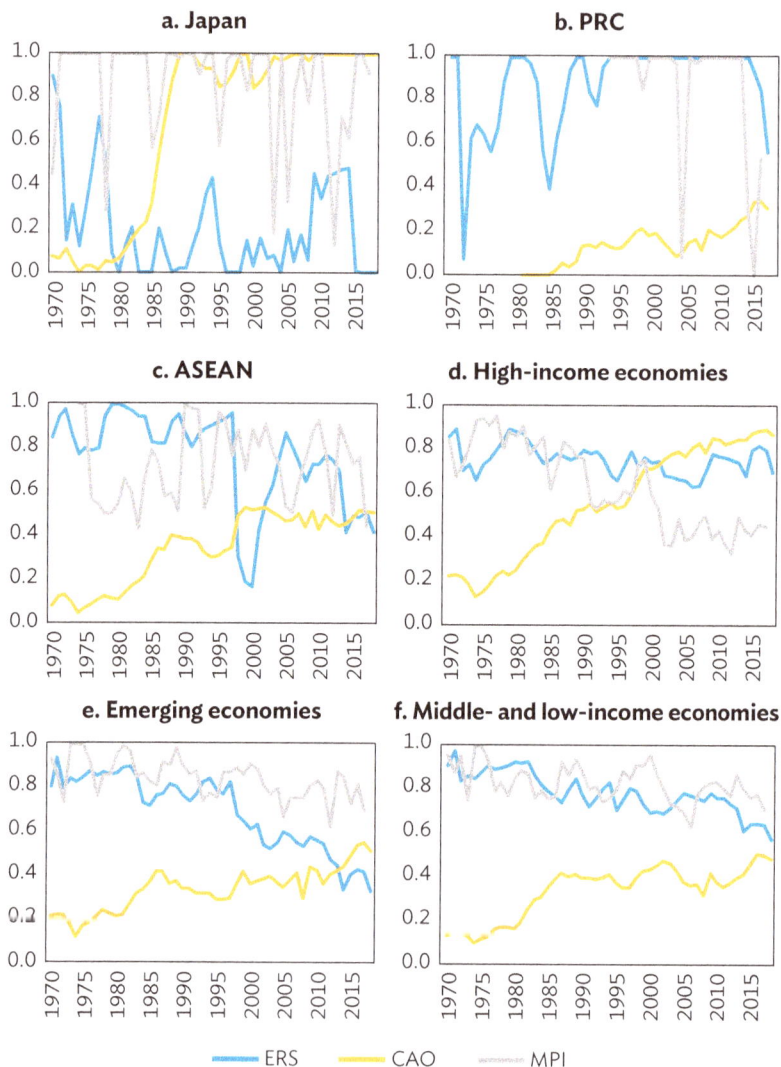

a. Japan

b. PRC

c. ASEAN

d. High-income economies

e. Emerging economies

f. Middle- and low-income economies

ERS — CAO — MPI

CAO = capital account openness; ERS = exchange rate stability; MPI = monetary policy independence; PRC = People's Republic of China.

Note: The groupings of "high-," "middle-," and "low-income" economies are based on the World Bank's classifications. "Emerging economies" refer to Argentina; Brazil; Chile; the People's Republic of China; Colombia; Czech Republic; Egypt; Hungary; India; Indonesia; Israel; Jordan; the Republic of Korea; Malaysia; Mexico; Morocco; Pakistan; Peru; the Philippines; Poland; the Russian Federation; South Africa; Thailand; Turkey; and Venezuela. ASEAN includes the 10 member states except the Lao People's Democratic Republic due to lack of data. The data are created using the method of Ito and Kawai (2014).

Source: Authors.

stability declining moderately over time. Emerging economies exhibit similar patterns to middle- and low-income economies, except their capital account openness has steadily risen to an intermediate level while exchange rate stability has gone steadily down.

The three indexes for ASEAN countries show similar trends to the group of emerging economies, except that exchange rate stability plummeted during the Asian financial crisis and for a few years after. Interestingly, ASEAN countries have regained exchange rate stability, accompanied by sacrificing monetary policy independence. The level of capital account openness rose in two steps, in the mid-1980s and then in the late 1990s. ASEAN countries appear different from other developing and emerging economies in that they have been on a steady path toward greater capital account openness, even following the Asian and global financial crises. Nonetheless, capital account openness still lags high-income economies, suggesting there is room for further opening.

Not surprisingly, the two biggest Asian economies—the PRC and Japan—have cast distinctively different trajectories in their trilemma combinations. While the PRC has pursued exchange rate stability since the early 1990s, Japan adopted a flexible exchange rate regime after the breakdown of the Bretton Woods system in the early 1970s. Japan also started liberalizing its capital account in the mid-1980s and completed it in the early 1990s. The PRC, on the other hand, has ample room for further capital account liberalization. Being quite large, both economies have tended to pursue greater monetary policy independence for most of the sample period. Although not shown in Figure 3.7, the Republic of Korea used to manage exchange rates heavily to limit rate flexibility and also maintain a relatively closed capital account until the mid-2000s. Since the second half of the 2000s, it has opened up the capital account in a significant way and moved toward much greater exchange rate flexibility. Over the entire transition, the country's monetary authorities have preserved policy independence.

Trilemma Configuration for Selected ASEAN+3 Economies

The most intuitive way of illustrating combinations of the three policy choices—exchange rate stability, capital account openness, and monetary policy independence—for a particular economy is to set the combinations within the prism of the trilemma triangle, using metrics that represent the extent of actual achievement in the three policy choices.[15] To our knowledge, plotting a combination of the three policies in a trilemma triangle is the first attempt in the literature of international macroeconomics.

Figure 3.8a presents the trilemma triangles with the three indexes for 5-year ranges from 1986–1990, 2001–2005, and 2016–2017, and for different groups: high-income economies, emerging economies, and ASEAN+3 economies.

Several observations can be made. Generally speaking, while high-income economies used to have many combinations of the three policy choices, over time they have moved toward a high degree of capital account openness. By the 2000s, two types of high-income economies had emerged: one group pursuing strong exchange rate stability and capital account openness, most notably the euro area economies, and another group of economies that achieved a high degree of capital account openness and monetary policy independence with exchange rate flexibility, such as Australia and Japan. High-income economies seem to be able to attain the "corner solution" of a fully flexible exchange rate regime, full capital account openness, and full monetary policy independence. This is rarely observed among middle- or low-income economies.

While most high-income economies have steadily increased their capital account openness, this generally has not happened in emerging economies. In the second half of the 2000s, emerging economies could be classified into three groups: first, with full monetary policy independence but varying degrees of exchange rate stability and capital account openness; second, with full exchange rate stability and varying degrees of monetary policy independence and capital account openness; and third, with intermediate levels in all three choices.

Among ASEAN+3 economies, Japan has been close to the corner solution. Indonesia and the Republic of Korea have approached the corner over time. Singapore has moved from a position of exchange rate stability with a relatively open capital account toward higher levels of exchange rate flexibility and capital account openness. Other economies started from a combination of relatively stable exchange rates and independent monetary policy, and moved to positions with greater monetary policy independence while giving up exchange rate stability to some degree, partly reflecting the abandonment of fixed exchange rate regimes after the Asian financial crisis.

---

[15] For more details, refer to Ito and Kawai (2014).

Figure 3.8a: Trilemma Triangles for ASEAN+3 Economies and Global Economy Groups, 1986–2017

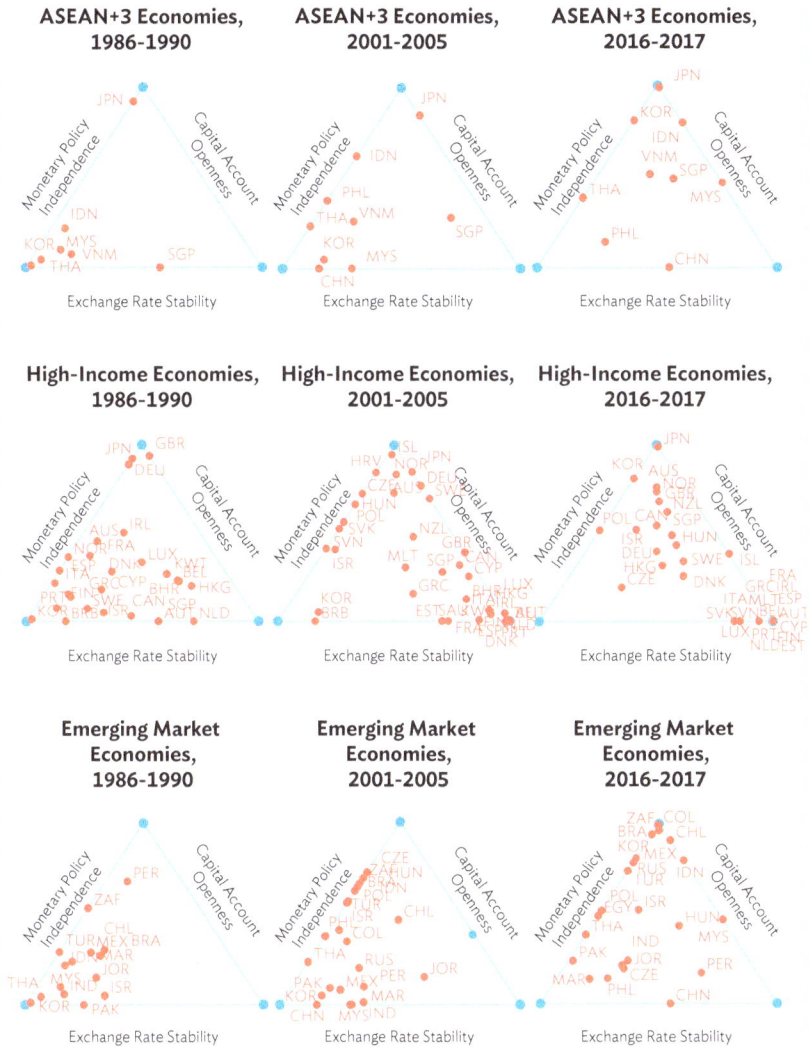

ASEAN+3 Economies, 1986-1990 — Monetary Policy Independence / Capital Account Openness / Exchange Rate Stability

ASEAN+3 Economies, 2001-2005

ASEAN+3 Economies, 2016-2017

High-Income Economies, 1986-1990

High-Income Economies, 2001-2005

High-Income Economies, 2016-2017

Emerging Market Economies, 1986-1990

Emerging Market Economies, 2001-2005

Emerging Market Economies, 2016-2017

Note: Abbreviations match the 3-figure country codes of the International Organization for Standardization.
Source: Authors.

Figure 3.8b illustrates the trilemma triangles for selected ASEAN+3 economies over 1970–2017. The year in the triangle refers to the last year of each 5-year period. As widely discussed, the PRC has maintained exchange rate stability and monetary policy independence by limiting capital account openness. Despite the government announcing it would increase exchange rate flexibility in 2005, the triangle plot suggests that the country has retained a fixed exchange rate arrangement without significant openness of its capital account. Other ASEAN+3 economies, on the other hand, have weakened their exchange rate stability after the Asian financial crisis and retained monetary policy independence. ASEAN+3 emerging economies do not appear to have opened their capital account significantly. Interestingly, many ASEAN economies in recent years appear to have increased exchange rate stability but not their capital account openness.

Figure 3.8b: Trilemma Triangles for Selected ASEAN+3 Economies, 1970–2017

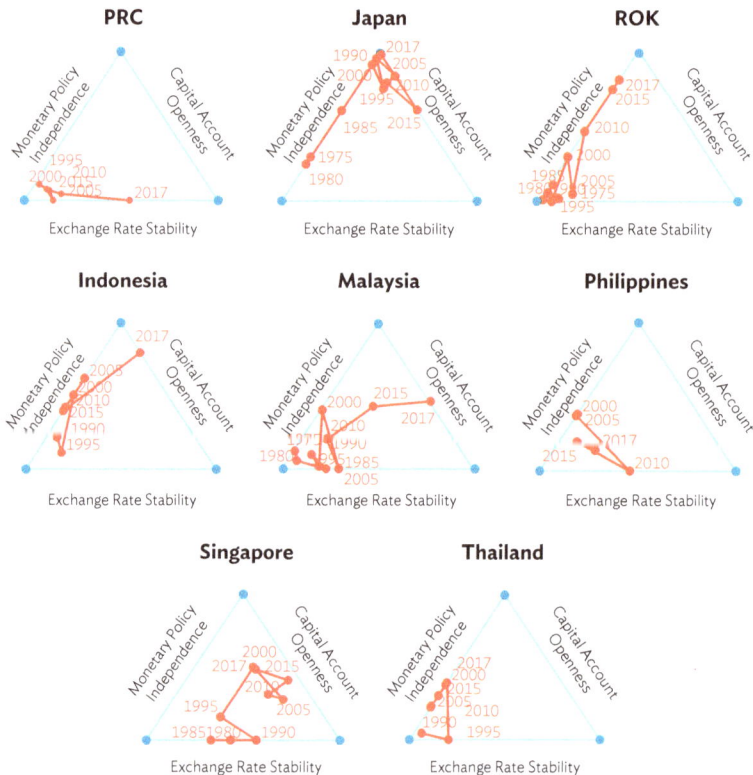

PRC = People's Republic of China, ROK = Republic of Korea.
Source: Authors.

Overall, most economies in the world have moved toward capital account openness, while some have moved toward exchange rate stability and others toward monetary policy independence. Only high-income economies seem able to reach a "corner solution," and most emerging economies seem to end up being "somewhere inside the triangle," which is also the case with ASEAN+3 emerging economies.

Although the trilemma hypothesis does not predict the use of a particular major currency or national currency for international transactions, trilemma configurations can have implications for an economy's choice of international currencies. That is, an economy with a stable or managed exchange rate regime likely uses its anchor currency for international transactions, while the currency of an economy without an open capital account is unlikely to be used for international purposes. Once an economy opens its capital account, it must face a crucial issue of choosing the home currency, partner currency, or major international currencies for denominating and settling cross-border capital flows.

3.4 Use of Regional Currencies in ASEAN+3 Economies

This section examines the current state and progress in using regional currencies for trade, investment, financial transactions, and exchange-rate management as nominal anchors in the ASEAN+3 region. It evaluates how far ASEAN+3 currencies have functioned as international currencies and identifies factors impeding their use for economic and policy purposes.

Foreign Exchange Markets and International Settlements

Figure 3.9 attempts to capture the extent to which ASEAN+3 currencies are traded in global foreign exchange markets and used for overall international settlements. It is essentially the ASEAN+3 version of Figures 3.2a and 3.1b in Section 3.2. Figure 3.9a shows that the Japanese yen is by far the most frequently used internationally among ASEAN+3 currencies in the foreign exchange markets, followed by the yuan, Hong Kong dollar, Republic of Korea won, and Singapore dollar. Other currencies are not much used. It is notable that the won has limited use despite its economy being the 11th largest in the world in 2020, with income at $31,500 per person. A major reason for this is that the Republic of Korea, unlike Japan and the PRC, has not made internationalizing its currency a policy priority and has not promoted the international use of the won.

Figure 3.9: Shares of ASEAN+3 Currencies in Foreign Exchange Market Turnover and Overall International Settlements
(%)

a. Foreign exchange market turnover   b. Overall international settlements

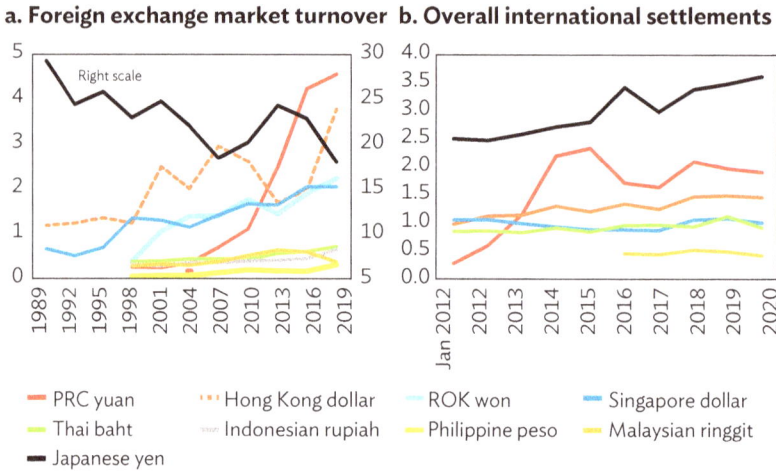

RC = People's Republic of China, ROK = Republic of Korea.
Note: The Japanese yen share in panel a is measured by the right scale.
Source: Authors, based on BIS, *Triennial Central Bank Survey: Foreign Exchange Turnover* (accessed September 2019) and from SWIFT, *RMB Tracker*, various issues (accessed July 2021).

Figure 3.9b also shows that the yen, yuan, and Hong Kong dollar, Singapore dollar, and Thai baht are most frequently used for overall international settlements. Two important observations can be made: first, although the extent of yuan use rose fast between 2012 and 2014 and peaked in 2015, it has declined since; and second, the won does not play a visible role as an international settlement currency.

Trade Invoicing and Settlement

Among the ASEAN+3 economies, the PRC, Indonesia, Japan, the Republic of Korea, and Thailand publish data on trade invoicing or settlement by currency. IMF work by Boz et al. (2020) has also collected currency invoicing/settlement data for Cambodia, Malaysia, and the Philippines, among others. Combining these data, one can make important observations about the pattern of currency invoicing and/or settlement for trade (Figure 3.10).

Figure 3.10: Shares of US, Home, and ASEAN+3 Currencies in Trade for Selected ASEAN+3 Economies

(%)

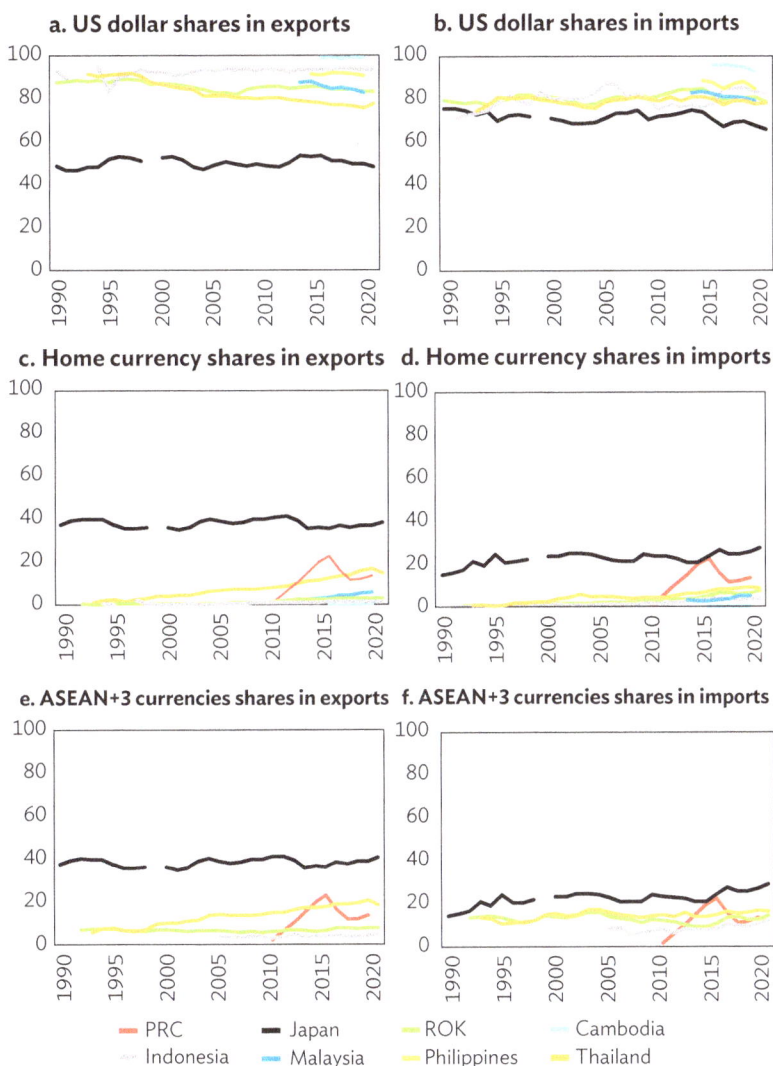

a. US dollar shares in exports

b. US dollar shares in imports

c. Home currency shares in exports

d. Home currency shares in imports

e. ASEAN+3 currencies shares in exports

f. ASEAN+3 currencies shares in imports

- PRC
- Japan
- ROK
- Cambodia
- Indonesia
- Malaysia
- Philippines
- Thailand

PRC = People's Republic of China; ROK = Republic of Korea; US = United States.
Note: The PRC authorities provide the yuan share in total trade, not export and import separately, so in the figure the same yuan shares are plotted for PRC exports and imports.
Source: Authors, based on Boz et al. (2020) (accessed July 2012); Bank of Indonesia, Indonesia Financial Statistics (accessed July 2021); Bank of Korea, Economic Statistics System (accessed August 2021); Bank of Thailand, Statistics–International Trade; Government of Japan, Customs, Share of Currency in Trade (accessed June 2021); and People's Bank of China, *RMB Internationalization Report* (accessed August 2021).

First, as anecdotally argued, ASEAN+3 economies rely heavily on the dollar for international trade. While Japan settles about half of its exports in US dollars, Indonesia, the Republic of Korea, Thailand, and other countries settle higher proportions of exports in dollars. The use of the dollar for export invoicing has been consistently around 80%–90% for the time period available for these countries, although the trend is declining slightly, particularly for Thailand. The dollar share on the import side is higher than the export side in their trade for Japan, but with a mild declining trend. It is higher for other countries, hovering at more than 75% without any sign of slippage.

Second, the share of home currency in trade invoicing and/or settlement is the highest for Japan at about 40% for exports and close to 30% for imports. The PRC and Thailand follow. The yuan share in total PRC trade rose rapidly until 2015, to more than 20%, and began declining to about 10% in the late 2010s. The share of the baht for Thai trade settlement has been rising, particularly on the export side, reaching about 15% in 2020. In contrast, the share of the won in the Republic of Korea's trade settlement is much lower even as it has risen slowly over the years. Essentially, home currency is not the most important invoicing and/or settlement currency for ASEAN+3 economies' overall trade with the world, even for Japan.

Many researchers have conducted empirical analysis to identify factors that determine trends in the use of currencies in trade invoicing and settlements.[16] Ito and Chinn (2015) find that countries with higher per capita income tended to have lower shares of US dollar export invoicing and higher shares of invoicing exports in their home currencies. Ito and Kawai (2016) find that an economy with unstable macroeconomic conditions (e.g., high inflation, high exchange rate volatilities) tended to invoice its trade in the deutschemark (before the launch of the euro) or the dollar and an economy with a deeper and larger financial market or more open financial market was less likely to invoice its exports in dollars, suggesting such an economy tended to invoice its exports more in home currency than major currencies.

Japan, the Republic of Korea, and Thailand publish disaggregated data on the shares of US, home, and other currencies used for settling trade with different trading partners. While detailed time series figures for each country are shown in Appendix Figure 3.1, a snapshot for the most recent year is shown in Figure 3.11. The figure confirms that it is the dollar that

[16] Refer to Boz et al. (2020), Ito and Chinn (2015), and Ito and Kawai (2016) for reviews of the literature.

plays the dominant role in these countries' overall trade, but variations in dollar and home currency use are considerable and depend on who these countries trade with. In trade with the US, countries tend to use the dollar much more heavily than the home currency, but in trade with the European Union and Japan, the Republic of Korea and Thailand favor the partner and home currencies.

Figure 3.11: Shares of the US, Home and Other Currencies in Japan, the Republic of Korea, and Thailand's Trade with Partners, 2020

(%)

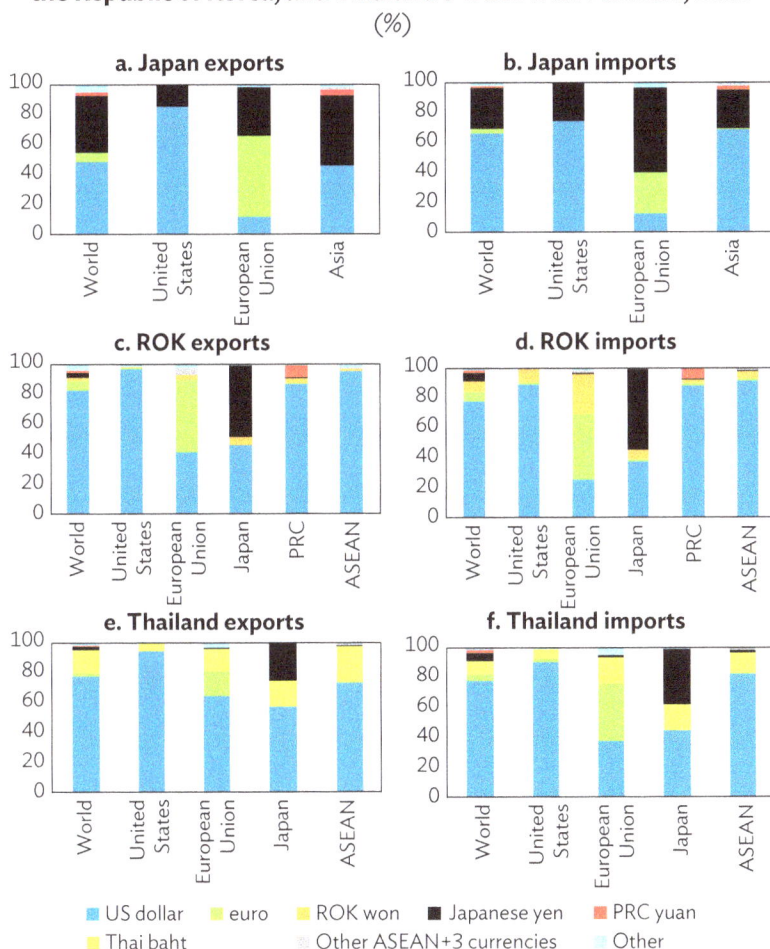

PRC = People's Republic of China, ROK = Republic of Korea, US = United States.
Note: For Thailand trade, the European Union refers to 14 member countries, not the entire membership.
Source: Authors, based on Bank of Korea, Economic Statistics System (accessed August 2021); Bank of Thailand, Statistics–International Trade (June 2021); and Government of Japan, Customs, Share of Currency in Trade (accessed June 2021).

For example, Japan uses the euro and the yen predominantly for trade settlement with the European Union (with the euro preferred for Japan's exports and the yen preferred for Japan's imports) and the US dollar is used for only 10% of settlements. In Japan's trade with Asia, the yen is used as frequently as the dollar on the export side (about 45% each), while the dollar dominates the import side (accounting for 70% of settlements).

The Republic of Korea is an interesting case. In its trade with the European Union, the euro is the most important trade settlement currency (accounting for 52% in the Republic of Korea's exports and 45% in its imports). The won is not used much in the Republic of Korea's exports to the European Union but is used almost as frequently as the dollar to pay for imports from the European Union (a 24% share in won and 27% share in dollars). In the Republic of Korea's trade with Japan, the yen is the most important trade settlement currency, accounting for 47% for exports and 53% for imports, followed by the dollar. The won is used only for 5%–6% of the Republic of Korea's trade with Japan. In contrast, the dollar is far more dominant in the Republic of Korea's trade with ASEAN and the PRC, accounting for more than 90% of settlements, with the won having limited use and the yuan used to settle only 5%–7% of transactions with the PRC.

Thailand's data suggest that the baht is used more frequently as a settlement currency in Thai trade than the won is in the Republic of Korea's trade. On the other hand, in trade with the European Union and Japan, Thailand tends to settle more with the US dollar and less with the currencies of the two trading partners than does the Republic of Korea. That said, Thailand does not use the baht as much as the Republic of Korea uses the won to settle these transactions. In Thailand's trade with ASEAN, the dollar accounts for more than 70% of total settlement, but this is below its use in the Republic of Korea's trade with ASEAN.

Therefore, even as the US dollar remains the most dominant currency in the three countries' trade settlements, there are clear variations between them. In terms of home currency for trade settlement, Japan uses the most, followed by Thailand, and then the Republic of Korea. This is particularly so in trade with the European Union and other ASEAN+3 economies. Still, the dollar dominates payments in the ASEAN+3 supply chain network, suggesting that it is not an easy task to increase the use of regional currencies for trade among countries that participate in the network.

Cross-Border Financial Transactions

The extent to which ASEAN+3 economies use their home currencies for international financial transactions, i.e., in cross-border bank liabilities and international debt securities issuance, is an important part of the narrative. Many researchers have pointed out the difficulties of emerging and developing economies borrowing abroad in their home currency and their tendency to hold foreign-currency-denominated debts and liabilities, a phenomenon called the "original sin" (Calvo and Reinhart 2002; Eichengreen, Hausmann, and Panizza 2002; Hausmann and Panizza 2003, 2010; Ize and Levy-Yeyati 2003, Chang and Velasco 2006). Foreign currency borrowing can make borrowing economies vulnerable to external financial shocks due to potential currency mismatches.

Cross-border bank liabilities

Most ASEAN+3 economies find it a challenge to receive international loans in their home currency and overcome the "original sin," as such, loans tend to be provided in major international currencies. Figure 3.12 presents the composition of three major currencies (the US dollar, euro, and yen) for cross-border bank liabilities using BIS data.[17] The BIS does not provide information on cross-border bank loans and liabilities extended in emerging economy currencies, so it is not possible to identify with any clarity the extent that ASEAN+3 currencies other than the yen are used. Data suggest that in some countries, the magnitude of cross-border bank loans denominated in emerging economy currencies is non-negligible though not as significant as the dollar.

The figure shows that the four economies represented in the ASEAN+3 region, i.e., the PRC, Japan, the Republic of Korea, and ASEAN, receive cross-border bank loans mainly in US dollars. The Republic of Korea relies on dollar bank loans most heavily among the four economies followed by ASEAN, which has exhibited a rising trend since the mid-2000s. The two other economies have stable dollar shares. The use of euro-denominated bank loans by the four economies is not so high and has been relatively stable. The PRC, the Republic of Korea, and ASEAN used to have high shares of Japanese yen-denominated bank loans in the 1990s and early

---

[17] The BIS international banking database by location reports 47 countries' assets and liabilities relative to more than 190 economies. Data used in that collection and in the subsequent one on cross-border bank *liabilities* are the bank *assets* of the reporting countries relative to the sample countries. Information on currencies for cross-border liabilities is available only for the three major currencies, plus the pound sterling and Swiss franc.

2000s, but yen shares are on the decline. For Japan, not surprisingly, the yen share has remained high at 45% and is comparable to the US dollar share in 2020.

Figure 3.12: Shares of Major Currencies in Cross-Border Bank Liabilities of the PRC, Japan, the Republic of Korea, and ASEAN
(%)

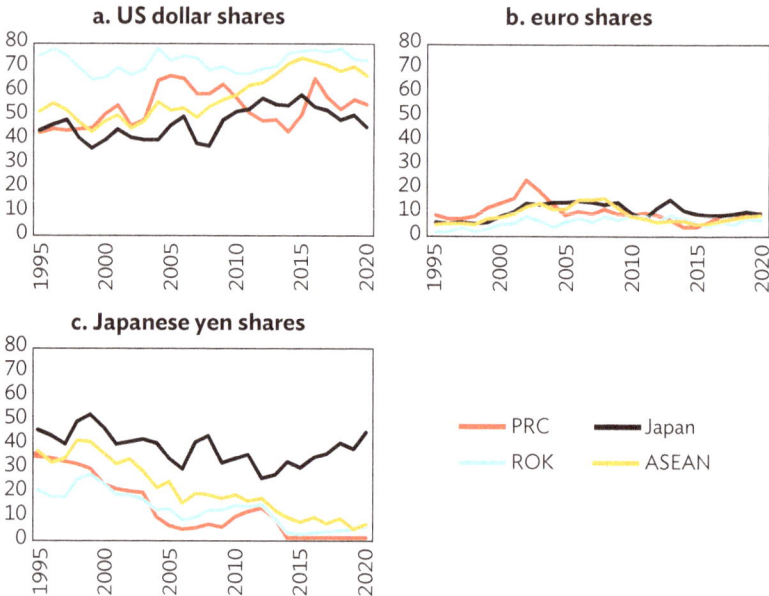

ASEAN = Association of Southeast Asian Nations, PRC = People's Republic of China, ROK = Republic of Korea, US = United States.
Note: Data for ASEAN are the aggregated average for the 10 ASEAN member countries.
Source: Authors, based on BIS, *Locational Banking Statistics*, Immediate borrower basis (accessed August 2021).

Figure 3.13 summarizes the currency compositions of cross-border bank liabilities for all ASEAN+3 economies as of end-2020. Time-series data for individual economies are plotted in Appendix Figure 3.2. Figure 3.13 clearly demonstrates the importance of the dollar, whose share ranges from 83% for Viet Nam to 45% for Japan, followed by the euro and Japanese yen. Yen-denominated cross-border bank liabilities take the largest shares in Japan (45%), followed by Singapore (8%), and the Philippines (7%). Large shares for other currencies in cross-border bank liabilities are notable for the PRC (32%), Brunei Darussalam (29%), and Cambodia (28%). Such loans may include loans from emerging ASEAN+3 economies, like the PRC, but detailed information is not yet available.

Figure 3.13: Shares of Major Currencies in Cross-Border Bank Liabilities of ASEAN+3 Economies
(%)

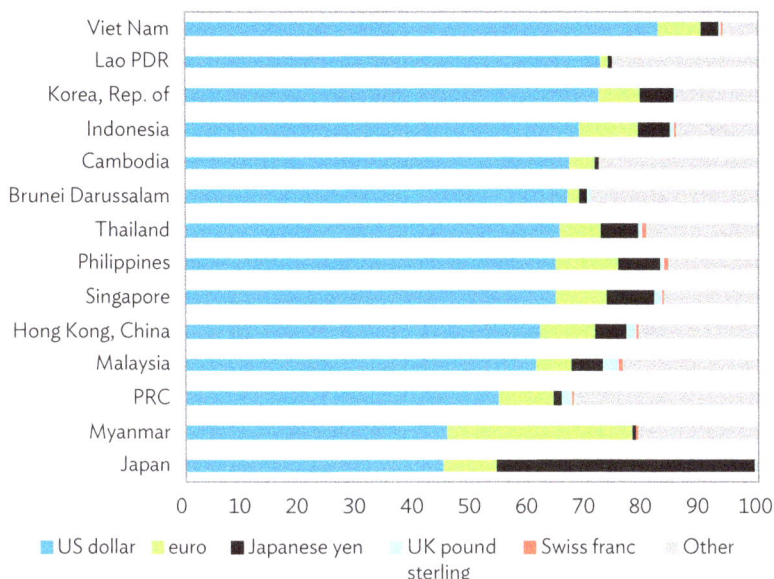

ASEAN+3 = Association of Southeast Asian Nations plus the People's Republic of China, Japan, and the Republic of Korea; PRC = People's Republic of China; Lao PDR = Lao People's Democratic Republic; UK = United Kingdom; US = United States.
Note: Information on currency shares is available only for the US dollar, euro, Japanese yen, pound sterling, and Swiss franc for each country or economy.
Source: Authors, based on BIS, *Locational Banking Statistics*, Immediate borrower basis (accessed August 2021).

International debt securities issued

ASEAN+3 economies also borrow abroad by issuing international debt securities. Figure 3.14 presents currency compositions of such issuance by the PRC, Japan, the Republic of Korea, and the 10 ASEAN member countries, based on a BIS debt securities database. The BIS collects international debt data by nationality and on a residence basis and reports currency information only for the US dollar, euro, and home currency for each issuing economy. This is an advantage over cross-border bank loans as debt data provide information on the use of home currencies for international debt issuance.

Figure 3.14: Shares of Major and Home Currencies in International Debt Securities Issued by the PRC, Japan, the Republic of Korea, and ASEAN
(%)

a. Nationality data

US dollar shares · Euro shares · Home currency shares

b. Residence data

US dollar shares · Euro shares · Home currency shares

PRC — Japan — ROK — ASEAN

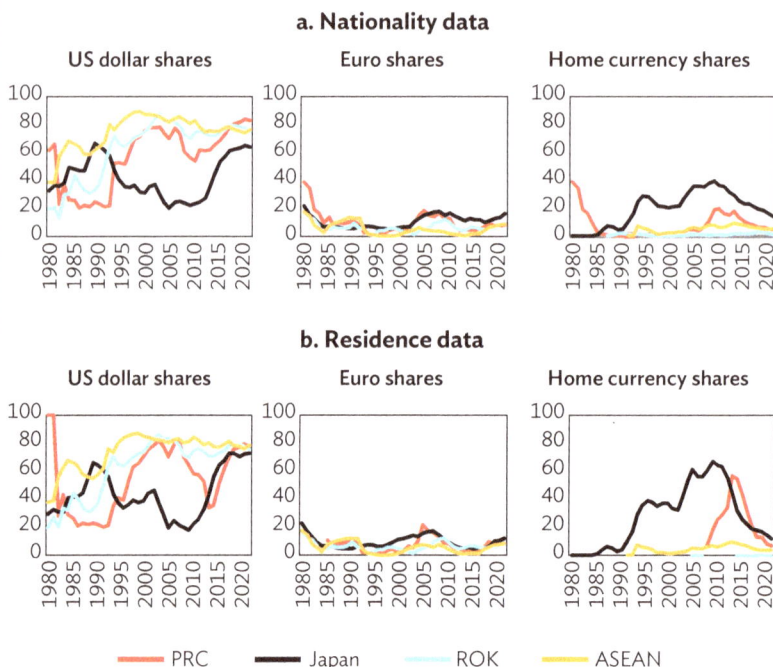

ASEAN= Association of Southeast Asian Nations; PRC = People's Republic of China; ROK = Republic of Korea; US = United States.
Note: Data for international debt securities issued are measured on the basis of nationality or residence of issuers. Information on currencies is available only for the US dollar, euro, and home currency for each country or economy.
Source: Authors, based on BIS, *Debt Securities Statistics* (accessed August 2021).

The figure illustrates changing reliance on the US dollar for international debt securities issued by the four economies. The PRC's reliance on the dollar for debt denomination was initially high in the beginning of the 1980s, declined in the early 1980s till the early 1990s, and began to rise in the mid-1990s, reaching 80% in 2020. Japan's reliance on the dollar also fluctuated, initially in directions opposite to the PRC's dollar reliance, but began to synchronize with the PRC in the 2000s and 2010s, reaching 60% in 2020. The Republic of Korea and ASEAN's reliance on the dollar moved in tandem, peaking in the late 1990s and early 2000s, and recording about 75% in 2020.

The four economies' reliance on the euro for international debt denomination is relatively limited. The PRC and Japan issued international debt securities in their own currencies in the late 2000s and early 2010s, but home currency issues shrank in the late 2010s. The yen share in Japan's international debt issued was surprisingly low in 2020 given that the yen is a major international currency. The Republic of Korea is particularly notable in not issuing much international debt in its own currency and the same applies to ASEAN issuance. This likely reflects the persistence of "original sin" for these economies.[18]

Figure 3.15 summarizes the currency compositions of international debt securities from selected ASEAN+3 economies for which end-2020 data are available. (Time-series data for individual economies are plotted in Appendix Figure 3.3.) Figure 3.15 clearly demonstrates the importance of the US dollar, whose share ranges from 100% for Cambodia and Viet Nam to 60%–70% for Singapore, with the Lao PDR an outlier at a 25% dollar share. The euro and home currencies are next in significance. The home currency share is high for Japan (14% on a nationality basis and 12% on a residence basis); Singapore (13% and 8%); Hong Kong, China (9% and 8%); Thailand (8% and 0%); Malaysia (6% and 0%); and the PRC (5% and 7%). Difference between shares based on nationality and residence are notable in some cases, suggesting that ASEAN+3 firms (except those from the PRC) tend to issue international debt securities in their own currencies in foreign jurisdictions while firms operating in an ASEAN+3 economy do not issue much of them in the resident jurisdiction. Also of note, the Republic of Korea rarely issues international debt securities in won, despite it being one of the richest economies in the region.

---

[18] Ito and Rodriguez (2020) also find that the extent of fall in foreign currency reliance for international debt issuance has been quite modest.

Figure 3.15: Shares of Major and Home Currencies in International Debt Securities Issued by ASEAN+3 Economies, 2020
(%)

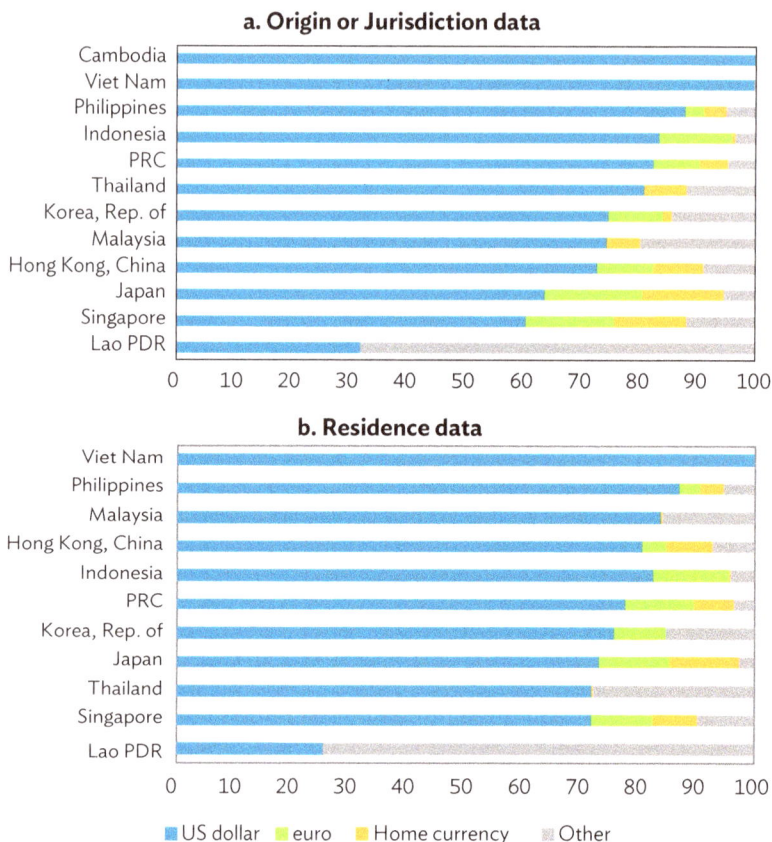

a. Origin or Jurisdiction data

b. Residence data

ASEAN+3 = Association of Southeast Asian Nations plus the People's Republic of China, Japan, and the Republic of Korea; PRC = People's Republic of China; Lao PDR = Lao People's Democratic Republic.
Note: Data for international debt securities issued are measured by a nationality or residence basis as issuers. Information on currencies is available only for the US dollar, euro, and home currency for each country or economy.
Source: Authors, based on BIS, *Debt Securities Statistics* (accessed June 2021).

Ito and Rodriguez (2020) investigate the determinants of the extent of reliance on the dollar, euro, and home currency for denominating international debt securities. They find that countries with better economic prospects, deeper financial development, and greater investment opportunities do not tend to rely on the dollar, though they may continue to depend on major currencies (such as the euro). Also, countries with greater "fiscal space" tend to denominate international debt less in major currencies, suggesting that they can afford to issue debt more in home currency in the international financial markets.[19] Given that ASEAN economies tend to have strong economic prospects, ample investment opportunities, and relatively sound fiscal conditions, deeper financial development may enable them to issue more international debt securities in home currency.

Anchor Currencies for Exchange-Rate Management

Countries often try to stabilize or manage their exchange rate movements against a certain anchor currency or a basket of anchor currencies. The main motive is to reduce exchange rate volatility and currency risk, facilitate smooth international trade, investment and financial transactions, and help achieve stable economic growth. To identify a country's anchor currency or anchor basket of currencies, this section draws on results obtained by Kawai and Pontines (2015). As explained in Section 3.2 in the discussion on the dominance of the US dollar zone, the Kawai–Pontines method yields superior and more stable and robust estimates on US dollar and yuan weights in an economy's implicit currency basket than the traditional Frankel–Wei method.

Figure 3.16 summarizes estimation results on the dollar, yuan and yen weights for selected ASEAN+3 economies in two periods. The first, from June 2000 to June 2005, was when the yuan was officially pegged to the dollar and in the second, June 2010 to July 2013, the PRC embarked on yuan internationalization and left the currency repeg that had followed the global financial crisis.

The figure demonstrates that the US dollar was the major anchor currency for ASEAN+3 economies in both periods. The yuan weights for 8 out of 13 economies increased from the first to the second period and became statistically significant and positive, although still smaller than the dollar weights. The yen weights were significantly positive in six economies in the first period but became much smaller in value and less statistically significant by the second period. Thus, the yuan has taken on importance in the implicit currency baskets of a number of ASEAN+3 economies and this appears to have occurred at the expense of the yen. One important reason for this is the rapid expansion of the PRC economy and its trade with its neighbors and the relative decline of the Japanese economy globally and regionally.

---

[19] Having strong trade ties with the US or the euro area helps a country in choosing the dollar or euro for international debt issuance. In the case of developing countries, however, the degree of reliance on the dollar or euro for international debt issuance tends to be affected by factors other than trade relations.

Figure 3.16: Weights of the US Dollar, Yen, and Yuan as Anchor Currencies for Selected ASEAN+3 Economies

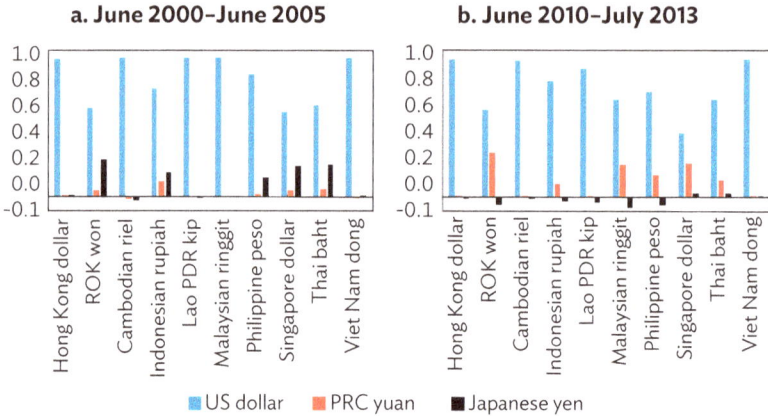

a. June 2000–June 2005

b. June 2010–July 2013

ASEAN+3 = Association of Southeast Asian Nations plus the People's Republic of China, Japan, and the Republic of Korea; Lao PDR = Lao People's Democratic Republic; US = United States; PRC = People's Republic of China; ROK = Republic of Korea.
Note: The estimation follows the Kawai–Pontines method.
Source: Authors, based on Kawai and Pontines (2015).

Even as ASEAN+3 is the largest economic grouping in the world, the region continues to rely on the dollar instead of regional currencies. Despite its rise, the yuan has not grown into a major international currency because it is not fully convertible on capital account. The yen, which is the only fully convertible currency from a large economy in the region, has its own hurdle because the global shares of Japanese GDP and trade are shrinking. The challenge for ASEAN+3 economies is to promote further integration in trade, investment, and finance; and to establish open, deep, broad, and liquid financial markets within the region. Then one can expect a rise in either the yen, the yuan, or a basket of ASEAN+3 currencies as the regional currency used for its trade, investment, and financial transactions.

3.5 ASEAN+3 Policy Initiatives

Global reliance on the US dollar poses significant challenges for emerging economies such as through volatile capital outflows in dollars and the type of currency turbulence experienced during the global financial crisis, the taper tantrum, and the COVID-19 pandemic. Several options have been proposed to solve the issue, such as transforming the Federal Reserve into a global central bank, the promotion of the IMF's special drawing rights as a major reserve asset, and the creation of a global single currency. None are realistic, at least in the foreseeable future. One of the possible ASEAN+3 approaches would be the creation of a new monetary and financial system based on regional currencies.

An important implication of Section 3.4 is that it would be difficult to increase the use of regional currencies in the supply chain network among ASEAN+3 economies without all supply-chain participating countries collaborating to promote regional currency use. Thus, ASEAN+3 authorities need to work together to promote the use of regional currencies for intraregional trade, investment, and other international transactions. This section discusses the policies ASEAN+3 authorities have pursued to promote regional currency use in trade settlements and currency exchanges. The Local Currency Settlement Framework is one such attempt, currently made by several ASEAN countries, and it also has further potential for internationalizing ASEAN+3 currencies.

Efforts at Currency Internationalization

In the ASEAN+3 region, a few countries introduced policy initiatives to internationalize their currencies. Japan's attempt in the 1980s and 1990s and the PRC's effort in the 2010s are well-known examples. Less known is Thailand's initiative of creating a baht zone in Indochina in the early 1990s. This part of the section examines these currency internationalization efforts and experiences and evaluates their successes and failures.

Japan's yen internationalization initiative

The revision of the Foreign Exchange and Foreign Trade Control Law in 1980 liberalized all cross-border transactions and provided a legal basis for yen internationalization. Responding both to the US' demand for domestic financial market liberalization and opening for yen internationalization, the Japanese government agreed to set up the "Yen-Dollar Committee"[20] in November 1983 and started discussions with the US to open Japan's financial market and promote yen internationalization. Facing large current account deficits, particularly against Japan, the US objective was to see the liberalization and opening of the Japanese financial market, greater external demand for yen assets, and a stronger yen against the dollar. The committee's 1984 report proposed measures to integrate the Japanese

---

[20] The official name of the committee was the "Joint Japan-US Ad Hoc Group on Yen/Dollar Exchange Rate, Financial and Capital Market Issues."

financial market with global finance and internationalize the yen by liberalizing interest rates in the interbank and short-term government bond markets and by eliminating exchange controls. Through these measures, Japan substantially opened its capital account in the mid-1980s to support a market-driven process for internationalizing the yen.

Japanese authorities initially were not keen on promoting yen internationalization because they did not want the yen to appreciate (due to higher demand for yen assets, which the US wanted to see) or to lose control over monetary policy.[21] But by the early 1990s, they became more active and the yen achieved about 8.5% share of global foreign exchange reserves. Use of the yen for cross-border bank liabilities and international debt issues reached about 15% of the world total in the mid-1990s. The yen also became important as a trade invoicing or settlement currency for ASEAN+3 economies.

Figure 3.17 shows that the yen invoicing or settlement shares in the Republic of Korea and Thailand's trade with the world were relatively high in the 1990s, particularly on the import side, recording around 13% for the Republic of Korea and 10% for Thailand until the mid-2000s. The yen share for Indonesia was lower but still recorded 5% levels on its import side in the second half of the 2000s. However, the yen share has continued to decline since the mid-2000s. An important factor behind the decline is a relative decline of Japan as a trade partner for these ASEAN+3 countries. Even though these countries have maintained relatively high yen invoicing/settlement shares for trade with Japan (see Appendix Figure 3.1b and 3.1c for the Republic of Korea and Thailand, respectively), the declining importance of Japan for these countries' trade has led to overall diminishing shares of yen invoicing/settlement.

While Japan uses its home currency for international trade and financial transactions more than other ASEAN+3 economies do, the yen has not become a truly international currency commensurate with Japan's economic size, even if not comparable to the dollar or euro. There are several reasons for this. First, Japan achieved post-war economic growth as a US dollar-zone economy and has not fully grown out of it. Second, Japan's Asian neighbors are also US dollar-zone economies that prefer the dollar for their international transactions, including with Japan. Third, Japan imports natural resources and foodstuffs which tend to be invoiced and settled in the dollar. In addition, Japanese trading companies and

---

[21] See Frankel (2011).

multinational corporations with capacity to manage currency risks do not have much interest in using yen for their international transactions (Kawai 1996). Fourth, economic stagnation after asset price bubbles burst in the 1990s reduced Japan's per capita income, its share in global trade, and the presence of Japanese banks abroad, limiting yen use for invoicing trade (Ito and Kawai 2016). The prolonged economic stagnation in the 1990s and 2000s prevented the yen from becoming a truly international currency. Finally, dollar dominance has prevented the yen from playing a significant role because of associated network externalities and inertia effects.

Figure 3.17: Japanese Yen Shares in Trade Invoicing or Settlement for Indonesia, the Republic of Korea, and Thailand

a. Yen shares in exports to world (%)

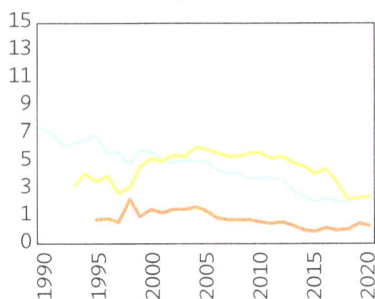

b. Yen shares in imports from world (%)

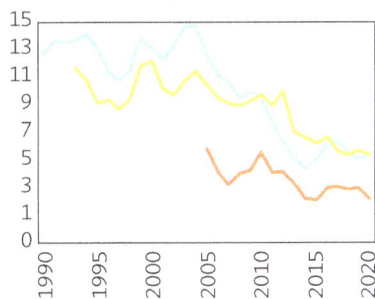

Republic of Korea — Indonesia — Thailand

Source: Authors, based on Bank Indonesia, Indonesia Financial Statistics (accessed July 2021), Bank of Korea, Economic Statistics System (accessed August 2021), and Bank of Thailand, Statistics–International Trade (accessed June 2021).

Thailand's internationalization of the baht

Thailand launched a "Baht Economic Zone" plan in the early 1990s. After achieving current account convertibility and becoming an IMF Article-VIII country in May 1990, Thailand began liberalization of domestic interest rates, foreign exchange regulations, and international capital flows. In March 1993, 47 domestic and foreign banks received approval under the Bangkok International Banking Facilities (BIBF) initiative to conduct offshore transactions. The idea was to transform Bangkok into the international financial center for Indochina, expecting that Thai trade and investment with Cambodia, the Lao PDR, Myanmar, and Viet Nam would grow rapidly. The BIBF was expected to channel funds from global and

Asian financial markets into Indochina neighbors through Bangkok (called "out-out" financial flows), rather than see them go through Singapore or Hong Kong, China. At the same time, Thai authorities encouraged the baht to be used for international transactions, particularly trade, thereby promoting its internationalization.

The BIBF initiative also encouraged foreign funds to flow into Thailand ("out-in"). That was a time when domestic investment demand was rising in Thailand and a large amount of foreign funds entered the economy given its favorable growth prospects and high domestic interest rates, while out-out financial transactions were limited. External funds that entered Thailand through the BIBF were used largely to speculate in real estate and the stock market, building financial vulnerabilities that led to the Thai economy into financial crisis in 1997.

Although Thai authorities never revived the Baht Economic Zone program after the financial crisis, the baht's use in trade with some Indochina countries has risen. Figure 3.18 summarizes the shares of the US dollar, baht, and other currencies used in Thai trade with ASEAN countries, especially Cambodia, the Lao PDR, Myanmar, and Viet Nam in 2020. Baht use in trade with other ASEAN countries has risen over the last 20 years to reach 24% in Thai exports and 14% in imports. Notably, baht use in trade with the Lao PDR in 2020 reached 66% (in Thai exports) and 34% (in Thai imports), its use in trade with Myanmar was at 58% (in exports), and its use in trade with Cambodia was 43% (in exports) and 35% (in imports). Baht use in trade with Viet Nam is about the same as the ASEAN average. Although lack of currency invoicing and settlement data for the Lao PDR and Cambodia themselves makes it hard to judge if in effect these two countries are baht economic zone countries, the baht has clearly played a significant role in their trade with Thailand.

Figure 3.18: US Dollar and Baht Shares in Thai Trade with ASEAN, Cambodia, the Lao PDR, Myanmar, and Viet Nam, 2020

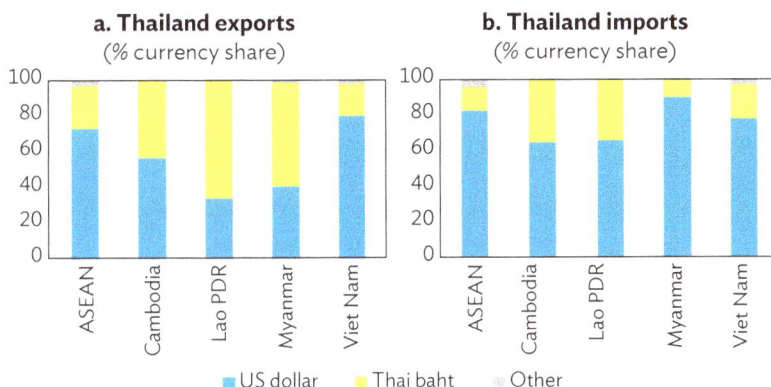

ASEAN = Association of Southeast Asian Nations, Lao PDR = Lao People's Democratic Republic, US = United States.
Source: Authors, based on Bank of Thailand, Statistics–International Trade (accessed June 2021).

The PRC's yuan internationalization

The PRC launched a yuan internationalization initiative following the Lehman Brothers shock of 2008. It started with the use of the yuan for trade settlement and expanded to outward and inward foreign direct investment (FDI) settlement and inward portfolio investment. The PRC has used Hong Kong, China as a major platform for yuan internationalization, where an offshore yuan (called the CNH) market has been developed. The yuan Cross-border Interbank Payment System (CIPS) was established in 2015 to become the main channel of cross-border yuan clearing and settlement. In addition, the PRC had concluded bilateral currency swap arrangements with 39 central banks and monetary authorities by end-2019 so they could hold and use yuan for trade and FDI settlements. As a result, rapid and substantial progress has been made in yuan use for current and capital account settlements, offshore deposits, and offshore bond issuance.[22] A major milestone was the inclusion of the yuan in the IMF's special drawing rights basket in October 2016.[23]

---

[22] The market size of the yuan in the world's foreign exchange trading was the eighth largest in 2019, accounting for 4.3% of the world total. The size of yuan reserves was the fifth largest in the IMF members' total foreign exchange reserves, with a share of 2.3% in end-2020. The yuan ranked fifth as a payment settlement currency globally, with a market share of 1.9% in end-2020.

[23] The yuan was included in the special drawing rights basket on the grounds that the PRC was a large exporter and that the yuan was judged to be freely usable, i.e., freely used and traded by IMF member authorities in the PRC onshore market.

The share of yuan settlements in the PRC's overall cross-border transactions by nonbank sectors expanded rapidly from virtually zero in 2009 to 29% in 2015, then declined somewhat in 2016–2017 and started to rise again in 2018, reaching 37% in 2020 (Figure 3.19). In contrast, the US dollar share declined as a trend from 83% in 2010 to 56% in 2020. Similarly, the yuan share in total trade settlements expanded rapidly from zero in 2010 to a peak of 23% in 2015, and then declined after that to 13% in 2019.

Figure 3.19: Yuan Cross-Border Settlements for International Transactions
(%)

a. Shares of major currencies in the PRC's overall cross-border settlements by nonbank sectors

b. Yuan settlement shares in the PRC's goods trade, current account, and all cross-border transactions

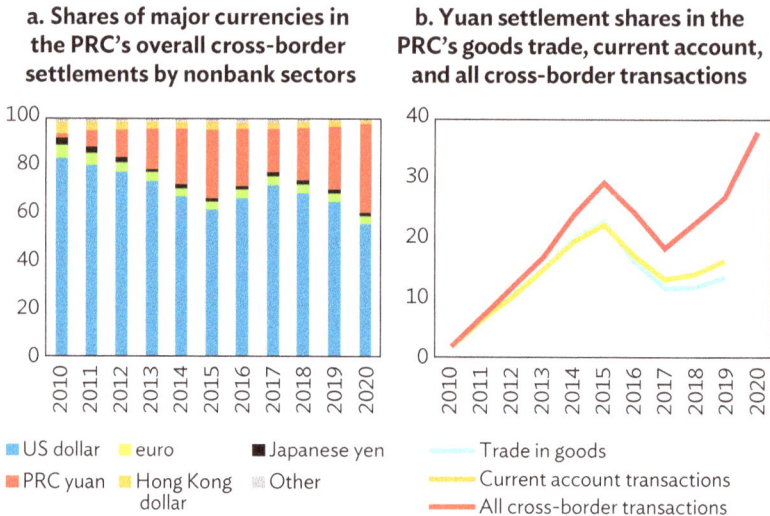

US dollar   euro   Japanese yen
PRC yuan   Hong Kong dollar   Other

Trade in goods
Current account transactions
All cross-border transactions

PRC = People's Republic of China, US = United States.
Note: The yuan values of cross-border settlements for trade in goods and current account transactions are obtained from the People's Bank of China (PBOC), and the yuan values of cross-border settlements for all cross-border transactions by nonbanking sectors are obtained from the State Administration of Foreign Exchange (SAFE) of the PBOC. These values are divided by the corresponding total values by nonbanking sectors obtained from SAFE.
Source: Authors, based on PRC, *RMB Internationalization Report* 2017–2020; and State Administration of Foreign Exchange of the PBOC, Cross-border Receipts and Payments by Non-banking Sectors (accessed August 2021).

The available data for selected ASEAN+3 economies' use of the yuan for trade invoicing or settlement show a much lower share in their overall trade (Figure 3.20). For example, only close to 2.3% of Japan's overall exports and 1.3% of its imports were invoiced in yuan in 2020. In the Republic of Korea, the yuan shares in overall exports and imports were 2.0% and 1.5%. These ratios are 1.0% and 3.3% for Indonesia's overall exports and imports, and 0.5% and 1.5% for Thailand's.[24]

Figure 3.20: Yuan Shares in Trade Invoicing and/or Settlement for Selected ASEAN+3 Economies

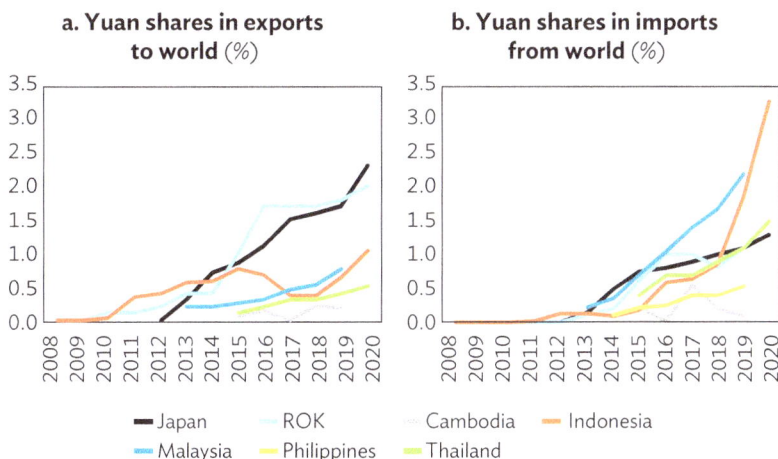

a. Yuan shares in exports to world (%)

b. Yuan shares in imports from world (%)

Japan   ROK   Cambodia   Indonesia
Malaysia   Philippines   Thailand

ASEAN+3 = Association of Southeast Asian Nations plus the People's Republic of China, Japan, and the Republic of Korea; ROK = Republic of Korea.
Source: Authors, based on Boz et al. (2020); Georgiadis et al. (2021); Bank of Indonesia, Indonesia Financial Statistics (accessed July 2021); Bank of Korea, Economic Statistics System (accessed August 2021); Bank of Thailand, Statistics–International Trade (accessed June 2021); Government of Japan, Customs, Share of Currency in Trade (accessed June 2021); and People's Bank of China, *RMB Internationalization Report* (accessed August 2021).

One of the most significant achievements of yuan internationalization is that the currency has been playing an important role as a partial nominal anchor for exchange-rate management in many Asian economies, particularly in ASEAN+3. The currency weight of the yuan in the implicit basket of exchange rate movements has risen to more than 20% for the Republic of Korea, Malaysia, and Singapore (Figure 3.16).

However, the pace of yuan internationalization has slowed and even reversed in recent years. From late 2014 to 2016, the PRC encountered massive capital outflows, yuan depreciation, and a loss of almost $1 trillion in foreign exchange reserves between mid-2014 and early 2017. The People's Bank of China (PBOC), perhaps to put the exchange rate in line with the market fundamentals, devalued the yuan in three consecutive

---

[24] However, yuan shares in a country's bilateral trade with the PRC are higher. For example, in the case of the Republic of Korea, the only ASEAN+3 economy that publishes bilateral currency settlement data vis-à-vis the PRC, the yuan shares are 7.4% for exports and 6.4% for imports in 2020.

days in August 2015 amid market turmoil, accelerating capital outflows that had started in mid-2014 and worsening exchange market pressure. Capital outflows and large exchange rate depreciations had significant spillover effects on financial markets globally. In response, the authorities resorted to capital outflow controls and currency market interventions to stop the yuan value from plunging. This reversed trends toward capital account opening and exchange rate flexibility. As a result, yuan internationalization has slowed and prospects for the process have become uncertain.

Implications

The currency internationalization efforts in the PRC, Japan, and Thailand have not necessarily produced intended outcomes, although all achieved some success in increasing international use of the currencies. For the ROK, one reason for the low degree of internationalization of the won might be the lack of a comprehensive policy to achieve this. Even so, currency internationalization involves benefits and costs (Box 3.1). It particularly poses macroeconomic and financial stability challenges as it requires capital account convertibility, which would further require certain preconditions for success. These include sound macroeconomic management, financial market development and openness,[25] an effective financial regulatory and supervisory framework, and readiness to allow exchange rate flexibility. Therefore, a drive for currency internationalization makes it vital to optimize the trilemma configuration of international finance. Not all ASEAN+3 economies have reached this stage, implying that the priority is for step-by-step improvements to the macroeconomic and financial market fundamentals in laggard economies and to prepare gradually for capital account opening, if not currency internationalization.

---

[25] Ito and Kawai (2018) empirically show that financial market opening without quality development of financial markets tends to worsen macroeconomic performance.

Box 3.1: Costs and Benefits of Currency Internationalization

Several countries have pursued "currency internationalization," promotes the use of a home currency for international transactions, such as trade, foreign direct investment, and cross-border financial transactions, and as official foreign exchange reserves and exchange rate anchors for other authorities. Currency internationalization requires both current and capital account convertibility, as otherwise residents and nonresidents cannot freely use the currency for international purposes. All high-income economies and most emerging and developing economies have achieved current account convertibility by accepting the obligations of the International Monetary Fund's Article VIII. Most high-income economies have achieved full capital account convertibility, but many emerging and developing economies have not. To achieve capital account convertibility, a country needs to satisfy certain preconditions, which many emerging and developing economies consider too costly to fulfil. The benefits and costs of currency internationalization can be summarized as follows:

Benefits:

- Avoidance of exchange risk associated with international transactions.
- Reduced costs of currency transactions due to currency being traded frequently.
- Increased international business opportunities for banks and nonbank financial firms due to low domestic funding costs.
- "Exorbitant privilege" of not facing binding current account and fiscal disciplines or binding "trilemma" constraints for a country with a dominant international currency.

Costs:

- Increased financial instability caused by large capital inflows and outflows (due to capital account convertibility).
- Loss of monetary policy control due to nonresidents' holding and trading of the currency.
- Intensified exchange rate volatility, overshooting and misalignment (due to the adoption of exchange rate flexibility).
- Enlarged responsibility of providing international liquidity during global liquidity shortages and financial crises for a country with a dominant international currency.

Source: Author's compilation.

ASEAN+3 Initiatives: ASEAN Economic Community, Local Currency Settlement Framework , and Other Bilateral Cooperation

Several ASEAN+3 economies have recently taken conscious approaches to expanding cross-border use of their own currencies, particularly for trade and FDI. ASEAN's drive for regional cooperation focuses on the deepening of the ASEAN Economic Community (AEC), while the PRC is motivated by the desire to pursue economic integration of "Belt and Road Initiative" countries, particularly through yuan internationalization, and Japan is interested in promoting regional economic and financial integration and yen internationalization.

Local Currency Settlement Framework

Indonesia, Malaysia, and Thailand have been promoting their own currencies for use in bilateral transactions through the Local Currency Settlement Framework (LCSF), which the Philippines has recently joined. This is a set of bilateral agreements among central banks to use their own currencies for cross-border settlements of mutual trade and FDI through commercial banks designated as appointed cross-currency dealers (ACCDs). ACCDs conduct direct exchanges of currencies without the triangular transactions of going through the US dollar as a vehicle currency. Banks appointed as ACCDs can also provide several foreign currency services for domestic clients, such as financing and deposit services in the partner currency and currency hedging to manage exchange risks between the two currencies.

The LCSF was initiated by the Malaysian and Thai central banks, Bank Negara Malaysia (BNM) and the Bank of Thailand (BOT), in March 2016. Under this framework, eligible international transactions for local currency settlement were limited to trade in goods and services, three banks were designated as ACCDs in each country, and direct exchanges of the ringgit and baht were introduced in interbank markets. Then Bank Indonesia (BI) joined the framework in December 2017 and the BNM–BOT–BI LCSF was officially launched, effective January 2018. Eligible transactions for ringgit-rupiah and baht-rupiah settlements were limited to trade in goods and services initially, while the Malaysian and Thai central banks agreed to expand eligible transactions for ringgit-baht settlements to include FDI. The three central banks designated their commercial banks as ACCDs for each of the two pairs, i.e., BI–BNM and BI–BOT on bilateral bases, while the Malaysian and Thai central banks enlarged their lists of ACCDs.

The Philippines central bank, Bangko Sentral ng Pilipinas (BSP), signed three separate letters of intent on LCSF with BI, BNM, and BOT in April 2019, with the next step being to identify ACCDs to conduct cross-border settlements and associated currency exchanges. In the meantime, the BI–BOT LCSF was expanded in December 2020 to include FDI in eligible transactions, add more commercial banks as ACCDs in each country, and further relax foreign exchange rules and regulations, such as allowing flexible documentation requirements.

Several objectives motivate the introduction and development of the LCSF. The most important are to promote home currency use in cross-border trade and FDI settlements, reduce the risks from dependence on the dollar, and to achieve greater economic and financial stability. Reliance on the dollar for conducting international transactions would make countries vulnerable to rapid swings in US monetary policy and dollar liquidity shortages during times of global financial market stress. Thus, the use of regional currencies in trade and investment would mitigate such risks and contribute to the diversification of international settlement currencies. Another objective is to stimulate trade and investment and economic growth by reducing currency risks among LCSF participating countries. A final objective is to help deepen economic and financial integration in ASEAN. This is in line with the ASEAN Economic Community (AEC) 2025 Blueprint, which aims to stimulate intra-ASEAN trade, investment, and connections among the region's commercial banks. Finance sector integration is central to AEC building under the Blueprint.[26]

The PRC's drive for yuan cross-border settlements and direct currency exchange

PRC authorities have taken several routes to promoting cross-border settlements of trade, FDI, and other transactions in yuan as part of the country's currency internationalization policy. First, they have set up offshore yuan-clearing banks and direct exchange markets between the yuan and partner currencies. By end-2019, the PBOC had established clearing banks in 25 countries and regions. The most successful is Hong Kong, China, where offshore yuan trading has rapidly expanded. Second,

---

[26] *AEC 2025 Blueprint* points out six key elements of a highly integrated and cohesive ASEAN economy and one of these is financial integration, inclusion, and stability (ASEAN Secretariat 2015). It encourages ASEAN states to liberalize financial services through the ASEAN Trade in Services Agreement and provide greater market access and operational flexibility for Qualified ASEAN Banks (QABs) through the ASEAN Banking Integration Framework (ABIF), based on each country's readiness and on a reciprocal basis.

the PBOC has created and developed the Cross-Border Interbank Payment System (CIPS) since 2015. With banks and financial institutions from 47 countries and regions participating, CIPS has played a significant role in clearing and settling cross-border transactions in yuan. Finally, the PRC has been setting up bilateral currency swap arrangements (BCSAs) with 41 central banks globally (including some not yet active) and maintaining active ones with most ASEAN+3 economies. These are intended to promote yuan settlements for trade and investment and provide yuan liquidity in the event of financial difficulties in partner countries. They have contributed to the cross-border use of the yuan for international transactions.

The PRC has been developing direct exchange markets at home and abroad between the yuan and other regional currencies as part of the internationalization efforts. For example, the PRC and Japan launched direct trading of their currency pair in Shanghai and Tokyo in June 2012 to reduce the role of the US dollar in bilateral trade. In the same manner, direct exchange with the won became available in Shanghai in June 2016, with 14 banks designated as market makers to sell and buy the two currencies. This marked the first time the won was directly traded outside the Republic of Korea. In late 2018, a Bank of China-sponsored trading association for the yuan signed an agreement with 13 Filipino banks to allow direct exchange with the peso. In September 2020, the PBOC signed a memorandum of understanding with Indonesia to establish a framework promoting trade and FDI, including the direct exchange rate quotation and interbank trading for their currency pair.

Japan's bilateral currency cooperation with several ASEAN+3 economies

Japan has been promoting yen use for international transactions and the development of direct exchange markets between the yen and other regional currencies such as the yuan, baht, Philippine peso, and rupiah. The country has also renewed several bilateral currency swap arrangements with regional central banks.

The Japanese Ministry of Finance announced in June 2017 a comprehensive plan to launch direct currency trading with other economies in the region to further promote yen internationalization. As a start, the ministry signed a memorandum of cooperation with the BOT to promote the use of regional currencies in March 2018. It signed a letter of intent with BSP, on the establishment of a yen–peso direct trading framework in May 2019. The ministry also announced with BI in August 2020 a framework for cooperation to promote the use of their currencies for the settlement of bilateral trade and FDI.[27] The announcement was significant as it not only stated that "(t)he framework includes, among others, promotion of the direct quotation between the Indonesian Rupiah and the Japanese Yen as well as the relaxation of relevant rules and regulations to enhance the usage of local currencies," but also appointed several banks in each country as ACCDs to carry out rupiah–yen transactions.

Both the Japanese Ministry of Finance and the Bank of Japan (BOJ) have renewed or added bilateral currency swap agreements to promote the yen in currency swaps. For example, agreements renewed with BSP (October 2017), the Monetary Authority of Singapore (MAS, May 2018), BOT (July 2018), BI (October 2018), and BNM (September 2020) added the yen as a swap currency for counterpart central banks except BNM. The BOJ went on to conclude a local currency–yen swap with the PBOC in October 2018, extended one with the MAS in November 2019, and signed one with the BOT in March 2020.

Implications and challenges

There are several implications of the development of the LCSF and similar initiatives undertaken by the PRC and Japan. First, the LCSF applies greater flexibility to existing foreign exchange regulations and rules regarding the use of domestic currency in partner countries for currency trading and the provision of related financial services (domestic currency financing, deposit services, and currency hedging) by partner countries' ACCDs. This has forced some participants which prefer to retain certain foreign exchange restrictions to avoid excessive market volatilities—including Malaysia which regulates offshore trading of the ringgit—to allow flexibilities to foreign exchange regulations and administrative rules, so contributing to greater financial integration through designated commercial banks.

Second, the appointment of domestic commercial banks as ACCDs allows them to offer partner currency financing and deposit accounts and currency hedging services to domestic businesses. This arrangement complements the Qualified ASEAN Bank (QAB) initiative of the ASEAN Banking Integration Framework (ABIF) under the AEC 2025 Blueprint.

---

[27] A list of bilateral agreements is published on the website of the Japanese Ministry of Finance, https://www.mof.go.jp/english/international_policy/financial_cooperation/in_asia/bilateral_financial_cooperation/index.htm

Agreeing on QABs has been difficult because they must be banks (i) headquartered in the ASEAN region and majority-owned by the region's citizens, and (ii) approved both by country-partner authorities and the ABIF's Taskforce.[28] In contrast, given that ACCDs are appointed only by country authorities, they are not subject to the same stringency. Amid slow progress in developing a QAB network across the region, this suggests the ACCD arrangement is one of the ways to expand the area of financial services that foreign banks can provide and so partially complements the QAB initiative. Closer information exchange, policy dialogue, and surveillance between central banks involved would contribute to deeper financial integration among LCSF countries and eventually in ASEAN as a whole.

Third, the PRC and Japan's efforts to promote the use of regional currencies together with LCSF central banks would in effect expand the ASEAN-led LCSF to the wider ASEAN+3 region. This would not only reduce foreign exchange risk associated with trade and investment and currency transaction costs, but also contribute to ASEAN+3 financial integration.

On the other hand, significant challenges exist in reaping the benefits of the LCSF and the PRC and Japan's supporting efforts. As Sussangkarn (2019) explains, the LCSF is intended to reduce transaction costs in exchanging local currencies to the point where direct exchanges are less costly than transactions triangulated through the US dollar, leading to a persistent increase in regional currency use for trade and FDI settlement.

Several policy recommendations can be made to stimulate regional currency use. First, participating countries are advised to pursue greater liberalization and coordination of foreign exchange regulations and rules and cross-border settlement practices. For example, the amount of local currency that nonresidents can hold can be raised. The Japanese Bankers Association is encouraged to extend its yen-clearing system, now only available at home, to Japanese banks operating in ASEAN+3 economies to speed up cross-border yen transfers. Second, eligible underlying transactions should be expanded to include wider long-term capital flows, particularly cross-border investment in local currency bonds. This would create synergies between cross-border settlements in local currencies for trade and FDI and those of intraregional local currency bond transactions. Third,

---

[28] Only two Malaysian banks have been established as QABs in Indonesia so far (which feature in the Joint Statement of the 6th ASEAN Finance Ministers and Central Bank Governors' Meeting, 2 October 2020, https://asean.org/joint-statement-of-the-6th-asean-finance-ministers-and-central-bank-governors-meeting-afmgm/).

LCSF countries should be expanded to other ASEAN members—and in particular include Singapore as it is among the most developed financial centers in the region. Fourth, authorities in participating countries should focus on developing deep and liquid foreign exchange markets to reduce transaction costs. This is crucial as the holding of currencies that are not very liquid involves greater exchange risks and higher fees, which discourage demand and the use of regional currencies. Finally, closer coordination of exchange rate policies among participating countries is desirable to ensure greater exchange rate stability among LCSF currencies. The reason is that if exchange rates are volatile, then regional currencies would be costly to use and the US dollar would tend to continue to dominate settlements for intraregional trade and investment.

Central Bank Digital Currencies

ASEAN+3 economies have taken various approaches to the issuance of a central bank digital currency (CBDC), which is the digital form of an economy's legal tender. Instead of printing paper money, a central bank may issue a CBDC backed by the full faith and credit of the government. While Cambodia has already introduced the digital riel under the "Bakong" project, Brunei Darussalam, the Lao PDR, Myanmar, Malaysia, and Viet Nam have not made moves (Table 3.1). Other ASEAN+3 economies are either studying CBDCs or have initiated test runs and pilot programs. The PRC has taken the most significant action by rapidly developing its own CBDC for official issuance by 2022.

Table 3.1. State of Preparation for Central Bank Digital Currencies in ASEAN+3 Economies

Economy	Issuing body (including potential)	CBDC status	No. of users (millions)	Current situations
PRC	People's Bank of China (PBOC)	Pilot	1,439.3	Trials of DCEP carried out in major cities in April 2020; exploring real-time cross-border settlements with HKMA, BOT, and CBUAE; plan to issue DCEP by February 2022.
Hong Kong, China	Hong Kong Monetary Authority (HKMA)	Pilot	7.5	Test of a cross-border corridor network carried out with BOT in 2019; undertaking cross-border pilot programs for CBDC with PBOC, BOT, and CBUAE.

continued on next page

Table 3.1 (continued)

Japan	Bank of Japan	Development	126.5	The first phase experiment started in April 2021 to develop a test environment, the second phase planned in 2022 to implement CBDC in the test environment, and then consider a pilot program.
Korea, Republic of	Bank of Korea	Pilot	51.3	Launch of research on legal and technical implications of a CBDC in April 2020; pilot program during August to December 2021.
Brunei Darussalam	Monetary Authority of Brunei Darussalam	Inactive	0.4	--
Cambodia	National Bank of Cambodia	Other	16.7	Bakong launched as a DLT-based interbank and retail payment system with its digital currency in October 2020.
Indonesia	Bank Indonesia	Research	273.5	Under study to launch a digital rupiah
Lao PDR	Bank of the Lao PDR	Inactive	7.3	--
Malaysia	Bank Negara Malaysia	Inactive	32.4	No plan to issue CBDC
Myanmar	Central Bank of Myanmar	Inactive	54.4	--
Philippines	Bangko Sentral ng Pilipinas	Research	109.6	Under study in accordance with the Digital Payments Transformation Roadmap.
Singapore	Monetary Authority of Singapore	Pilot	5.9	Testing of CBDC through Project Ubin; the first successful international transaction of CBDCs with Canada conducted in 2019.
Thailand	Bank of Thailand (BOT)	Pilot	69.8	Testing of a prototype decentralized CBDC for domestic interbank transfers in 2018; testing of cross-border transfers with HKMA in 2019, expanded to include PBOC and CBUAE in February 2021; plan to launch a retail CBDC pilot in the second quarter of 2022.
Viet Nam	State Bank of Viet Nam	Inactive	97.3	No development yet
United States	Federal Reserve	Research	331.0	Under study; Boston Fed is working with MIT researchers to develop and test a CBDC.
Euro area	European Central Bank	Development	340.9	Launch of the "digital euro" project in July 2021, starting with a 24-month investigation phase.

CBDC = central bank digital currency, CBUAE = Central Bank of United Arab Emirates, DCEP = Digital Currency Electronic Payment, DLT = distributed ledger technology, Lao PDR = Lao People's Democratic Republic, MIT = Massachusetts Institute of Technology, PRC = People's Republic of China.
Note: The number of users is the population of the country or economy.
Source: Authors, based on Atlantic Council, *Central Bank Digital Currency Tracker* (accessed August 2021).

A country would have several reasons to introduce a CBDC. They include: reducing the cost of issuing and managing fiat currency; improving the functions of the domestic and cross-border payments system; protecting the integrity of legal tender from cryptoassets (such as Bitcoin) and stablecoins (such as Tether, USD Coin, Amazon Pay, Apple Pay, Google Pay, Alipay, WeChat Pay, Facebook's proposed Diem, and the like) thereby maintaining monetary sovereignty; increasing interoperability between existing private digital currencies and allowing users to enjoy low-cost, low-risk, and efficient financial transactions in real time; promoting financial inclusion to enable those who are unbanked or underbanked to have easier and safer access to money on their mobile phones; tracking financial flows and limiting money laundering, terrorist financing, tax evasion, and other illicit activity; and enhancing the effectiveness of fiscal and monetary policy.

Cambodia's "Bakong" project

In October 2020, the National Bank of Cambodia (NBC) launched "Bakong," which is a real-time interbank payment system based on a distributed ledger technology (DLT) and supports its digital currency. "Bakong" uses a two-tier system where financial institutions replace money deposited by end users with electronic money and offer the latter to them. To use electronic money, end users must deposit cash at a financial institution, open "Bakong" accounts under the domain of that institution, and transfer money to the "Bakong" accounts.[29] Then, the NBC collects physical cash (riel and US dollar notes) from the financial institution and creates electronic money (in riel and US dollars). Finally, end users can make payments by using electronic payment accounts (or e-wallets) created at the financial institution. Thus, "Bakong" follows a prefunded model where end-users must deposit in their "Bakong" accounts before making transactions. The NBC can change the quantity of electronic money (in riel) in circulation, which is a *de facto* CBDC, for the purpose of monetary control.[30]

---

[29] End users have two separate accounts to allow for transactions for the riel and US dollar. Alternatively, they can open "Bakong" accounts on the Bakong App under the domain of any participating institution and make a direct cash deposit through them. End users must utilize the physical services of participating banks or institutions to convert riel into dollar, or vice versa, as they cannot do that on the system.

[30] But the NBC cannot change the size of dollar-electronic money in circulation as its supply is limited and cannot be altered by the central bank.

The NBC has been motivated primarily by the need to modernize its payments system, which was severely underdeveloped with no Real Time Gross Settlement (RTGS) capabilities in the interbank network or between merchants and banks. DLT adoption has improved interoperability of retail payments among banks and payment service institutions, which was a challenge.[31] In addition, the NBC has viewed "Bakong" as helping expand financial inclusion because most citizens are unbanked even though mobile phone penetration is rising. Finally, the introduction of electronic money in riel as a *de facto* CBDC is expected to help restore the effectiveness of monetary policy and eventually reduce the extent of dollarization.

Development of the digital yuan

The PBOC began efforts to issue digital currency (later named as Digital Currency Electronic Payment [DCEP]) in 2014. Having conducted research, particularly through the Digital Currency Institute established in 2017, and the basic designs and drafting of legislation, the PBOC piloted the digital yuan in four cities in April 2020. Commercial banks were allowed to run internal tests such as conversions between cash and digital currency, account-balance checks, and payments. The PBOC expanded the pilot program to many cities in August and launched full-scale demonstration tests in major cities such as Shenzhen, Suzhou, Beijing, Xi'an, and Hainan in October. The PBOC also announced it would test cross-border settlements of the digital yuan with the Hong Kong Monetary Authority (HKMA), Bank of Thailand (BOT), and Central Bank of the United Arab Emirates (CBUAE). It aimed for widespread domestic use of the digital yuan by 2022 and considered allowing foreign athletes and visitors to use it during the 2022 Winter Olympics in Beijing.

Like most other planned CBDCs, the digital yuan has a two-tier system. The technology to support it is a combination of DLT and a newly developed technology based on existing electronic payments. From monetary policy perspectives, the PBOC appears to prefer a CBDC based on a central rather than decentralized technology. However, the joint project with the HKMA, BOT, and CBUAE, is reportedly exploring DLT capabilities in developing a proof-of-concept prototype to support cross-border foreign exchange payment-versus-payment transactions in multiple jurisdictions, and operating 24/7.

---

[31] DLT was selected as it was believed to allow the payments system to leapfrog the traditional way of connecting all players and become more efficient, reliable, and resilient to cyberattacks than the traditional one, especially when connecting to payment service providers (NBC 2020).

The digital yuan functions like existing mobile payments (such as Alipay and WeChat Pay) for end users but differs from them in a significant way: it is a legal tender, the user's transaction information is captured by authorities through commercial banks rather than private payment providers, and offline payments are possible. Thus, the digital yuan enables authorities to keep track of financial flows as it allows only "controlled anonymity" in comparison to fully anonymous cash transactions. In addition, the PBOC has required mobile payments service providers (such as Alibaba's Ant Financial and Tencent) to put 100% of their customer funds in central bank accounts as interest-free reserve deposits so that it can monitor nonbank payments firms and control financial risk.

In addition to usual reasons for issuing a CBDC, the PRC's push for the digital yuan appears to have another important motivation. That is, by issuing the digital yuan capable of being used for cross-border settlements, the PBOC can establish CBDC alliances with other countries and regions, set international standards on technology and regulations related to a CBDC, and enjoy first-mover advantage. If the digital yuan is increasingly used for the cross-border settlement of trade and investment particularly with the Belt and Road Initiative countries, it is possible that the yuan-based economic and currency zone is created and expanded rapidly. Even though the PRC has not achieved full capital account convertibility, the digital yuan could be used for current account and limited capital flows (such as FDI and long-term bank loans) by a large number of countries. In the eyes of the US, Europe, and Japan, this could threaten the existing international monetary system based on the dollar, euro, and yen.

Approaches taken by major advanced economies

Given that the PRC is racing ahead, major advanced economies are likely to accelerate plans to issue their own CBDCs. In addition, they are urged to respond to the spread of stablecoins—privately issued digital currencies pegged to a fiat currency like the dollar and euro (Tether, USD Coin, and bigtech e-money coins)—and potentially the digital yuan, in order to conduct effective monetary policy and achieve financial stability within the existing international monetary system. However, of the three largest advanced economies (the US, euro area, and Japan), the US is furthest behind, according to the Atlantic Council's Central Bank Digital Currency Tracker.

The US is studying the benefits and costs of a CBDC, but remains cautious. The Federal Reserve has done research to examine whether a digital dollar can complement existing systems and serve the needs of households and businesses and to identify the implications for monetary policy, financial stability, consumer protection, and legal and privacy issues. Views diverge within the central bank on the need for, and usefulness of, a CBDC. Federal Reserve Board members seem to want to make sure any CBDC is built on a solid foundation. Individual Federal Reserve banks are also working with various stakeholders on their research. Most importantly, the Federal Reserve Bank of Boston is collaborating with the Massachusetts Institute of Technology to experiment with existing and new prototypes of payments systems that could be used for a digital dollar. Once decisions are made to start a pilot phase and issue a digital dollar, many other countries are likely to follow suit.

The European Central Bank (ECB) has been pursuing its analytical work and experimentation on the feasibility of a digital euro more proactively than the US Federal Reserve. ECB priorities seem to be to retain monetary sovereignty amid expanding use of stablecoins and to avoid bank disintermediation and maintain financial stability. The ECB began joint DLT experiments for a wholesale CBDC with the BOJ in 2016 and internal preliminary experimentation in October 2020. The focus was on issues of the digital euro ledger, privacy and anti-money laundering, limits on a digital euro in circulation, and end-user access and inclusiveness. In July 2021, following the preliminary experimentation phase, the ECB launched the "digital euro project" as a 24-month investigation phase. This aims to assess the possible impact of a digital euro on the market; identify design options; create a riskless, accessible, and efficient form of a CBDC; and define a business model for supervised intermediaries in the digital euro ecosystem. This move came after preliminary experimentation found no major technical obstacles and established that architectures combining centralized and decentralized elements were feasible. Launch of a digital euro is expected within 4 years.

Following internal research on a CBDC and joint DLT experiments for a wholesale CBDC with the ECB for several years, the BOJ in April 2021 entered the proof-of-concept process to test the technical feasibility of the core functions and features required for a general-purpose CBDC in two phases (Bank of Japan 2020). In the first phase, the BOJ develops a test environment for the CBDC system and conducts experiments on core functions of a CBDC as a payment instrument. The BOJ then plans to move to the second phase in the spring of 2022 to test the feasibility of other functions. After this, the BOJ may consider a pilot program involving banks, other private payment service providers, and end users. The BOJ takes the position that it has no plan to issue a CBDC at this point but will be ready if one is needed. The BOJ focuses on universal access, security, resilience (availability at 24/7/365 and offline use during system and network failures), instant payment capability, and interoperability. Besides banking sector soundness, its emphasis is on security and resilience, because of the heavy use of cash in retail payments, the importance of the banking system in the economy, and the 2011 earthquake and tsunami, which caused widespread disruption.

Importance of fundamental forces

As ECB (2021) notes, a CBDC can promote use of a currency for cross-border payments but is not necessarily a "game changer." When it comes to international currency status, fundamental forces such as stable economic fundamentals; economic size in terms of trade and finance; financial market depth, breadth, liquidity and openness; and inertia in international currency use are the most important determinants. Nonetheless, the US and the euro area are accelerating the process of CBDC development partly because they do not wish to lag behind the PRC in establishing *de facto* standards on technology, regulations, and cross-border settlements involving CBDCs. If some ASEAN+3 currencies are to become truly international, the relevant economies must focus on strengthening these fundamentals, while developing their own CBDCs.

3.6 Conclusion

This chapter has used a wide variety of data and verified that the US dollar is the most dominant international currency in many aspects of cross-border use—trade, investment, finance, international reserve holding, and exchange-rate management. It is clear that the ASEAN+3 region is highly reliant on the dollar in international exchanges and finance. This suggests that the development of regional currencies for international economic transactions is a daunting challenge.

Comparison of ASEAN+3 economies with others from the "trilemma" perspective has exhibited how policy makers have balanced a trade-off in making two out of three policy choices: exchange rate stability, capital account openness, and monetary policy independence. The result shows that ASEAN+3 economies have increased their capital account openness gradually over the last few decades. Along with that, many economies have chosen to retain monetary policy independence by giving up a degree of exchange rate stability, while a few others have decided to retain exchange rate stability and forego a degree of monetary policy independence.

The chapter has also revealed that the PRC; along with Hong Kong, China; and most ASEAN countries have persistently belonged to the US dollar zone. Consistent with that, ASEAN+3 economies have used the dollar as a settlement or invoicing currency in international trade, which also applies to large economies such as the PRC, Japan, and the Republic of Korea. Interestingly, despite the dollar being the most important settlement and vehicle currency, own and partner currencies are also increasingly used for trade among ASEAN+3 economies and with the European Union. For example, Japan's exports to Asia and the Republic of Korea's trade with Japan involve greater use of ASEAN+3 currencies (the yen, yuan, and won) than the US dollar and that Japan and the Republic of Korea's trade with— and Thailand's imports from—the European Union have shifted from reliance on the dollar to own and partner currencies. The use of the baht in Thailand's trade has been rising steadily, and the currency is now dominant in settlements for its exports to the Lao PDR and Myanmar.

In international financial transactions involving cross-border bank loans and international debt security issues, the dollar share has been persistently high for ASEAN+3 economies, while the yen share has been declining. The use of regional currencies for international debt issuance remains limited in the ASEAN+3 region.

All these findings suggest that the US dollar is dominant even as ASEAN+3 do have some increasingly notable roles in certain areas. The problem is that dollar-centric international finance, a key feature for the region, keeps the economies vulnerable to monetary and financial spillover effects from the US. As developing and emerging economies, more so than developed economies, are more exposed to global financial cycles (Rey 2018), changes in economic and financial conditions or macroeconomic policies of the US could easily have significant, adverse impact on these economies in the region through volatile capital flows.

To shield from external shocks, ASEAN+3 economies have been cooperating to increase the use of regional currencies. The Local Currency Settlement Framework (LCSF) pursued by Malaysia, Thailand, and Indonesia—and now the Philippines—has the potential to increase the use of the ringgit, baht, rupiah, and peso for trade and FDI among these economies. The PRC and Japan, which have been promoting international use of their own currencies, have also started to work with the framework participants. The challenge is to get to the point where direct exchange of regional currencies is cheaper than triangular transactions through the US dollar, and where regional currency use for trade and FDI settlement is on a persistent uptrend.

ASEAN+3 economies can further strengthen currency cooperation in a way that accelerates the use of regional currencies between them. They can strengthen the LCSF to settle more bilateral trade and FDI in regional currencies. The rising role of the baht in Thai trade settlements suggests that other economies can also increase home currency use in their trade. Measures would include: greater liberalization and coordination of foreign-exchange regulations and rules; expansion of eligible transactions to include local currency bond investment; participation of other ASEAN member countries in the settlement framework; development of deep and liquid foreign exchange markets; and greater coordination of exchange rate policy among participating countries.

ASEAN+3 economies can also encourage mutual holdings of sovereign bonds denominated in regional currencies as official reserve assets. Authorities may encourage the region's banks to extend cross-border loans in ASEAN+3 currencies. These policy initiatives will likely contribute to the deepening of markets for regional currencies. Lastly, authorities can strengthen policy dialogue and information exchange and establish a regional exchange rate surveillance process by using a regional basket of currencies, such as the ASEAN+3 currency unit (ACU), as a reference indicator. The ACU, much like the European Currency Unit created before the introduction of the euro, might also be developed for settlements of intraregional trade, FDI, and financial transactions, while strengthening the LCSF. This would also allow vulnerable economies to access ASEAN+3 liquidity when they face financial instability.

Although the introduction of a CBDC is not necessarily a game-changer for the international monetary system, ASEAN+3 economies other than the PRC will be under increasing pressure to develop sound CBDCs if they wish to promote home currency use for international transactions. The PRC needs to pursue further capital account opening and exchange rate flexibility in order to promote the digital yuan as a truly international currency. With the spread of CBDCs among ASEAN+3 economies, authorities will have to cooperate to establish settlement arrangements for efficiently conducting foreign exchange transactions involving CBDCs across different payments systems.

References

Aizenman, J., M. D. Chinn, and H. Ito. 2013. The 'Impossible Trinity' Hypothesis in an Era of Global Imbalances: Measurement and Testing. *Review of International Economics*. 21 (3), August. pp. 447–58. https://doi.org/10.1111/roie.12047.

_____. 2021. *The Trilemma Indexes*. Updated as of 31 August. http://web.pdx.edu/~ito/trilemma_indexes.htm.

Aizenman, J., H. Ito, and G. K. Pasricha. 2021. Central Bank Swap Arrangements in the COVID-19 Crisis. *NBER Working Paper*. No. 28585 (August). Cambridge, MA: National Bureau of Economic Research. https://www.nber.org/system/files/working_papers/w28585/w28585.pdf.

Aizenman, J. and G. K. Pasricha. 2010. Selective Swap Arrangements and the Global Financial Crisis. *International Review of Economics and Finance*. 19 (3). pp. 353–65. https://doi.org/10.1016/j.iref.2009.10.009.

ASEAN Secretariat. 2015. *ASEAN Economic Community Blueprint 2025*. November. Jakarta: ASEAN Secretariat. https://aseandse.org/wp-content/uploads/2021/02/AEC-Blueprint-2025-FINAL.pdf.

Atlantic Council. *Central Bank Digital Currency Tracker*. https://www.atlanticcouncil.org/cbdctracker/#:~:text=A%20Central%20Bank%20Digital%20Currency%20(CBDC)%20is%20the%20digital%20form,and%20credit%20of%20the%20government (accessed August 2021).

Bank for International Settlements. Debt Securities Statistics. https://www.bis.org/statistics/secstats.htm (accessed June and August 2021).

_____. *Locational Banking Statistics*. https://www.bis.org/statistics/bankstats.htm (accessed August 2021)

_____. *Triennial Central Bank Survey of Foreign Exchange and Over-the-counter (OTC) Derivatives Markets*. https://stats.bis.org/statx/srs/table/d11.3 (accessed September 2019).

Bank Indonesia. *Indonesia Financial Statistics*. https://www.bi.go.id/en/statistik/ekonomi-keuangan/seki/Default.aspx#headingFour (accessed July 2021).

Bank of Japan. 2020. The Bank of Japan's Approach to Central Bank Digital Currency. Released 9 October. Tokyo: Bank of Japan. https://www.boj.or.jp/en/announcements/release_2020/rel201009e.htm/.

Bank of Korea. *Economic Statistics System*. http://ecos.bok.or.kr/flex/ClassSearch_e.jsp?langGubun=E&topCode=022Y007 (accessed August 2021).

Bank of Thailand. *Statistics–International Trade*. https://www.bot.or.th/English/Statistics/EconomicAndFinancial/Pages/StatInternationalTrade.asp (accessed June 2021).

Board of Governors of the Federal Reserve System n.d. Central Bank Liquidity Swap Lines. https://www.federalreserve.gov/regreform/reform-swaplines.htm.

Boz, E., C. Casas, G. Georgiadis, G. Gopinath, H. Le Mezo, A. Mehl, and T. Nguyen. 2020. Patterns in Invoicing Currency in Global Trade. *IMF Working Paper*. WP/20/126 (July). Washington, DC: International Monetary Fund. https://www.imf.org/-/media/Files/Publications/WP/2020/English/wpiea2020126-print-pdf.ashx.

Calvo, G. and C. Reinhart. 2002. Fear of Floating. *Quarterly Journal of Economics*. 98 (2). pp. 379– 408. https://doi.org/10.1162/003355302753650274.

Chang, R. and A. Velasco. 2006. Currency Mismatches and Monetary Policy: A Tale of Two Equilibria. *Journal of International Economics*. 69 (1). pp.150–175. https://doi.org/10.1016/j.jinteco.2005.05.008.

Chinn, M. D. and J. A. Frankel. 2007. Will the Euro Eventually Surpass the Dollar as Leading International Reserve Currency? In R. Clarida, ed. *G7 Current Account Imbalances: Sustainability and Adjustment*. pp. 285–322. Chicago: University of Chicago Press.

_____. 2008. Why the Dollar Will Rival the Euro. *International Finance*. 11 (1). pp. 49–73.

Eichengreen, B. 2010. Managing a Multiple Reserve Currency World. In Wing Thye Woo, ed. *The 21st Century International Monetary System*. Manila: Asian Development Bank.

_____. 2011. *Exorbitant Privilege: Dollar and the Future of the International Monetary System*. Oxford: Oxford University Press.

Eichengreen, B., Hausmann, R., and Panizza U. 2002. Original Sin, The Pain, The Mystery and The Road to Redemption. Unpublished manuscript. Cambridge, MA, and Berkeley, CA: Harvard University and UC Berkeley.

Eichengreen, B. and M. Kawai, eds. 2015. *Renminbi Internationalization: Achievements, Prospects and Challenges*. Tokyo and Washington, DC: Asian Development Bank Institute and Brookings Institution. https://www.adb.org/sites/default/files/publication/159835/adbi-renminbi-internationalization-achievements-prospects-challenges.pdf.

European Central Bank. 2021. *The International Role of the Euro*. June 2021. Frankfurt. https://www.ecb.europa.eu/pub/pdf/ire/ecb.ire202106~a058f84c61.en.pdf.

Frankel, J. 2011. Historical Precedents for Internationalization of the RMB. A CGS/IIGG Working Paper. Washington, DC: Council on Foreign Relations. https://scholar.harvard.edu/files/frankel/files/interntnlztnrmb_cgs-iigg_wp17_frankel_0.pdf.

Frankel, J. and S. J. Wei. 1994. Yen Bloc or Dollar Bloc? Exchange Rate Policies in East Asian Economies. In T. Ito and A. Krueger, eds. *Macroeconomic Linkage: Savings, Exchange Rates, and Capital Flows*. pp. 295–329. Chicago: University of Chicago Press.

Georgiadis, G., H. Le Mezo, A. Mehl, and C. Tille. 2021. Markets vs. Policies: Can the US Dollar's Dominance in Global Trade be Dented? Unpublished manuscript. March 25. Frankfurt: European Central Bank.

Gopinath, G. 2015. The International Price System. Paper presented to the Federal Reserve Bank of Kansas City Jackson Hole Symposium (August, revised November). https://scholar.harvard.edu/files/gopinath/files/paper_083115_01.pdf.

Gopinath, G. and J. Stein. 2018a. Banking, Trade, and the Making of a Dominant Currency. *NBER Working Paper Series*. No. 24485. Cambridge, MA: National Bureau of Economic Research. https://doi.org/10.3386/w24485.

_____. 2018b. Trade Invoicing, Bank Funding, and Central Bank Reserve Holdings. *American Economic Review*. 108 (May). pp. 542–46. https://doi.org/10.1257/pandp.20181065.

Government of Japan, Customs. Share of Currency in Trade. https://www.customs.go.jp/toukei/shinbun/trade-st/tuukahappyou.htm (accessed June 2021).

Government of the People's Republic of China. *Cross-border Receipts and Payments by Non-banking Sectors*. https://www.safe.gov.cn/en/2019/0919/1561.html (accessed August 2021).

Hausmann, R. and U. Panizza. 2003. On the Determinants of Original Sin: An Empirical Investigation. *Journal of International Money and Finance.* 22 (7). pp. 957–90. https://doi.org/10.1016/j.jimonfin.2003.09.006.

⸻. 2010. Redemption or Abstinence? Original Sin, Currency Mismatches and Counter-Cyclical Policies in the New Millennium. *Center for International Development Working Paper.* No. 194. Cambridge, MA: Harvard University. https://doi.org/10.2202/1948-1837.1127.

International Monetary Fund (IMF). 2016. *Strengthening the International Monetary System: A Stocktaking.* Washington, DC: International Monetary Fund. https://www.imf.org/external/np/pp/eng/2016/022216b.pdf.

⸻. Currency Composition of Official Foreign Exchange Reserves. https://data.imf.org/?sk=E6A5F467-C14B-4AA8-9F6D-5A09EC4E62A4 (accessed August 2021).

⸻. World Economic Outlook database, April 2021. https://www.imf.org/en/Publications/WEO/weo-database/2021/April (accessed June 2021).

Ito, H. and M. Chinn. 2015. The Rise of the 'Redback' and China's Capital Account Liberalization: An Empirical Analysis on the Determinants of Invoicing Currencies. In B. Eichengreen and M. Kawai, eds. *Renminbi Internationalization: Achievements, Prospects, and Challenges.* pp. 111–58. Tokyo and Washington, DC: Asian Development Bank Institute and Brookings Institution. https://www.adb.org/sites/default/files/publication/159835/adbi-renminbi-internationalization-achievements-prospects-challenges.pdf.

Ito, H. and M. Kawai. 2014. Determinants of the Trilemma Policy Combination. *ADBI Working Paper.* No. 456 (January). Tokyo: Asian Development Bank Institute. https://www.adb.org/sites/default/files/publication/156311/adbi-wp456.pdf.

⸻. 2016. Trade Invoicing in Major Currencies in the 1970s–1990s: Lessons for Renminbi Internationalization. *Journal of the Japanese and International Economies.* 42. pp. 123–145. https://doi.org/10.1016/j.jjie.2016.10.005.

⸻. 2018. Quantity and Quality Measures of Financial Development: Implications for Macroeconomic Performance. *Public Policy Review.* 14 (5), September. pp. 803–34. https://www.mof.go.jp/english/pri/publication/pp_review/ppr14_05_01.pdf

Ito, H. and C. Rodriguez. 2020. Clamoring for Greenbacks: Explaining the Resurgence of the US Dollar in International Debt. *International Finance*. 23 (2). pp. 370–91. https://doi.org/10.1111/infi.12370.

Ize, A. and E. Levy-Yeyati. 2003. Financial Dollarization. *Journal of International Economics*. 59 (2). pp. 323–47. https://doi.org/10.1016/S0022-1996(02)00017-X.

Kawai, M. 1996. The Japanese Yen as an International Currency: Performance and Prospects. In R. Sato, R. V. Ramachandran, and H. Hori, eds. *Organization, Performance and Equity: Perspectives on the Japanese Economy*. pp. 305–55. Boston, London, Dordrecht: Kluwer Academic Publishers.

Kawai, M. and V. Pontines. 2015. The Renminbi and Exchange Rate Regimes in East Asia. In B. Eichengreen and M. Kawai, eds. *Renminbi Internationalization: Achievements, Prospects, and Challenges*. pp. 159–204. Tokyo and Washington, DC: Asian Development Bank Institute and Brookings Institution Press. https://www.adb.org/sites/default/files/publication/159835/adbi-renminbi-internationalization-achievements-prospects-challenges.pdf.

————. 2016. Is There Really a Renminbi Bloc in Asia? A Modified Frankel-Wei Approach. *Journal of International Money and Finance*. 62 (April). pp. 72–97. https://doi.org/10.1016/j.jimonfin.2015.12.003.

Krugman, P. 1980. Vehicle Currencies and the Structure of International Exchange. *Journal of Money, Credit and Banking*. 12 (3), August. pp. 513–26. https://doi.org/10.2307/1991725.

————. 2007. Will There be a Dollar Crisis? *Economic Policy*. 22 (51). pp. 436–67. https://doi.org/10.1111/j.1468-0327.2007.00183.x.

Maggiori, M., B. Neiman, and J. Schreger. 2019. The Rise of the Dollar and Fall of the Euro as International Currencies. *AEA Papers and Proceedings*. 109. pp. 521–26. https://doi.org/10.1257/pandp.20191007.

People's Bank of China. *RMB Internationalization Reports*. http://www.pbc.gov.cn/en/3688110/3688259/3689026/index.html (accessed August 2021).

Prasad, E.S. 2014. *The Dollar Trap: How the US Dollar Tightened Its Grip on Global Finance*. Princeton: Princeton University Press.

Rey, H. 2001. International Trade and Currency Exchange Source. *Review of Economic Studies*. 68 (2). pp. 443–64.

_____. 2018. Dilemma not Trilemma: The Global Financial Cycle and Monetary Policy Independence. *NBER Working Papers.* No. 21162 (February). Cambridge, MA: National Bureau of Economic Research. http://dx.doi.org/10.3386/w21162

Rogoff, K. and T. Tashiro. 2015. Japan's Exorbitant Privilege. *Journal of the Japanese and International Economies.* 35 (March). pp. 43–61. https://doi.org/10.1016/j.jjie.2014.11.003.

Society for Worldwide Interbank Financial Telecommunication (SWIFT). *RMB Tracker.* Brussels. https://www.swift.com/our-solutions/compliance-and-shared-services/business-intelligence/renminbi/rmb-tracker/document-centre.

Sussangkarn, C. 2019. Promoting Local Currency Usage in the Region. Chapter 3 in *Local Currency Contribution to the Chiang Mai Initiative Multilateralization.* January. AMRO Research Collaboration Program RCP/19-01. Singapore: ASEAN+3 Macroeconomic Research Office. https://www.amro-asia.org/local-currency-contribution-to-the-chiang-mai-initiative-multilateralisation/.

Tovar, C. E. and T. Mohd Nor. 2018. Reserve Currency Blocs: A Changing International Monetary System? *IMF Working Paper.* No. WP/18/20 (January). Washington, DC: International Monetary Fund. https://www.imf.org/-/media/Files/Publications/WP/2018/wp1820.ashx.

United Nations Conference on Trade and Development (UNCTAD). Data Centre. https://unctadstat.unctad.org/wds/ReportFolders/reportFolders.aspx?sCS_ChosenLang=en (accessed August 2021).

Appendix Figure 3.1: Shares of US Dollar, Home, and Other Currencies in Trade with Partners

a. Japan—Currency shares in trade with different partners
(%)

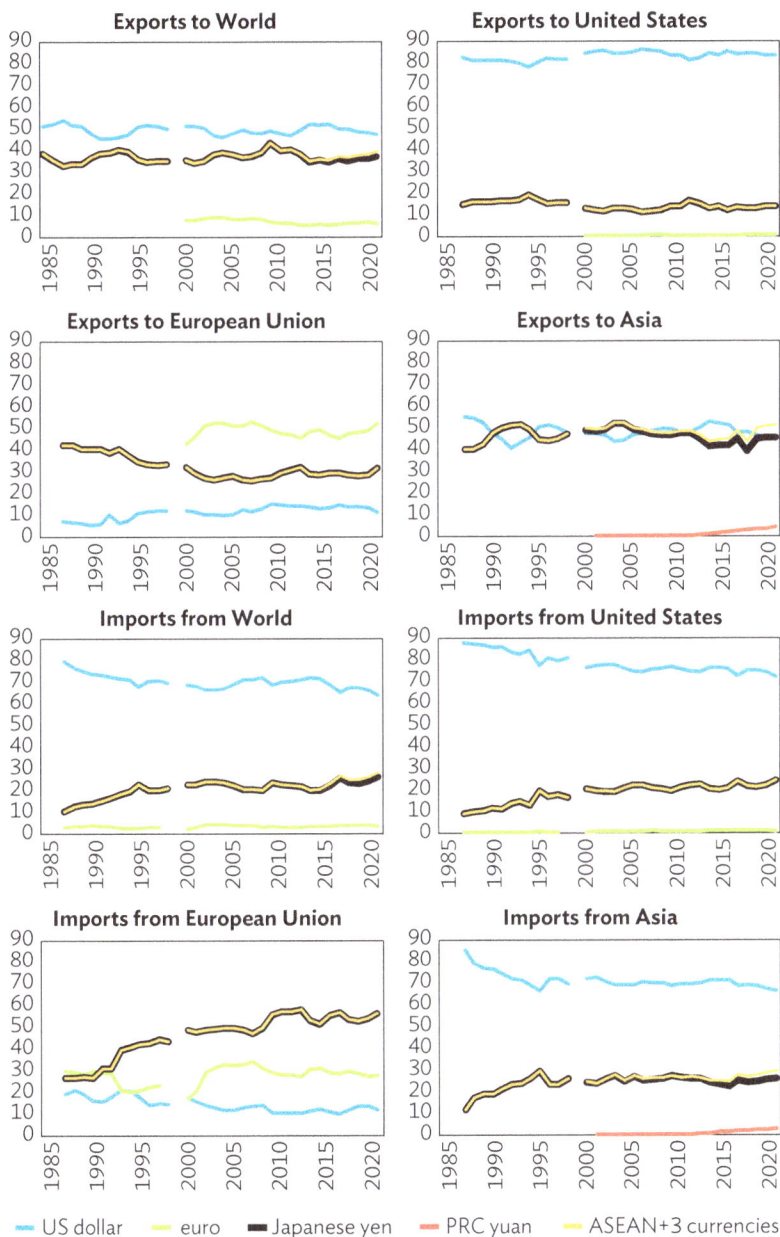

Exports to World

Exports to United States

Exports to European Union

Exports to Asia

Imports from World

Imports from United States

Imports from European Union

Imports from Asia

— US dollar   — euro   ▬ Japanese yen   — PRC yuan   — ASEAN+3 currencies

b. Republic of Korea—Currency shares in trade with different partners
(%)

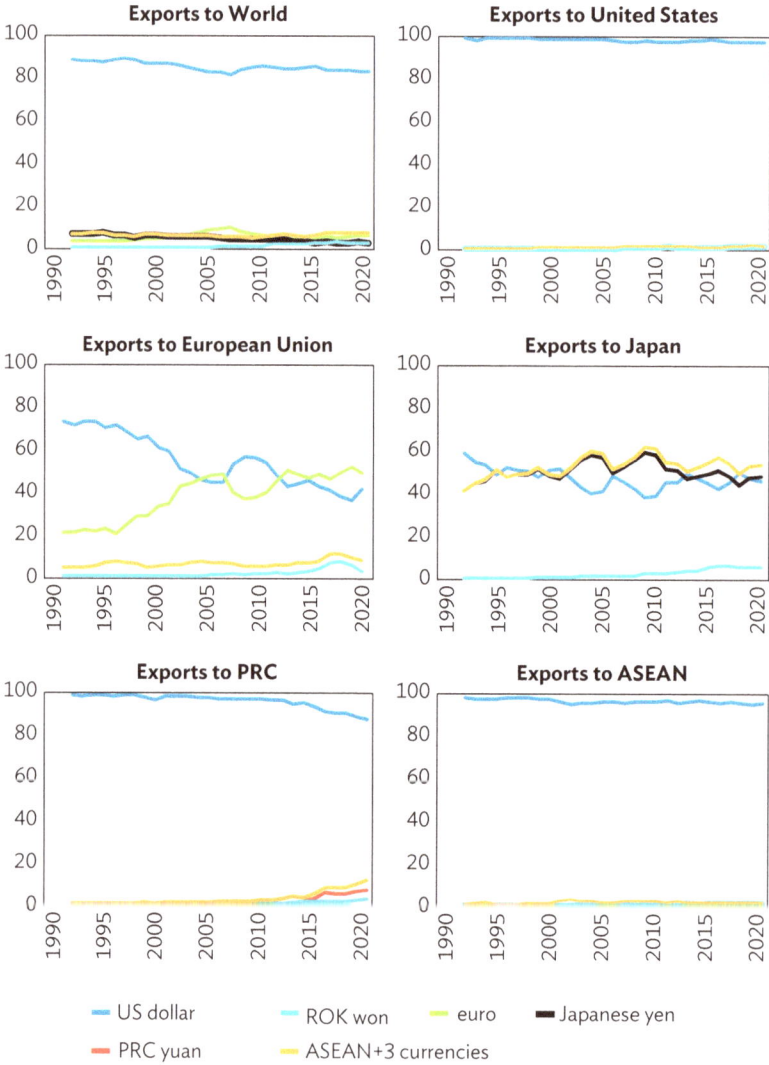

Exports to World

Exports to United States

Exports to European Union

Exports to Japan

Exports to PRC

Exports to ASEAN

━━ US dollar   ━━ ROK won   ━━ euro   ━━ Japanese yen
━━ PRC yuan   ━━ ASEAN+3 currencies

b. Republic of Korea—Currency shares in trade with different partners
(%)

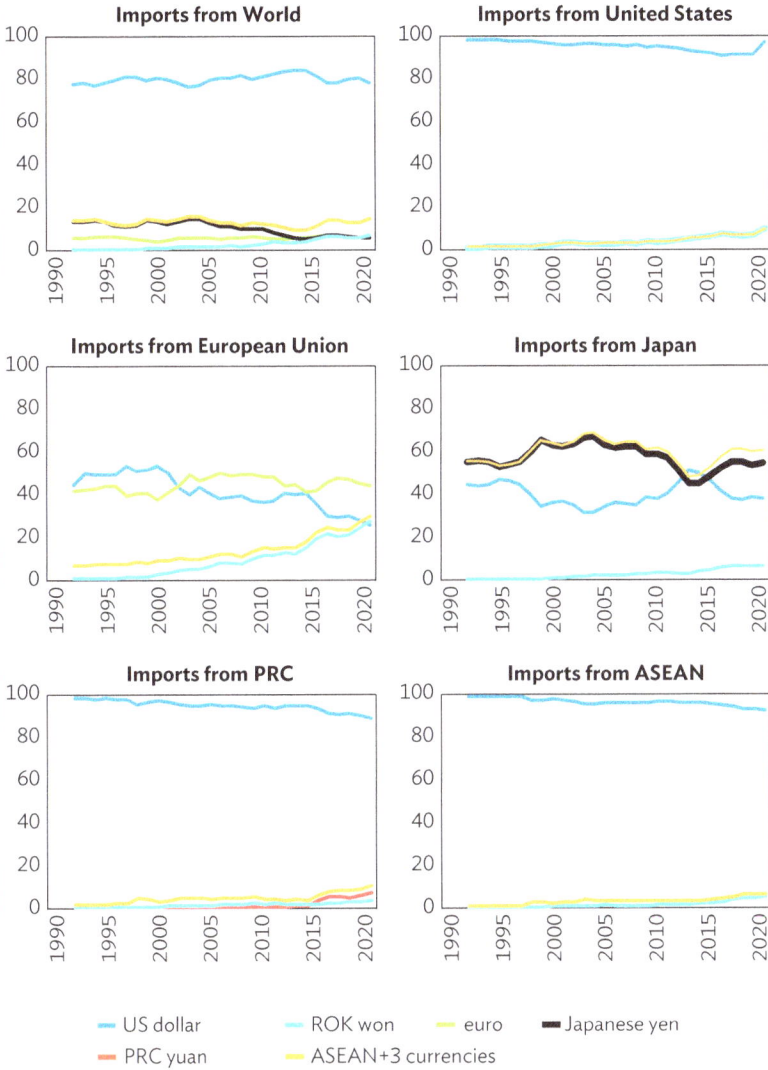

Imports from World

Imports from United States

Imports from European Union

Imports from Japan

Imports from PRC

Imports from ASEAN

Legend:
- US dollar
- ROK won
- euro
- Japanese yen
- PRC yuan
- ASEAN+3 currencies

c. Thailand—Currency shares in trade with different partners
(%)

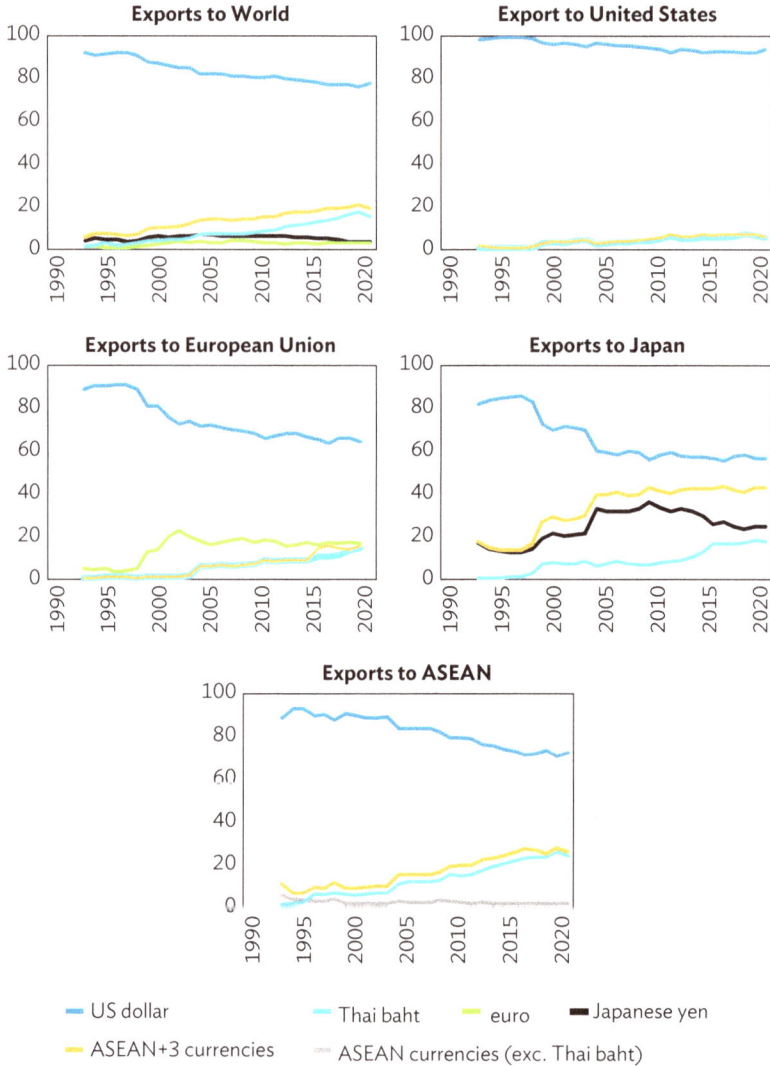

Exports to World

Export to United States

Exports to European Union

Exports to Japan

Exports to ASEAN

Legend:
- US dollar
- Thai baht
- euro
- Japanese yen
- ASEAN+3 currencies
- ASEAN currencies (exc. Thai baht)

c. Thailand—Currency shares in trade with different partners
(%)

Imports from World

Imports from United States

Imports from European Union

Imports from Japan

Imports from ASEAN

Legend:
- US dollar
- Thai baht
- euro
- Japanese yen
- ASEAN+3 currencies
- ASEAN currencies (exc. Thai baht)

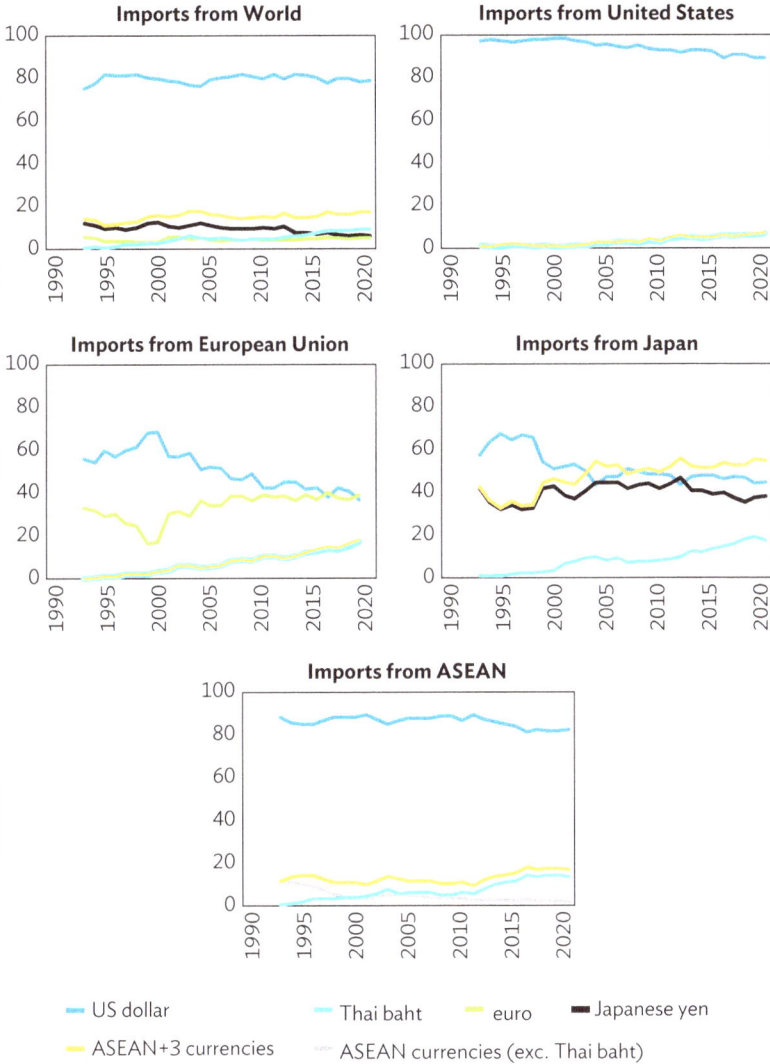

ASEAN+3 = Association of Southeast Asian Nations plus the People's Republic of China, Japan, and the Republic of Korea; PRC = People's Republic of China; ROK = Republic of Korea; US = United States.
Source: Authors, based on Bank of Thailand, Statistics–International Trade (accessed June 2021).

Appendix Figure 3.2: Currency Compositions of Cross-Border Bank Liabilities, ASEAN+3 Economies
(%)

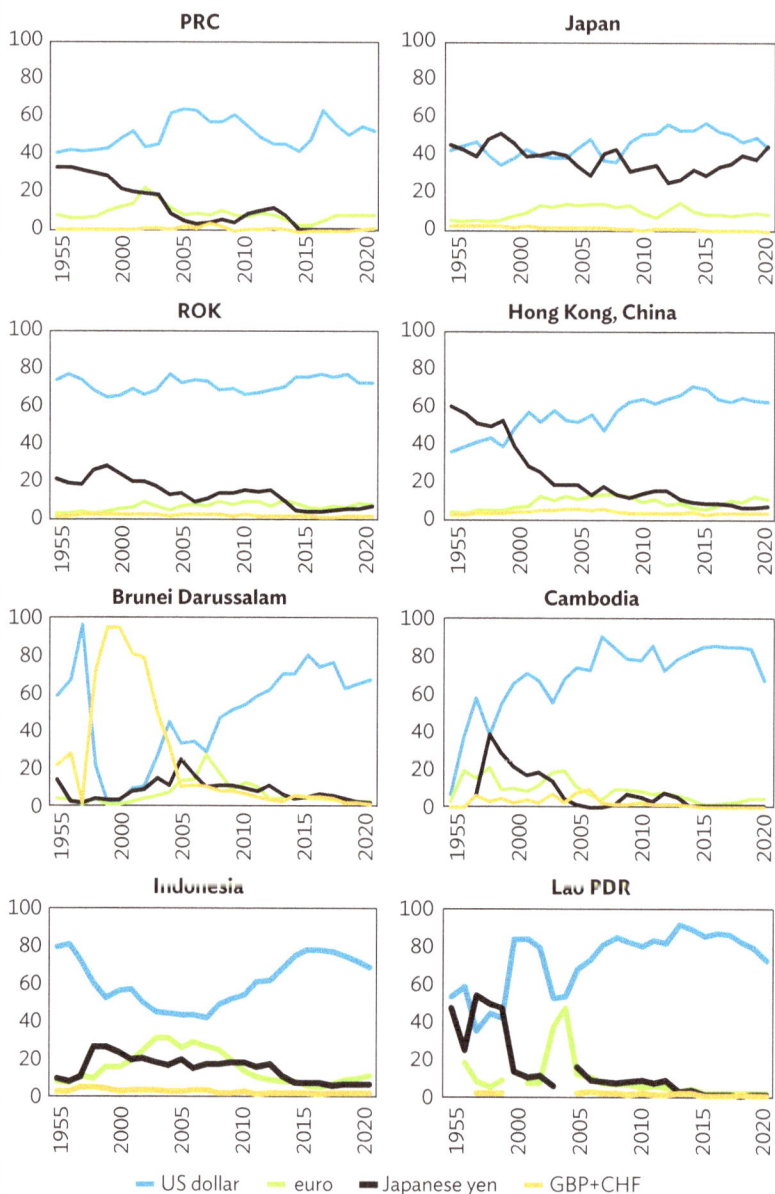

PRC

Japan

ROK

Hong Kong, China

Brunei Darussalam

Cambodia

Indonesia

Lao PDR

— US dollar — euro — Japanese yen — GBP+CHF

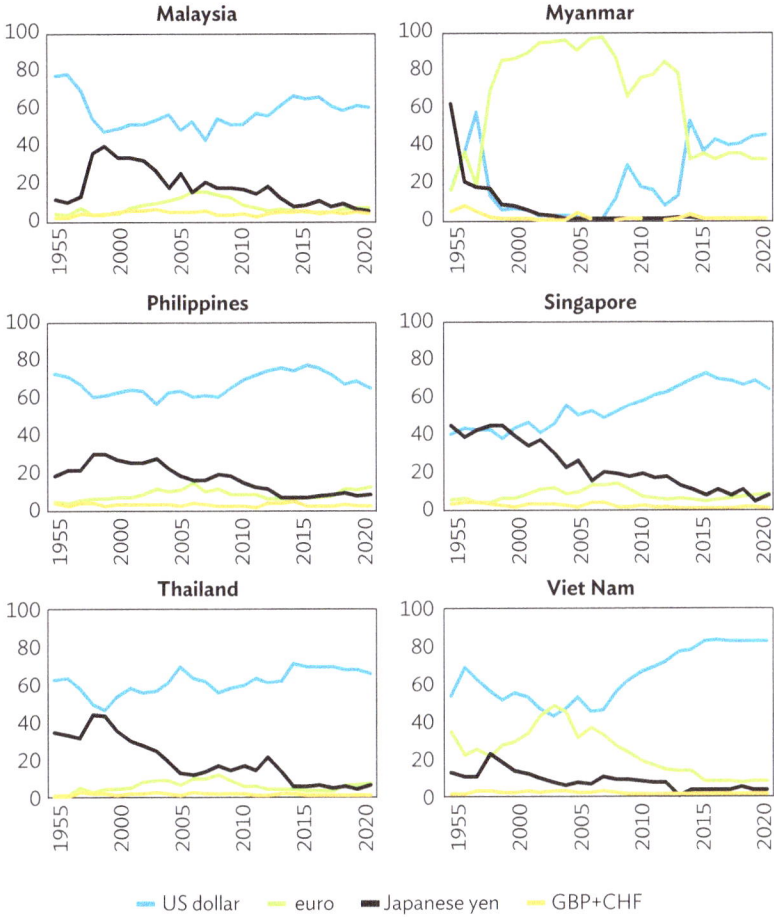

Malaysia

Myanmar

Philippines

Singapore

Thailand

Viet Nam

— US dollar   — euro   ■ Japanese yen   — GBP+CHF

ASEAN+3 = Association of Southeast Asian Nations plus the People's Republic of China, Japan, and the Republic of Korea; CHF = Swiss franc; GBP = United Kingdom pound sterling; Lao PDR = Lao People's Democratic Republic, PRC = People's Republic of China, ROK = Republic of Korea; US = United States.
Source: Authors, based on BIS, *Locational Banking Statistics*, Immediate borrower (accessed August 2021).

Appendix Figure 3.3: Currency Compositions of International Debt Securities Issued by ASEAN+3 Economies, 1980–2020

a. Origin or Jurisdiction (%)

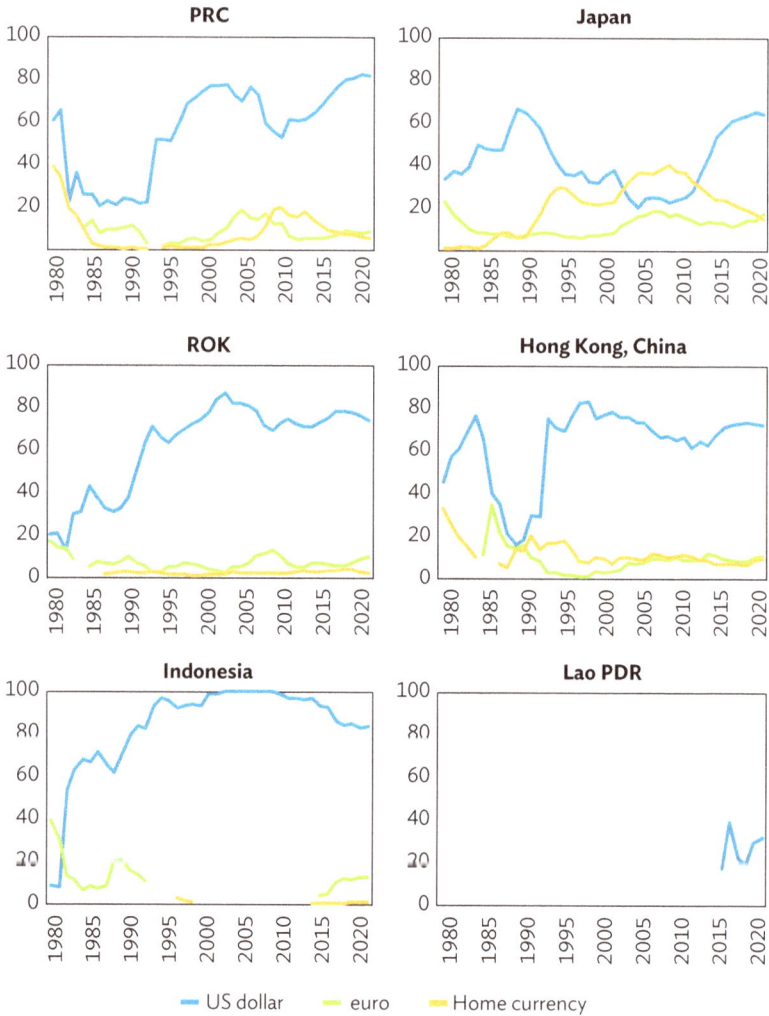

PRC, Japan, ROK, Hong Kong, China, Indonesia, Lao PDR

— US dollar   — euro   — Home currency

a. Origin or Jurisdiction (%)

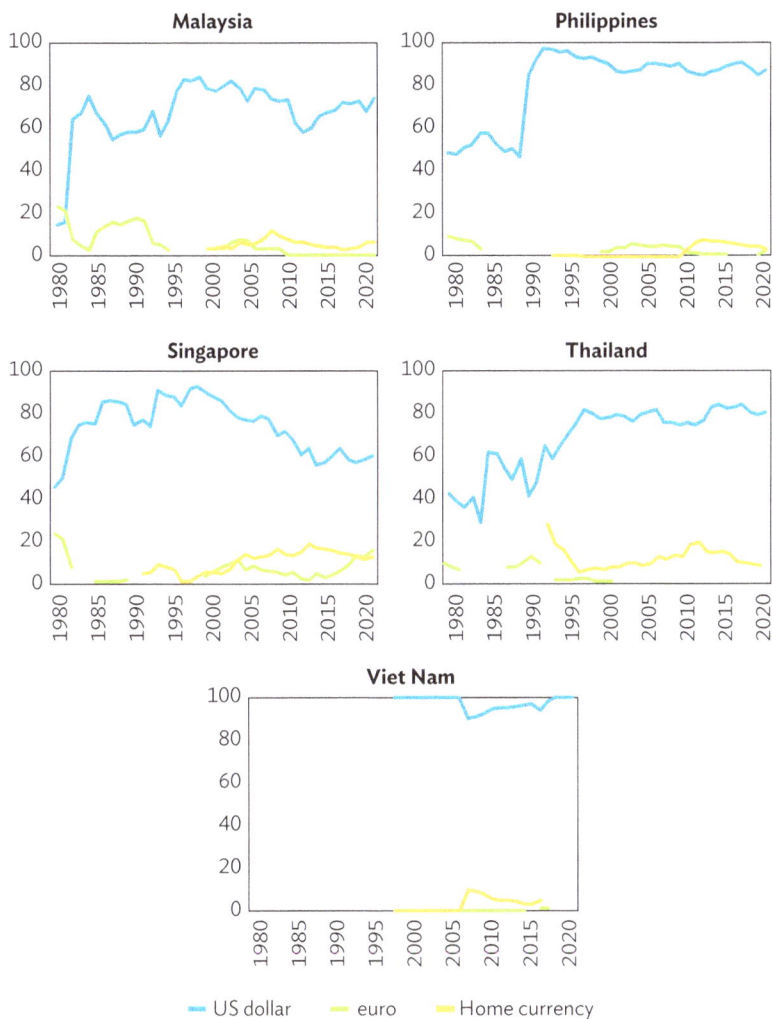

Malaysia

Philippines

Singapore

Thailand

Viet Nam

— US dollar   — euro   — Home currency

b. Residence data

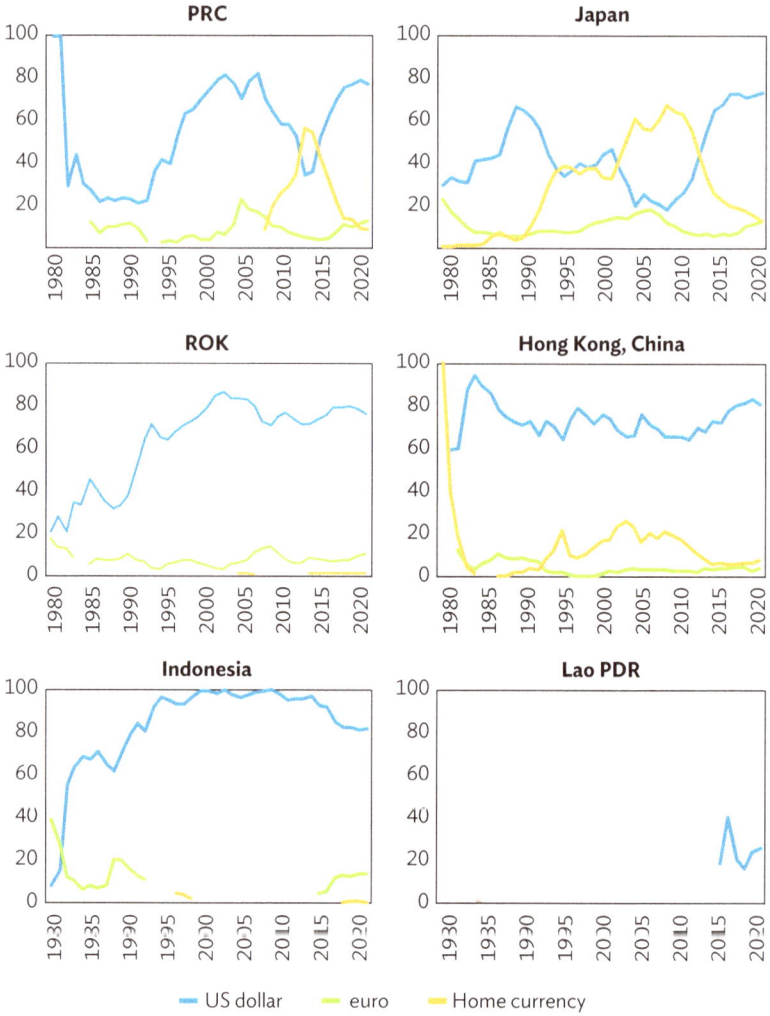

PRC

Japan

ROK

Hong Kong, China

Indonesia

Lao PDR

— US dollar   — euro   — Home currency

b. Residence data

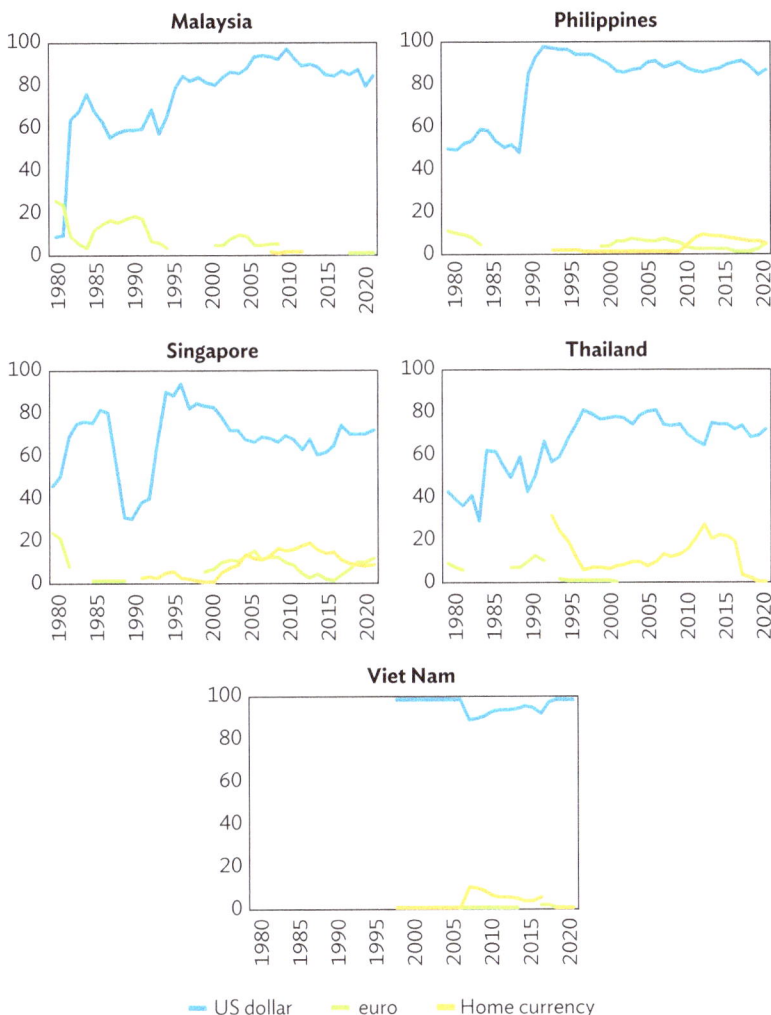

Malaysia

Philippines

Singapore

Thailand

Viet Nam

— US dollar   — euro   — Home currency

Lao PDR = Lao People's Democratic Republic, PRC = People's Republic of China, ROK = Republic of Korea, US = United States.
Note: The origin or jurisdiction data, before the introduction of the euro, refer to the sum of the European Currency Unit and the legacy currencies now included in the euro.
Source: Authors, based on BIS, *Debt Securities Statistics* (accessed June 2021).

4 Fintech in ASEAN+3 and Implications for Financial Inclusion and Financial Stability

Peter Morgan and Bihong Huang

4.1 Introduction

Financial technology (fintech) is a promising tool to promote financial inclusion, that is, to broaden the access of excluded households and small firms to financial products and services. Fintech uses software, applications, and digital platforms to deliver financial services to consumers and businesses through digital devices such as smartphones. Financial inclusion in turn can help promote more inclusive growth by providing the previously unbanked with access to mechanisms for savings, investment, smoothing consumption, and insurance.

In 2010, the Group of Twenty (G20) endorsed the Financial Inclusion Action Plan and established the Global Partnership for Financial Inclusion to coordinate and implement it. The action plan was updated at the 2014 G20 Leaders' Summit in Brisbane. Acknowledging the importance of fintech, the action plan commits to implementing the G20 Principles for Innovative Financial Inclusion under a shared vision of universal access (BIS and WBG 2016).

Among the important challenges, however, significant gaps in financial inclusion and financial literacy separate men and women, urban and rural residents, those with higher and lower incomes, and small and large firms, among others. While digital finance (or alternative finance) has been expected to help reduce such gaps, early adopters tend to be people with higher education, income, and digital financial literacy, and urban dwellers. Thus, even though fintech may promote financial inclusion by making it easier to access financial services, it may also tend to widen gaps in financial access, income, and wealth.

The coronavirus disease (COVID-19) pandemic, meanwhile, has increased demand for fintech services, but also presents greater challenges to financially excluded disadvantaged groups and micro, small, and medium-sized enterprises (MSMEs), which may not have adequate internet access or digital financial literacy.

A second key challenge is the potential threat to financial stability and monetary policy effectiveness. Fintech's promise for financial inclusion can only be realized if the accompanying risks are managed to maintain trust in the system and avoid a build-up of risks that could lead to financial instability. For example, the development of peer-to-peer (P2P) lending could undermine the stability of banks, by reducing both deposits and loans. The development of cryptoassets could lead to destabilizing fund flows outside of the control of traditional instruments of central banks and a loss of information about the actual amount of liquidity in the system, thereby potentially weakening the transmission mechanism and the effectiveness of monetary policy. The development of central bank digital currencies (CBDCs) could also reduce the demand for bank deposits, potentially undermining the stability of banks. The rapid pace of change in the fintech space makes it particularly difficult for authorities to assess and respond to risks (e.g., credit, liquidity) in the financial system. To be sure, the development of alternative finance may well imply a need for longer-term restructuring of the traditional banking sector, with weaker banks dropping out and others accelerating their technological development.

This chapter reviews the development of fintech in the ASEAN+3 region and considers the potential implications for financial inclusion and financial stability. It also examines other fintech-related financial risks, including microfinancial risks, money laundering, terrorist financing, illicit transfers, and risks to consumer and investor protection. In addition, it looks at the implications fintech holds for monetary policy transmission; regulatory challenges associated with the rising adoption of fintech (for fintech firms, bigtech firms, and traditional financial institutions such as banks); and the scope for regional cooperation to address these issues.

The next section describes the overall development of fintech in the ASEAN+3 region. Section 4.3 reviews the current status of financial inclusion in Asia and the contribution of fintech. Section 4.4 examines the implications of COVID-19 for fintech development in the region. Section 4.5 considers the implications of fintech for financial stability, while the section after develops implications of fintech for administrative and regulatory frameworks to ensure financial stability. Section 4.7 does the same for the design of monetary and financial policies. Section 4.8 considers the role of regional cooperation, and the final section summarizes the discussion.

4.2 Development and Current Status of Fintech in Asia

Digital financial services are defined as financial services which rely on digital technologies for their delivery and use by consumers (Pazarbasioglu et al. 2020). Fintech broadly refers to the latest wave of innovations in digital financial services, driven by developments such as smartphones, artificial intelligence (AI), machine learning, and big data. Fintech typically excludes more traditional digital transactions such as those using credit cards or internet banking, although the divide can be somewhat arbitrary.

The Financial Stability Board (FSB) defines fintech as "technologically enabled financial innovation that could result in new business models, applications, processes, or products with an associated material effect on financial markets and institutions and the provision of financial services" (FSB 2017). These functions may be viewed as continuing efforts to reduce financial frictions, such as information asymmetries, incomplete markets, negative externalities, misaligned incentives, network effects, and behavioral distortions (FSB 2017).

The FSB classifies fintech activities into five major categories of financial services:

- Digital payments, clearing and settlement: Electronic money (e-money), mobile phone wallets, digital currencies (including cryptoassets—both unlinked and stablecoins—and CBDCs) remittance services, value transfer networks, digital exchange platforms, etc.

- Deposits, lending and capital raising (alternative finance): Crowdfunding, P2P lending, online balance sheet lending, invoice and supply chain finance, etc.

- Insurance: Insuretech.

- Investment management: Internet banking, online brokers, robo advisors, cryptoasset trading, personal financial management, mobile trading, cryptoassets.

- Market support: Portal and data aggregators, ecosystems, data applications, distributed ledger technology (DLT), security, cloud computing, internet of things/mobile technology, artificial intelligence, and machine learning (FSB 2017).

Financial institutions are investigating the use of DLT for applications such as cross-border interbank payments, credit provision, capital raising, and for digital clearing and settlement. The ability of DLT to transfer and record ownership of digital assets and store information securely and unchangeably is an advantage that reduces information asymmetries. DLT may change the way record keeping, accounting, payment, settlement, and other key aspects of financial markets are carried out. The technology may also increase transparency and reduce counterparty risk. A number of central banks are experimenting with or researching DLT for use in financial market infrastructure. Potential benefits include increased efficiency as a result of improving end-to-end processing speed and enhancing network resilience through distributed data management (IMF 2019). Digital identity verification can also increase information security and lower transaction costs (FSB 2017). Smart contracts may also have wide potential application.

Fintech is also supported by what the FSB refers to as "policy enablers," including digital identification, the promotion of application program interfaces (widely known as APIs) to support open banking, data protection and cybersecurity, and innovation facilitators (Ehrentraud et al. 2020). All these add up to a complex and rapidly changing ecosystem.

Moreover, an analysis of fintech cannot ignore the implications of so-called bigtech firms. Bigtech refers to large globally active technology firms with a relative advantage in digital technology, such as Apple, Facebook, Google, Ant Financial, and Tencent. Bigtech firms typically provide internet-based services (search engines, social networks, e-commerce, etc.) and/or IT platforms or supply infrastructure services such as data storage and processing capabilities which other firms can use to provide products or services (BCBS 2018). Bigtech firms can rapidly gain a large world market share when launching a new financial product or service. These firms can also affect markets given the size of their operations and their investment capacity. Many banks, financial institutions, and fintech firms are partnering with bigtech firms, which then become important third-party providers of financial services, i.e., subcontractors of specific services to financial institutions. Therefore, it will become important to properly monitor and assess their concentration risk, since they could become systemically important (BCBS 2018).

The focus of this chapter is on issues related to the development of the two major segments of the fintech industry most likely to significantly impact financial inclusion and financial stability and that are most relevant for regional cooperation in ASEAN+3. These are payments, clearing and settlement and deposits, as well as lending and capital raising (alternative finance).

Digital Payments, Clearing, and Settlement

Digital payment systems encompass digital payments and clearing and settlement mechanisms, and comprise the largest share of fintech activity by transaction value. There is no standard definition of digital (or electronic) payments, but they generally refer to "… transfers of value which are initiated and/or received using electronic devices and channels to transmit the instructions" (Better than Cash Alliance 2020). This definition notwithstanding most discussions of digital payments typically exclude the following more traditional kinds of payments, since they represent an earlier stage of development of payment services:

- Conventional credit card payments using a merchant's point-of-sale (POS) terminal.
- Bank transfers, even if done via the internet or ATMs.

Among other methods, such payments can be made through electronic money (e-money), "… an electronic store of monetary value on a technical device that may be widely used for making payments to entities other than the e-money issuer. The device acts as a prepaid bearer instrument which does not necessarily involve bank accounts in transactions" (ECB 2021). E-money can be classified as either hardware or software. The former includes things such as stored-value cards (PASMO or Suica) and the latter includes e-wallets (or digital wallets)—that is, a software system that securely stores users' payment information and passwords for numerous payment methods and websites.

This section focuses on the segments most relevant for issues related to financial inclusion and financial stability: digital payments, including mobile money, wallets, and P2P payments; digital remittances; and digital currencies including private cryptoassets and CBDCs.

Digital payments

The digital payments market segment is led by consumer transactions and "… includes payments for products and services which are made over the Internet as well as mobile payments at point-of-sale via smartphone applications," as defined by Statista. Not included in this segment are transactions between businesses (business-to-business payments), bank transfers initiated online (not in connection with products and services purchased online), and payment transactions at the point of sale where mobile card readers (terminals) are used (Statista 2020a).

Digital payments comprise two major subcategories: mobile POS payments and digital commerce. Mobile money (a payment system which does not require bank accounts and instead relies on agent-banking outlets) represents a third category of digital payments not included in the Statista definition, since it does not necessarily involve either POS transactions or Internet-based transactions.

It is difficult to find comparative figures for fintech-related and conventional payment transaction volumes, although Chaudhuri et al. (2020) provide the ranges for advanced and emerging Asian economies (Table 4.1). Cash is still king in most countries, but its role is declining. What are called "digital" transactions here include mobile money and mobile payments, so these range from 5% to 35% of the total for advanced economies and from 5% to 55% for emerging economies.

Table 4.1: Comparison of Fintech and Conventional Payments in Asia
(% of total)

	Advanced Economies	Emerging Asia
Consumer	100	100
Cash	40–95	40–95
Credit cards	≤25	<5
Digital transactions	5–35	5–55
Retail merchants	100	100
E-commerce	≤20	≤20
Others	≥80	≥80

Note: Advanced economies include Hong Kong, China; Japan; the Republic of Korea; Singapore; and Taipei,China. Emerging Asia includes the People's Republic of China, Indonesia, Malaysia, Thailand, and other economies.
Source: Authors based on Chaudhuri et al. (2020).

Mobile POS payments: The mobile POS payments segment includes transactions at POS terminals processed via smartphone applications (so-called mobile wallets). Well-known providers of mobile wallets include ApplePay, Google Wallet, and Samsung Pay. Payments are made by a contactless interaction of the smartphone app with a suitable payment terminal. The data transfer can be made using wireless standard near-field communication or by scanning a quick response (QR) code. A buyer pays via a mobile wallet by making an online bank transfer or by using a digitally stored credit or debit card.

Digital commerce: This covers all consumer transactions made online for products and services. Online transactions can be settled via various payment methods (credit cards, direct debit, invoice, or online payment providers such as PayPal and AliPay). The category includes more than just fintech-related payments, but there are no data on the breakdown between fintech-related payments and others.

Table 4.2 shows the estimated value of these transactions for selected countries. Figure 4.1 shows the recent trend of total digital payments and their projection through 2024. Total transaction value in digital payments is projected to reach close to $2.5 trillion in 2020. The market's larger segment is digital commerce, with projected total transaction value of about $1.6 trillion. Total transaction value is expected to grow 16.3% annually and thus to reach almost $4.5 trillion by 2024. Mobile POS payments are projected to grow 27.5% and digital commerce 8.8% in the same period. Transaction value is highest in the People's Republic of China (PRC) ($1.9 trillion) (Statista 2020a).

Digital commerce is clearly a more mature segment than mobile POS payments.

Table 4.2: Value of Digital Payments Transactions, 2020 Estimated
($ billion)

	Mobile POS	Digital Commerce	Total
PRC	755.5	1,165.0	1,920.5
Japan	...	...	165.2
Korea, Rep. of	...	...	113.5

... = not available, PRC = People's Republic of China, POS = point of sale.
Source: Statista (2020a).

Figure 4.1: Growth of Digital Payments Transaction Value in Asia
($ trillion)

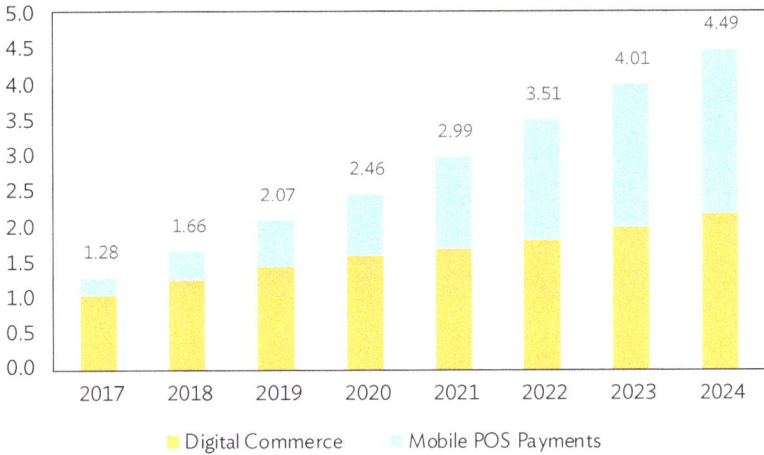

POS = point of sale.
Note: Asia includes Bangladesh, Bhutan, Brunei Darussalam, Cambodia, the People's Republic of China, Indonesia, Japan, Kazakhstan, the Kyrgyz Republic, the Lao People's Democratic Republic, Malaysia, Mongolia, Nepal, Pakistan, the Philippines, the Republic of Korea, Singapore, Sri Lanka, Tajikistan, Thailand, Timor-Leste, Turkmenistan, Uzbekistan, Viet Nam, and other economies. Users refer to active paying accounts. Penetration rate refers to the ratio of active paying accounts to population.
Source: Statista (2020a).

In 2019, total users of mobile POS transactions were estimated at 693 million and digital commerce users at 1.93 billion. Figure 4.2 shows the development of users of digital payments in Asia, including projections through 2024. The penetration rate of digital commerce in 2019 was 44.2% and is projected to hit 64.3% by 2024.

Figure 4.3 shows the share of mobile transactions in payments in stores in some ASEAN+3 countries. The PRC has by far the largest share, at 86%, followed by Thailand and Viet Nam. Indonesia, Malaysia, Singapore, and the Philippines all have shares in the 40% range.

Figure 4.4 shows the penetration of users of the two main providers of digital payments services in the PRC—Alipay and WeChat. These bigtech firms seem to have gained access to almost all adult users in the PRC.

Figure 4.2: Penetration Rate of Users of Digital Payments in Asia
(%)

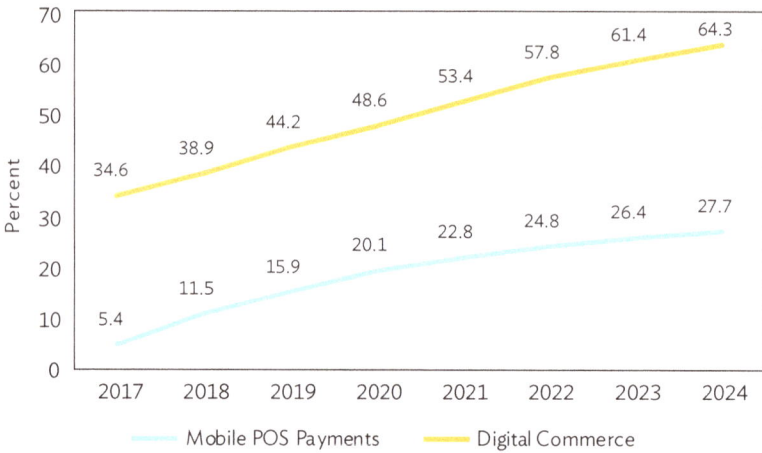

POS = point of sale.
Note: Asia includes Bangladesh, Bhutan, Brunei Darussalam, Cambodia, the People's Republic of China, Indonesia, Japan, Kazakhstan, the Kyrgyz Republic, the Lao People's Democratic Republic, Malaysia, Mongolia, Nepal, Pakistan, the Philippines, the Republic of Korea, Singapore, Sri Lanka, Tajikistan, Thailand, Timor-Leste, Turkmenistan, Uzbekistan, Viet Nam, and other economies. Users refer to active paying accounts. Penetration rate refers to the ratio of active paying accounts to population.
Source: Statista (2020a).

Figure 4.3: Share of Consumers Using Mobile Payments, 2019
(% share)

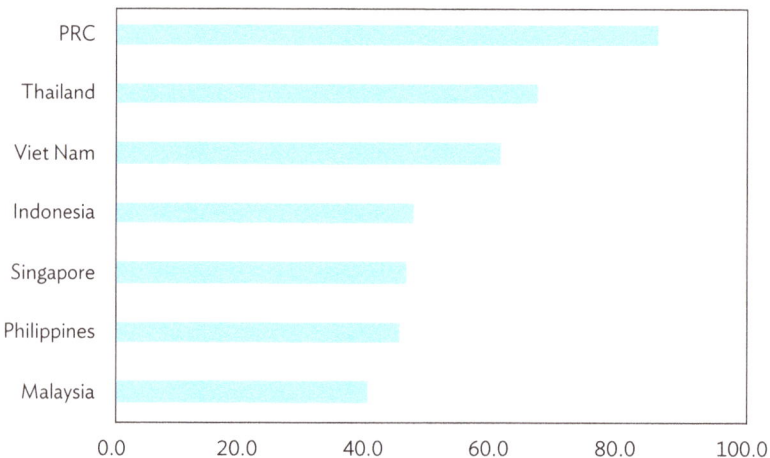

PRC = People's Republic of China.
Source: PwC Global Consumer Insights Survey (PwC 2019).

**Figure 4.4: Penetration of Users of Digital Payments
in the People's Republic of China**
(million)

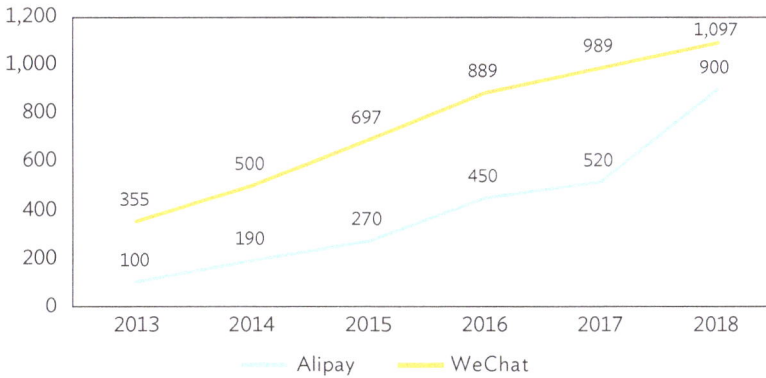

Note: Users refer to individuals who have used digital payments.
Source: Klein (2019).

Mobile money: This is also a subcategory of digital payments, but is separate from mobile POS and digital commerce, and hence is not counted in the Statista statistics given above. The GSM Association (GSMA) (2020) defines a mobile money service by the following characteristics:[1]

- It includes transferring money and making and receiving payments using a mobile phone.

- It must be available to the unbanked, i.e., people who do not have access to a formal account at a financial institution.

- It must offer a network of physical transaction points which can include agents, outside of bank branches and ATMs that make the service widely accessible. The agents enable cash to be added to or withdrawn from an individual's e-wallet without requiring a bank deposit, i.e., a "cash-in, cash-out" service. This makes it available to the unbanked.

The GSMA definition of mobile money excludes the following:

- Mobile banking or payment services that offer the mobile phone as just another channel to access a traditional banking product.

- Payment services linked to a traditional banking product or credit card.

---

[1] The GSMA represents more than 750 mobile operators with almost 400 related companies, including handset and device makers, software companies, equipment providers, and internet companies, as well as organizations in adjacent industry sectors. See gsma.com.

In other words, the definition excludes more conventional payment services linked directly to bank accounts or credit cards. Since the mobile POS and digital commerce services described above typically have some link to a bank account or credit card, they are not included in this definition.

Mobile money transactions have significant advantages over other channels.

(i)   First, they reduce variable costs considerably by taking advantage of the fixed costs of the mobile network already in place. As a result, even low-value and low-volume transactions can be profitable, unlike transactions through conventional banking channels.

(ii) Second, mobile money relies on an agent network, which is much less costly than a bank branch network.

(iii) Third, if accompanied by appropriate risk-based regulations that exempt clients with a smaller number and size of transactions from cumbersome documentation requirements, large parts of the population in the informal economy can have access to such payments. (Beck 2020).

Total mobile payments amounted to $68.1 billion in 2019, with somewhat over one-third in East Asia and the Pacific and somewhat below two-thirds in South Asia. The overall average compound growth rate since 2016 was 36%, and the growth rate in East Asia (53%) and the Pacific (28%) was considerably faster than in South Asia. P2P payments dominate, making up half of the total overall, followed by cash-in and cash-out, respectively, which are probably mostly related to P2P payments. The shares for other categories are relatively small—merchant payments make up only 2.6% of the total and international remittances only 0.4%, which suggests that the potential for these transactions remains largely unexploited, especially in South Asia (GSMA 2020).

The number of active accounts (used within the last 90 days before the survey) reached 151.2 million in East Asia, the Pacific, and South Asia by December 2019, almost a ninefold increase relative to the end of 2014. The number of agent outlets in East Asia, the Pacific, and South Asia has tripled over the past 5 years, and the number of mobile money agents is seven times that of ATMs and 20 times bank branches (GSMA 2020). Total active agents in East Asia, the Pacific, and South Asia reached 2.15 million in December 2019, up by 4.5% from the previous year.

It is interesting that, as part of the shift from in-kind payments to cash transfers, humanitarian organizations are increasingly using digital transactions. Since 2017, mobile money platforms have been used to deliver money and voucher assistance in at least 44 countries—almost half of all countries with a live mobile money service. As a result, the mobile money industry has been able deliver financial assistance to over 2.7 million accounts used by people affected by various crises (GSMA 2020).

Remittances and international money transfers

The World Bank estimates that inward remittances and international money transfers from migrants in ASEAN+3 in 2019 totaled $158 billion, about 21% of global inflows, growing at a compound rate of 6.1% over the previous decade.[2] However, it is estimated to have fallen about 7% in 2020 due to the pandemic. Four countries accounted for most of the ASEAN+3 total in 2019, including the PRC (43%), the Philippines (22%), Viet Nam (11%), and Indonesia (7.4%).

The great bulk of these transfers are still made via traditional routes such as Western Union, but digital transactions are growing rapidly. Digital remittances can be accomplished using a web browser or an app, combined with the use of a mobile phone, tablet, or computer; and a digital funding mechanism. Digital remittances can be funded through various means, including bank accounts, cryptoassets, and mobile money. Growth of digital remittances has been boosted by the entry of digital-first money transfer organizations, and the established of these have responded by rapidly introducing digital initiation and funding capacities in response (VEEI 2021). The emergence of digital-first money transfer organization has helped substantially reduce transfer costs, making them more affordable.

According to Statista (2020a), total digital remittances in 2019 reached $73.9 billion, or about 11.1% of total global remittances, and the total number of users reached 7.1 million. Applying the same share figure to total Asian remittances would imply a value of total digital remittances of $34.8 billion. Digital remittances are projected to grow an average of 14%, over twice the rate of overall remittances, so the share will gradually increase.

[2]   World Bank Annual Remittances Data (updated as of October 2020). Migration and Remittances Data. Washington, DC: World Bank. https://www.worldbank.org/en/topic/migrationremittancesdiasporaissues/ brief/migration-remittances-data (accessed April 2021).

Digital currencies

According to the Bank for International Settlements (BIS) (2018b) a digital currency is an asset that only exists electronically and can be used as a currency (means of payment, store of value, unit of account) although it is not legal tender.[3] Digital currencies sometimes use distributed ledger technology (DLT) systems to record and verify transactions made using the digital currency. These include private currencies and digital versions of national bank currencies. Digital currencies that use cryptographic techniques to verify transactions are called "cryptocurrencies" or "cryptoassets".[4] Digital currencies issued as liabilities of central banks are called central bank digital currencies (CBDCs) and are legal tender.

Cryptoassets: Cryptoassets such as Bitcoin enable transfers and payments to be made without using banks, instead of using public DLT. Currently, there are about 9,200 cryptoassets with a total market capitalization of around $2.06 trillion as of 12 April 2021.[5] This compares, for example, with the value of the US dollar monetary base of about $6 trillion. However, widespread adoption of cryptoassets for purchases and transfers, rather than speculation, has been limited by various factors, including price volatility, regulatory concerns due to transaction anonymity—raising anti-money laundering/counterterrorist financing (AML/CFT) issues—and lack of scalability (BCBS 2018). Scalability refers to the ability to greatly increase the volume of transactions that can be processed in real time. Stablecoins such as Tether and the Diem project, whose values are linked to those of national currencies, may overcome the issue of price volatility and potentially compete more with fiat currencies, although scalability may still be an issue, as discussed in section 6.

Central bank digital currencies: Many central banks are actively researching the potential development of CBDCs, although actual implementation is still rare. Proponents of CBDCs claim that they can lower costs, expand financial inclusion, increase the efficiency of monetary policy implementation, counter competition from private digital currencies, ensure competition and contestability of the payment market, and offer a risk-free payment

---

3   The last part of the definition seems to be out of date, since CBDCs are digital currencies but presumably are legal tender.

4   The terms cryptocurrencies and cryptoassets are used interchangeably by institutions such as the FSB and the BIS. However, G20 documents refer to them as cryptoassets, so that terminology is adopted here.

5   Coinmarketcap. All Cryptocurrencies Database (accessed April 2021). https://coinmarketcap.com/all/views/all/.

instrument to the public (IMF 2019, BIS 2021). CBDC proposals are of three types:

- Account-based CBDC targeting the general public.
- Value-based or digital-token-based CBDC targeting the general public.
- CBDC based on DLT targeting financial institutions (Shirai 2020).

In some advanced economies such as Sweden, the declining use of cash and the potential to have negative interest rates have motivated the study of CBDC as an alternative, robust, and convenient payment method. A CBDC could increase contestability of the payment market, thus reducing the risk of a few large private payment providers dominating the market. In developing countries, the focus is more on improving operational and cost efficiency. In countries with underdeveloped financial systems and a large portion of unbanked citizens, a CBDC is viewed as way to increase financial inclusion and support digitalization (IMF 2019, BIS 2021).

CBDCs can have varying degrees of anonymity in transactions. A non-anonymous CBDC could make the monitoring of transactions easier. Many central banks seem to favor a hybrid approach that allows the authorities to trace large-value transactions, which are more important for detecting tax avoidance, money laundering, terrorist financing, and other illicit purposes, while small transactions remain anonymous. Several central banks are focusing research on a two-pronged approach with anonymous tokens for small holdings/transactions, and traceable currency for large ones (IMF 2019).

A CBDC can have features similar to cash or deposits, and can be interest-bearing. A CBDC that closely competes with deposits would tend to lower bank credit and output, while a cash-like CBDC could lead to the disappearance of cash. Therefore, the optimal CBDC design balance would maintain bank intermediation while keeping a diverse portfolio of payment instruments. When network effects matter, i.e., an increase in the number of users of a service increases the convenience of that service, an interest-bearing CBDC could alleviate the central bank's concern about the potential disappearance of cash by increasing the distinction of the CBDC from cash (Agur, Ari, and Dell'Ariccia 2019). However, these trade-offs may be lessened by having a two-tier system where banks or other financial institutions distribute the CBDCs to individuals or firms.

Central banks in ASEAN+3 are exploring the potential use of CBDCs (Table 4.3). The People's Bank of China (PBOC) is one of the most active in developing a retail CBDC. The PRC's version of a sovereign digital currency—the so-called Digital Currency Electronic Payment —has been managed by the PBOC since 2014 under a centralized system and does not use blockchain technology. The PBOC has been conducting tests involving its Digital Currency Electronic Payment system in four cities— Suzhou, Xiongan, Shenzhen, and Chengdu, at 20 private firms, as well as at sites for the 2022 Beijing Winter Olympics. PBOC governor Yi Gang said in May 2020 that the PRC had "basically completed" the top-level design, standard setting, research on functions, and integration tests of the digital yuan (PBOC 2020). State media reported in August 2020 that major state-owned banks were conducting large-scale internal testing of a digital wallet application, moving closer toward the official launch of a CBDC.[6] According to Huang (2020), the PBOC's planned digital currency is a coupled hybrid of digital currency and electronic payment, issued by the central bank, but operated and exchanged by authorized operators. This makes it a two-tier system, where the central bank does not directly interact with the public. This structure would help avoid competition with private financial institutions, and thus limit the risk of financial disintermediation. Notably it is token-based, and therefore does not require a link to a bank account. This would make it accessible to foreigners as well as Chinese residents.

The National Bank of Cambodia became the first central bank in Asia to implement such a system with the launch of its blockchain-powered payment system, named Project Bakong, in October 2020. The P2P payment system runs on top of the Hyperledger Iroha blockchain designed by the Japanese technology company Soramitsu. Unlike many CBDC prototypes, it does not involve the exchange of central-bank-backed tokens, but is based on fiat currencies and supports transactions in both Cambodian riel and US dollar. This quasi-central bank digital currency is similar to m-Pesa developed in Kenya, and the goals are to reduce money transfer costs and increase financial inclusion. Bakong connects all financial institutions and payment service providers under a single payment platform which allows for fund transfers to be processed on real-time basis without the need of a centralized clearing house (NBC 2020).

---

[6]   See the report by Reuters at https://es.reuters.com/article/marketsNews/idUSL4N2F80SA for more information.

Table 4.3: Research and Development in ASEAN+3 Related to Central Bank Digital Currency

Country/ Project Name	Characteristics	Progress
Cambodia Project Bakong	Retail two-tier issuance; blockchain based system, but using Cambodian riel and US dollars, so technically not CBDC	Implemented 2020
PRC Digital Currency Electronic Payment	Retail two-tier-tier issuance; Hybrid (central and DLT payment network)	Conducting tests in Suzhou, Xiongan, Shenzhen, and Chengdu; "top-level design" basically completed
Japan Project Stella	No plans to issue CBDC, but research focuses on implications of DLT for financial market infrastructure	Experiments; Phase 4 explores how confidentiality and auditability could be balanced in a DLT environment; CBDC experiments to start Spring 2021
Korea, Rep. of	No plans to issue CBDC, but conducting mock tests of DLT-based interbank payment and settlement systems	Experiments
Hong Kong, China	Studying retail CBDC together with the BIS; studying local use of e-CNY; participating in the mCBDC Bridge wholesale CBDC project with the PRC, Thailand, and the United Arab Emirates	Study stage
Singapore Project Ubin	Wholesale, a collaborative project with the industry to explore the use of blockchain and DLT for clearing and settlement of payments and securities	Experiments, 5 phases of project completed in July 2020
Thailand Project Inthanon	Proof-of-concept for wholesale CBDC for interbank and cross-border settlements; also prototype development project for CBDC for business	Experiments

CBDC = central bank digital currency, CNY = Chinese yuan, DLT = distributed ledger technology, PRC = People's Republic of China, US = United States.
Source: Bank of Japan and European Central Bank (2020), Bank of Thailand (2021), Huang (2020), Kishi (2019), Monetary Authority of Singapore (2020a), Shirai (2019), and Supadulya et al. (2019).

The Monetary Authority of Singapore (MAS) in November 2016 embarked on the collaborative Project Ubin with the financial industry to explore the use of DLT for clearing and settlement of payments and securities. The project aims to help the MAS and the industry better understand the technology and the potential benefits it may bring (FSB 2017). In December 2016, the Bank of Japan and the European Central bank launched a joint research project on DLT and jointly studied the use of DLT for financial market infrastructure. The Bank of Korea and the Bank of Thailand have also been conducting research projects.

However, none besides the PBOC has announced plans to set up a CBDC, much less a retail CBDC. A number of reasons have been cited for the PBOC's rapid move toward adoption of retail CBDC, including the intention to promote financial inclusion (Huang 2020). It may also have been prompted by concerns about the dominance of the two main private payment systems and their resulting accumulation of transaction-related information and the potential spread of private stablecoins such as Facebook's Diem, which could constrain internationalization of the yuan.

Alternative Finance: Crowdfunding, P2P Lending, and Online Balance Sheet Lending

After digital payments, alternative finance is the second largest fintech segment providing financial access for households and small firms. Table 4.4 shows the development of an online alternative finance market in ASEAN+3 based on the survey data reported by the Cambridge Centre for Alternative Finance (CCAF 2020, 2021); and CCAF, the Academy of Internet Finance at Zhejiang University, and the Asian Development Bank Institute (ADBI, CCAF, and AIFZU 2018). It shows a boom-and-bust pattern of online alternative finance markets and the dominance of the PRC market in the region until 2019. The PRC market rapidly grew from 2013 to 2017 but then plummeted by over 99% by 2019 as a result of tighter regulation of the P2P lending sector. A similar trend can be seen in the total market volume of ASEAN+3. By 2020, total volume of the region dropped about 98% from the peak in 2017 due to the PRC market drop. In contrast, market volume in Japan, the Republic of Korea, and Southeast Asian economies has continued to increase, although erratically in some cases. Most growth of the ASEAN market was contributed by Indonesia, which reached almost $1.45 billion in 2018 compared to only $80.00 million in 2017, although it has been flat since then.

Table 4.4: Online Alternative Finance Market Value
and Development of ASEAN+3
($ million)

Year	PRC Value	Growth (%)	Japan Value	Growth (%)	Korea, Rep. of Value	Growth (%)	ASEAN Value	Growth (%)	ASEAN+3 Value	Growth (%)
2013	5,560	...	87	...	2	...	11	...	5,660	...
2014	24,240	336.0	115	32.5	2	13.7	26	141.4	24,384	330.8
2015	102,000	320.8	351	205.6	40	1,642.7	47	76.2	102,438	320.1
2016	243,000	138.2	398	13.5	376	830.8	216	362.9	243,991	138.2
2017	358,000	47.3	349	-12.5	1,130	200.3	325	50.4	359,803	47.5
2018	215,400	-39.8	1,069	206.6	753	-33.4	2,190	574.2	219,412	-39.0
2019	84,346	-60.8	599	-44.0	1,605	113.1	2,271	3.7	88,820	-59.5
2020	1,161	-98.6	1,141	90.6	1,304	-18.8	2,705	19.1	6,310	-92.9

PRC = Peoples' Republic of China.
Note: Online alternative finance includes P2P lending, balance sheet lending, invoice trading, securities, crowdfunding, profit sharing, and others. The ASEAN economies included in the aggregation exclude Brunei Darussalam and the Lao People's Democratic Republic.
Source: CCAF (2020); and CCAF, AIFZU, and ADBI (2018), Global Alternative Finance Benchmarks Database (accessed July 2021).

Within alternative finance, lending, and crowdfunding are the two major segments. Table 4.5 breaks down the lending and crowdfunding segments in total volume of business in 2020. Lending is by far the largest segment in both Asia and the Pacific (excluding the PRC) and the PRC, dominated by P2P lending. Within crowdfunding, P2P consumer lending is the largest category in both the Asia and the Pacific (excluding PRC) and the PRC. Invoice trading is a separate and relatively small segment. Alternative lending in the PRC has shrunk dramatically since 2017 as a result of tighter regulation of the sector and the exit of many platforms. The clampdown attempted to bring order to what previously had been a very lightly regulated sector and to weed out unethical and fraudulent practices such as investor guarantees by platforms and thefts of investor funds by platform operators.

Table 4.5: Total Transaction Value of Major Alternative Finance Segments in Asia and the Pacific, 2020

Model	Definition	Transaction Volume ($ million)	
		Asia and the Pacific ex-PRC	PRC
Marketplace/P2P consumer lending	Individuals or institutional funders provide a loan to a consumer borrower.	2,363.6	7.0
Marketplace/P2P Business Lending	Individuals or institutional funders provide a loan to a business borrower.	1,819.7	0.3
Marketplace/P2P property lending	Individuals or institutional funders provide a loan for a property of a consumer or business borrower.	541.8	0.0
Balance sheet business lending	The platform entity provides a loan directly to a business borrower using its own balance sheet.	2,266.5	1,132.0
Lending subtotal		**6,991.6**	**1,139.3**
Revenue sharing/ profit sharing, crowdfunding	Individuals or institutions purchase securities from a company, such as shares or bonds, and share in the profits or royalties of the business.	51.5	0.0
Real estate crowdfunding	Individuals or institutional funders provide equity or subordinated-debt financing for real estate.	351.8	0.0
Equity-based crowdfunding	Individuals or institutional funders purchase equity issued by a company.	333.5	0.0
Other crowdfunding		938.6	8.3
Crowdfunding subtotal		**1,675.4**	**8.3**
Invoice trading	Individuals or institutional funders purchase invoices or receivable notes from a business at a discount.	241.8	13.5
Total alternative finance		**8,908.8**	**1,161.1**

P2P = peer-to-peer, PRC = People's Republic of China.
Note: Asia and the Pacific here includes economies in East Asia, Southeast Asia, South Asia, Central Asia, and Oceania, consistent with the Asian Development Bank's country groupings, excluding the PRC.
Source: CCAF, AIFZU, and ADBI (2018), Global Alternative Finance Benchmarks Database (accessed July 2021).

Alternative finance is still tiny compared with conventional finance. Table 4.6 compares alternative finance loans with conventional loans as a percentage of gross domestic product in 2019. Only the PRC's figure exceeded 0.1% and the figure for the PRC fell drastically in 2020 due to tighter regulation of this sector. The share of equity-related alternative finance is similarly tiny compared with conventional stock market issuance volumes.

**Table 4.6: Comparison of Alternative Finance Lending and
Conventional Lending, 2019**

	Loans (% of GDP)				
	(1)	(2)	(3)	(4)	(5)
Economy	Total Conventional (2)+(3)+(4)	Commercial Banks	Credit Unions and Credit Cooperatives	Microfinance Institutions	Alternative Finance
Brunei Darussalam	29.1	29.1	...	...	0.0
Cambodia	117.3	90.6	...	26.7	0.0
PRC	111.4	108.4	3.0	...	0.6
Indonesia	35.5	35.5	...	...	0.1
Japan	133.4	101.5	31.9	...	0.0
Republic of Korea	117.1	88.7	28.4	...	0.1
Lao PDR	46.0	45.3	0.1	0.6	0.0
Malaysia	109.4	109.4	...	...	0.0
Myanmar	24.3	22.8	...	1.5	0.0
Philippines	34.0	34.0	0.0	...	0.0
Singapore	136.4	136.4	...	...	0.1
Thailand	83.3	70.8	12.5	...	0.0
Viet Nam	134.9	133.0	2.0	...	0.0

... = not available, GDP = gross domestic product, PRC = People's Republic of China, Lao PDR = Lao People's
Democratic Republic.
Source: Authors' estimates; Cambridge Centre for Alternative Finance's Global Alternative Finance
Benchmarks Database; IMF Financial Access Survey Database; and IMF World Economic Outlook April 2021
Database (accessed July 2021).

4.3 Current Status of Financial Inclusion in Asia and Role of Fintech

Current Status of Financial Inclusion in ASEAN+3

According to the World Bank, financial inclusion means "… that individuals
and businesses have access to useful and affordable financial products
and services that meet their needs—transactions, payments, savings,
credit and insurance—delivered in a responsible and sustainable way"
(World Bank 2018). Actual usage of financial services is also important
for financial inclusion, as are financial literacy and education. Financial
inclusion is considered an enabler for 7 of the 17 Sustainable Development
Goals, and the G20 committed to advance financial inclusion worldwide
and reaffirmed its commitment to implement the G20 High-Level Principles
for Digital Financial Inclusion (GPFI 2016).

Financial inclusion has been adopted as a high-priority target by the ASEAN+3 countries and the Asian Development Bank (ADB). Improved financial access enables firms and households to smooth consumption, make long-term investment plans, and cope with unexpected emergencies. People who hold accounts at banks or other financial institutions are more likely to use other financial services, such as credit and insurance, to start and grow businesses, invest in education or health, manage risk, and smooth consumption against shocks, which can improve their quality of life (GPFI 2016).

Individuals: Financial accounts

The most commonly cited measure of financial inclusion is the percentage of adults of age 15 and above who have an account at a formal financial institution. This can be either a bank, some other savings institution, or a microfinance institution. Figure 4.5 shows the evolution of this figure for the PRC, Japan, the Republic of Korea, and most ASEAN countries from 2014 to 2017, based on the World Bank's Global Findex Survey results from those years. The figure shows three distinct clusters: high-income countries with financial inclusion rates of over 90% (Japan, Republic of Korea, and Singapore); upper middle-income countries with financial inclusion rates of 80%–90% (the PRC, Malaysia, and Thailand); and middle-income countries in the range of 15%–50% (Cambodia, Indonesia, the Philippines, and Viet Nam). The figure for the Lao People's Democratic Republic (Lao PDR) was not available in 2014, but was 29% in 2017, putting it in the third group as well. Most countries improved modestly in the 2 years, except Indonesia, which showed a large increase of 12 percentage points, and Viet Nam, with a slight decrease. The level of financial inclusion correlates well with other development-related measures such as per capita GDP and overall financial development.

Figure 4.6 shows the share of the adult population that have used digital payments based on the World Bank's Global Findex Database in 2014 and 2017. Digital payments in the figure include credit card payments, so the definition is broader than that given in section 4.2. Countries appear to be divided into the same three groups as for the holding of financial accounts. Digital payments are quite common in the Republic of Korea, Japan, and Singapore, with Japan coming on top in both years. Around 95% of the Japanese population made or received digital payments in 2017, up by six percentage points from 2014. Presumably the bulk of these are traditional credit card payments, but use of e-money is increasing as well. Increasing use of digital payments can be seen in all countries except Cambodia, with especially large increases in Thailand (up 29 percentage points) and the PRC (up 22 percentage points).

Figure 4.5: Share of Adult Population with a Financial Institution Account, 2014 and 2017
(%)

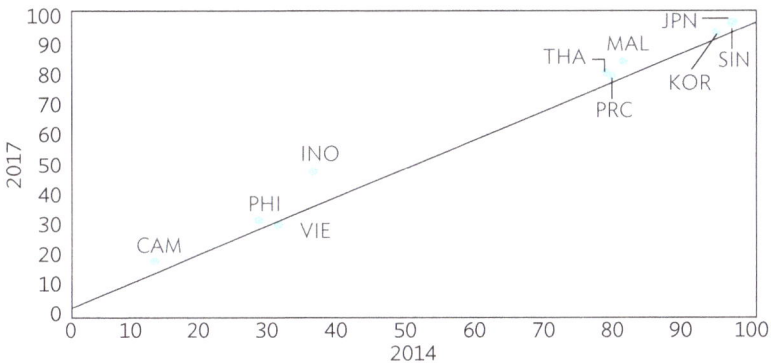

CAM = Cambodia, INO = Indonesia, JPN = Japan, KOR = Republic of Korea, MAL = Malaysia, PHI = Philippines, PRC = People's Republic of China, SIN = Singapore, THA = Thailand, VIE = Viet Nam.
Source: World Bank Global Findex Database 2018 (accessed May 2020).

Figure 4.6: Share of Adult Population Using Digital Payments
(%)

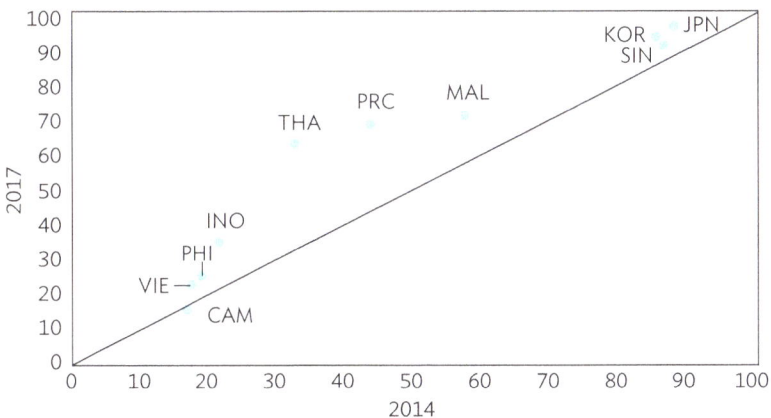

CAM = Cambodia, INO = Indonesia, JPN = Japan, KOR = Republic of Korea, MAL = Malaysia, PHI = Philippines, PRC = People's Republic of China, SIN = Singapore, THA = Thailand, VIE = Viet Nam.
Note: The data refer to the percentage of adults (age 15+) who made or received digital payments in the past year.
Source: World Bank Global Findex Database 2018 (accessed May 2020).

Figure 4.7 shows inclusion rates for adults with a mobile money account for the same periods. Data for the PRC, Japan, Republic of Korea, and the Lao PDR are not available. All countries except Cambodia showed increases, with the largest increases seen in Malaysia and Thailand. The reason for the large decline in Cambodia is not clear. The market is still relatively small, with no country having a share above 11%. Nevertheless, this segment is likely to show rapid growth.

Figure 4.7: Share of Adult Population with a Mobile Money Account (%)

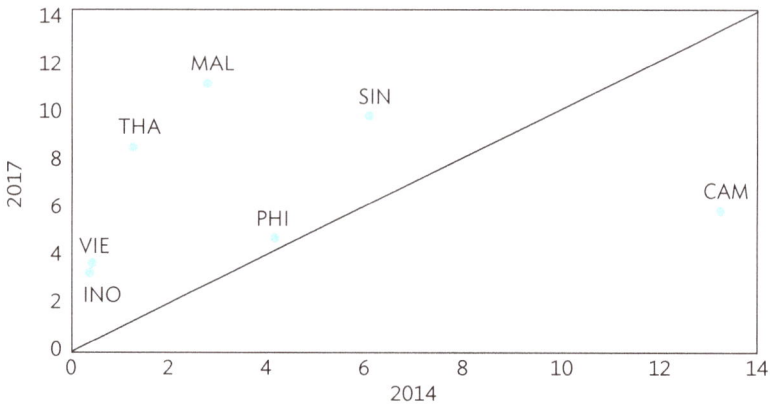

CAM = Cambodia. INO = Indonesia, JPN = Japan, KOR = Republic of Korea, MAL = Malaysia, PHI = Philippines, PRC = People's Republic of China, SIN = Singapore, THA = Thailand, VIE = Viet Nam.
Source: World Bank Global Findex Database 2018 (accessed May 2020).

Implications of fintech for income and wealth distribution

One key challenge is significant gaps in financial inclusion and financial literacy between men and women, urban and rural residents, those with higher and lower incomes, and small and large firms, among others. While digital finance has been expected to help reduce such gaps, its early adopters tend to be those with higher education, income, and financial literacy, or those who live in urban areas. For example, studies of fintech adoption in the PRC, Japan, and Viet Nam showed that individuals in higher-income groups are significantly more likely than those in low-income groups to adopt fintech services, and that men are significantly more likely than women to adopt fintech services (Huang, Wu, and Yang 2020, Morgan and Trinh 2020; Yoshino, Morgan, and Trinh 2002). Thus, even though fintech may promote financial inclusion, it has the potential to widen gaps in financial access, income, and wealth.

Figure 4.8 shows usage gaps in fintech products by gender, location (urban versus rural), and income group in the PRC and Viet Nam. In both countries, gender gaps appear to be small, although many other countries exhibit large gender gaps. However, the gaps in fintech adoption among rural and urban residents and among income groups in both countries are large. For example, only 2% of PRC rural residents own fintech products, while 14% of urban residents do. The share of the poor (those below the PRC's poverty line) who hold fintech products is only about one-third the share of those with higher incomes (Huang, Wu, and Yang 2020). A similar pattern is also seen in Viet Nam (Morgan and Trinh 2020).

Figure 4.8: Gaps in Usage and Awareness of Fintech Products in the PRC and Viet Nam
(% of total respondents)

a. PRC

b. Viet Nam

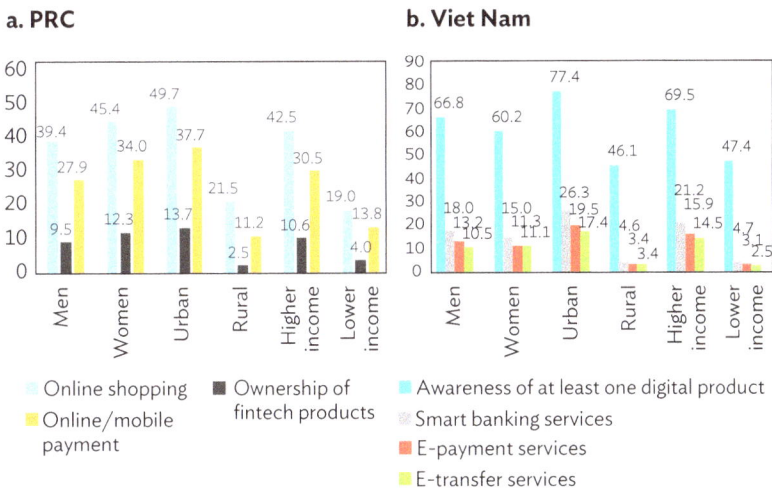

PRC = People's Republic of China.
Note: The poorer group in the PRC is defined as those under the PRC poverty line. Viet Nam's poorer group consists of those in households with total income less than 85 million dong (equal to 75% of the median household income in our sample).
Source: Huang, Wu, and Yang (2020) and Morgan and Trinh (2020).

The COVID-19 pandemic has increased demand for fintech services, but also presents greater challenges to vulnerable groups, including the elderly, the less educated, owners of small and medium-sized enterprises (SMEs) and start-up firms, rural residents, and women, who may not have adequate access to online services or the knowledge to use them appropriately and safely. This suggests that, in addition to promoting investment in internet access for disadvantaged groups, it is also necessary to promote digital financial literacy; design tools to assess it; and develop programs to promote digital financial education, including specialized programs for disadvantaged groups.

Micro, small, and medium-sized enterprises: Issues of access

Micro, small, and medium-sized enterprises (MSMEs) are the backbone of ASEAN+3 economies, accounting for 47%–97% of employment and 30%–60% of GDP (ADB 2015). They are, thus, crucial in spreading economic gains down to the base of the economy, which can help reduce poverty, create better quality jobs, address informality, and broaden economic inclusivity (IFC 2013, OECD 2017). They are likewise key in generating value added, promoting innovation, fostering environmental sustainability, and maximizing the benefits of digitalization (OECD 2017).

Nevertheless, it is well known that MSMEs have difficulty accessing finance for a number of reasons, including higher risk, lack of adequate or traditional collateral, and lack of reliable accounting data. Actual data on lending to MSMEs is limited. Figure 4.9 shows the ratio of commercial bank loans to SMEs as a percentage of GDP for countries, with available data in the IMF's Financial Access Survey.[7] The figures differ widely, with shares well below 10% in Indonesia, but over 35% in the PRC and the Republic of Korea, and in the range of 15%–30% in Malaysia and Thailand. However, these are well below the shares of SMEs in GDP.

The range of ratios of bank lending to SMEs to total lending in ASEAN is similarly wide. The latest publicly available data (Table 4.7) show that it is less than 1% in Brunei Darussalam, less than 7% in Singapore and the Philippines, close to 20% in Indonesia and the Lao PDR, and over 30% in Thailand.[8] ADB (2020) data further indicate that the share of SMEs in banks' lending portfolios generally declined between 2015 and 2019, except in Indonesia.

---

[7]   IMF Financial Access Survey Database. https://data.imf.org/?sk=E5DCAB7E-A5CA-4892-A6EA-598B5463A34C (accessed July 2021).

[8]   ADB Asia SME Monitor 2020 Database. https://data.adb.org/dataset/2020-adb-asia-sme-monitor-vol1-country-regional-reviews (accessed July 2021).

Figure 4.9: Commercial Bank Loans to SMEs
(% of GDP)

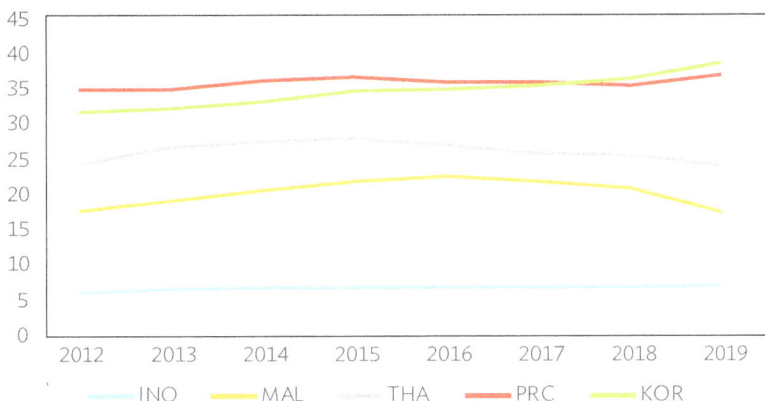

INO = Indonesia, KOR = Republic of Korea, MAL = Malaysia, PRC = People's Republic of China,
SMEs = small and medium-sized enterprises, THA = Thailand.
Source: IMF Financial Access Survey 2020 (accessed July 2021).

Table 4.7: Share of SME Loans in Total Bank Loans, ASEAN
(%)

Economy	2015	2019ᵃ
Brunei Darussalam	...	0.2
Indonesia	19.3	19.6
Lao PDR	30.9	19.8
Malaysia	18.7	14.6
Philippines	7.9	6.1
Singapore	6.3	5.8
Thailand	33.5	30.9

... = not available, Lao PDR = Lao People's Democratic Republic, SMEs = small and medium-sized enterprises.
ᵃ The data of Singapore are for 2018.
Source: ADB (2020), Asia Small and Medium-Sized Enterprise Monitor Volume 1: Country and Regional
Reviews Database (accessed July 2021).

Role of Fintech in Expanding Financial Inclusion

Notably, digital payments have significantly penetrated nonbanked or
underbanked groups.[9] Figure 4.10 shows that 25% of digital payment
customers in ASEAN countries are unbanked, the highest penetration for
any fintech segment, and another 16% are underbanked. This underscores

[9]   Individuals who have a bank account but limited to no access to other financial products and services are
classified as being underbanked.

the strong potential for digital payments to expand financial inclusion. Presumably these are people with mobile money accounts, which do not require the holder to have a bank account. Digital lending (part of alternative finance) has the next highest penetration rate of the unbanked, at 19% of the total.

Figure 4.10: Banked Status of Fintech Customers in ASEAN, 2019

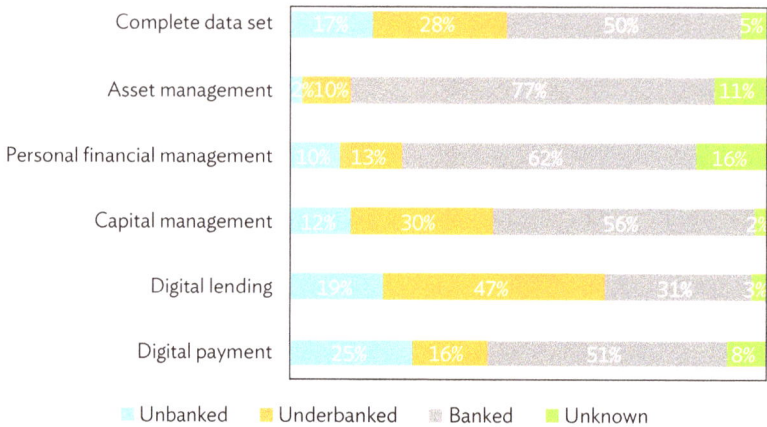

Note: The data for ASEAN exclude Brunei Darussalam and the Lao People's Democratic Republic. Complete data set refers to average of all of the segments shown below it.
Source: CCAF, ADBI, and FinTechSpace (2019).

For example, in Thailand, digital payments are viewed as a critical element for fintech development and adoption. The adoption of digital payments can be a first step toward development and adoption of digital (online) banking (savings and borrowing), and other online financial products such as investment and insurance (Moenjak, Komprajya, and Monchaitrakul 2020).

Digital finance such as P2P lending and crowdfunding can significantly expand the access of individuals and MSMEs to finance. This can be accomplished in various ways, such as using nontraditional data including bill-paying records to generate credit scores and using distributed ledger technology (DLT) to record nontraditional assets as collateral. However, despite rapid growth in recent years, penetration remains low overall. Table 4.8 shows levels of new digital finance as a share of GDP in various ASEAN+3 countries. Aside from the PRC, the figures are tiny, less than 0.1% of GDP, and far smaller than the figures for commercial bank loans to SMEs as a share of GDP shown in Figure 4.9. This reflects the small size of such loans, and their limited use mainly for working capital. It may also reflect basic limitations of the model, such as the lack of collateral or collection mechanisms in case of default. Inadequate access to the internet may also inhibit participation, especially in rural areas. This suggests that concerns about the competition of digital finance with traditional bank lending should not be exaggerated, at least in the near term.

It may take further technological and other innovations to fully unlock the potential of alternative finance to support financial inclusion. One possible approach is to integrate fintech into other financial inclusion policies. Two such examples from the Philippines include the following: (i) regulations were changed to allow banks to open microfinance windows to cater to MSME demand for small loans without collateral; and (ii) the central bank established a nationwide Credit Surety Fund for MSMEs' loans with participating banks. Loans granted under this scheme did not require collateral and credit history.

Table 4.8: Digital Finance Outstanding, Share of GDP
(%)

	PRC	Japan	Korea, Rep. of	ASEAN	ASEAN+3
2013	0.06	0.00	0.00	0.00	0.03
2014	0.23	0.00	0.00	0.00	0.13
2015	0.92	0.01	0.00	0.00	0.53
2016	2.16	0.01	0.03	0.01	1.20
2017	2.91	0.01	0.07	0.01	1.67
2018	1.55	0.02	0.04	0.07	0.93
2019	0.59	0.01	0.10	0.07	0.37
2020	0.01	0.02	0.08	0.09	0.03

ASEAN = Association of Southeast Asian Nations; ASEAN+3 = the ASEAN members plus the People's Republic of China (PRC), Japan, and the Republic of Korea; GDP = gross domestic product.
Note: The data refer to outstanding credit. The data for ASEAN exclude Brunei Darussalam and the Lao People's Democratic Republic.
Sources: CCAF (2020); CCAF, AIFZU, and ADBI (2018), Global Alternative Finance Benchmarks Database (accessed July 2021); and World Bank, *World Development Indicators* (accessed July 2021).

However, fintech credit options can vitally complement the banking sector in addressing the financing needs of the MSMEs and nonbank financial institutions, whose outstanding credit is also still relatively small but continues to expand.[10] MSME participation in the capital markets remains limited. According to ADB (2020), MSME equity market capitalization in 2019 was about 14.8% of GDP in Viet Nam, the Lao PDR (5.9%),

---

[10] ADB Asia SME Monitor 2020 Database. https://data.adb.org/dataset/2020-adb-asia-sme-monitor-vol1-country-regional-reviews (accessed July 2021).

Cambodia (2.6%), Singapore (1.9%), Malaysia (1.4%), Thailand (1.3%), and the Philippines (0.1%). Development of MSME bond markets in the region remains nascent (Shinozaki 2014). In addition, burgeoning bank-fintech partnerships and open banking initiatives indicate that fintech is not only influencing bank operations through competition, but also through adoption of new ways to develop products, approach the market, and assess the risks (Chuard 2021, Fintech News Philippines 2021).

4.4 COVID-19 and Fintech Adoption

In response to social distancing, quarantining, and lockdowns to slow COVID-19's spread, individuals have increasingly adopted digital finance and fintech platforms. Using data from mobile apps in 74 countries from January to May 2020, Fu and Mishra (2020) find that downloads of financial applications (apps) have increased substantially since the outbreak of COVID-19 in January 2020. Except in Europe, financial app downloads grew from 24% to 32% in major regions. Figure 4.11 shows the sharp increase of fintech mobile app downloads since February 2020, when the first lockdowns outside of the PRC were implemented. The 14-day lead moving average number of daily downloads jumped from around 12,000 to more than 17,000 within a month and have kept growing at slower rates since then. The Android market drove growth, while the iOS market remained flat.

Use of financial apps also grew. At the end of March 2020, social distancing, lockdowns, and isolation led to a 72% increase in their use in Europe (deVere Group 2020). Between December 2019 and March 2020, use of financial apps grew significantly in Japan, the Republic of Korea, the US, the PRC, and several other major countries in Europe. Weekly growth was 55% in Japan and 35% in the Republic of Korea, and by about 20% in the PRC and the US (Statista 2020b). Developing economies, meanwhile, tended to report very large increases in digital payments and remittances, and smaller increases in digital lending, digital capital raising, digital banks, and digital deposits, according to a global survey of financial regulators. However, some economies reported significant decreases in digital lending, due to lower credit demand resulting from the economic downturn (World Bank and CCAF 2020).

The pandemic also prodded governments to expand efforts to provide financial aid and other cash transfers to their constituents electronically, as they are more efficient, cheaper, and reduce direct human contact, including visits to bank branches. For example, the Philippine government boosted promotion of digital currency by raising to 56 the number of government institutions that accept digital payment through EGov Pay, the government's e-payments platform, by the end of March 2021 (Endo 2020).

Figure 4.11: Impact of COVID-19 on Adoption of Fintech Mobile Apps

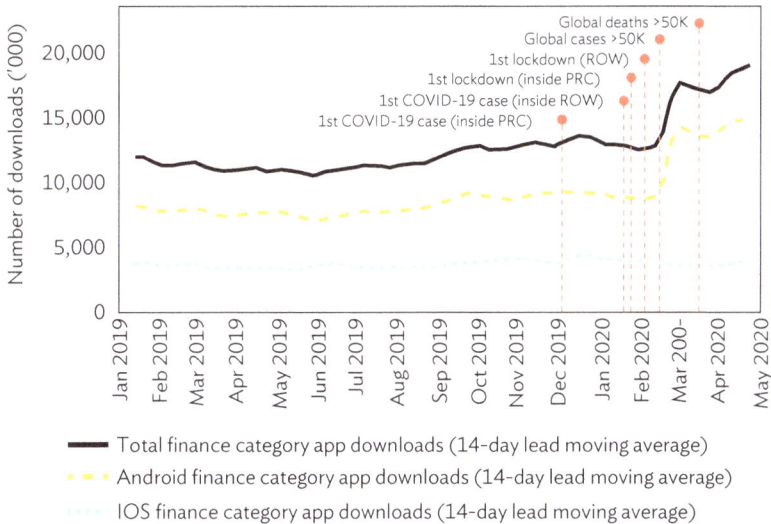

PRC = People's Republic of China, ROW = rest of the world
Source: Fu and Mishra (2020).

Roles, Opportunities, and Future of Fintech

The spread of COVID-19 highlights the role fintech and digital finance can play in helping individuals and firms adapt to shifting norms. Fintech allows individuals and businesses to access financial services cheaply, efficiently, and conveniently—especially money transfers and payments—while maintaining social distancing and reducing human contact (Arner et al. 2020, Ozili 2020, WAIFC 2020).

In developing countries, where the urgency of financial inclusion has become clearer amid the pandemic and economic slowdown, fintech is essential to better financial inclusion, because many people in those countries mainly use mobile handsets to access financial services (Haidar 2020). The fintech industry also plays a significant role in government crisis responses, benefiting from multiple measures from several central banks promoting fintech and digital finance to eliminate physical contact (Berg et al. 2020). The top three areas where fintech was having impact were digital disbursement of payments and remittances, delivery of government relief/stimulus funding, and healthcare, according to a global survey of financial regulators (World Bank and CCAF 2020).

Nonetheless, several risks associated with fintech also increased during the pandemic, such as cyberattacks, money laundering, and threats to data privacy (Zachariadis, Ozcan, and Dinçkol 2020). World Bank and CCAF (2020) also found that cybersecurity risks were financial regulators' biggest concern, followed by operational risks and consumer protection. Security and trust in fintech clearly need to improve (Ozili 2020). Korobov (2020) predicts several possible changes in the fintech industry after COVID-19 passes. First, fintech and retail services might merge, leading to all-in-one fintech apps which offer multiple services on one platform. Second, new collaborations between banks and fintech firms may arise as pressure mounts on banks to innovate. Third, governments and central banks will need to enact new regulations to monitor banking and fintech industries.

Challenges

Yet, the fintech industry, like other industries, is facing several challenges, such as economic slowdown, tighter financing conditions, and reduced investment. Fintech funding plunged in many regions (CB Insights 2020). In January–March 2020, fintech funding dropped 69% in Asia and fintech deals 23%, while venture-backed fintech funding dropped to $6 billion. GP Bullhound's fintech index dropped by $24 billion in January–March 2020, while fintech mergers and acquisitions and funding also slowed (Fintechnews Switzerland 2020).

COVID-19 also made life more difficult for financial regulators. Nonetheless, World Bank and CCAF (2020) reported high organizational preparedness, resilience, and adequacy of resources, although this was truer of advanced economies than of developing economies. This mainly reflects general resilience and adaptability amid COVID-19, rather than preparedness for a pandemic of this magnitude.

4.5 Implications of Fintech for Financial Stability

Fintech's widespread use has potential positive and negative implications for financial stability. This section focuses on the implications of the two main fintech sectors of interest—digital payments and alternative finance.

On the positive side, FSB (2017) argues that, theoretically, technology-enabled innovation in financial services has positive effects on economic growth and financial stability through multiple transmission channels, including decentralization and diversification, greater efficiency, transparency, and the access and convenience of financial services.

Yet, fintech can pose microfinancial and macrofinancial risks. Microfinancial risks leave individual firms, financial market infrastructure, or sectors particularly vulnerable to shocks. These include financial risks (maturity mismatch, liquidity mismatch and leverage) and operational risks (governance/process control, cyber risks, reliance on third parties, legal/regulatory risks, and business risks of critical financial market infrastructure). These apply to both incumbent banks and new fintech entrants (BCBS 2018). Macrofinancial risks are system-wide vulnerabilities that can amplify shocks to the financial system, raising the likelihood of financial instability. They include unsustainable credit growth, contagion, procyclicality,[11] excess volatility of markets, and systemically important financial institutions (FSB 2017). Table 4.9 categorizes the kinds of risks arising from fintech, and they are described in more detail in the following subsections.

The entry of nonfinancial "bigtech" firms into financial services has implications for regulation, both for financial stability and consumer protection. The growing use by bigtech and other firms of exploding amounts of personal data raises important questions about consumer protection and privacy (Beck 2020, Carstens 2021).

Moreover, consumer protection becomes a greater concern as financial innovators introduce new products and services and increase financial inclusion. Lack of trust in financial services, partly due to experiences of fraudulent activities and financial crises, has been an important factor hindering the increase of financial inclusion (Beck 2020).

---

[11] Procyclicality refers to forces that tend to magnify the volatility of economic cycles, such as positive feedback loops between the real and financial sectors of the economy.

Table 4.9: Fintech-Related Macrofinancial and Microfinancial Risks

| | | Microfinancial | |
Sector	Macrofinancial	Financial	Operational
Payment systems	Systemically important financial market infrastructure,	Financial market infrastructure failure	Cyber risks, third-party contractors
	Systemically important bigtech firms		
Remittances	Encourage volatile capital flows		Cyber risks
Digital currencies			
Cryptoassets			
Unlinked		DLT settlement finality	Cyber risks
		Exchange failure	Weak code and cryptography
Stablecoin	Weakening of banking sector	DLT settlement finality	Cyber risks
	Weaken monetary policy transmission	Exchange failure	Strength of code, cryptography
	Encourage volatile capital flows		
CBDC	Weakening of banking sector		Cyber risks
	Weaken monetary policy transmission		
	Encourage volatile capital flows		
Alternative finance			
Lending	Weakening of banking sector	Moral hazard of lending platforms	Cyber risks
	Contagion risks	Maturity mismatch, leverage	
	Procyclicality	Platform failure	
Equity-related		Platform failure	Cyber risks

CBDC = central bank digital currency, DLT = distributed ledger technology.
Source: Authors.

The lack of data and information on fintech activities constrains assessment of the implications for financial stability. Industry and academic groups are voluntarily collecting data on fintech activities, but these efforts are nascent. Also, the kinds of data regulators and supervisors need may differ (FSB 2017). So far, based on current estimates, fintech firms are not regarded as systemically important. Based on a study of 75 fintech firms quoted on the Nasdaq and Frankfurt stock exchanges using variance-covariance analysis, Franco et al. (2020) estimate that within the US financial system, fintech firms increase systemic risk by around 0.03%, while in Europe they contribute close to 0%.

Based on this and other studies, the Committee on the Global Financial System and the Financial Stability Board (CGFS and FSB 2017) concluded that, so far, fintech-related credit is generally still small enough not to pose a systemic risk. Nonetheless, this conclusion could change if fintech services grow further. Particularly, the recent entry of bigtech firms, which have a competitive advantage due to the massive amounts of data on consumer spending behavior they possess, presents new and difficult regulatory trade-offs between financial stability, competition, and data protection (BIS 2019, Amstad 2019).

General Fintech Risks

Cyberattacks increasingly threaten the entire financial system, and fintech could raise this risk. The BIS cites cyber risk as perhaps the biggest fintech-related threat to financial stability, at least in the short term. The susceptibility of financial activity to cyberattacks is likely to increase as systems of different institutions become increasingly connected, if one of them proves to be a weak link (FSB 2017).

The computer code underpinning digital finance raises information asymmetry risks. The inability to know whether the code, public or otherwise, does what it is supposed to do increases uncertainty, particularly when a computer code (or proof of work or consensus finding) takes the place of a third party (Amstad 2019).

Decentralization may also increase information asymmetry, e.g., when comparing an initial coin offering with an initial public offering, since the latter is vetted by a central exchange, while the former is not. However, decentralization could also lower information asymmetries, following the general argument that decentralized markets are more efficient than a centrally planned economy and thus can allocate resources better (Amstad 2019).

Some fintech activities could increase reliance on third-party (outside contractor) service providers. For example, concentration of cloud computing services among a small number of firms could have significant implications for cloud-based financial services if operational problems arise. Disruptions to third-party services—such as operational problems—

are more likely to pose systemic risks if such third parties connect increasingly with systemically important institutions or markets (FSB 2017).

Payment System Risks

If innovative payment and settlement services develop into systemically important financial market infrastructure, their losses could impair the supply of important services and become an obstacle to recovery or orderly resolution. Some of these important services may be provided by a parent company in other business lines, such as bigtech firms, whose other operational priorities might conflict with the offering of financial services, and could be outside the normal financial regulatory scope (FSB 2017). Network effects and economies of scale and scope could also tend to promote greater market concentration and the emergence of nonfinancial players as systemically important entities, which could reduce system resilience.

As noted, because of their relatively small size, cryptoassets are not yet considered a systemic risk. Moreover, given the low probability of a private cryptoasset such as Bitcoin ever accounting for a significant share of transactions, the likelihood of a private cryptoasset ever becoming systemically important is low. However, this situation could change if one or more of them is widely adopted (FSB 2017). These risks are discussed below.

Operational risk is probably the main microfinancial risk related to cryptoassets, especially those that are decentralized and have little or no formal governance structure. Enforcing operational requirements to ensure the efficiency and stability a cryptoasset that that has no governance structure and allows anyone to participate as part of the infrastructure would no doubt be challenging (FSB 2017). For example, private cryptoassets can work only if the incentives incorporated into their design support transactions in an environment where participants do not trust each other. These incentive structures have performed relatively well so far, but only at a relatively low scale. The risk remains that a private cryptoasset system could be introduced whose design is unstable (FSB 2017).

Individual users of cryptoassets face risks, e.g., the insolvency of critical third-party service providers of cryptoasset infrastructure such as exchange platforms. Bitcoin exchanges have failed numerous times to sufficiently safeguard the Bitcoins held by users, leading to millions of dollars of losses.

Widespread use of digital currencies (either private cryptocurrencies or CBDCs) might reduce demand for cash and related payment infrastructure, which could damage the ability of the payment infrastructure to provide efficient and reliable services. Regulation and supervision of a private cryptoasset would inherently be more difficult in view of its borderless nature. Digital currencies and digital wallets could displace traditional bank-based payment systems, while payment aggregators could become the main channel for accessing banks and applying for new bank accounts and loans, thereby becoming systemically important. Other oligopolies or monopolies may also develop, for example, in the collection and processing of customer data (FSB 2017).

Widespread use of cryptoassets might also diminish central bank control over monetary policy and economies and inhibit the effectiveness of lender-of-last-resort interventions, with negative implications for financial stability since monetary policy actions also support that. Section 4.7 discusses this issue further.

If the transaction volume of a global stablecoin increases dramatically, it is not clear that the issuer would be able to continue to supply it without disrupting payments and creating substantial volatility in the stablecoin value. In an economy with an unstable, unreliable government, the availability of a global stablecoin might increase the risk of capital flight. Therefore, a shift in holdings from a domestic fiat currency to a stablecoin may not only reduce the effectiveness of monetary policy but may also lead to significant depreciation of some currencies (Shirai 2020).

The Group of 20 leaders saw a need for monitoring the development of cryptoassets, noting that "… [W]hile crypto-assets do not pose a threat to global financial stability at this point, we are closely monitoring developments and remain vigilant to existing and emerging risks" (G20 2019). The G20 leaders also expressed concerns about stablecoins in their November 2020 communique, noting that "… [n]o so-called 'global stablecoins' should commence operation until all relevant legal, regulatory and oversight requirements are adequately addressed through appropriate design and by adhering to applicable standards" (G20 2020).

DLT solutions entail a number of new risks. In post-trade clearing and settlement, settlement finality is a legally well-defined moment, normally underpinned by a statutory, regulatory, or contractual framework related to a given financial transaction. Conversely, in a DLT solution based on majority votes, multiple parties have permission to update a shared ledger.

These parties must agree on the particular state of the ledger by consensus, meaning that the finality of settlement using this model may only be probabilistic (FSB 2017).

A key question for new technologies such as DLT is whether they can be implemented and operated securely across a wide range of adverse conditions. A DLT system is not immune to cyberattacks. It is vulnerable within software and hardware components, and hence could face increased risk of cyberattacks through its distributed network of participants validating transactions and updating the distributed ledger.

The strength of cryptography is another operational challenge for DLT solutions. If the system's encryption is compromised, a DLT solution may be at risk. As risks and threats are continually changing, the operators of DLT solutions must ensure that procedures and controls are continually assessed, improved, and adapted. This may be especially difficult in an open and "permissionless" system.[12]

There are also concerns about risks and limits to the smooth, not to mention feasible, operation of a payment system operating using DLTs. Morris and Shin (2018) develop a model in which banks using DLT-based payment systems have the option to delay payment. Depending on the parameters of the system, they find that banks would have an incentive to delay payments, which could lead to a "stalemate" of the system. Only a central bank would be able to break this stalemate, thereby undermining the argument for a decentralized system. BIS (2018a) also raises numerous questions about the feasibility of DLT-based payment systems, including scalability, a potential deficit of trust due to the fragility of the consensus approach to transaction verification, congestion issues leading to volatility of fees,[13] and volatile prices.

Potential gridlocks or deadlocks may also pose major systemic risks. Such a situation could occur if participants lack sufficient liquidity to settle transactions, which could lead to settlement queues.[14]

---

[12] A permissionless system is one where the number of participants on the network is unlimited, and no one needs to get permission from another user in order to take part in it.

[13] In settlement systems for cryptocurrencies, transaction fees can rise sharply when the number of transactions increases, especially if transactors desire rapid settlement.

[14] This eventuality is normally addressed through liquidity saving mechanisms and queue management in existing Real-Time Gross Settlement systems.

The implications of DLT for wholesale and retail payments need to be carefully studied. DLT solutions are still at an early stage as a financial service instrument, and major work is needed to sufficiently evaluate their effectiveness.

Alternative Finance Risks

Fintech developments may accelerate the finance industry's recent tendency to shift credit intermediation away from commercial banks to nonbanks, a diverse and growing sector. To be sure, the alternative finance sector is still tiny and, were it to grow dramatically as result of penetration by bigtech firms, it probably would be subject to tighter regulation.

P2P lending is a major example of this. Greater competition from fintech lenders such as P2P lending platforms could reduce the profitability of traditional banks. The "unbundling" of bank business lines, as banks respond to competitive pressures by outsourcing certain activities to reduce costs, could shrink banks' revenue bases, making them more subject to losses and reducing their cushion of retained earnings as a source of internal capital.

The P2P lending business model carries inherent risks for financial stability (Nemoto, Storey, and Huang 2019). There are problematic incentives for platforms to originate loans without holding the risk of these loans. For example, P2P platforms usually receive revenue as a function of the loan volume generated, which could incentivize them to maximize loan origination at the expense of credit standards. In several countries, including the PRC, P2P platforms have committed fraudulent behavior and run Ponzi-like schemes. In response, Chinese regulators have largely shut down the sector.

Funding for these platforms mainly comes from individual investors who are not protected by deposit insurance, unlike bank deposits, which are insured in many countries.[15] If lending platforms use their own balance sheet to intermediate funds, this could lead to maturity mismatches. On the other hand, P2P lending platforms are not seen as performing maturity transformation, so liquidity mismatch does not seem to be an issue. Leverage is not generally perceived to be an issue either, although

---

[15] Moral hazard arises when investor returns are guaranteed by platforms, because investors would have no incentive to distinguish among risk categories.

it could be if P2P or crowdfunding platforms leverage their own balance sheets to fund lending activities (FSB 2017).

Lending platforms are also subject to macrofinancial risks. For example, large and unexpected losses suffered by a single fintech lending platform could lead to expectations of losses across the sector, possibly triggering contagion risks. Also, unstable interactions between investors and borrowers on fintech lending platforms could develop if a sudden unexpected rise in nonperforming loans leads to a sharp reduction of new funds. Having a large share of retail investors could raise this risk (FSB 2017).

A rising share of fintech credit could tend to lower lending standards and lead to more procyclical supply of credit. If fintech platforms grow to the extent that certain segments of the real economy rely heavily on credit from them, then any difficulties in those platforms could lead to a reduction in credit supply.[16]

4.6 Administrative and Regulatory Frameworks for Ensuring Financial Stability

Macroprudential and Microprudential Risks Related to Fintech

According to the FSB (2017), regulation of fintech so far has focused mostly on consumer and investor protection, market integrity, financial inclusion, and promoting innovation or competition. Few regulatory authorities have cited financial stability as an objective for recent or planned regulatory reforms related to fintech.

Rapid innovation in fintech and its multifaceted aspects pose particular challenges for regulation. Most importantly, regulators need to balance requirements for microfinancial and macrofinancial stability against the benefits of innovation and financial inclusion. Regulation of fintech for financial stability also needs to be squared with the demands of regulation for consumer and investor protection, cybersecurity, data protection and anti-money laundering/counterterrorist financing (AML/CFT). Finally, "cross-border" issues involving the regulation of telecommunication firms and bigtech firms need to be considered. Countries differ in their emphasis on promoting fintech as opposed to regulating it (IMF 2019).

---

[16] As noted in Section 4.3, this does not seem to be a risk in the near term.

Potential macrofinancial risks brought about by fintech include non-sustainable credit growth, increased interconnectedness or correlation, incentives for greater risk-taking by incumbent institutions, procyclicality, contagion, and systemically important financial institutions (SIFIs) (FSB 2017). Macrofinancial issues pertaining to systemic importance are contained in the FSB's SIFI framework, which recommends that financial institutions identified as systemically important be subject to stronger supervisory oversight, higher loss resilience, and recovery and resolution plans (FSB 2017).[17]

Potential microfinancial risks include both financial risks (maturity mismatch, liquidity mismatch, and leverage) and operational risks (governance/process control, cyber risks, reliance on third parties, legal/regulatory risks, and business risks of critical FMIs). Financial risks can be addressed mainly by regulating alternative finance platforms. Basic principles of such regulation would include forbidding platforms from providing guarantees to investors, forbidding them to use their own capital for investment activities, and requiring them to register and report regularly to regulatory authorities. Operational risks such as cyber risks may be addressed by appropriate supervision, although this probably will require developing new capacities on the part of regulators.

General Approach to Regulation of Fintech

The Bali Fintech Agenda, supported by the IMF and the World Bank, is perhaps the most comprehensive attempt in one framework to address these issues related to fintech. Table 4.10 shows its main elements, which underline the complex nature of the problem.

The relevant standard-setting bodies have also issued guidelines and standards related to fintech. As examples, the Basel Committee's Core Principles are applicable for assessing innovations in banking and the interaction between banks and fintech firms; the IOSCO Objectives and Principles are applicable for use of fintech in securities markets; the International Association of Insurance Supervisors (IAIS) Insurance Core Principles are relevant for fintech applications in insurance (InsurTech); and the Committee on Payments and Market Infrastructures (CPMI)-IOSCO Principles for Financial Market Infrastructures are applicable to fintech uses in payments, clearing and settlement (FSB 2017). In some

---

[17] Bigtech firms that are engaged in fintech should also be defined as SIFIs if their scales become significant in the future.

countries, prudential authorities do not have authority over nonbanks, and some services previously conducted by banks are now being provided by firms not regulated by bank supervisors (BCBS 2018). In such cases, a new regulatory perimeter will have to be defined to promote systemic financial stability.

Table 4.10: Bali Fintech Agenda Elements: Balancing Opportunities and Risks

No.	Elements
1	Embrace the opportunities of fintech
2	Enable new technologies to enhance financial service provision
3	Reinforce competition and commitment to open, free, and contestable markets
4	Foster fintech to promote financial inclusion and develop financial markets
5	Monitor developments closely to deepen understanding of evolving financial systems
6	Adapt regulatory framework and supervisory practices for orderly development and stability of the financial system
7	Safeguard the integrity of financial systems
8	Modernize legal frameworks to provide an enabling legal landscape
9	Ensure the stability of monetary and financial systems
10	Develop robust financial and data infrastructure to sustain fintech benefits
11	Enhance collective surveillance and assessment of the financial sector

Source: IMF (2018).

To the extent that fintech activities are innovative and are not covered by existing legislation or regulation, legal and regulatory frameworks will need to be adapted and expanded. This applies to the full range of financial services, from customer interfaces to back-office systems and infrastructure (FSB 2017). The BIS classifies fintech-related regulatory innovations and policy responses into three categories: (i) those that adjust the regulatory perimeter and/or directly target fintech activities, (ii) those that focus on the use of new technologies in the provision of financial services standard-setting; and (iii) those that facilitate financial innovation or promote digital financial services more broadly (Ehrentraud et al. 2020).

Financial sector private laws, especially laws which pertain to payment and securities transfers, require a high degree of legal certainty to be effective. However, in contrast to previous efforts, which were responses to greater computing power and high-speed telecommunications, the continual need to better understand the rapidly evolving fintech environment is a key challenge (IMF 2019).

Fintech developments pose at least three challenges to legal certainty. First, various fintech business models have developed at high speed. They have moved within just a few years from basically zero to taking a key role in debates about the financial system. This contrasts with the normally drawn out processes for new regulations commonly seen in a system of public consultation with the most important involved stakeholders. The second challenge is related to the sheer number of government bodies involved. Financial regulation in many jurisdictions is spread across a number of institutions, including the central bank, financial supervisory bodies, other government departments such as the tax authorities, legislative, and the AML regulator. Third, for both regulators and market participations, fintech increasingly requires knowledge of computer coding on top of the normal legal and financial market knowledge (Amstad 2019).

Regulatory authorities may need to adjust their supervisory architecture and practices to fintech. Most regulatory authorities supervise fintech activities in line with ongoing supervisory processes in those firms' current organizational structures, yet some have significantly revised that structure (Ehrentraud et al. 2020).

Another challenge is to define the regulatory perimeter, i.e., what institutions and market participants fall under financial stability regulation and supervision, and hence also under the financial safety net (Beck 2020). Regulatory perimeter issues may affect the ability of authorities to follow fintech-related developments, depending on how flexible the existing regulatory framework is.

As bigtech firms increasingly enter financial markets as direct competitors of traditional financial institutions, financial authorities face new challenges on both a national and international level. A key question related to fintech and bigtech firms is whether one should regulate only financial activities or the whole entities. The activities of bigtechs are closely integrated and data from one operation is used in others as well. An example is Alibaba's Ant Financial and Alipay. Activity-based regulation may not be sufficient to treat banks and bigtech firms equally, because bigtechs are not subject to entity-based prudential regulation (Carstens 2021).

Regulatory fintech sandboxes, accelerators, and innovation hubs can be an important source of information about new activities and business models, and can provide important information to understand their risks and incentives. However, even though sandboxes give policy makers valuable insights, they cannot be relied on as an all-encompassing solution for understanding the implications of and regulating fintech. They can be supplemented by "innovation facilitators," such as accelerators and innovation hubs (IMF 2019).

Finally, regulations on consumer protection and programs for financial literacy must also take into account the need to extend them to digital financial services. Digital financial literacy encompasses knowledge different from conventional financial literacy, including knowledge about fintech services, their risks, how to protect oneself from those risks, and how to seek redress if one suffers damages (Morgan, Huang, and Trinh 2019). Without adequate knowledge, consumers are likely to make inappropriate use of fintech products and may suffer losses due to fraud or identity theft.

Digital Payment Services

Many countries have implemented fintech-specific regulations for digital payment services. Some countries aim to facilitate nonbank access to the payments market. In Japan, the Payment Services Act of 2009 allows nonbank firms to perform fund transfers, previously reserved exclusively for banks. However, unlike bank transfers, these nonbank transfers are limited to a maximum of ¥1 million. In Singapore, the pre-2019 framework was split into two pieces of legislation that regulated payment systems, stored value facilities, and money-changing and remittance businesses separately (Ehrentraud et al. 2020).

Many countries have a separate regulatory framework for e-money services. There are two broad types of e-money licensing regimes. In the first, e-money services are treated as a banking business and subject to bank-like prudential regulation. In the second type, nonbank e-money service providers need to obtain a particular license from the authority, subject to specific requirements (Ehrentraud et al. 2020).

Many countries have issued or plan to issue new regulations covering mobile payments and digital currencies. These regulations often aim to increase financial inclusion and provide greater access to consumers for payment services, as well as ensuring the smooth functioning of the payments systems, in line with existing responsibilities for payments infrastructure (FSB 2017).

Tokenization is developing in parallel to the spread of open application program interfaces or APIs, promoted by global payment card providers. The growing trend of third-party apps getting access to bank accounts and payment card accounts has focused more attention on the question of how to authenticate customers reliably (IMF 2019).

One of the most important challenges to developing a regulatory approach for cryptoassets is the lack of a common categorization. Regulators' definitions of cryptoassets usually share the following elements: (i) form of the asset—whether it is a digital or electronic representation of value; (ii) properties of the asset—if it can be transferred, stored, and traded electronically; and (iii) function of the asset—if it can be used as a means of payment or exchange, store of value, or unit of account. Usually, regulators use the underlying economic function as the main criterion for classifying cryptoassets and determining whether they fall within the regulatory perimeter and, if so, which regulation applies. In the case of stablecoins, the underlying assets criterion is also being used to determine regulatory requirements. In light of the risks of criminal and terrorist misuse of cryptoassets, countries are revising their regulatory frameworks to incorporate international AML/CFT guidance (Ehrentraud et al. 2020).

The Banking Sector

The development of fintech sectors will affect bank operations and, potentially, their financial stability through multiple channels. Although fintech firms often compete with banks and other traditional financial institutions, collaboration based on complementarities of comparative advantages is also widespread. Both trends are likely to accelerate following the pandemic.

On one hand, fintech firms provide services to groups not normally well served by banks, including the poor and MSMEs, and in this sense complement traditional providers. Banks have also benefited from the provision of innovative technologies by third parties (FSB 2019). Fintech firms have helped banks create a variety of new business models, shift them toward digital means of service provision (e.g., mobile and online banking), reach out to new customers with state-of-the-art platforms, and set up in-house incubators and innovation labs.

On the other hand, competition between fintech firms and other established financial institutions is emerging. For instance, purely digital banks such as Webank are directly competing for customers from traditional banks and even attracting new ones with their technological advantages and low-cost services. Bigtech firms are entering financial services at a rapid pace. Starting with payments, bigtech firms such as Alipay and WeChat Pay have expanded into other services including lending, insurance, and savings and investment products, either on their own or with financial institution partners. Compared with the incumbents, bigtech firms have the advantages of big data analysis, large networks, and economies of scale and scope, which might lead to greater concentration (Frost et al. 2019). Big banks are beginning to feel these competitive pressures and are responding in different ways, such as buying up small fintech firms or investing heavily in fintech.

In response to these developments, bank supervisors should promote safety and soundness by requiring that banks adopt appropriate risk management processes and control environments (BCBS 2018). Safety, soundness, and financial stability can be increased by implementing supervisory programs that make sure that banks have effective governance structures and risk management processes that suitably identify, manage, and monitor risks stemming from the use of fintech models, processes, or products (BCBS 2018).

Regarding third-party risk, safety, soundness, and financial stability can be improved by establishing supervisory programs to make sure that banks have suitable risk management practices and processes regarding any operation outsourced to or supported by a third party, including fintech firms, and that controls over outsourced services are maintained at the same level as those for operations that the bank conducts by itself (BCBS 2018). Risk management practices must be in line with portions of the Basel Committee's Principles for sound management of operational risk relevant to fintech developments (BCBS 2018).

Safety, soundness, and financial stability can also be improved by bank supervisors communicating and coordinating with relevant regulators and public authorities, including those responsible for data protection, consumer protection, fair competition, and national security. This is to make sure that banks using innovative technologies comply with the relevant laws and regulations (BCBS 2018). Finally, bank supervisors should review staffing and training programs to make sure that the knowledge, skills, and tools of staff stay relevant and effective in overseeing the risks of new technologies and innovative business models. Supervisors may need to add staff with specialized skills to complement existing expertise (BCBS 2018).

Money laundering stands out as a key risk to market integrity stemming from fintech. The recommendations by the independent intergovernmental body, the Financial Action Task Force, are regarded as the standard for global AML/CFT activities (Amstad 2019).

Many economies apply existing banking laws and regulations to digital banking. Only a few have implemented specific licensing regimes for digital banks, e.g., Singapore and Hong Kong, China. In June 2019, the Monetary Authority of Singapore (MAS) announced a new digital banking framework with two kinds of licenses: (i) a digital full bank license, which allows the licensee to provide a wide range of financial services and take deposits from retail customers; and (ii) a digital wholesale bank license, which allows the licensee to serve SMEs and other businesses but not accept deposits in Singapore dollars from individuals (except for fixed deposits of at least S$250,000) (Ehrentraud et al. 2020).

Alternative Finance

P2P lending: Increased access to credit, while benefiting some households and firms in the short term, could lead to excessive borrowing and in turn contribute to financial instability and impose costs on the financial system if the sector becomes sufficiently large. This highlights how important it is to monitor micro- and macrofinancial risks. To the extent that fintech firms carry out activities similar to those of banks, fintech credit platforms could be regarded as benefiting from regulatory arbitrage (FSB 2017).

Regulatory responses to P2P lending have varied greatly among countries. The United Kingdom (UK) and Japan have established regulatory sandboxes to permit innovating firms to experiment without being too burdened by legal constraints in their early-growth stages. However, P2P platforms in the US and the PRC are limited to the role of information intermediary, and therefore platforms in those countries need to depend on banks to originate the loans. Strict regulation in the US has limited the extent to which new entrants can compete with established platforms. The safeguarding of investors through provision funds, i.e., funds provided by the platform to protect investors against losses from nonperforming loans, is common in the UK, less seen in Japan and the US, and, although formerly widely used in the PRC, is now prohibited there. The main challenge for regulators is to encourage the growth of digital lending to transform small business funding and enhance economic growth, while at the same time protect the financial system against systemic risks and maintain a fair, safe, and competitive market.

Nemoto, Storey, and Huang (2019) proposed eight principles for P2P lending regulatory frameworks:

(i)   P2P lending should provide a safe and effective investment channel for a broad segment of society.

(ii) P2P lending should allow borrowers access to affordable and reliable capital on fair terms.

(iii) Lending should differentiate among borrowers based on risk of default.

(iv) Platforms should provide investors with an accurate understanding of credit risks and investors should hold at least some of the risk to prevent moral hazard.

(v)   Unviable lending platforms should be able to exit the market without causing losses to investors or funding shortfalls for borrowers.

(vi) Lending should be robust enough during economic downturns to prevent sudden stops in lending, excessive default rates, and problematic failures of lending platforms.

(vii) A competitive market between P2P platforms should be maintained to promote consumer choice; prevent rent seeking, monopolistic, or oligopolistic practices; and avoid the systemic risk of overreliance on one or a small number of platforms.

(viii) The sector should be socially useful and serve the real economy.

In addition, there should be principles limiting the risk of balance sheet lending.

Balance sheet lending: Most countries do not have specific regulations for fintech balance sheet lending. Many countries have introduced fintech-specific regulations that apply to both loan and equity crowdfunding. Consumer protection has been the policy objective most cited by authorities, followed by the need to establish a level playing field and maintain financial stability. For the most part, regulatory requirements focus on consumer and investor protection, AML/CFT, and operational resilience (Ehrentraud et al. 2020).

Equity crowdfunding: Many regulators have amended or clarified existing rules for equity crowdfunding and for online marketplace lending. This has also been a major focus of the International Organization of Securities Commissions. These changes include defining new licensing requirements and clarifying where existing rules continue to apply (FSB 2017).

4.7 Implications for Design of Monetary Policy

In theory, the overall effect of nonbank finance, including fintech, on monetary policy transmission could be either positive or negative. Although bank leverage is limited by prudential regulation, the increasing role of (potentially) highly leveraged nonbank intermediaries for overall credit supply might strengthen the transmission of monetary policy via the nonbank lending channel. An increasing gap between prudential regulation of banks and nonbanks could reduce the dampening effect of the bank-capital channel for monetary policy transmission. In a comprehensive study analyzing both aggregate and micro-level data on several advanced and emerging economies, IMF (2016) finds that nonbank finance tended to strengthen monetary policy transmission (Bernot, Gebauer, and Schäfer 2020).

The development of fintech poses several risks for monetary policy transmission and financial stability. New financial infrastructure systems may have hidden weaknesses undiscovered in early trials, which could lead to financial disruption and critical episodes such as "flash crashes." If privately issued cryptoassets become widely used for transactions, this may tend to reduce the use of official currencies and make it harder to track monetary aggregates. This could pose a challenge to obtaining information needed for setting monetary policy (Furche et al. 2017). In the near term, it seems unlikely that cryptoassets will be sufficiently large to have such an impact, but this will require closer monitoring. In particular, if global stablecoins become sufficiently popular, they could compete with domestic fiat currencies, undermining the effectiveness of national monetary policy (IMF 2020).

The introduction of central bank digital currencies (CBDCs) potentially presents the greatest challenges for implementing monetary policy. The features of a CBDC would largely determine its potential attractiveness to investors and hence the potential demand for it. A CBDC that pays interest and is readily transferable could prove attractive to institutional financial market participants and become a substitute for money market instruments such as government bills, reverse repos, central bank bills, and foreign-exchange swaps. It could also be a liquid and credit-risk-free asset facilitating final settlement. A CBDC of a major currency usable by nonresidents could substitute for internationally used banknotes, bank deposits, and international reserve assets, and thereby become an important component of international capital flows (CPMI-MC 2018).

On the positive side, retail CBDCs could provide individuals with a new, safer, and more liquid asset; improve the effectiveness of monetary policy; and give central banks increased ability to track payment and settlement transactions (Shirai 2020). One possible benefit of a retail CBDC (especially an account-based CBDC) is that helicopter money or monetization of government debt could be implemented more easily if the public can directly hold deposit accounts with a central bank (Shirai 2020). Also, transactions using cryptoassets are traceable, and a positive or negative interest rate can be charged, potentially improving the effectiveness of monetary policies such as a negative interest rate policy (Shirai 2020).

On the negative side, during financial stress, domestic investors may consider a CBDC to be more attractive than private bank deposits, leading to a possible outflow of deposits from the banking system, with consequential implications for banking system stability. Also, central banks may be cautious for fear they would suffer reputational losses if their implementation of retail CBDC would not succeed (Shirai 2020).

On the whole, CPMI-MC (2018) concludes that the introduction of a CBDC would only have a minor impact on central banks' monetary policy implementation, i.e., how they carry out operations on their balance sheets to affect short-term interest rates. While a central bank would need to accommodate demand for a CBDC, flows into a CBDC would drain reserves in the system in the same way as flows into other assets such as banknotes and central bank deposits held by nonmonetary counterparties currently do (e.g., the treasury, foreign central banks, or financial market infrastructure).

CPMI-MC (2018) also concludes that the net effects of CBDC on the term structure of interest rates are difficult to predict, since they would depend on many factors. Depending on the specific assets held by the central bank to accommodate the issued CBDC, it would need to carry out various kinds of maturity, liquidity, and credit risk transformations. It is hard to predict how these effects would balance out in terms of the structure of interest rates across asset classes and maturities. The implications of a CBDC relative to other instruments most probably will depend on each country's specific circumstances.

Fintech could potentially lead to new forms of cross-border financial flows. New instruments are being developed for transactions in capital markets, including international transactions, such as tokenized securities and blockchain bonds. Crowdfunding transactions may also occur cross-border. These developments could gradually hinder the role of traditional centralized financial intermediaries, with possible negative implications for the global financial system (IMF 2019). Both global stablecoins and CBDCs could pose financial stability risks for emerging market economies. For example, if residents of countries with high inflation or monetary policy systems with low credibility can invest in global stablecoins or CBDCs of a low-inflation country, this currency substitution effect could trigger capital outflows and weaken the domestic currency, as well as impair the effectiveness of monetary policy (CPMI-MC 2018, IMF 2020).

4.8 Role of Regional Cooperation

Regional financial cooperation in ASEAN+3 has tended to proceed cautiously, due to differences in economic and financial systems, levels of economic and financial development, concerns about the negative impacts of volatile capital flows, and the desire of countries to maintain sovereignty. Even within ASEAN, the principle of voluntary cooperation has been maintained. Liberalization of loan and equity flows has been substantial, but allowing direct investment in the financial sector, such as establishment of branches of one country's bank in another, has proceeded more slowly. In ASEAN, this is now encouraged through the so-called Qualified ASEAN Banks (QABs) program. Nonetheless, these qualified banks need to comply with both international standards and those prescribed by specific ASEAN country authorities, and the number of allowed cases is still small. The question is whether the common challenges posed by fintech can provide a lever to promote further cooperation in financial stability, financial integration, cooperation in cross-border payments and settlement, and harmonization of regulations and fintech practices, as well as learning from each other's fintech experiences.

Increased Focus on Fintech Risks

According to the Financial Stability Board (FSB), international bodies and national authorities need to increase their focus on fintech when making regular risk assessments and developing micro- and macroprudential regulatory frameworks in the following areas:

- Managing operational risks from third-party service providers

- Mitigating cyber risks

- Monitoring macrofinancial risks

- Cross-border legal issues and regulatory arrangements

- Governance and disclosure frameworks for big data analytics (FSB 2017)

Countries have called for greater international cooperation in many areas, including cybersecurity; AML/CFT; development of legal, regulatory, and supervisory frameworks; payment and securities settlement systems; and cross-border payments and capital flows. Standard-setting bodies also need to revise or develop international standards (IMF 2019).

The ASEAN+3 Macroeconomic Research Office is the logical body to assess these risks and propose coordination measures. However, this may require a substantial increase in staff since coverage of these issues will require expertise in new areas. These issues can also be taken up at the ASEAN and ASEAN+3 finance ministers' and central bank governors' meetings. A logical starting point would be to hold comprehensive policy dialogue for a wide range of issues on fintech within the ASEAN+3 finance group. More concretely, the ASEAN+3 finance ministers and central bank governors may launch a high-level working group on regional cooperation in fintech, discuss key issues, explore areas of cooperation, and implement cooperative initiatives step by step.

Work in this area has already started. Under the auspices of the ASEAN finance ministers and central bank governors, the ASEAN Working Committee on Financial Inclusion together with the World Bank carried out a broad assessment of activities relating to digital financial inclusion in the region. Given disparate rates of development of digital financial services, they emphasize the need for regional cooperation. "The broad spectrum of digital financial services development calls for greater intraregional knowledge exchange and cross-border investment. Aligning or standardizing regulatory frameworks throughout the ASEAN region, or at least among the largest economies in the region with similar levels of financial development, would facilitate such exchanges" (Aviles, Sitorus, and Trujillo Tejada 2019).

They singled out cyber risks as an area that "... would even benefit from a coordinated regional approach" (Aviles, Sitorus, and Trujillo Tejada 2019). Finally, they noted that "... the ASEAN region's broad digitization strategies and cooperation agreements should complement and be coordinated with [national financial inclusion strategies] and other strategies specific to the financial sector" (Aviles, Sitorus, and Trujillo Tejada 2019). The ASEAN Working Committee on Financial Inclusion report identifies the ASEAN Bankers Association and the ASEAN Financial Innovation Network as promising forums to advance public–private cooperation in these areas.

For cross-border banking, a pivotal regional mechanism is the ASEAN Banking Integration Framework (ABIF) endorsed in 2014. The framework, part of the commitment under the ASEAN Framework Agreement on Services, allows designation of QABs to banking institutions that meet the criteria subject to assessment and bilateral agreement. The designation will give the banks greater access to the other ASEAN economies (ASEAN 2015). Under the scheme, two Malaysian banks were granted the qualification to operate in Indonesia (ASEAN 2020, ASEAN Secretariat 2020). However, the overall pace of designating QABs in the region has been measured despite the willingness expressed by the national authorities.

ASEAN authorities have backed a study on the changing financial landscape in the region brought about by digitalization in preparation for the review of the ABIF Guidelines (ASEAN 2021). The initiative is arguably relevant and timely as ASEAN has made some progress in cross-border investment in digital banking. In December 2020, the MAS awarded digital banking licenses to four entities, including a consortium of Singapore Telecommunications Ltd (Singtel) and Grab Holding Inc (Grab); a consortium of Greenland Financial Holdings Group Co. Ltd, Linklogis Hong Kong Ltd and Ant Financial; and Beijing Co-operative Equity Investment Fund Management Co. Ltd. Among these, the first two got digital full bank licenses while the latter two PRC-based firms obtained digital wholesale bank licenses. The Philippines awarded its first digital bank license to Neobank Tonik in March 2021 (Tonik 2021). This could provide a boost to encouraging cross-border investment by more traditional banks as well.

Standardization and harmonization of systems in the area of capital markets are another important area for cooperation. At the level of ASEAN+3, the ASEAN+3 Bond Market Forum and the Cross-Border Settlement Infrastructure Forum are currently discussing the role of standardization to ensure interoperability of different systems.

In view of the current and potential global growth of fintech and bigtech firms, global financial stability can be improved by increased supervisory coordination and information-sharing for cross-border fintech that may affect banks, including the activities of bigtech firms (BCBS 2018).

The emergence of global stablecoins also poses new risks that make it desirable for authorities to coordinate on both the national and international level. Introduction of CBDCs should also be reviewed for possible side-effects on other member countries. The lack of harmonized standards and interoperability in some enabling technologies such as DLT represents another major challenge for authorities to overcome (Ehrentraud et al. 2020).

Supervisors can learn from each other's approaches and practices (BCBS 2018). Safety, soundness, and financial stability could be improved by supervisors studying the potential of new technologies to improve their methods and processes, and they share their practices and experiences with each other (BCBS 2018). The ASEAN Working Committee on Financial Inclusion report notes that "... intraregional knowledge exchanges, facilitation of cross-border payment systems based on country readiness, and partnerships between the private and public sectors to support innovation could greatly enhance development and use of digital financial services. In particular, countries in the region with more advanced digital financial services systems could continue regional and bilateral initiatives to share their experience and expertise with less developed neighbors" (Aviles, Sitorus, and Trujillo Tejada 2019).

Data sharing: Sharing of data for regulatory purposes is an important but controversial area. The use of digital financial data not only increases the amount of data, but makes it easier to share. Nonetheless, countries are likely to be reluctant to share sensitive private data. At least, the issue should be added to the agenda of areas for possible cooperative action. This also ties in with the possible use of big data for regulatory purposes, i.e., regulatory technology or regtech. Financial regulators can use big data to monitor systemic risk, with potential benefits for regional stability from sharing that information.

Trade finance: Fintech has shown great potential in utilizing big data, reducing the cost of delivering finance, and speeding up transaction processes. However, many institutional and legal barriers confronting fintech need to be solved through regional cooperation. Trade finance for SMEs is one important example. SME exporters are innovative, often young, and competitive. Yet, globally, banks reject 52% of their applications for trade finance, resulting in a very large global trade finance gap of $1.5 trillion. As the main driver of world trade, Asia and the Pacific accounts for 77% of global export letters of credit, reflecting the region's high dependence on traditional documentary credits. Consequently, 40% of the global gap in trade finance is estimated to occur in this region, especially in developing economies such as the PRC (Di Caprio, Beck, and Kim 2017). Both banks and firms have high expectations that fintech, in particular blockchain-based transactions, will fill this gap. However, digital solutions have yet to be widely applied and traditional problems associated with providing financial support to SMEs in trade persist.

To reduce financing gaps for trade, fintech approaches need to address due diligence challenges associated with performance and compliance (AML/CFT) risks. For example, SMEs should be encouraged to use a Legal Entity Identifier, a standardized and globally harmonized identification number that can make the transaction visible; reduce the cost of conducting due diligence; facilitate collection; and track credit, performance, and commercial dispute data. Mutual recognition of individual digital identification would help as well. Regional or global cooperation is needed to achieve this. Moreover, establishing digital standards in trade, both technical and regulatory, would address the difficulties of creating metadata needed to underpin due diligence on performance and other risks that inhibit financial institutions or fintech platforms from providing more support to SMEs (Dicaprio, Beck, and Kim 2017). The ASEAN Free Trade Area Council would be one entity to guide this cooperation.

Central bank digital currency: The development of CBDCs is another potential area for regional cooperation. Perhaps, the main challenge is to develop mechanisms for carrying out foreign exchange transactions between CBDCs. This holds out the promise of substantially reducing the cost of foreign exchange transactions and increasing transparency. Multiple CBDC Bridge is one such development. First, initiated bilaterally by the Hong Kong Monetary Authority and the Bank of Thailand under the name Inthanon-LionRock, the project was renamed Multiple CBDC Bridge when the PBOC and the Central Bank of the United Arab Emirates joined. The project explores the capabilities of DLT and studies the application of

CBDC in enhancing multicurrency cross-border payments. By tackling pain points such as inefficiencies, high cost, low transparency, and complexities related to achieving regulatory compliance, Multiple CBDC is expected to build a real-time, 24-hour payment bridge between Asia and the Middle East (Auer, Haene, and Holden 2021).

The Singapore–Canada (Ubin–Jasper Project) effort is another example. It handles transactions between tokenized depositary receipts of the respective currencies. It has tested cross-border payments with DLT systems under different models including wholesale CBDC, and has proved a prototype commercial blockchain network for multicurrency payments to improve cross-border payment functionality (KPMG 2018). Also, Phase 3 of Project Stella involving the Bank of Japan (BOJ) and European Central Bank (ECB) investigated the feasibility of a ledger-agnostic protocol that synchronizes payments across different types of ledgers. It also assessed the safety and efficiency implications of a variety of payment methods which could be used in the cross-ledger payment. It found that such systems were feasible, but that various legal, compliance, technology, and cost/benefit analysis issues would need to be addressed before such a system could be implemented (BOJ and ECB 2019).

4.9 Conclusion

Fintech has been recognized as a promising tool to promote financial inclusion, allowing excluded households and small firms to gain access to financial products and services. Its use is increasing rapidly in ASEAN+3 economies, especially where financial systems are more traditional and less developed. However, it presents many challenges as well. First, left by itself, fintech may actually tend to widen gaps in financial inclusion, income, and wealth. Second, it potentially has positive and negative implications for financial stability. Fintech potentially poses both microfinancial and macrofinancial financial stability risks. COVID-19 has accelerated the shift toward fintech use by firms and individuals, underscoring the need for adequate regulatory frameworks. Among fintech segments, digital payments and alternative finance are most likely to pose risks for financial stability, which can be addressed by enhanced regulation and supervision and potentially by greater regional cooperation.

Digital payments are expanding rapidly and will likely play the most important role in promoting financial inclusion among the unbanked and underbanked. Payment systems which bypass the legacy channels of bank deposits and credit cards, such as e-wallets and agent systems, are expanding the options and lowering costs for the financially underserved. The size of cryptoassets is very small, and they face various barriers to widespread use as stores of value or means of exchange, especially their high price volatility. Stablecoins could mount a more sustained challenge to legacy payment systems, however, and this trend needs to be monitored closely by G7 and G20 authorities. CBDCs could be implemented by central banks to stave off the challenge of stablecoins, but they also face difficulties in their implementation and potential limits to their usefulness.

Alternative finance is growing fast, but the scale remains very small relative to more traditional bank-centered finance. This reflects the small size of transactions, which are used mainly for working capital rather than investment, and perhaps basic limitations of the model, such as the lack of collateral or collection mechanism in case of default. However, if alternative finance models evolve to handle larger transactions, they may pose a more sustained threat to traditional banking.

Regulatory frameworks for fintech must address a complex intersection of issues. First, they need to balance the positive aspects of financial innovation against the needs for financial stability, consumer protection, cybersecurity, data protection, and AML/CFT efforts. Second, they must take account of the increasing role of bigtech firms and telecommunication firms not normally within the regulatory perimeter. The development of alternative lending platforms and digital currencies, either private or central bank, could have negative implications for the stability of the banking sector. Regulators must also work hard to upgrade their expertise and stay on top of rapidly evolving technologies and markets.

Fintech also has potential implications for the effectiveness of monetary policy and its operation. The development of alternative payment systems and digital currencies may make it more difficult for central banks to track developments of liquidity in the economy. The large presence of alternative forms of liquidity may also hinder the transmission of monetary policy. Fortunately, at this stage, the magnitude of such alternative instruments is judged too small to be a significant hindrance, although this could change. Regarding cryptoassets, stablecoins are more likely to pose a challenge than traditional cryptoassets such as Bitcoin, whose prices are very volatile, but even stablecoins face important limitations in scalability, congestion, and finality of transactions. On the other hand, if alternative currencies are interest-bearing, they could actually aid the transmission of monetary policy. CBDCs would compete with other financial assets as substitutes for central bank reserves. However, it does not seem that their existence would significantly alter the ways central banks use their balance sheets to operate monetary policy.

Fintech offers many fruitful areas for international cooperation, including cybersecurity; AML/CFT; development of legal, regulatory, and supervisory frameworks; sharing of data; payment and securities settlement systems; cross-border payments and capital flows; and trade finance. If CBDCs develop in the region, mechanisms for enabling foreign exchange transactions involving them need to be implemented. Increased supervisory coordination and information-sharing is appropriate for cross-border fintech that affects banks, bigtech firms, and capital flows. Fintech may also provide a wedge for banking integration by permitting greater direct investment by fintech banks in other regional markets. Other cross-border challenges include dealing with the emergence of global stablecoins and harmonizing standards. In doing so, supervisors and regulators will find it useful to compare experiences and best practices in dealing with rapidly developing technologies and markets. These issues can be addressed by regional institutions such as ASEAN+3 Macroeconomic Research Office, the ASEAN and ASEAN+3 finance ministers' and central bank governors' meetings, the ASEAN+3 Bond Market Forum, the ASEAN+3 Cross-Border Settlement Infrastructure Forum, the ASEAN Free Trade Area Council, the ASEAN Bankers Association, the ASEAN Financial Innovation Network, and the ASEAN Working Committee on Financial Inclusion.

References

Agur, I., A. Ari, and G. Dell'Ariccia. 2019. Designing Central Bank Digital Currencies. *ADBI Working Paper*. No 1065. Tokyo: Asian Development Bank Institute. https://www.adb.org/publications/designing-central-bank-digital-currencies.

Amstad, M. 2019. Regulating Fintech: Objectives, Principles, and Practices. In *Central Bank Digital Currency and Fintech in Asia*, edited by M. Amstad, B. Huang, P. Morgan, and S. Shirai. Tokyo: Asia Development Bank Institute. https://www.adb.org/sites/default/files/publication/539801/adbi-central-bank-digital-currency-and-fintech-asia.pdf.

Arner, D.W., J.N. Barberis, J. Walker, R.P. Buckley, and D.A. Zetzsche. 2020. Digital Finance & The COVID-19 Crisis. *University of Hong Kong Faculty of Law Research Paper*. No. 2020/017. University of New South Wales (UNSW Law Research). http://dx.doi.org/10.2139/ssrn.3558889.

Asian Development Bank (ADB). 2015. *Asian SME Finance Monitor 2014*. Manila. https://www.adb.org/sites/default/files/publication/173205/asia-sme-finance-monitor2014.pdf.

Association of Southeast Asian Nations (ASEAN). 2015. *ASEAN Banking Integration Stronger Regional Banks, More Robust and Inclusive Growth*. Jakarta. https://www.asean.org/storage/images/2015/October/outreach-document/Edited%20ASEAN%20Banking%20Integration%20Framework-1.pdf.

_____. 2020. Joint Statement of the 6th ASEAN Finance Ministers and Central Bank Governors' Meeting (AFMGM). Jakarta. https://asean.org/storage/2020/10/AFMGM6_JMS_Final-003.pdf.

_____. 2021. Joint Statement of the 7th ASEAN Finance Ministers and Central Bank Governors' Meeting (AFMGM). Jakarta. https://asean.org/storage/Joint_Statement_of_the_7th_AFMGM.pdf.

Association of Southeast Asian Nations (ASEAN) Secretariat. 2020. ASEAN 2020: Cohesive and Responsive. *ASEAN Annual Report 2019–2020*. Jakarta. https://asean.org/storage/2020/09/Annual-Report-ASEAN-2019–2020-Web-Version-v2.pdf.

Auer, R., P. Haene, and H. Holden. 2021. Multi-CBDC Arrangements and the Future of Crossborder Payments. *BIS Paper*. No 115. Basel: Bank for International Settlements. https://www.bis.org/publ/bppdf/bispap115.pdf.

Aviles, A.M., D. Sitorus, and V.P. Trujillo Tejada. 2019. *Advancing Digital Financial Inclusion in ASEAN: Policy and Regulatory Enablers*. Washington, DC: World Bank Group. http://documents.worldbank. org/curated/en/856241551375164922/Advancing-Digital-Financial-Inclusion-in-ASEAN-Policy-and-Regulatory-Enablers.

Bank for International Settlements (BIS). 2018a. Cryptocurrencies: Looking Beyond the Hype. *BIS Annual Report 2018*. Basel. https://www.bis. org/publ/arpdf/ar2018e5.pdf.

_____. 2018b. *Sound Practices: Implications of Fintech Developments for Banks and Bank Supervisors*. Basel. https://www.bis.org/bcbs/publ/ d431.pdf.

_____. 2019. Big Tech in Finance: Opportunities and Risks. *Annual Economic Report 2019*. Basel. https://www.bis.org/publ/arpdf/ ar2019e3.pdf.

_____. 2021. CBDCs: An Opportunity for the Monetary System. *BIS Annual Economic Report 2021*. https://www.bis.org/publ/arpdf/ ar2021e3.pdf.

Bank for International Settlements and the World Bank Group (BIS and WBG). 2016. *Payment Aspects of Financial Inclusion*. Basel and Washington, DC. https://www.bis.org/cpmi/publ/d144.pdf.

Bank of Japan and European Central Bank (BOJ and ECB). 2019. *Project Stella: Synchronised Cross-border Payments*. https://www.boj.or.jp/en/ announcements/release_2019/data/rel190604a1.pdf.

_____. 2020. *Project Stella: Balancing Confidentiality and Auditability in a Distributed Ledger Environment*. https://www.boj.or.jp/en/ announcements/release_2020/data/rel200212a1.pdf.

Bank of Thailand (BOT). 2021. Results of the Central Bank Digital Currency (CBDC) for Business Prototype Development Project. *BOT Press Release*. No. 13/2021. Bangkok. https://www.bot.or.th/English/ PressandSpeeches/Press/2021/Pages/n1364.aspx.

Basel Committee on Banking Supervision (BCBS). 2018. *Sound Practices: Implications of Fintech Developments for Banks and Bank Supervisors*. Basel: Bank for International Settlements. https://www.bis.org/bcbs/ publ/d431.pdf.

Beck, T. 2020. Fintech and Financial Inclusion: Opportunities and Pitfalls. *ADBI Working Paper*. No. 1165. Tokyo: Asian Development Bank Institute. https://www.adb.org/sites/default/files/ publication/623276/adbi-wp1165.pdf.

Berg, G., M. Guadamillas, H. Natarajan, and A. Sarkar. 2020. COVID-19 will Shape the Trajectory of FinTech Development in the Europe and Central Asia Region. *World Bank Blogs*. https://blogs.worldbank.org/psd/covid-19-will-shape-trajectory-fintech-development-europe-and-central-asia-region.

Bernot, K., S. Gebauer, and D. Schäfer. 2017. Monetary Policy Implications of Financial Innovation. *Politikberatung kompakt*. 120. Berlin: Deutsches Institut für Wirtschaftsforschung. https://www.diw.de/documents/vortragsdokumente/220/diw_01.c.560187.de/v_2017_sch%C3%A4fer_implications_econ.pdf.

Better than Cash Alliance. 2020. *How to Define Digital Payments?* United Nations Capital Development Fund. https://www.betterthancash.org/tools-research/toolkits/payments-measurement/focusing-your-measurement/introduction.

Cambridge Centre for Alternative Finance (CCAF). 2020. *The Global Alternative Finance Market Benchmarking Report: Trends, Opportunities and Challenges for Lending, Equity and Non-Investment Alternative Finance Models*. Cambridge, UK: University of Cambridge Judge Business School. https://www.jbs.cam.ac.uk/fileadmin/user_upload/research/centres/alternative-finance/downloads/2020-04-22-ccaf-global-alternative-finance-market-benchmarking-report.pdf.

_____. 2021. *The 2nd Global Alternative Finance Market Benchmarking Report: Trends, Opportunities and Challenges for Lending, Equity and Non-Investment Alternative Finance Models*. Cambridge, UK: University of Cambridge Judge Business School. https://www.jbs.cam.ac.uk/faculty-research/centres/alternative-finance/publications/the-2nd-global-alternative-finance-market-benchmarking-report/.

Cambridge Centre for Alternative Finance, Asian Development Bank Institute, and FinTechSpace (CCAF, ADBI and FinTechSpace). 2019. *ASEAN FinTech Ecosystem Benchmarking Study*. Cambridge, UK: University of Cambridge Judge Business School. https://www.jbs.cam.ac.uk/faculty-research/centres/alternative-finance/publications/the-asean-fintech-ecosystem-benchmarking-study/.

Cambridge Centre for Alternative Finance, the Academy of Internet Finance at Zhejiang University, and Asian Development Bank Institute (CCAF, AIFZU, and ADBI). 2018. *3rd Asia Pacific Region Alternative Finance Industry Report*. Cambridge, UK: University of Cambridge Judge Business School. https://www.jbs.cam.ac.uk/fileadmin/user_upload/research/centres/alternative-finance/downloads/2019-04-3rd-asia-pacific-alternative-finance-industry-report.pdf.

Carstens, A. 2021. Public Policy for Bigtechs in Finance. Conversations on Central Banking: Finance as Information. *Presentation.* 21 January. Asia School of Business in collaboration with MIT Sloan School of Management. https://www.youtube.com/watch?v=n8i9AMuQnTo.

CB Insights. 2020. *The State of Fintech Q1'20 Report: Investment & Sector Trends to Watch.* https://www.cbinsights.com/research/report/fintech-trends-q1–2020/.

Chaudhuri, C., J. Dahl, B. Sattanathan, and J. Sengupta. *2020. The Future of Payments in Asia.* Singapore and Hong Kong, China: McKinsey & Company. https://www.mckinsey.com/~/media/McKinsey/Industries/Financial%20Services/Our%20Insights/The%20next%20frontier%20in%20Asia%20payments/The-future-of-payments-in-Asia-vF.pdf.

Chuard, M. 2021. *What's Next for Open Banking?* Geneva: World Economic Forum. https://www.weforum.org/agenda/2021/04/open-banking-future-of-finance/.

Committee on Payments and Market Infrastructures: Markets Committee (CPMI-MC). 2018. *Central Bank Digital Currencies.* Basel: Bank for International Settlements. https://www.bis.org/cpmi/publ/d174.pdf.

Committee on the Global Financial System-Bank for International Settlements and the Financial Stability Board (CGFS and FSB). 2017. *FinTech Credit: Market Structure, Business Models and Financial Stability Implications.* Basel. https://www.fsb.org/wp-content/uploads/CGFS-FSB-Report-on-FinTech-Credit.pdf.

deVere Group. 2020. Coronavirus Lockdown: Massive Surge in the use of Fintech Apps. https://www.devere-group.com/news/Coronavirus-lockdown-Massive-surge-in-the-use-of-fintech-apps.aspx.

Di Caprio, A., S. Beck, and K. Kim. 2017. Trade Finance Gaps Continue Despite Fintech Breakthroughs. *Asian Development Blog.* https://blogs.adb.org/blog/trade-finance-gaps-continue-despite-fintech-breakthroughs.

Ehrentraud, J., D. Garcia Ocampo, L. Garzoni, and M. Piccolo. 2020. Policy Responses to Fintech: A Cross-country Overview. *FSI Insights on Policy Implementation.* No 23. Basel: Bank for International Settlements. https://www.bis.org/fsi/publ/insights23.pdf.

Endo, J. 2020. Digital Payment Grows in Philippines amid COVID-19 Fears. *Nikkei Asia.* 19 July. https://asia.nikkei.com/Business/Companies/Digital-payment-grows-in-Philippines-amid-COVID-19-fears.

European Central Bank (ECB). 2021. *Electronic Money*. Frankfurt. https://www.ecb.europa.eu/stats/money_credit_banking/ electronic_money/html/index.en.html#:~:text=Electronic%20 money%20(e%2Dmoney),than%20the%20e%2Dmoney%20 issuer.&text=E%2Dmoney%20products%20can%20be,to%20 store%20the%20monetary%20value.

Financial Stability Board (FSB). 2017. *Financial Stability Implications from FinTech: Supervisory and Regulatory Issues that Merit Authorities' Attention*. Basel. https://www.fsb.org/wp-content/uploads/R270617.pdf.

_____. 2019. *FinTech and Market Structure in Financial Services: Market Developments and Potential Financial Stability Implications*. Basel. https://www.fsb.org/wp-content/uploads/P140219.pdf.

Fintech News Philippines. 2021. FinScore Inks Partnership With UnionBank for Data-Driven Credit Scoring. 12 January. https://fintechnews. ph/44369/financial-inclusion/finscore-inks-partnership-with-unionbank-for-data-driven-credit-scoring/.

Fintechnews Switzerland. 2020. COVID-19 Crisis to Give Fintech Enablers a Boost. 13 May. https://fintechnews.ch/covid19/covid-19-crisis-to-give-fintech-enablers-a-boost/35802/.

Franco, L., A. L. García, V. Husetović, and J. Lassiter. 2020. Does Fintech Contribute to Systemic Risk? Evidence from the US and Europe. In *Macroeconomic Stabilization in the Digital Age*, edited by J. Beirne and D. Fernandez. Tokyo: Asian Development Bank Institute. https://www.adb.org/sites/default/files/publication/653306/adbi-macroeconomic-stabilization-digital-age.pdf.

Frost J., L. Gambacorta, Y. Huang, H.S. Shin, and P. Zbinden. 2019. BigTech and the Changing Structure of Financial Intermediation. *BIS Working Papers*. No 779. Basel: Bank for International Settlements. https://www.bis.org/publ/work779.pdf.

Fu, J. and M. Mishra. 2020. The Global Impact of COVID-19 on Fintech Adoption. *Swiss Finance Institute Research Paper Series*. No. 20–38. Zurich: Swiss Finance Institute. https://www.zora.uzh.ch/id/ eprint/187776/1/SSRN-id3588453.pdf.

Furche, P., C. Madeira, M. Marcel, and C. Medel. 2017. FinTech and the Future of Central Banking. *Economic Policy Papers*. No 63. Santiago, Chile: Central Bank of Chile. https://www.bcentral.cl/ documents/33528/0/DPE_63.pdf/16c8d359-2a6f-979d-0a94-ff20c148a09d?t=1588788358453.

Global Partnership for Financial Inclusion (GPFI). 2016. G20 High-Level Principles for Digital Financial Inclusion. Global Partnership for Financial Inclusion. https://www.gpfi.org/sites/gpfi/files/documents/G20%20High%20Level%20Principles%20for%20Digital%20Financial%20Inclusion%20-%20Full%20version-.pdf.

Global System for Mobile Communications Association (GSMA). 2020. State of the Industry Report on Mobile Money 2019. London. https://www.gsma.com/sotir/wp-content/uploads/2020/03/GSMA-State-of-the-Industry-Report-on-Mobile-Money-2019-Full-Report.pdf.

Group of 20 (G20). 2019. G20 Osaka Leaders' Declaration. 28–29 June. https://www.mofa.go.jp/policy/economy/g20_summit/osaka19/en/documents/final_g20_osaka_leaders_declaration.html.

———. 2020. Leaders' Declaration. 21–22 November. https://www.mofa.go.jp/files/100117981.pdf.

Haidar, B. 2020. COVID-19 Underlines the Importance of Fintech in Emerging Markets. Geneva: World Economic Forum. https://www.weforum.org/agenda/2020/05/covid-19-importance-mobile-solutions-emerging-markets/.

Huang, B., Y. Wu, and J. Yang. 2020. Digital Finance and Financial Literacy: An Empirical Investigation of Chinese Households. ADBI Working Paper Series. No. 1190. Tokyo: Asian Development Bank Institute. https://www.adb.org/sites/default/files/publication/668351/adbi-wp1209.pdf.

Huang, Y. 2020. Fintech Development in the People's Republic of China and its Macroeconomic Implications. In Macroeconomic Stabilization in the Digital Age, edited by J. Beirne and D. Fernandez. Tokyo: Asian Development Bank Institute. https://www.adb.org/sites/default/files/publication/653306/adbi-macroeconomic-stabilization-digital-age.pdf.

International Finance Corporation (IFC). 2013. IFC Jobs Study: Assessing Private Sector Contributions to Job Creation and Poverty Reduction. Washington, DC. https://documents1.worldbank.org/curated/en/157191468326714061/pdf/835080WP0IFC0J00Box382079B00PUBLIC0.pdf.

International Monetary Fund (IMF). 2016. Monetary Policy and the Rise of Nonbank Finance. Global Financial Stability Report—Fostering Stability in a Low-Growth, Low-Rate Era. Washington, DC. https://www.imf.org/external/pubs/ft/gfsr/2016/02/pdf/text.pdf.

_____. 2018. The Bali Fintech Agenda: A Blueprint for Successfully Harnessing Fintech's Opportunities. *Press Release*. No. 18/388. Washington, DC: International Monetary Fund. https://www.imf.org/en/News/Articles/2018/10/11/pr18388-the-bali-fintech-agenda#:~:text=The%20International%20Monetary%20Fund%20and,services%2C%20while%20at%20the%20same.

_____. 2019. *Fintech: The Experience So Far. Washington*, DC: International Monetary Fund. https://www.imf.org/-/media/Files/Publications/PP/2019/PPEA2019024.ashx.

_____. 2020. *Digital Money Across Borders: Macro-Financial Implications*. Washington, DC: International Monetary Fund. https://www.imf.org/en/Publications/Policy-Papers/Issues/2020/10/17/Digital-Money-Across-Borders-Macro-Financial-Implications-49823.

Kishi, M. 2019. Project Stella and the Impacts of Fintech on Financial Infrastructures in Japan. In *Central Bank Digital Currency and Fintech in Asia*, edited by M. Amstad, B. Huang, P. Morgan, and S. Shirai. Tokyo: Asia Development Bank Institute. https://www.adb.org/sites/default/files/publication/539801/adbi-central-bank-digital-currency-and-fintech-asia.pdf.

Klein, A. 2019. Is China's New Payment System the Future? Washington, DC: Center on Regulations and Markets, Brookings Institution. https://www.brookings.edu/wp-content/uploads/2019/06/ES_20190620_Klein_ChinaPayments.pdf.

Korobov, G. 2020. How the Post-COVID-19 Reality will Change Banks and Fintech. *Blog Article*. 13 May. Finextra. https://www.finextra.com/blogposting/18749/how-the-post-covid-19-reality-will-change-banks-and-fintech.

KPMG. 2018. Cross-border Interbank Payments and Settlements: Emerging Opportunities for Digital Transformation. https://www.mas.gov.sg/-/media/MAS/ProjectUbin/Cross-Border-Interbank-Payments-and-Settlements.pdf?la=en&hash=5472F1876CFA9439591F06CE3C7E522F01F47EB6.

Moenjak, T., A. Kongprajya, and C. Monchaitrakul. 2020. FinTech, Financial Literacy, and Consumer Saving and Borrowing: The Case of Thailand. *ADBI Working Paper*. No. 1100. Tokyo: Asian Development Bank Institute. https://www.adb.org/sites/default/files/publication/575576/adbi-wp1100.pdf.

Monetary Authority of Singapore (MAS). 2020a. Project Ubin: Central Bank Digital Money Using Distributed Ledger Technology. *Schemes and Initiatives*. Singapore. 8 December. https://www.mas.gov.sg/schemes-and-initiatives/project-ubin.

_____. 2020b. MAS Announces Successful Applicants of Licences to Operate New Digital Banks in Singapore. *Media Releases*. 4 December. Singapore. https://www.mas.gov.sg/news/media-releases/2020/mas-announces-successful-applicants-of-licences-to-operate-new-digital-banks-in-singapore.

Morgan, P., B. Huang, and L.Q. Trinh. 2019. The Need to Promote Digital Financial Literacy for the Digital Age. *Policy Brief*. T20 Japan Task Force 7: The Future of Work and Education for the Digital Age. https://t20japan.org/policy-brief-need-promote-digital-financial-literacy/.

Morgan, P. and L.Q. Trinh. 2020. Fintech and Financial Literacy in Viet Nam. *ADBI Working Paper Series*. No. 1154. Tokyo: Asian Development Bank Institute. https://www.adb.org/sites/default/files/publication/616781/adbi-wp1154.pdf.

Morris, S. and H.S. Shin. 2018. Distributed Ledger Technology and Large Value Payments: A Global Game Approach. *Presentation*. 9 November. Conference on Cryptocurrencies and Blockchains. University of Chicago Becker Friedman Institute.

National Bank of Cambodia (NBC). 2020. Project Bakong: Next Generation Payment System. *White Paper*. Phnom Penh: National Bank of Cambodia. https://bakong.nbc.org.kh/download/NBC_BAKONG_White_Paper.pdf.

Nemoto, N., D. Storey, and B. Huang. 2019. Optimal Regulation of P2P Lending for Small and Medium-Sized Enterprises. *ADBI Working Paper*. No. 912. Tokyo: Asian Development Bank Institute. https://www.adb.org/sites/default/files/publication/478611/adbi-wp912.pdf.

Organisation for Economic Co-operation and Development (OECD). 2017. Enhancing the Contributions of SMEs in a Global and Digitalised Economy. *Meeting of the OECD Council at Ministerial Level*. Paris. https://www.oecd.org/industry/C-MIN-2017-8-EN.pdf.

Ozili, P.K. 2020. Financial Inclusion and Fintech during COVID-19 Crisis: Policy Solutions. *The Company Lawyer Journal*. 8. http://dx.doi.org/10.2139/ssrn.3585662.

Pazarbasioglu, C., A. Garcia Mora, M. Uttamchandani, H. Natarajan, E. Feyen, and M. Saal 2020. *Digital Financial Services*. Washington, DC: World Bank Group. https://pubdocs.worldbank.org/en/230281588169110691/Digital-Financial-Services.pdf.

Peoples' Bank of China (PBOC). 2020. Interview with PBOC Governor Yi Gang by Financial News and China Finance on Key Issues During "Two Sessions". *Speeches*. Beijing. May 30. http://www.pbc.gov.cn/en/3688110/3688175/4031198/index.html.

PwC. 2019. It's Time for a Consumer-Centred Metric: Introducing 'Return on Experience'. *Global Consumer Insights Survey 2019*. https://www.pwc.com/gx/en/consumer-markets/consumer-insights-survey/2019/report.pdf.

Shinozaki, S. 2014. Capital Market Financing for SMEs: A Growing Need in Emerging Asia. *ADB Working Paper Series on Regional Economic Integration*. No. 121. Manila: Asian Development Bank. https://www.adb.org/sites/default/files/publication/31179/reiwp-121.pdf.

Shirai, S. 2019. Money and Central Bank Digital Currency. In *Central Bank Digital Currency and Fintech in Asia*, edited by M. Amstad, B. Huang, P. Morgan, and S. Shirai. Tokyo: Asia Development Bank Institute. https://www.adb.org/sites/default/files/publication/539801/adbi-central-bank-digital-currency-and-fintech-asia.pdf.

———. 2020. *Growing Central Bank Challenges in the World and Japan: Low Inflation, Monetary Policy, and Digital Currency*. Tokyo: Asia Development Bank Institute. https://www.adb.org/sites/default/files/publication/611476/adbi-growing-central-bank-challenges-world-japan-low-inflation-monetary-policy-digital-currency.pdf.

Statista. 2020a. *Digital Payments Report 2020: Asia*. https://www.statista.com/outlook/296/101/digital-payments/asia.

———. 2020b. Growth in Average Weekly Usage of Finance Apps during the COVID-19 Pandemic in Selected Counties from December 29, 2019 to March 1, 2020. https://www.statista.com/statistics/1116563/fintech-apps-growth-usage-covid19/ (accessed April 2021).

Supadulya, C., K. Tansanguan, V. Sethaput, W. Wattanasiriwiroj, and K. Areechitranusorn. 2019. In *Central Bank Digital Currency and Fintech in Asia*, edited by M. Amstad, B. Huang, P. Morgan, and S. Shirai. Tokyo: Asia Development Bank Institute. https://www.adb.org/sites/default/files/publication/539801/adbi-central-bank-digital-currency-and-fintech-asia.pdf.

Tonik. 2021. Tonik Launches as First Neobank in the Philippines. *News.* 18 March. https://tonikbank.com/news/tonik-launches-first-neobank-philippines.

Visa Economic Empowerment Institute (VEEI). 2021. *The Rise of Digital Remittances: How Innovation is Improving Global Money Movement.* Washington, DC: Visa. https://usa.visa.com/content/dam/VCOM/global/ms/documents/veei-the-rise-of-digital-remittances.pdf.

World Alliance of International Financial Centers (WAIFC). 2020. *How Global Financial Centers Can Help Combat the COVID-19 Pandemic.* Brussels. https://waifc.finance/assets/files/c7a00b63-4ec7-49ee-bfef-3964dfd816ef.3e0b86c21ccc0f4dfcbda4e9df93e028.pdf.

World Bank. 2018. Overview. *Financial Inclusion.* Washington, DC. World Bank. https://www.worldbank.org/en/topic/financialinclusion/overview (accessed October 2020).

World Bank and Cambridge Centre for Alternative Finance (CCAF). 2020. The Global COVID-19 FinTech Regulatory Rapid Assessment Report. Washington, DC: World Bank Group and Cambridge, UK: University of Cambridge. https://www.jbs.cam.ac.uk/wp-content/uploads/2020/10/2020-ccaf-report-fintech-regulatory-rapid-assessment.pdf.

Yoshino, N., P.J. Morgan, and L.Q. Trinh. 2020. Financial Literacy and Fintech Adoption in Japan. *ADBI Working Paper.* No. 1095. Tokyo: Asian Development Bank Institute. https://www.adb.org/publications/financial-literacy-fintech-adoption-japan.

Zachariadis, M., P. Ozcan, and D. Dinçkol. 2020. The COVID-19 Impact on Fintech: Now Is the Time to Boost Investment. *LSE Business Review Blog Post.* 13 April. http://eprints.lse.ac.uk/104463/3/businessreview_2020_04_13_the_covid_19_impact_on_fintech_now_is_the.pdf.

5 Financing Sustainable Infrastructure Investment in ASEAN+3

Naoyuki Yoshino, Saloni Lakhia, and Josef T. Yap

5.1 Introduction

Infrastructure development is a key component of inclusive economic growth. Better access to physical infrastructure has increased firm-level competitiveness, reduced poverty, and improved welfare. The primary mechanism for these outcomes is enhanced economic productivity. Infrastructure encourages efficiency by lowering distribution costs and making goods and services more affordable (ADB 2017). Meanwhile, by allowing access to better health and educational services and fostering greater social and economic mobility, infrastructure bestows benefits equitably across income classes.

To maintain the beneficial contribution of infrastructure to economic development, plans and programs that articulate its role and design can be guided by the UN Sustainable Development Goals (SDGs) and the Principles for Promoting Quality Infrastructure Investment espoused by the Group of 20 (G20). A common link between these two sets of tenets is the objective of incorporating environmental considerations. This is one of the components of sustainability considered in this chapter. The other is closing a financing gap that threatens the implementation of these plans and programs.

Financing Gaps Constrain Infrastructure Investment

While developing Asia has made great strides in the last 5 decades in building infrastructure, major shortfalls remain. The Asian Development Bank (ADB 2017) estimated that over 400 million Asians still lack electricity; roughly 300 million have no access to safe drinking water and

1.5 billion people lack basic sanitation. In 2017, the Asian Development Bank (ADB) estimated that total investment needs for 2016–2030 for its 45 developing member countries would be $22.6 trillion (in 2015 prices). The amount covers transport, power, telecommunications, and water supply and sanitation. However, if the costs of climate mitigation and adaptation are included, the amount rises to $26.2 trillion. This is equivalent to 5.1% of projected gross domestic product (GDP) during that period.

Using data for 25 of these developing Asian countries, which cover 96% of the region's population and include seven Southeast Asian economies, an annual infrastructure gap was calculated for 2016–2020 (Table 5.1). This provided a benchmark for analysis, with the gap expected to extend beyond 2020. Including climate-related needs led to a gap of about $459 billion annually or 2.4% of projected GDP. Without the People's Republic of China (PRC), the gap in the climate-adjusted scenario as a share of remaining economies' GDP was 5%.

**Table 5.1: Estimated Infrastructure Investments and Gaps,
25 Developing Asian Economies, 2016–2020**
($ billion in 2015 prices)

Economy Coverage	Estimated Current Investment (2015)	Baseline Estimates			Climate-Adjusted Estimates		
		Annual need	Gap	Gap (% of GDP)	Annual need	Gap	Gap (% of GDP)
Total (25)	881	1,211	330	1.7	1,340	459	2.4
Total without PRC (24)	195	457	262	4.3	503	308	5.0
Central Asia (3)	6	11	5	2.3	12	7	3.1
South Asia (8)	134	294	160	4.7	329	195	5.7
Southeast Asia (7)	55	147	92	3.8	157	102	4.1
Pacific (5)	1	2	1	6.2	2	2	6.9
Indonesia	23	70	47	4.7	74	51	5.1
PRC	686	753	68	0.5	837	151	1.2

GDP = gross domestic product, PRC = People's Republic of China.
Note: The numbers in parentheses refer to the number of selected economies. The gap as a percent of GDP is based on the annual average of projected GDP from 2016 to 2020. The 25 economies covered here are listed in Appendix 3.1 of ADB (2017, 95).
Source: ADB (2017).

Sustainable Infrastructure Investment

This chapter examines the role of the public and private sector in providing resources for infrastructure investment. A key issue is to align the process and outcome with the concept of sustainability, resulting in *sustainable infrastructure investment.* Sustainability is defined along three dimensions: macroeconomic stability, environmental soundness, and encouraging and maintaining private sector participation.

Mobilizing public sector resources for infrastructure projects should not lead to unsustainable debt levels. Meanwhile, climate mitigation measures—primarily focused on the reduction of greenhouse gas emissions—and climate adaptation measures should be incorporated in investment plans in line with the SDGs and the Principles for Promoting Quality Infrastructure Investment.[1] Given relatively limited public sector resources, particularly to support environment-friendly infrastructure, the private sector has to be incentivized to broaden and deepen its participation in infrastructure finance.

Figure 5.1 summarizes the mechanisms through which public and private sectors can finance infrastructure. Sources of public infrastructure finance include national and subnational governments, development financial institutions—which include multilateral development banks, national development banks, and other financial institutions (for example, the China Development Bank in the PRC—and official development assistance.

Figure 5.1: Sources of Public and Private Sector Infrastructure Finance

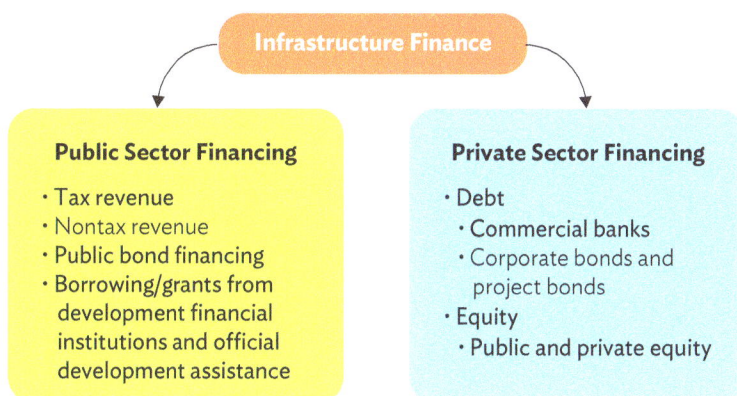

Infrastructure Finance

Public Sector Financing

- Tax revenue
- Nontax revenue
- Public bond financing
- Borrowing/grants from development financial institutions and official development assistance

Private Sector Financing

- Debt
  - Commercial banks
  - Corporate bonds and project bonds
- Equity
  - Public and private equity

Source: ADB (2017).

---

[1] These are referred to as green investment or green projects. Apart from climate change mitigation and climate change adaptation, economic activities related to environmental sustainability are the use and protection of water and marine resources; the transition to a circular economy; pollution prevention and control; and the protection and restoration of biodiversity and ecosystems.

Section 5.2 describes the role of public finance and the importance of debt sustainability. Developing Asia has relied heavily on the public sector for financing infrastructure investment. In 2017, this was estimated at 92% (ADB 2017). However, public funds are not sufficient to cover the estimated gap for 2016–2030. Demand for public resources created by the coronavirus disease (COVID-19) pandemic has exacerbated this shortfall, making the need for private sector financing more critical.

Private sector infrastructure finance primarily relies on user fees—the revenue stream that supports financing through either public or private equity or debt, e.g., borrowing from commercial banks or by issuing bonds. User fees are relatively low in developing economies. As a result, the risk-return profile of infrastructure projects has diverted from those that are normally undertaken by the private sector. Figure 5.2 shows that the return from user fees, i.e., the benchmark yield, is usually lower than the expected or desired return of private investors. This has led to the relative scarcity of bankable infrastructure projects, which has impeded the participation of the private sector. Section 5.3 tackles this issue and proposes measures to encourage private sector participation. The section also discusses how public and private finance can be combined to deliver infrastructure services—such as public–private partnership (PPP) infrastructure projects.

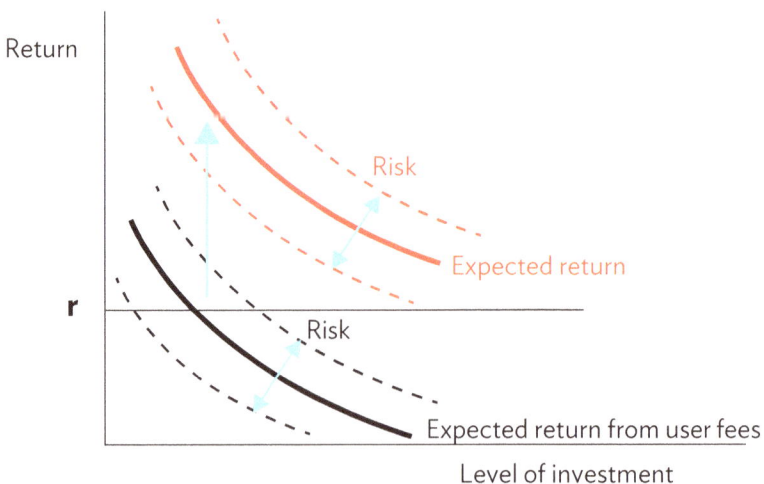

Figure 5.2: Expected Rate of Return and Risk Profile of Project Bonds versus Benchmark Yield

Source: Authors.

Two crosscutting issues that run between public and private finance are: (i) the need to raise resources for the infrastructure components related to climate mitigation and adaptation, so-called green finance; and (ii) the impact of COVID-19 on the availability of resources and the attractiveness of green projects. Sections 5.4 and 5.5 deal with these issues separately. The three components of sustainability in this chapter are, therefore, interwoven in several ways. One, exploring how to incentivize the private sector to support green infrastructure projects. Two, evaluating the government response to the added burden from climate-adjusted infrastructure requirements and relief and recovery measures necessitated by the pandemic. And three, how economic recovery measures can dovetail with green projects.

Figure 5.3 presents the key challenges confronting most economies in green projects and how the pandemic has magnified problems. Related to the ability to mobilize savings, government recovery strategies to address the pandemic must plan to better leverage resources for attracting capital from nonpublic sources including PPPs; institutions (pension funds, commercial banks, etc.); and the capital markets, together grouped as private, institutional, and commercial sources (ADB 2020a).

Figure 5.3: Challenges in Promoting Green Infrastructure

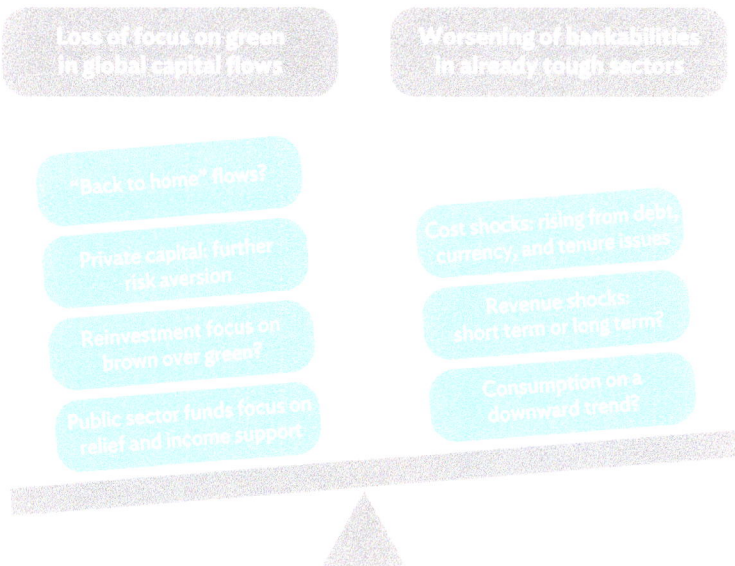

Loss of focus on green in global capital flows

Worsening of bankabilities in already tough sectors

"Back to home" flows?

Private capital: further risk aversion

Reinvestment focus on brown over green?

Public sector funds focus on relief and income support

Cost shocks: rising from debt, currency, and tenure issues

Revenue shocks: short term or long term?

Consumption on a downward trend?

Source: ADB (2020a).

The penultimate section examines how regional cooperation can support sustainable infrastructure investment. Progress in previous efforts is reported, particularly the development of local currency bonds. These are juxtaposed against more recent measures that focus on green finance. The last section concludes.

5.2 Role of Public Finance

As noted, the public sector has played a dominant role in the provision of infrastructure investment.[2] In 2017, this was estimated at 92% of total infrastructure investment. Data in Tables 5.2 and 5.3 indicate this trend has continued in recent years for the ASEAN+3 economies,[3] at least in the ratio to GDP. Table 5.2 is obtained from ADB (2017) and shows the average of both public and private infrastructure investment for 2010–2014. Data on private sector infrastructure investment could not be replicated for later years. Data for general government gross fixed capital formation for 2005 to 2019 were obtained (Table 5.3). The bulk of this expenditure category is public infrastructure investment, and it can be gleaned from Tables 5.2 and 5.3 that, as a ratio to GDP, public infrastructure investment has remained fairly steady in East Asia.

The heavy reliance on the public sector in this context stems from the public goods nature of the bulk of infrastructure investment. Many projects yield low private rates of return but high social rates of return. This section examines the role of public finance, with particular attention on fiscal space and debt sustainability.

Table 5.2: Public and Private Infrastructure Investment in Asia, 2010–2014
(% of GDP)

	Private	Public
25 ADB Developing Member Countries	0.4	5.1
East Asia	app. 0	6.3
South Asia	1.8	3.0
Central and West Asia	0.3	2.6
Pacific	0.3	2.5
Southeast Asia	0.5	2.1
People's Republic of China	app. 0	6.3
Indonesia	0.3	2.3

ADB = Asian Development Bank, GDP = gross domestic product.
Note: The numbers are based on 25 selected countries listed in Appendix 3.1 of ADB (2017).
Source: ADB (2017).

---

[2] The main reference for discussion in this section is ADB (2017, pp. 55–59).

[3] Association of Southeast Asian Nations plus the People's Republic of China, Japan, and the Republic of Korea

**Table 5.3: General Government Gross Fixed Capital Formation
in ASEAN+3**
(% of GDP)

Economy	2005	2010	2015	2019
Brunei Darussalam	3.4	5.9	5.4	1.7
Cambodia	3.6	8.2	3.7	3.4
People's Republic of China	18.6	17.7	15.3	17.3
Hong Kong, China	4.3	4.7	6.2	5.8
Indonesia	2.9	2.4	3.3	3.4
Japan	5.9	5.2	5.0	5.0
Korea, Rep. of	5.8	5.2	4.3	4.8
Lao PDR	4.3	6.4	6.0	...
Philippines	1.5	2.2	2.2	3.7
Singapore	4.2	4.5	5.1	4.7
Thailand	5.8	5.1	5.2	5.0
Viet Nam	3.8	5.6	5.4	5.8

GDP = gross domestic product, PRC = People's Republic of China, Lao PDR = Lao People's Democratic Republic.
Note: The variables refer to the general government investment (gross fixed capital formation) in billions of constant 2011 international dollars and GDP in billions of constant 2011 international dollars.
Source: International Monetary Fund Investment and Capital Stock Dataset May 2021 Update (accessed July 2021).

Three Considerations for Fiscal Space

Even prior to the pandemic, a fiscal gap in available resources for physical infrastructure investment was forecast (ADB 2017). Public finance reforms in 24 of the 25 economies referred to in Table 5.1 were determined to narrow the gap, but only approximately 40% of the shortfall for 2016–2020 could be covered. Figure 5.4 indicates that debt service in the Asia and the Pacific is relatively high, even further constraining public sector ability to provide adequate infrastructure services.

Fiscal sustainability is the primary concern in public sector finance here. To assess fiscal space for infrastructure investment, three areas can be explored. First, policy makers need to determine to what extent tax efforts can be raised through higher rates or reforms aimed at greater administrative efficiency in tax collection. Second, opportunities exist whereby public spending can be reoriented toward infrastructure investment and away from inefficient items such as poorly targeted subsidies. Third, policy makers can assess the extent to which government can borrow while maintaining sustainable public debt. This is normally done by analyzing the economy's growth prospects—which represents the capacity to pay—and prevailing interest rates.

Figure 5.4: Debt Service in Selected Developing Asian Economies, 2019 and 2020

a. Debt Service on External Debt to Total External Debt, 2019 (%)

b. Debt Service on External Debt to Total Revenues, 2020 (%)

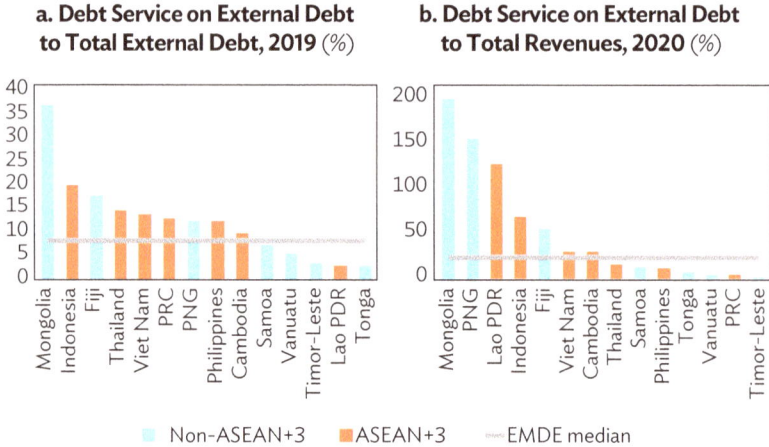

Non-ASEAN+3   ASEAN+3   EMDE median

EMDE = emerging market and developing economies, Lao PDR = Lao People's Democratic Republic, PNG = Papua New Guinea, PRC = People's Republic of China.
Note: The EMDE medians are based on the calculations and definitions of World Bank (2021a). Total revenues refer to general government revenues.
Source: World Bank (2021a).

Public transfers of tax revenues—whether current or future—are the main source of public sector infrastructure financing. Table 5.4 shows general government revenue as a percentage of GDP for ASEAN+3 countries. Other sources are user charges for publicly provided infrastructure services, tools such as land value capture, and international transfers which usually come in the form of official development assistance. Future tax revenues are important in the context of debt sustainability.

Most economies in the region can sustainably increase revenues through changes in tax policy, improving tax administration, or a combination of the two. At the time the 2017 ADB report was written, in most economies, specific policies had already been identified and their impact on revenues quantified. Overall, IMF estimates at that time suggested that 22 of the 25 developing Asian economies analyzed could sustainably increase revenues via policy reform. In the case of ASEAN+3 economies, the performance of general government revenue has improved between 2005 and 2020, or at least remained steady (Table 5.4). The performance is comparable with other emerging market middle-income economies, except those in Europe.

Reorienting other budget expenditures toward public investment can also increase resources for infrastructure investment. Energy subsidies are one major source. Studies show subsidies are often poorly targeted, with most benefits accruing to the wealthiest households. They also lead to energy overconsumption, which harms the environment. Reforms of unprofitable state-owned enterprises are another area for consideration. IMF estimates at that time suggested at least 14 developing Asian economies could reorient expenditures toward public investment.

Table 5.4: General Government Revenue in ASEAN+3
(% of GDP)

Economies	2005	2010	2015	2020
Cambodia	11.9	17.1	19.6	22.5
PRC	16.9	24.7	28.8	25.6
Hong Kong, China	17.2	20.7	18.6	19.7
Indonesia	17.9	15.6	14.9	12.4
Japan	29.1	28.7	33.6	34.1
Korea, Rep. of	19.7	20.1	20.3	22.8
Lao PDR	12.8	20.9	20.2	12.1
Malaysia	21.7	22.3	22.2	20.4
Myanmar	9.9	9.2	21.4	16.0
Philippines	17.1	16.1	18.5	19.6
Singapore	14.9	15.9	17.3	17.7
Thailand	21.8	20.9	22.3	20.6
Viet Nam	19.7	21.5	19.2	16.2
Emerging Market and Middle-Income Economies Groups				
G20	25.2	27.0	27.4	25.3
Asia	17.9	22.5	26.2	23.6
Europe	36.2	34.1	33.4	34.3
Latin America	27.6	29.9	26.4	25.8
MENA and Pakistan	35.7	31.7	27.1	23.8

G20 = Group of Twenty, Lao PDR = Lao People's Democratic Republic, MENA = Middle East and North Africa , PRC = People's Republic of China.
Note: Brunei Darussalam is not included in the data set. The emerging market and middle-income economies groupings are based on the definitions of the source.
Source: International Monetary Fund Fiscal Monitor Database (accessed July 2021).

Assessing Debt Sustainability

Meanwhile, any discussion of fiscal space must deal with public borrowing capacity and debt sustainability. High debt makes public finance and the broader economy vulnerable to growth and interest rate shocks. Debt servicing costs would consume a large share of government expenditures, restricting other priority spending. High public debt can also hurt the private sector, as the prospect of tax hikes or cutbacks in government spending to service debt can dampen investor sentiment and economic activity. Increased government borrowing can crowd out private investment.

Debt sustainability analysis helps assess how much spending can increase while keeping debt levels manageable. For a given set of macroeconomic assumptions, one can compute the primary balance—fiscal balance excluding interest payments—that will stabilize or raise public debt. Stabilizing public debt may not make sense in all cases—where those with low debt burdens could allow an increase to provide more room for priority spending. Normally, for economies with public debt greater than 50% the target is to stabilize public debt at current levels. On the other hand, low-debt economies—with public debt below 50% of GDP—can raise public debt toward the 50% of GDP threshold over a decade.

The fundamental point for developing Asia is that—considering revenue and expenditure measures along with debt sustainability—regional economies have fiscal space to increase infrastructure investment. Looking at individual countries, some have more than others.

This analysis has focused on the quantifiable aspects of fiscal space for infrastructure investment, but several other important (but less quantifiable) factors also shape policy makers' public infrastructure investment decisions. First, governments often have other pressing priorities, such as health and education expenditures, which compete for the available fiscal space of governments. Second, contingent liabilities— emanating from the financial sector or disaster risk, for example—are often difficult to quantify and can reduce available fiscal space. Third, governments can squeeze more out of each investment dollar by improving the efficiency of the public investment process. Fourth, maturity dates of current public debt have to be accounted for. Bunching up of maturities may affect the feasibility of some infrastructure projects. Finally, there is much scope for governments in the region to increase infrastructure-related revenues. These include user fees that governments can charge for infrastructure services, which are more common for some types of infrastructure such as piped water, energy, and highways, but where prices are often set below cost recovery. Additional revenue can also arise from the increased economic activity generated by infrastructure projects, in some cases mitigating the burden of debt servicing.

Another infrastructure-related revenue stream—one underutilized by many countries as a means of financing infrastructure—is land value capture, a method by which the increase in property or land value due to public infrastructure improvements is captured through land-related taxes or other means to pay for the improvements. Essentially, it enables increases in private real estate value generated by public investments to flow to the public sector. Value capture works best for specific types of projects. In general, it produces the highest return in areas undergoing rapid urban growth. Development drives up land prices, creating an ideal opportunity to raise significant revenues. While value capture can be applied to a wide range of sectors, it is most appropriate for three project types: (i) new land development; (ii) major capital projects, particularly in transportation; and (iii) infrastructure that supports basic services such as water supply, wastewater treatment, and drainage. The benefits arising from these projects contribute directly to raising the value of the surrounding land, making value capture ideal.

5.3 Expanding Involvement of the Private Sector

Because of the anticipated shortfall in financial resources in 2016–2030 and the current strain on public finance, the role of the private sector has to be expanded. Table 5.5 shows that the access of the private sector in ASEAN+3 countries to credit resources has improved between 2015 and 2020. Mechanisms have to be designed to channel these funds to infrastructure investment.

The discussion of private sector financing in this section focuses on: (i) the progress of local bond markets—particularly those denominated in local currency—and how regional financial cooperation could continue its constructive role; (ii) specific tools to attract more private sector investment: (a) floating-interest-rate infrastructure bonds anchored on spillover tax revenues of the underlying project; (b) land trust methods, which can help overcome some right-of-way issues; and (iii) the regulatory and institutional framework for private sector participation, with a focus on PPPs.

The Nature of Private Finance

Since public finance reforms could cover only approximately 40% of the infrastructure finance shortfall for 2016–2020, it is deemed critical to expand the role of private sector finance. The latter can be broadly divided into project and corporate finance. Project finance—otherwise known as limited recourse financing—utilizes a special purpose vehicle to raise funds for acquiring or constructing an infrastructure asset. Once operational, the cash flows generated by the project special purpose vehicle are used to pay its costs. In corporate finance, projects are undertaken by companies themselves and funded through their own balance sheets. While corporate finance is more flexible and less complicated than project finance, companies can only take on as much debt as their equity allows. Moreover, large projects may cause excessive balance sheet exposure. Thus, corporate finance is commonly used in relatively smaller infrastructure projects.

Table 5.5: Sources of Private Sector Credit in ASEAN+3
(% of GDP)

Economy	Domestic Credit to Private Sector by Banks			Equity Market Capitalization[a]			Local Currency Corporate Bonds		
	2015	2019	2020	2015	2019	2020	2015	2019	2020
Brunei Darussalam	41.1	34.9	38.8	...	...	...	...	...	...
Cambodia	74.2	114.2	...	1.0	2.6	9.5	...	...	...
PRC	152.6	165.4	182.4	77.1	60.1	78.5	24.0	30.6	35.7
Hong Kong, China	208.8	237.5	258.5	1,029.2	1,341.7	1,767.6	28.7	38.1	45.4
Indonesia	33.1	32.5	33.2	42.3	45.9	45.2	2.2	2.8	2.8
Japan	102.0	109.6	...	109.6	120.1	128.8	14.7	15.3	16.6
Korea, Rep. of	132.1	151.7	165.5	87.1	89.1	122.2	72.3	78.6	84.6
Lao PDR	...	...	...	10.3	5.9	...	...	...	...
Malaysia	123.1	120.8	134.1	139.7	109.2	123.9	43.1	50.0	56.0
Myanmar	17.7	26.3	28.7	...	0.6	0.6	...	...	...
Philippines	39.9	48.0	51.9	80.2	71.5	73.0	5.8	7.7	9.0
Singapore	122.4	120.0	132.7	213.7	183.6	183.8	33.1	32.3	37.0
Thailand	115.9	111.2	125.0	91.4	100.3	104.0	18.3	22.4	23.5
Viet Nam	111.9	137.9	...	31.0	57.5	68.2	1.2	1.7	4.5

PRC = People's Republic of China, Lao PDR = Lao People's Democratic Republic.
[a] The exchanges are: Cambodia Securities Exchange (Cambodia), Shanghai and Shenzhen Stock Exchanges (PRC), Hong Kong Exchanges and Clearing (Hong Kong, China), Indonesia Stock Exchange (Indonesia), Japan Exchange Group (Japan), Korea Exchange (Republic of Korea), Lao Securities Exchange (Lao PDR), Bursa Malaysia (Malaysia), Yangon Stock Exchange (Myanmar), Philippine Stock Exchange (Philippines), Singapore Exchange (Singapore), The Stock Exchange of Thailand (Thailand), and Ho Chi Minh and Hanoi Stock Exchanges (Viet Nam).
Source: Authors based on CEIC, domestic sources, and World Federation of Exchanges Statistics Portal; AsianBondsOnline; and World Bank, *World Development Indicators* (accessed July 2021).

Large infrastructure projects historically receive relatively little private financing for two main reasons. First, the risk-reward profile of many infrastructure projects is not financially attractive, either in absolute terms or in comparison to alternative investment choices. If these investment transactions were to occur, a financial viability gap would result, or other investment choices would simply be more attractive.

Second, even where infrastructure projects might be financially attractive, capital markets and information gaps may prevent private capital from coming in. For example, capital market gaps in green projects are often the result of the "newness" of the technology or the process, and thus generate unfounded perceptions of excessive risk. Factors preventing private financing flows are generally related to either high perceptions of risk or high project or capital costs (for a given level of returns), or a combination of the two.

The importance of these constraints can be gleaned from the amount of investible funds available from the private sector. Of the estimated $50 trillion private capital managed globally by pension funds, sovereign wealth funds, insurance companies, and other institutional investors, only 0.8% has been allocated to infrastructure in recent years (ADB 2017, citing The Economist 2014). Moreover, savings are high in Asia and the Pacific. To channel available resources into infrastructure finance, an overall regulatory, legal, institutional, and financing framework that provides an effective risk allocation and risk transfer mechanism is needed to generate a pipeline of bankable projects—one that expands financial sources and instruments.

Credit Enhancement Mechanisms

Meanwhile, institutional investors, such as pension funds and insurance companies, are looking to diversify their portfolios, and are typically mandated to invest in low-risk assets. Infrastructure assets offer a viable investment alternative given their long-term, predictable income streams; low sensitivity to business cycles; and low correlation in rates of return to other asset classes. However, most infrastructure bonds in developing countries—even those for completed projects—have ratings below those required by institutional investors. Thus, credit enhancement mechanisms can help boost ratings, protecting senior creditors by absorbing the "first loss" in the case of default—through credit guarantees where a third party acts as the guarantor in exchange for a fee. These can either be privately provided by banks or specialized institutions, or publicly by governments, official agencies, and multilateral development banks.

A lack of credible credit ratings also constrains investment, particularly for project bonds, fueled by insufficient data to determine default probabilities. Credit enhancement instruments require rating agencies to provide a standalone rating to bonds and advise on the extent of the credit enhancement (guarantee cover) required to raise the rating to the desired level. Investors will only invest in the credit-enhanced bonds if the rating agency guidance is credible.

Stronger rating agencies will also support liquidity in instruments such as "green bonds"—corporate, project, and sub-sovereign bonds for clean energy assets—and in enabling securitization of asset-backed securities (whereby bonds are backed by a pool of infrastructure loans and sold to investors through capital markets). In this way, credible credit ratings can inject much-needed liquidity into infrastructure bonds, especially in markets where investors cannot yet assess the bankability of infrastructure projects. The role of credit guarantees and credit enhancement instruments is discussed further in section 5.4. The moral hazard dimension of credit guarantees must be taken into consideration. Any future losses will have to be covered by the guarantors and this may lead to unfair outcomes.

The role of the public sector in credit enhancement mechanisms must be tempered by the possibility of moral hazard. While attracting private finance by guaranteeing a rate of return, it may result in an unsustainable public sector debt level. Optimal allocation of risk is crucial, and this can be achieved by instruments described in subsequent subsections.

Long-Term Finance and Bond Markets

The Asian Bond Markets Initiative (ABMI) was established in December 2002 to develop efficient and liquid local currency bond markets to better channel Asia's vast savings to more productive long-term investments (Park et al. 2017). In turn, broader and deeper bond markets could mitigate currency and maturity mismatches. Table 5.6 looks at local currency (LCY) bond market progress in Asia. Data show that the share of emerging market economies (EME) bonds denominated in local currency increased from 75% in 2001 to 87% in 2011. The value of local currency bonds was $7,070 in 2011, which was 87% of $8,119 billion.

Table 5.6: Development of Local Currency Bond Markets, 2001–2011

Economy	Total $ billion	2011 $ billion	2011 % of GDP	2011 % of total	2006 % of GDP	2006 % of total	2001 % of GDP	2001 % of total
Advanced economies	74,371	67,912	164	91	134	91	107	93
Euro area advanced economies	22,106	20,147	157	91	133	91	94	89
Other advanced economies	22,857	19,134	140	84	104	81	84	87
United States	29,409	28,630	191	97	158	96	131	98
Emerging market economies	8,119	7,070	32	87	31	83	26	75
Europe	699	500	24	72	30	77	25	76
Latin America	1,406	1,053	22	75	20	70	19	54
Asia	5,667	5,260	41	93	39	90	33	88
PRC	2,956	2,938	40	99	27	98	18	95
Hong Kong, China	116	45	18	39	19	53	15	54
Indonesia	113	84	10	74	15	87	27	96
Korea, Rep. of	1,265	1,117	100	88	94	91	85	91
Malaysia	260	233	81	90	59	79	57	77
Pakistan	34	32	15	94	15	90	22	96
Philippines	101	63	28	62	26	50	21	48
Singapore	130	90	37	69	40	60	35	69
Thailand	175	170	49	97	37	89	28	80
Other emerging market economies	347	255	11	74	11	69	10	50
Russian Federation	156	91	5	59	3	41	2	13
South Africa	191	164	40	86	39	90	32	87

GDP = gross domestic product, PRC = People's Republic of China.
Source: Burger, Warnock, and Warnock (2015).

The data represent both government and corporate bonds. Table 5.6 is not readily updated and more recent performance is presented. For example, Silva et al. (2020) show even more substantial progress for local currency bonds between 2011 and 2018 for Asia and Pacific economies (Figure 5.5). However, there has been hardly any progress if the PRC is excluded. Meanwhile, ADB (2019) provides a useful update on the progress of ABMI. According to the Asian Economic Integration Report, since the ABMI was established in 2002, local currency bond markets in ASEAN+3 economies have grown steadily, and today are comparable in size to the United States (US) Treasury and euro-denominated bonds issued by residents in the euro area.

In May 2019, ADB published *Good Practices for Developing a Local Currency Bond Market: Lessons from the ASEAN+3 Asian Bond Markets Initiative.* Though every market has its own unique features—there is no "one-size-fits-all" approach—sharing experiences and lessons learned from the ABMI can help foster the process of local currency bond market development across developing Asia. The ASEAN+3 Multi-Currency Bond Issuance Framework is an ABMI policy initiative designed to help facilitate intraregional transactions by standardizing bond and note issuance, along with investment processes. This can help facilitate the process of recycling savings within the region more pragmatically and efficiently. The ASEAN+3 Multi-Currency Bond Issuance Framework helps intraregional bond and note issuance and investment by creating common market practices; utilizing a common document for submission—the single submission form (SSF); and highlighting transparent issuance procedures documented in implementation guidelines for participating markets.

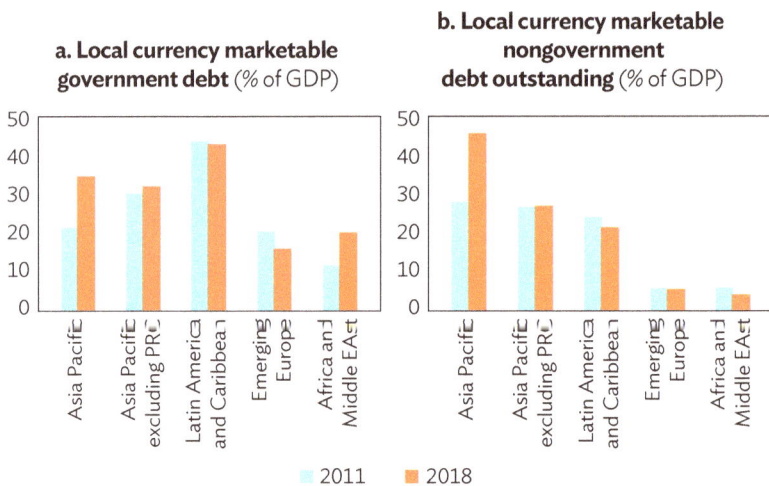

Figure 5.5: Local Currency Marketable Government Debt in Emerging Markets
(% of GDP)

GDP = gross domestic product, PRC = People's Republic of China
Note: The country groupings are based on the definitions of the source.
Source: Silva et al. (2020).

Floating-Interest-Rate Infrastructure Bonds

One issue that usually constrains private sector participation in large infrastructure projects is the relatively low fees that can be charged to users. There is a conflict of interest between the actual beneficiaries of the infrastructure project and the investors (Figure 5.6). A trade-off exists between the level of user fees and the attractiveness of the project to private investors.

Figure 5.6: Conflict of Interest between Users and Investors

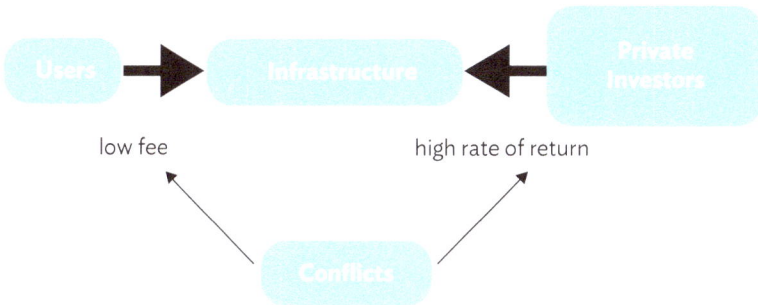

Source: Authors.

Floating-interest-rate infrastructure bonds are an innovative method to attract private finance in infrastructure projects by offering a higher rate of return. They are designed to capture part of spillover tax revenues created by infrastructure projects and can help reduce the trade-off between attracting private investors and affordable user charges (Box 5.1).[4]

Unlike the usual government bond, which provides a fixed interest rate, the proposed floating- interest-rate infrastructure bond provides a return on investment that depends on spillover tax revenues. When user charges and the return from spillover tax revenues are below the interest rate of the fixed-rate government bond, the interest rate will equal the fixed rate of the government bond. In other words, the latter acts as a floor. As the spillover effect of infrastructure investment increases, the rate of return from the

---

[4]   For instance, in the case of water supply, government injects extra funds into water supply companies, which are taken from property tax revenues assuming that water supply increases property values. Another example is private railways which develop station areas for shopping malls to get spillover profits to compensate for low revenues from user charges. In Hong Kong, China, subway companies can obtain the land in a station area which they can develop for shopping malls, apartments, etc., to receive spillover revenues in addition to user charges.

investment will become greater than the fixed rate of the government bond so infrastructure bond holders start receiving interest earnings higher than the floor rate. The spillover tax revenues in the latter stage can compensate losses in the first period.

Notably, the overall package includes paying interest equivalent to the fixed rate of the government bond during the construction period. This feature addresses a concern among private investors that the return to investment is zero during the construction period.

In Figure 5.7, the period from T_0 to T_1 is the project construction period. For simplicity, return on investment is zero in this diagram. The operation of the infrastructure starts at time T_1. User charges and spillover effect from infrastructure are not so large from the start of the operation until Point T_3, after which user charges and 50% of spillover tax return become higher than the government bond's interest rate.[5] Between T_0 and T_3, where not enough revenues are created by the infrastructure, the interest rate of the infrastructure bond is the same as the government bond.

From Point T_3, 50% of spillover tax revenues, in addition to user charges, become higher than the interest rate of the government bond. After this point, the floating-rate bond will start paying a higher rate of interest than the government bond. The rate of return on the floating-rate bond is the upward-moving red line in Figure 5.7. Revenue for the issuer of floating-interest-rate infrastructure bond is generated from two sources: infrastructure user charges and part of spillover tax revenues.

The issuer of the floating-interest-rate infrastructure bond could cap the interest paid to bond holders. If the spillover effect is very large, the cap on the floating interest rate will be high. However, the issuer must set the cap in advance, prior to bond issuances. Otherwise, private investors would be very skeptical of the cap level of the floating-rate bond.

Alternatively, the cap can be set such that it is conditional on the amount of spillover effects. In this scenario, the contract between government and private investors must stipulate the conditions clearly at the beginning of the project. This allows private investors to compute their expected future return even before the start of the project.

---

[5]   The choice of 50% is for illustrative purposes.

Extra revenues above the cap can be kept by the issuer as reserves to fund regular infrastructure maintenance and repairs and as a contingency for any future damage due to natural disasters. Maintenance and repairs are needed for infrastructure facilities especially after natural disasters, and such costs are usually covered by public funds (Yoshino, Azhgaliyeva, and Mishra 2020).

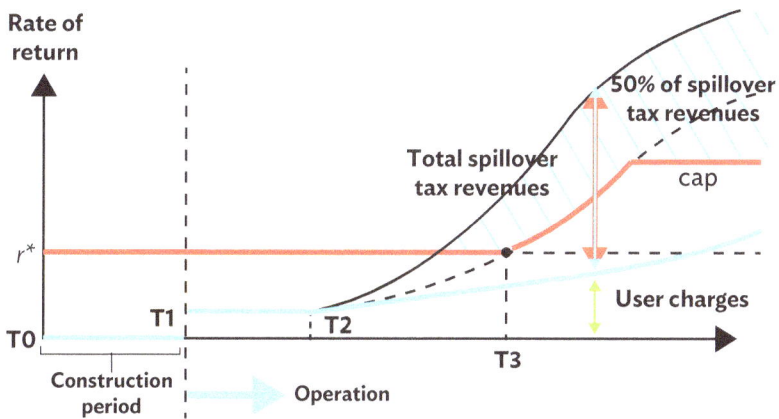

Figure 5.7: Structure of Proposed Floating-Rate Infrastructure Bonds

Source: Yoshino, Azhgaliyeva, and Mishra (2020).

Spillover tax revenues result from greater economic activity spurred by the infrastructure project and services. New businesses come to the region and new residential areas are constructed. The result is increased revenues from income tax, sales tax, and corporate business tax. Access to finance for new businesses is necessary for the spillover effect to materialize. When bank loans are not accessible or not affordable, hometown crowdfunding is one of the ways to finance small businesses and start-ups, which will increase economic activities in the region along the new infrastructure facilities (Yoshino 2013).

Box 5.1: Calculating the Spillover Tax Revenue

Spillover effects can be ascertained through the following procedures, presented diagrammatically in the first figure:

- Compute the national average growth rate of tax revenues in each tax category, such as corporate tax, personal income tax, property tax, and sales tax.
- Compute the growth rate of all tax revenues along the newly constructed infrastructure projects such as roads, highways, railways, and water supply.
- Take the difference in tax revenues between the affected region and non-affected region, and define the difference as the spillover effects.

Diagram of Spillover Tax Revenues

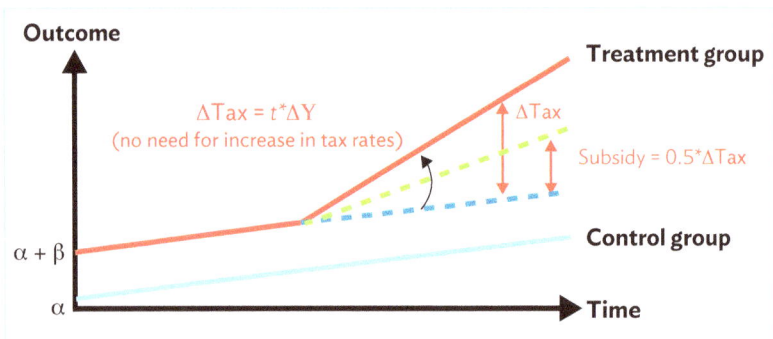

Source: Yoshino, Abidhadjaev, and Nakahigashi (2019).

Without investment in infrastructure, the government would not obtain the increased tax revenues. Part of the tax revenues could be distributed to private investors who financed the infrastructure, without decreasing existing tax revenues of local and central governments. In countries such as the Philippines, the central government finances much of the infrastructure development. However, local governments collect most of the spillover tax revenues. An agreement to share the spillover taxes must be forged between the national and local governments.

If local governments agree to share the spillover tax revenues with the central government, the latter can invest the proceeds to help mitigate poverty in rural regions. These projects would generate additional tax revenues from spillovers creating a virtuous cycle.

continued on next page

Box 5.1 (continued)

Following an econometric model (Equation 1), the difference in difference method is used to compare the differential impact of infrastructure investment in two different regions. One is the region which gained significantly from a transport infrastructure project. Another is the region located sufficiently far away so as not to be affected by the project. The difference between these two regions in either tax revenue or gross domestic product (GDP) can be obtained. Since monetary policy and fiscal policies affect all the countries, various economic variables will be used as explanatory variables to explain the fluctuations of tax revenue and GDP. Then add the dummy variable which represents specific infrastructure investment. Periods before the construction, during the construction, and during operation are compared to examine the impact of transport infrastructure investment (Yoshino and Abidhadjaev 2017a, 2017b).

Equation 1:
$$\Delta Y_{i,t} = \alpha_i + \phi_t + X'_{it}\beta + \delta(D_{gt\{2010:2009\}}) + \varepsilon_{it}$$

ΔY_{it} is the change in tax revenue or GDP of region i; X denotes time-varying covariates (vector of observed control variables); D is the dummy variable indicating whether the observation is in the affected group after the provision of the infrastructure services; g indexes groups of regions, affected and not affected; α_i is the sum of the autonomous and time-invariant unobserved region-specific rates of growth; ϕ_t is the year-specific growth effect; and ε_{it} is the error term, assumed to be independent over time.

There are ways to identify the impact of each infrastructure investment on spillover tax revenues. In staggered infrastructure projects, the use of annual dummy variables can identify spillover effects for each type of infrastructure project. Essentially, in this scenario, an increase in tax revenues resulting from one project can be isolated from an increase in tax revenues resulting from other projects. This allows the identification of different economic impacts in the region.

In simultaneous infrastructure projects, it is difficult to measure the impact of each infrastructure project on tax revenues created separately. There are many kinds of spillover effects derived from different kinds of infrastructure investments. The impact of an infrastructure project on the spillover tax revenues may not be easily distinguishable from the impact of the other infrastructure investments.

continued on next page

Box5.1 (continued)

Example 1: The Philippine Star Toll Highway

The table shows the case of the Star Highway in Manila (Yoshino and Pontines 2018). The periods *t*-1 and *t* indicate periods under construction. At the end of *t*, the highway had been completed and started operation. For Batangas City (last row), tax revenues increased from around ₱490 million before construction (*t*-2) to over ₱622 million and ₱652 million after construction had started (*t*-1 and *t*).

During the construction period, workers and related activities came to the area, which increased regional GDP. The Star Highway was completed at the end of *t*. Then at *t*-2, tax revenues diminished compared with the construction period until after the fourth year when tax revenues increased significantly. At *t*+4, tax revenues went up to as high as ₱1,209 billion, about twice the amount before the construction. These are the spillover tax increases emanating from infrastructure investment.

The relevant numbers are the increases in tax revenues. Thus, if the highway had not been constructed, incremental tax revenues would have likely remained at ₱490 billion as at *t*-2. Because of the highway construction and increased economic activities, Batangas City received tax revenues of ₱1,209 billion by *t*+4. If part of the incremental tax revenues (₱1,209 billion-₱490 billion) were to be returned to private investors, they would be more willing to invest their money to construct the highway.

Calculated Increase in Business Tax Revenues for the Beneficiary Group Relative to Non-Beneficiary Group (₱ billion)

Region	t-2	t-1	t	t+1	t+2	t+3	t+4
Lipa City	134.36	173.5	249.7	184.47	191.81	257.35	371.93
Ibaan City	5.84	7.04	7.97	6.8	5.46	10.05	12.94
Batangas City	490.9	622.65	652.83	637.83	599.49	742.28	1,209.61

Source: Yoshino and Pontines (2015).

continued on next page

Box5.1 (continued)

Example 2: Kyushu Railway Company (JR Kyushu)

The high-speed railway of Kyushu Railway Company (JR Kyushu) in Japan is one of case studies (Yoshino and Abidhadjaev, 2017b), where tax revenues are compared in three periods: (i) the construction period, (ii) the operational period without good connectivity, and (iii) the operational period with good connectivity to large cities such as Osaka and Tokyo. Total tax revenues, as well as revenues from personal income tax, corporate tax, and other taxes (including property tax) were compared (second figure). When construction started, speculators who anticipated a significant rise of property values started buying land along the high-speed railway. This caused property tax revenues to go up significantly (denoted in the figure as "other tax"). The project involved hiring many workers and construction companies in the region, which increased revenue from both personal and corporate taxes. During the operational period when there was no connectivity with large cities such as Osaka and Tokyo, revenues from personal income tax and corporate tax went down compared to the construction period. However, during the phase 2 of the operation, the improved connectivity between Osaka and Tokyo brought businesses and passengers into the region, which created a huge increase in corporate and individual income taxes. Interestingly, property tax revenues kept on rising because of the expected increase in property values, as is shown in "other tax" revenues.

Changes in Tax Revenues Resulting from the High-Speed Railway in Japan (¥ million)

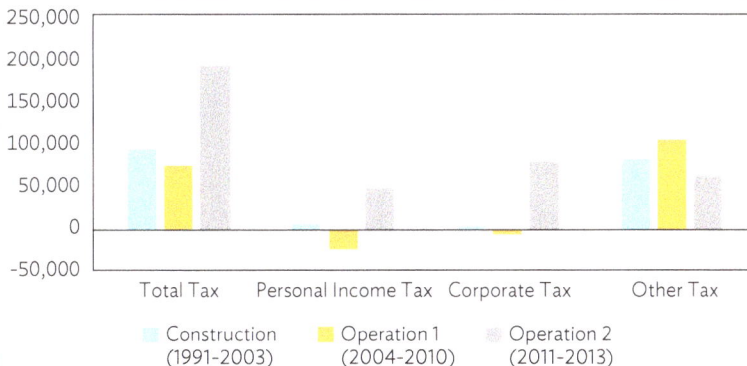

Note: The first bar is the period of construction, the second bar is the period after operation without connection to large cities, and the third bar is the period after the high-speed railway is connected to large cities such as Osaka and Tokyo.
Source: Yoshino and Abidhadjaev (2017b).

Land Trust Issue

Land acquisition for infrastructure investment continues to be a major barrier in many Asian countries. There is usually strong resistance among landowners to give up their land for development projects. This chapter proposes a land trust method as a solution to this barrier. Land trust allows the owners to retain their ownership of the land while it is leased for a stipulated period, for instance, 99 years for infrastructure projects in some cases in Hong Kong, China. In Japan, trust business can only be carried out by entities licensed under the Trust Business Act and financial institutions licensed under the Act for Financial Institutions' Trust Business.

As Yoshino and Lakhia (2020) explain, the process is to consolidate assets owned by individuals, assign them to the trust bank, thereby allowing more optimal use of the assets (Figure 5.8). It has a similar function to a trust for financial assets. Consolidating financial assets to operate more effectively is like consolidating land owned by various individuals who are not able to maximize the utility of their assets by themselves or do not have the know-how to do so. Assigning the land or financial assets to the trust bank can increase their utility.

Figure 5.8: Land Trust Structure and the Three Bodies of Trust

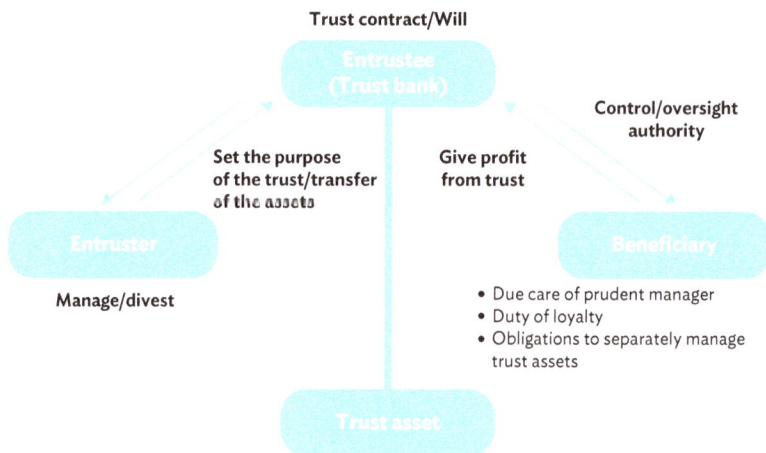

Source: Yoshino and Lakhia (2020).

For instance, Figure 5.9 shows that landowners, while retaining ownership, transfer the usage right to manage the land to the land trust, which further leases it to a railway company. The landowners will receive part of the profit as dividends. The proposed framework increases their profit by leasing land for infrastructure and development projects.

Figure 5.9: Land Trust for Infrastructure Investment

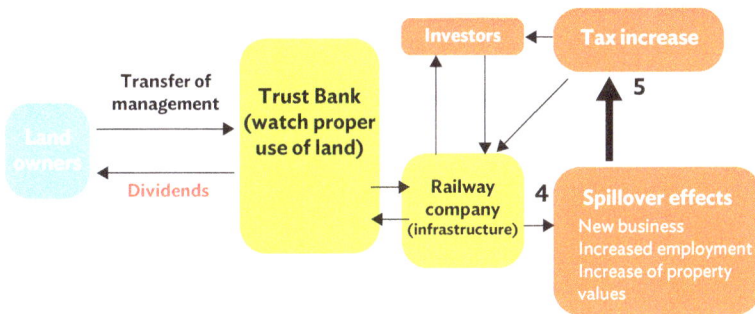

1. Reduction of costs of land purchase
2. Leasing contract
3. Future tax revenues can be used for repayment
4. Land owners keep their ownership

Source: Yoshino and Lakhia (2020).

Giving usage rights to infrastructure companies and city planning is one of the most efficient ways to develop infrastructure facilities. Infrastructure developers benefit as there is a significant reduction in land acquisition costs. With this method, they need to only pay for the rehabilitation costs of landowners and return an annual rent for the predetermined period to landowners. Meanwhile, the resulting spillover tax revenues from the infrastructure project can also help finance rental payments to landowners. The land trust method also reduces the time needed to negotiate with landowners. Instead of individual negotiations, the developer can deal with several landowners simultaneously. This process minimizes the problem of holdouts who may frustrate the entire transaction in the hope of getting a better deal. If the land were owned by a community instead of individuals, the community can receive rent every year from infrastructure operators.

Under this method, land acquisition is handled in a much more diplomatic and coordinated manner. Governance issues related to possible corruption are easily avoided because of the transparency involved. The landowners are readily relocated to a new place with some positive net earnings from the land. As a result, the benefits from a tax spillover can take place without waiting so many years for negotiation. Construction time is also reduced because there is less uncertainty about land acquisition.

However, transparency is not automatic. In regions where land grabbing is prevalent, particularly where land pooling or land readjustment is practiced, establishing laws that legalize a land trust system in the region is required. This will enable a clear, transparent, and corrupt-free land transaction mechanism in the region. The proposed trust bank will function as an arbiter between infrastructure operators, infrastructure investors, and landowners.

Disclosure of land prices openly to the public is also important in making land trusts transparent. A key reason for corruption and prevalence of land mafias is connected to the amorphous nature of land prices. The lack of regulation and transparency has enabled a thriving network of violators. This has also created mistrust between landowners and government. The land trust, complemented by transparency of land prices, seeks to challenge the role of the land mafia and aims to put an end to their prevalence. Land prices of the entire nation should be regularly disclosed to the public. In Japan, the Ministry of Land, Infrastructure, Transport and Tourism publishes all land purchase transactions, with the data accessible online.

To enable a more transparent and efficient method in the ASEAN+3 region, national licensing is also proposed for land evaluators. For instance, the Japanese government provides a certificate of national license to evaluators of land, obtained after passing national examinations on assessing land prices. In addition, the Japanese government established a Real Estate Transaction Price Search website where one can get the price of land by selecting the region. It shows the transacted price of land in each area without identifying the name of the owner.

Public–Private Partnerships

One mechanism to effectively channel private capital and funds toward a broader development agenda is to reinvent the relationship between the public and private sectors with the goal of sharing resources more efficiently.[6] The public–private partnership (PPP) mechanism has evolved, especially over the past 3 decades, to address development issues more effectively. Benefits from PPP-based delivery arise from its unique

---

[6] This section is based on ADB (2017, pp. 49–125); Deep, Kim, and Lee (2019); and Lee et al. (2019a).

structural and functional features: a life-cycle perspective on infrastructure provision and pricing, a focus on service delivery, and a sharing of risks between the public and private sectors. Instead of providing exclusively public assets and related services, governments have increasingly relied on the market for the direct provision of public goods and services. If appropriately deployed and managed, PPP facilitates the provision of adequate and efficient infrastructure services for users, profitable investment opportunities for the private sector, and a development mechanism that expands the capacity of the state.

Lee et al. (2019a) cite the four major channels through which PPPs can boost economic growth. The first and obvious channel is improving access to infrastructure services, particularly to a desired level of quality. The second channel highlights the benefits of building technical and institutional capacity, transparency, and good governance from partnerships with the private sector. The third channel emphasizes better allocation of public resources. The fourth channel is the potential of PPPs to attract private savings in long-term investments, such as pension and sovereign wealth funds.

Their empirical evidence supports the relevance of these channels. In particular, the infrastructure–growth link becomes stronger, especially when partnership arrangements emphasize the quality of infrastructure services, better maintenance, and delivering projects on time and within budget. Public sectors therefore need to strengthen their institutional capacity to carry out PPPs, and the legal and regulatory frameworks for PPP processes. And transparency and good governance must be another requirement in the practice of PPPs.

The role of the private sector in the provision of infrastructure services, therefore, should not be limited to closing the financing gap. To tap its comparative advantages, the private sector should help improve operational efficiency, participate in granting incentivized finance, and share innovation capacity. The primary goal is to deploy all the resources and expertise of the private sector in the provision of infrastructure services. The success of PPP depends on the optimal allocation of risk. Project finance for infrastructure extends beyond construction and well into the useful life of the asset. It depends entirely on cash flow generated by the project through user charges or revenues paid by the government. By allocating risk to the party best able to manage it, project finance aligns private profit incentives with the public interest. This makes project finance the preferred financing and governance structure for successful PPPs.

Although innovative methods for attracting private investment in infrastructure have been advocated in the literature for many years (Rillo and Zulfiqar 2018, Rowley 2020), one of the main difficulties that PPPs face is the scarcity of bankable projects due to the low rate of return from infrastructure projects that mainly depend on user charges. In some cases, the response has been for the pendulum to swing to the other extreme where the public sector is forced to agree to an inordinately high rate of return for the private investor because of lack of other options. The floating-interest-rate infrastructure bond can partially address this concern. Meanwhile, Susantono, Park, and Tian (2020) note that the barriers to attracting private investments in infrastructure include the complexity of PPPs, corruption in developing countries, and low rates of return. In addition, Lee et al. (2019b) summarize factors affecting PPP projects outcomes including (i) a project factor, (ii) macroeconomic conditions, and (iii) political/institutional indicators. The relatively long gestation period of some infrastructure projects makes them vulnerable to political cycles.

The main sources of project finance are equity and debt. The choice of financing method depends on project requirements and risks, the amount of capital available for direct investment as equity, and the quality of the financing consortium. Debt is the largest component of PPP financing, commonly more in the form of bank loans than bonds. Bonds are more desirable, though, as they allow for long-term financing. More financing can become available for infrastructure PPPs if bond issues allow access to abundant institutional savings, but this requires that project risks be appropriately mitigated.

The infrastructure financing gap is essentially a risk gap. The large infrastructure gap in Asia coexists with a substantial pool of long-term savings that can be mobilized if offered the appropriate balance of risk and return. Credit enhancement mechanisms can mitigate certain risks from PPPs to make them more attractive to a wider range of capital providers. These instruments include partial credit or revenue guarantees, off-take guarantees, subordinated debt, pooling and tranching, and infrastructure debt or equity funds. Multilateral development banks can do much more to promote credit enhancement products, unlock potential in private capital markets around the world, and bridge the risk gap.

5.4 Crosscutting Issue: Green Finance

As mentioned earlier, this chapter analyzes two cross-cutting issues that run between public and private finance. The first is the need to raise resources for the infrastructure components related to climate mitigation and adaptation, so-called green finance. Estimates presented in Table 5.1 showed that if the costs of climate mitigation and adaptation are included the amount needed for infrastructure rises from $22.6 trillion to $26.2 trillion for 2016–2030. Environmental soundness, therefore, has implications for fiscal sustainability and the required amount of private finance.

This section focuses on mobilizing private finance for so-called green infrastructure. The two main reasons why large infrastructure projects receive relatively little private financing—unattractive risk-reward profile and information gaps—are more critical for green projects. Consequently, finance remains disconnected from sustainable development for three core reasons:[7]

- Policies and prices in the real economy do not ensure that environmental and social costs are fully accounted.

- Fiscal resources are insufficient to close the viability gap.

- Rules governing the financial system do not ensure that financial decision-making takes account of social and environmental sources of risk and opportunity.

A framework recommended by United Nations Environment Programme (UNEP) (2015, 2016) provides a useful structure to systematically address these issues.

Financing Green and Greening Finance

In line with Goal 7 of the Sustainable Development Goals, the world is committed to achieving net-zero carbon emissions by 2050. Net zero means that, on balance, no more carbon is deposited into the atmosphere than is taken out. To demonstrate their commitment, many countries submitted their intended nationally determined contribution to the United Nations Framework Convention on Climate Change. The intended nationally determined contribution is a declaration by a country of its planned reduction in greenhouse gas emissions over a period. A country's

---

[7] See UNEP (2015).

intended nationally determined contribution is converted to a nationally determined contribution when it formally joins the Paris Agreement by submitting an instrument of ratification, acceptance, approval, or accession.

As of May 2021, all ADB developing member countries have declared their nationally determined contributions, and achieving these targets requires an unprecedented shift in investment away from greenhouse gases, fossil fuels, and natural-resource-intensive industries toward more resource-efficient technologies and business models. The financial sector will have to play a central role in this green transformation.

A World Bank (2020) report on mobilizing finance for nature details two channels through which private finance can be generated: (i) by monetizing cash flows from the provision of ecosystem services (financing green); and (ii) by driving better management of biodiversity risks (greening finance). The real and financial sectors are looking for investment opportunities arising from the conservation, restoration, and sustainable use of nature— "to *finance* green". Investors are also trying to avoid or limit biodiversity risk associated with investments— seeking "to *green* finance" Investment in this category aims to direct financial flows away from projects with negative impacts on biodiversity and ecosystem services to projects that mitigate negative impacts or pursue positive environmental impacts as a co-benefit. In general, investment and lending decisions are taken based on environmental screening and risk assessment to meet sustainability standards, as well as insurance services that cover environmental and climate risk.

The concepts of "financing green" and "greening finance" are also relevant for infrastructure projects directly related to the reduction of greenhouse gas emissions. The two combine as "green finance" which can be defined as comprising "all forms of investment or lending that consider environmental effect and enhance environmental sustainability" (Volz 2018). Or else, green financing deals with "how to enhance the ability of the financial system to mobilize private capital for green investment" (UNEP 2016).

Framework for Green Finance

Tables 5.7 and 5.8 present five approaches to align the financial system to sustainable development based on a framework developed by UNEP (2015). Definitions of each approach are shown below along with recent examples from Asia (ADB 2020). Box 5.2 contains examples in earlier years.

Enhancing market practice. In many countries, measures are directed to improve the efficiency and accountability of financial institutions and markets. In the ASEAN region, the issuance of green bonds and provision of green loans had almost doubled in 2019 from the previous year, reaching $8.1 billion (ADB 2020).

Harnessing the public balance sheet. Some countries are using the public balance sheet to improve risk-adjusted returns to investors in key areas. The ASEAN Catalytic Green Finance Facility is a green infrastructure financing facility under the ASEAN Infrastructure Fund, with funding commitments from several global development partners including the ADB. This innovative initiative was launched in 2019 to accelerate the development of green infrastructure projects across Southeast Asia in support of ASEAN members' climate change and environmental sustainability goals. The ASEAN Catalytic Green Finance Facility uses a de-risking approach in its fund—around $1.4 billion funding commitments from the ASEAN Infrastructure Fund as well as ADB and other development partners—to bridge the funding gap and create bankable green infrastructure projects that can catalyze private capital, technologies, and management efficiencies (ADB 2020).

Directing finance through policy (by reforming legal and market structures). In some countries, policies, requirements, and prohibitions are being used to direct where investment will be allocated. In the Philippines, the Department of Energy in October 2020, declared a moratorium on new applications for greenfield coal power plants. Such a policy should be accompanied by the authorization of "transition bonds". These are different from green bonds, which are designed for green industries alone, i.e., industries in those sectors defined in green taxonomies that are already on the road to reducing greenhouse gases. Transition bonds are a new asset class targeted at "brown" industries with high greenhouse gas emissions, which have a clear and explicit goal of becoming less brown or greener. In the context of the Philippines, the transition bonds can ease the financial burden on energy firms that will be hurt by this policy.

Encouraging cultural transformation in financial decision-making. Many countries are seeking to align financial behavior with sustainability through improved capabilities, culture, internal incentives, and societal engagement. Indonesia's Sustainable Finance Roadmap focuses on the sustainability skills of professionals. The Republic of Korea is aiming for net-zero emissions by 2050 and an end to coal financing (ADB 2020a).

The plan includes large-scale investments in renewable energy, the introduction of a carbon tax, the phase-out of domestic and overseas coal financing by public institutions, and the creation of the Regional Energy Transition Centre to support workers' transition to green jobs.

Upgrading governance architecture (Table 5.8). Internalizing sustainable development into financial decision-making can be consistent with the existing mandates of financial regulators and central banks. Globally aligned green frameworks with sector taxonomies and eligibility principles will be key to avoiding projects, companies, or countries seen as greenwashing or purpose-washing (ADB 2020a). For instance, the ASEAN Green Bond Standards, the ASEAN Social Bond Standards, and the ASEAN Sustainability Bond Standards were developed to align with the Green and Social Bond Principles and Sustainability Bond Guidelines of the International Capital Market Association.

Various tools designed to achieve the alignment toward more green finance under each approach are also listed in Tables 5.7 and 5.8. The tools are classified under various themes. To understand how these tools can effectively promote green finance, the inventory conducted by Volz (2018) for Asian countries will be useful. A succinct version is shown in Box 5.2.

Meanwhile, the main actors expected to implement these tools are the banking sector, bond issuers, equity investors, institutional investors, and the insurance sector. Proponents of measures listed in Box 5.2 come from at least one of the five groups. For a more concrete example, Box 5.3 discusses the tools available for bond issuers or what is called the debt capital market. Elucidation of both "financing green"—or green bonds per se—and "greening finance"—referred to as greening bond markets—are part of Box 5.3. Credit enhancement mechanisms described in section 5.3 are referred to in this discussion.

Implementing the various approaches in the framework has limitations. For instance, using the central bank balance sheet to incentivize green lending or even invest directly is frowned upon in orthodox central-banking circles. Likewise, directed credit allocation is associated with industrial policy and its soundness is a subject of extensive debate. Hence, the actual tools applied must be calibrated to the quality of governance in the country.

Table 5.7: UNEP Framework and Tools for Mobilizing Private Finance for Green Projects

Policy	Theme	Tool
Enhancing market practice	Financial responsibility	Fiduciary duty Fiduciary capability incentives
	Prudential regulation	Risk management Stress tests Capital requirements
	Disclosure and reporting by financial institutions	Policy Performance Accounting
	Disclosure and reporting by nonfinancial corporations	Standards and requirements Accounting frameworks
	Financial market criteria	Equity analysis Credit ratings Green assets indexes
Harnessing the public balance sheet	Fiscal incentives	Targeted fiscal incentives Review fiscal incentives
	Public financial institutions	Sustainability mandates Establishing new green institutions Blended finance instruments
	Central banks	Refinancing operations Asset purchase programs
	Public procurement	Procurement criteria
Reforming legal and market structures	Legal liability	Lender and other liabilities
	Capital requirements	Adjust capital requirements
	Directed investment and lending	Priority sector lending prohibitions
	Directed service provision	Directed provision Mandatory purchase requirements
Encouraging cultural transformation in financial decision-making	Financial capacity building	Consumer education Professional education Regulator capacity building
	Financial behavior	Remuneration regulation Codes of conduct Nonfinancial guidance
	Market Structure	Value-based financial institutions Market diversity Right-sizing financial institutions

UNEP = United National Environment Programme.
Source: UNEP (2015).

Efforts to enhance an economy's financial system to make it more aware and responsive to green concerns must be accompanied by cognizance of barriers in the real economy. Gaps in the enforcement of environmental regulation and the non-pricing of negative production and consumption externalities such as carbon emissions clearly reduce the demand for green investment. This is the same as the first reason for the disconnect between finance and sustainable development and stems from market failure (UNEP 2015). Price distortions from fossil-fuel subsidies constitute a particularly important challenge for most Asian economies. Addressing such real economy barriers through binding environmental regulation, emissions-trading schemes, or other policies that help to internalize negative externalities, is critical to mobilizing green investment.

Addressing shortcomings in the financial system itself remains the major challenge. Several proposals were put forth, including raising awareness among regulators and market participations in the financial sector on environmental and climate risks; developing capacities for environmental risk analysis and management; enhancing transparency through environmental, social, and governance (ESG) disclosure requirements, among others (Volz 2018).[8]

Table 5.8: Tools Specific to Upgrading Governance Architecture

Approach	Explanation
Principles	Adopt principles for a sustainable financial system to guide policy making
Policy and Legal Frameworks	Consider impacts on sustainability when developing and reviewing financial regulations
	Incorporate sustainability into financial sector development plans
	Ensure that opportunities for financial system reform are included into sustainability policies
	Introduce long-term strategies and roadmaps, supported by coordination mechanisms
	Strengthen the legal and judicial system to aid enforcement
Regulatory Mandates	Explore the impact of sustainability factors for existing mandates of central banks and financial regulators and adjust where necessary
Performance Measurement	Develop a performance framework to assess and guide progress in developing sustainable financial systems

Note: This table is separated from Table 5.7 because the actions to upgrade the governance architecture provide support across the toolbox.
Source: UNEP (2015).

---

[8]   See Volz (2018).

Box 5.2: Applying the UNEP Framework to Selected ASEAN+3 Economies

The inventory of Volz (2018) on examples of tools to align finance to green investments from Asia, following the United Nations Environment Programme (UNEP) Framework in Tables 5.7 and 5.8 in the main text, is shown below:

Enhancing Market Practice: Disclosure, Analysis, Risk Management

Sustainability disclosure: The Shanghai Stock Exchange introduced Guidelines on Listed Companies' Environmental Information Disclosure already in 2008. In 2010, the Singapore Stock Exchange released the Guide to Sustainability Reporting for Listed Companies. The Philippines Securities Exchange Commission requests an Annual Corporate Governance Report from listed firms since 2013. In Viet Nam, the State Securities Commission introduced a Sustainability Reporting Handbook for Vietnamese Companies in 2013.

Integrating environmental risks into financial regulation: The State Bank of Viet Nam issued the Directive on Promoting Green Credit Growth and Environmental Social Risks Management in Credit Granting Activities, requiring financial institutions to take environmental factors into account in their lending decisions.

Industry guidelines for sustainable market practice: The Association of Banks in Singapore (ABS) released ABS Guidelines on Responsible Financing in October 2015.

Upgrading Governance Architecture: Internalizing Sustainable Development into Financial Decision-Making of Financial Regulators and Central Banks

Inclusion of environmental risk to secure financial and monetary stability: Bank Indonesia is considering including environmental and climate risk into its macroprudential framework. In the People's Republic of China (PRC), the People's Bank of China (PBOC) is considering including the green credit performance of banks in the central banks' assessment of macroprudential risk.

Multi-stakeholder dialogue between financial authorities and the financial industry: In 2015, the PBOC established the Green Finance Committee to develop green

continued on next page

Box 5.2 *(continued)*

finance practices, environmental stress testing for the banking sector, and guidelines on greening the PRC's overseas investment.

Encouraging Cultural Transformation: Capacity Building, Behavior, Market Structure

Action to enhance the current skill set of financial professionals and regulators: Indonesia's Sustainable Finance Roadmap seeks to develop the sustainability skills of professionals. In Viet Nam, the central bank has also voiced its intent to organize training workshops for bank personnel.

Market development: With the new Green Financial Bond Directive, the PBOC has taken a first step to develop a new market segment for sustainable investment in the Chinese capital market.

Harnessing the Public Balance Sheets: Fiscal Incentives, Public Financial Institutions, and Central Banks

Fiscal incentives for investors: Thailand introduced a feed-in premium program in 2010 which has helped to more than double its installed clean-energy capacity.

Green credit and bond guarantees: Development banks such as the Asian Development Bank have offered risk-sharing facilities in various Asian countries where partial credit guarantees were provided to partner banks sharing the payment risk of underlying borrowers, for example for energy efficiency projects.

Public pension funds: In Japan, the Government Pension Investment Fund and the Pension Fund Association for Local Government Officials endorsed the Principles for Responsible Institutional Investors along with 160 other institutions within 6 months of its launch in February 2014 by Japan's Financial Services Agency. In 2017, Government Pension Investment Fund adopted an environmental, social, and governance (ESG) investment strategy. In 2014, the Korean National Assembly requested from the National Pension Service, the world's fourth largest pension fund, to enhance its ESG standards.

Source: Volz (2018).

Box 5.3: Role of Debt Capital Market in Green Finance

The bond market focuses on longer-term debt instruments issued by governments and corporations. It also allows lenders to convert illiquid assets into tradable asset-backed securities. Bonds are the largest single asset class in the financial system, currently valued at about $100 trillion. As capital requirements for bank debt tighten, bond markets are an increasingly important means of raising long-term debt, particularly for assets with relatively predictable risks and returns. In this case, there are two interlinked public policy priorities (table).

Applying the UNEP Framework to the Bond Market

Priority	Proposal Package: Key Tools
Green bonds	Product standards—green bond standards and verification
	Targeted fiscal incentives
	Credit enhancement (aggregation, securitization, and covered bonds)
	Greening asset purchase programs, strategic investment from public entities such as sovereign wealth funds
	Variations in capital requirements
Greening bond markets	Credit ratings
	Compacts and roadmaps

UNEP = United Nations Environment Programme.
Source: UNEP (2015).

The market for green bonds has grown rapidly, from $3.4 billion in 2012 to $156 billion in 2017 (Azhgaliyeva, Kapoor, and Liu 2020). However, the overall market for green bonds still has considerable potential to grow. The growth of the market can be partly explained by the comparable risk-adjusted financial returns of green bonds with non-green bonds, and the broad eligible issuer base. Any bond-issuing entity can issue a labeled green bond, because the requirements of using the label pertain to the use of proceeds being earmarked to qualifying green projects, not to whether the issuing entity is green. The label and earmarking make it easier for investors to identify green investments.

continued on next page

Box 5.3 *(continued)*

Investor demand for labeled green bonds is strong, evidenced by higher rates of oversubscription than non-green bonds. However, barriers to scaling up the market include the development of credible and ultimately verifiable standards.

Global cooperation is critical for international comparability and consistency. Ultimately, green bonds may need specific securities regulation to protect consumers, but initially, experimentation and development of standards is critical. Beyond such targeted measures is a broader need and potential to encourage a greening of bond markets, specifically to integrate environmental, social and governance factors into routine credit ratings. A first step would be greater transparency by credit rating agencies as to how such factors come into their analysis, which would allow for a more debate and method development process.

In the context of Southeast Asia (Azhgaliyeva, Kapoor, and Liu 2020), two distinct challenges that have been found for issuers include limited credit absorption capacity and costs of meeting green bond requirements. Challenges for investors include a limited investment pipeline; lack of data and analytical ability; and a lack of green bond indexes, listings, and ratings.

Measures to address these challenges are discussed in sections 5.4 and 5.6 of this chapter. The ASEAN Catalytic Green Finance Facility is an example of a mechanism to widen the investment pipeline. Meanwhile, part of section 5.6 proposes how the framework for supporting conventional local currency bonds can be extended to green local currency bonds. Country-specific measures are presented in Azhgaliyeva, Kapoor, and Liu (2020). The issuance of green bonds in Indonesia, Malaysia, and Singapore is driven by the support from the government. However, the nature of the support differs across these countries. In Indonesia, the government issues 99% of all green bonds. In contrast, the issuance of green bonds in Malaysia and Singapore is led by the private sector, but incentivized by government policies supporting green bond issuance, such as green bond grant schemes and tax incentives.

A related issue is the lack of accurate and unified environmental credit rating of investment. Currently, each rating agency provides different ratings to the same company since they have different criteria for environmental aspects.

continued on next page

The allocation of investors for green investment depends on which rating agency they follow. In order to avoid any distortions in portfolio allocation, a unified credit rating should be provided by an international organization (Yoshino and Yuyama 2021).

Source: Authors.

International and Regional Financial Cooperation

International cooperation can support national action. The increasing internationalization of national financial systems makes international cooperation a critical support in embedding sustainable development into financial decision-making. Fortunately, many venues for such cooperation and initiatives are already under way. International organizations and formal intergovernmental and interagency platforms are increasingly looking to this field of inquiry and action, such as the G20 and the Financial Stability Board, the IMF, the World Bank, regional multilateral development banks, and regional financial cooperation efforts.

The opportunities identified by UNEP (2015) for international cooperation fall into two main groups. One is specific to particular asset pools and financial market actors, and the other on opportunities to enhance the underlying financial system architecture.[9] These will be analyzed in the context of Asian regional financial cooperation in section 5.6.

5.5 Crosscutting Issue: COVID-19 Pandemic

Economic Impact of the Pandemic

The COVID-19 pandemic affected the flexibility and effectiveness of fiscal policy. In some countries, resources had to be realigned possibly reducing allocations in some areas such as physical infrastructure. However, the more prevalent experience in developing Asia is of rising public debt ratios resulting from slower economic growth and government spending measures to stem the impact of the pandemic. The drop in fiscal revenue, coupled with unplanned spending and countercyclical policies because

---

[9] See UNEP (2015) on areas on international cooperation across specific asset pools and actors, and on governing architecture.

of the pandemic, are expected to cause primary deficits to widen sharply. Based on *Asian Development Outlook Supplement—December 2020* (ADB 2020b) growth projections for 2020 and 2021, the average public gross debt ratio among ADB's developing members is projected at 50.9% of GDP by 2021, a significant increase from 42.5% of GDP in 2019 (Sawada and Sumulong 2021). Figure 5.10 shows the public debt ratios for 44 of developing members with available data using ADB's debt projection model (Ferrarini et al. forthcoming).

The region's past record of strong growth and a generally prudent fiscal stance kept public debt sufficiently low for most regional economies, now giving them the necessary fiscal space to run larger deficits in the short term. But policy space is not unlimited, so resuming growth and normalizing fiscal balances is critical to preserving debt sustainability. Even where pre-COVID-19 debt ratios are low enough to allow for some increase in debt ratios, maintaining debt sustainability inevitably requires that, soon enough, countries resume robust growth and rein in deficits from their crisis response. Otherwise, ballooning debt in gross terms would occur, and sustainability could possibly end up impaired in some parts of the region. Without growth resuming in earnest, countries are bound to face a policy dilemma from having to support their economies against the backdrop of shrinking policy space and rising debt ratios.

Figure 5.10: Comparing Public Debt in 2019 and 2021

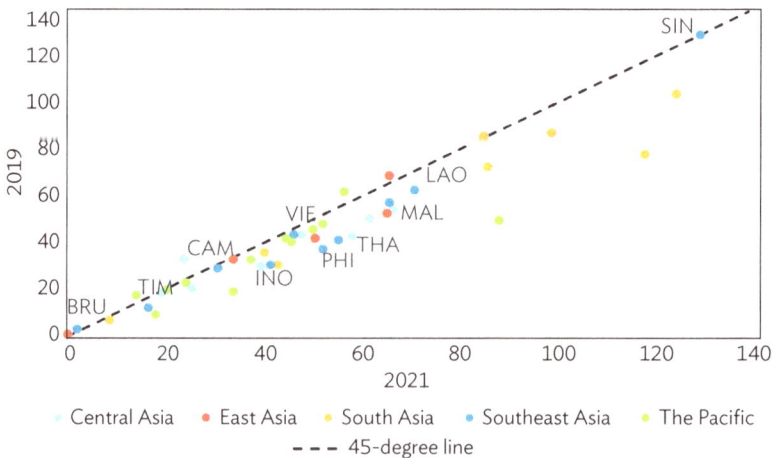

BRU = Brunei Darussalam, CAM = Cambodia, INO = Indonesia, LAO = Lao People's Democratic Republic, MAL = Malaysia, PHI = Philippines, SIN = Singapore, THA = Thailand, TIM = Timor-Leste.
Source: Sawada and Sumulong (2021), citing Ferrarini et al. (forthcoming).

This section explores possible responses to the economic impacts of the pandemic and how adverse effects on the environment can be mitigated at the same time. It would be useful for policy makers to apply the standard assessment that was needed to address the fiscal gap defined in section 5.1. First, policy makers need to determine to what extent tax revenues can be raised through higher tax rates or reforms aimed at greater administrative efficiency. And second, public spending can be reoriented toward infrastructure investment and away from inefficient items such as poorly targeted subsidies.

Green Fiscal Recovery Measures

Many governments responded appropriately to the pandemic by approaching the problem initially as a public health crisis. Measures to mitigate the adverse effects of the pandemic were analogous to disaster relief. These fiscal rescue measures were intended to offset income losses and address immediate human welfare concerns during lockdown periods. Broader aspects included protection of balance sheets of businesses, minimizing bankruptcies, and maintaining employment levels to the largest extent possible.

When the spread of the virus was controlled, governments shifted to stimulus packages or fiscal recovery measures. In the context of the energy sector, these recovery packages could be "brown," reinforcing the links between economic growth and fossil fuels or "green," decoupling emissions from economic activity, or "neutral." A silver lining during the pandemic was the sharp decline in greenhouse gas emissions. Globally, emissions likely fell by 8% or 2.6 gigatons of carbon dioxide in 2020 (IEA 2020a). This is more in absolute terms than in any other year on record.

The challenge is to encourage governments to sustain this momentum by adopting "green" fiscal recovery measures. It should be noted that the pandemic occurred at a time when renewable energy costs were declining, oil prices were persistently low, debt in the fossil fuel sector was rising, and investor concerns about the impact of fossil fuels on carbon emissions and environmental regulations were already lowering capital investment in the fossil fuel industry, while making renewable energy one of the fastest-growing industries (Khanna 2020). The pandemic, however, slowed down the momentum shift. As the International Energy Agency (IEA 2020b) succinctly described it: "The crisis has curbed investments in the energy sector and threatened to slow the expansion of clean energy technologies."

A distinct opportunity therefore exists to harness this earlier momentum and build on the desire of segments of society to "build back better" after experiencing a cleaner environment during lockdowns. This renewed thrust can be channeled to the recovery efforts with a parallel objective of expanding the use of renewable energy and low-carbon infrastructure. A lesson from the global financial crisis is that green recovery measures often have advantages over traditional fiscal stimulus. For instance, renewable energy generates more jobs in the short term when employment opportunities are scarce in the middle of a recession. In the long term, renewable energy conveniently requires less labor for operation and maintenance. This frees up labor as the economy returns to capacity. In addition, a recent global survey of economic experts indicates that some fiscal recovery measures rank favorably because of their relatively high multiplier effects but can be classified as green at the same time (Hepburn et al. 2020). These include building efficiency retrofits, natural capital investment, and clean research and development, among others. The extent to which these measures have been implemented largely depends on the priorities of policy makers.

Debt Service Suspension Initiative

While fiscal rescue and recovery measures mitigated the adverse impact of the pandemic, they contributed to the increase in public debt. Data show that public debt in emerging markets has surged to levels not seen in 50 years, and many developing countries have increasingly taken on debt on non-concessional terms—from private lenders and non-Paris Club members.[10]

To prevent the ballooning public debt from eroding the fiscal base of developing economies, the World Bank and the IMF urged G20 countries to establish the Debt Service Suspension Initiative. In all, 73 countries have become eligible for a temporary suspension of debt-service payments owed to their official bilateral creditors. Meanwhile, the G20 has also called on private creditors to participate in the initiative on comparable terms. The suspension period, originally set to end on 31 December 2020, has been extended through December 2021.

The World Bank and the IMF are supporting implementation of the Debt Service Suspension Initiative by monitoring spending, enhancing public debt transparency, and ensuring prudent borrowing. Initiative borrowers

---

[10] Refer to World Bank (2021b) for details.

commit to use freed-up resources to increase social, health, or economic spending in response to the crisis. This includes spending on infrastructure projects and therefore the initiative contributes to sustainable infrastructure investment.

Role of Environmental, Social, and Governance Bonds

The COVID-19 pandemic provides an opportunity to implement integrated responses that straddle economic, social, and environmental dimensions.[11] One option is to accelerate the mobilization of ESG bonds, or social bonds for short. Under the International Capital Market Association framework, there are three types of ESG bond instruments: (i) green bonds, which raise capital for projects with environmental benefits; (ii) social bonds, which raise funds for projects with social benefits; and (iii) sustainability bonds, which raise funds for projects with both green and social benefits. Many of the rating agencies include the governance component of ESG in their evaluation score (Yoshino and Yuyama 2021).

Global social bond issuance saw tremendous growth in 2020, as pandemic and economic lockdowns greatly increased market supply and demand for financing response and recovery efforts. Following year-on-year growth of 28% in 2018 and 44% in 2019, the issuance of global social bonds surged to $149.4 billion equivalent in 2020, an eightfold increase from 2019. Social bond issuance in Asia has consistently lagged European issuance, but recent growth in the region has been impressive (Figure 5.11). The equivalent performance for ASEAN+3 economies is shown in Figure 5.12.

In 2017, Asian social bond issuance comprised 12% of total global (excluding supranational) issuance; its share grew to 23% of the global total in 2020. From 2017 to 2020, the Asian social bond market grew 22.3 times, compared with growth of 9.8 times for Europe and 14.3 times for the world excluding Asia. Nonetheless, the Asian social bond market is still barely more than a third of the size of the European market in terms of its global issuance share, and the need for even faster growth is urgent.

It is generally agreed that the greatest obstacles to growth in the social bond space are the lack of clarity about measuring and assessing impact, as well as a supply-side shortage. More precisely, there has not yet been a coalescing around standardization in the measurement of impact, which is extremely difficult to do because social bond projects and assets are by

---

[11] The main reference for this subsection is ADB (2021).

their very nature much more diverse than green bond projects and assets. While the International Capital Market Association framework is a step forward, it falls well short of a standardized set of metrics that would enable comparison of impact performance across instruments.

Figure 5.11: Progress of Environmental, Social, and Governance Bonds in Asia
($ million)

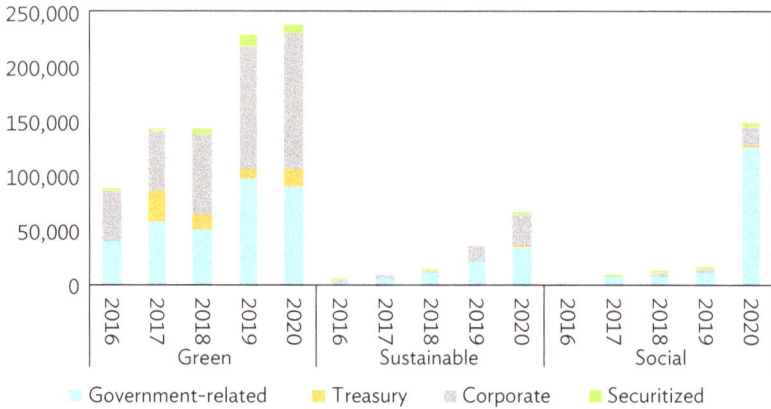

Source: ADB (2021).

Figure 5.12: Green, Social, and Sustainability Bond Issuance of Selected ASEAN+3 Economies by Issuer
($ billion)

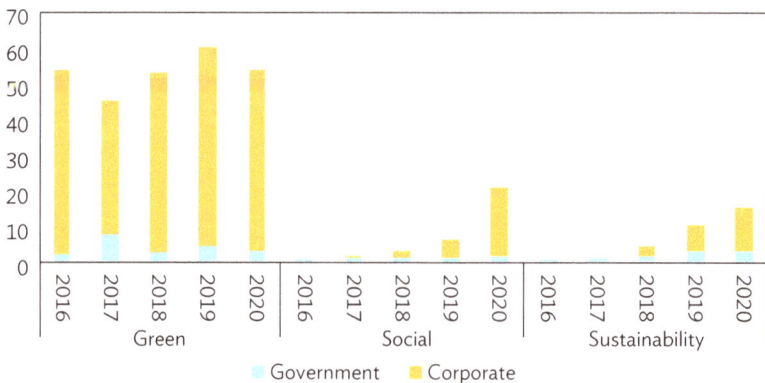

Note: The economies included in the calculation are the People's Republic of China; Hong Kong, China; Indonesia; Japan; Malaysia; the Philippines; the Republic of Korea; Singapore; and Thailand. The data include local and foreign currency issuance.
Source: Authors, based on AsianBondsOnline Database (accessed May 2021).

Without this clarity, the risk of "social washing," or overstating the social value of a bond, is very real, and investors are keenly aware of this risk. Indeed, even before the emergence of COVID-19 bonds, many market participants worried about "rainbow bonds" in which all manner of labels might go hand in hand with greenwashing or social washing. The need for higher issuance volume and diversity (i.e., more corporate issuers) is another significant obstacle to market growth.

This is a bit of a vicious cycle. Mainstream investors (i.e., those without a strong preference for ESG-linked investing) do not really understand the purpose and value of social bonds. This limits investor demand to niche status, which has then discouraged more widespread issuance and market development, thereby making it harder to explain what social bonds are for.

But COVID-19 brings an opportunity to turn this into a virtuous cycle, as attention is high and focused, and the need for financing is immense. However, different criteria used by different rating agencies for ESGs may bring distortions in the optimal investment portfolio unless a unified set of criteria is established (e.g., Yoshino, Taghizadeh-Hesary, and Otsuka 2021). These criteria should take into consideration unique circumstances brought about by the pandemic.

Issuing an ESG bond, which requires an ESG bond framework and second-party opinion, also typically requires the issuer to obtain an ESG evaluation by the second party, which takes time and preparation. This gives issuers a good reason to pre-commit to ESG so as to be ready when the crisis comes. Firms that did the ESG work ahead of time have come to market faster.

Of course, with every challenge comes an opportunity, and there is certainly a broad opportunity for market participants to develop this "holy grail": a widely accepted, standardized set of metrics to assess social impact. Various bodies—from the Sustainability Accounting Standards Board to European authorities—are pursuing a system of standardized reporting to include social impact. However, debate is continuing in the market about the right mix of regulatory oversight versus market-principles-based oversight.

The main takeaway from this discussion is that the factors relevant in aligning the financial system with sustainability goals are also relevant for the ESG bond market.

5.6 Regional Financial Cooperation in Support of Sustainable Infrastructure Investment

Regional financial cooperation has an important role in promoting sustainable infrastructure investment. In this chapter, several areas have been identified.

First, regional financial cooperation is needed to continue the progress of the ABMI, particularly in relation to the issuance of more local currency bonds. In particular, the framework for supporting conventional local currency bonds can be extended to green local currency bonds (ADB 2018). In this area, policy makers identified several regional policy priorities. These include the following:

(i)   Develop a regional technical assistance facility for green bond issuance

(ii) Provide specific coverage of green bonds on AsianBondsOnline

(iii) Consider requesting the International Capital Market Association to present annual updates on the Green Bond Principles and green bond market development globally to members of the ASEAN+3 Bond Market Forum

(iv) Consider encouraging the Credit Guarantee and Investment Facility to allocate a portion of the guarantee operations to involve green bonds

(v)   Continue working with market participants to address barriers to cross-border bond issuance and investment under the ASEAN+3 Bond Market Forum

(vi) Encourage regional and global public entities to issue local currency green bonds

(vii) Encourage regional and global public funds to commit to investing in local currency green bonds

Second, regional cooperation can support the establishment of a regional floating-interest-rate bond if the spillover of tax revenues of an infrastructure project involves several countries. An example is water transport infrastructure in the Mekong Region which covers many countries. Floating-interest-rate bonds can be sold to various investors in the Asian region to support the project. The expected rate of return will be higher by securing 50% of the estimated spillover taxes.

Third, multilateral development banks can narrow the risk gap of PPPs through credit enhancement which usually takes the form of sovereign risk mitigation. Involvement of multilateral development banks and other multilateral agencies can also be given as technical assistance, program lending, and specific advice.

Fourth, regional support on the framework for green bonds can be extended to ESG bonds. This includes the following actions: (i) regional cooperation to vet and adopt standards at the regional level, e.g., Social Bond Principles; (ii) develop a robust ESG bond market in the region, including establishing an ESG index; and (iii) regional cooperation in standardization of the measurement of impact of proceeds from ESG bonds.

Fifth, develop a common platform to ensure convergence of standards and to drive essential cross-border cooperation so that global bond and equity markets can most effectively raise capital to serve sustainable development.

Sixth, regional cooperation can help promote green finance measures. For example, scaling up the ASEAN Catalytic Green Finance Facility to the level of ASEAN+3, requires the involvement of the ASEAN+3 finance ministers' and the central bank governors' process. Continued involvement of multilateral development banks in green financing initiatives also requires financial cooperation at the regional level.

Seventh, the G20 Principles for Quality Infrastructure Investment should be taken into account. These are:

(i) Maximizing the positive impact of infrastructure to achieve sustainable growth and development

(ii) Raising economic efficiency in view of life-cycle costs implying that not only initial investment cost should be considered but also repairs and maintenance needed at a later stage

(iii) Integrating environmental considerations in infrastructure investments

(iv) Building resilience against natural disasters and other risks

(v) Integrating social considerations in infrastructure investment

(vi) Strengthening infrastructure governance

5.7 Conclusion

The infrastructure financing gap in the ASEAN+3 region is substantial. The public sector has shouldered a substantial portion of the financing burden. However, its resources are hardly adequate. COVID-19 has made the circumstances more challenging for governments as revenues drop and pandemic containment expenditures rise, increasing debt and tightening fiscal space for infrastructure investment. The circumstances call for a more vigorous drive to involve the private sector in infrastructure undertakings. Beyond the sheer size of the funding needed, the sustainability of the financing mechanisms is equally important.

PPPs are a viable option but developing Asia has more cancelled PPP projects than any other region globally. Studies show that project-related factors, macroeconomic conditions, and institutional quality tend to affect private sector investors' participation. One of the specific binding constraints is the low rate of return of infrastructure investment especially if the environmental, sociopolitical, and economic uncertainties are considered. Reliance on user fees alone is not a viable strategy in many cases.

Against this backdrop, this chapter has proposed the utilization of floating-interest-rate infrastructure bonds that carry a conditionality to share spillover tax revenues between the government and investors. This mechanism is geared toward augmenting the income stream from user fees, thus increasing the investor rate of return. The government partially compensates for the losses at initial stages of operation by paying interest at the prevailing rate of government bonds. The spillover tax revenues in the subsequent stages can then serve as a source for greater compensation.

Meanwhile, the analysis has made other proposals to operationalize the spillover taxation in various contexts. The success of the mechanism will depend on data transparency and accountability of the parties involved. To this end, governments can work on infrastructure projects with multilateral institutions. This will help curb corruption and strengthen the integrity of the entire process particularly in projects that involve multiple countries. In addition, regional organs and regional cooperation initiatives are critical in deepening long-term capital markets further without compromising the appropriate oversight frameworks.

The environmental impact of the infrastructure projects cannot be overlooked in the process of engaging the private sector. There are ample merits to bolster efforts to emphasize compliance of financing instruments with the ESG standards. A proposal to have a greenness-adjusted global taxation on carbon dioxide and other pollutants has been made in a bid to further promote green infrastructure.

More importantly, there is scope for ASEAN+3 economies to strengthen regional financial cooperation in infrastructure investment and in promoting green finance.

References

Asian Development Bank (ADB). 2017. *Meeting Asia's Infrastructure Needs.* Manila. https://www.adb.org/publications/asia-infrastructure-needs.

———. 2018. *Promoting Green Local Currency Bonds for Infrastructure Development in ASEAN+3.* Manila. http://dx.doi.org/10.22617/TCS189249–2.

———. 2019. *Asian Economic Integration Report 2019/2020: Demographic Change, Productivity, and the role of Technology.* Manila.

———. 2020a. *Green Finance Strategies for Post-COVID-19 Economic Recovery in Southeast Asia: Greening Recoveries for People and Planet.* Manila. http://dx.doi.org/10.22617/TCS200267–2.

———. 2020b. *Asian Development Outlook (ADO) 2020 Supplement: Paths Diverge in Recovery from the Pandemic.* Manila. http://dx.doi.org/10.22617/FLS200389–3.

———. 2021. *Primer on Social Bonds and Recent Developments in Asia.* Manila. http://dx.doi.org/10.22617/SPR210045–2.

———. AsianBondsOnline Database. https://asianbondsonline.adb.org/ (accessed July 2021).

Azhgaliyeva, D., A. Kapoor, and Y. Liu. 2020. Green Bonds for Financing Renewable Energy and Energy Efficiency in Southeast Asia: A Review of Policies. *ADBI Working Paper.* No. 1073. Tokyo: Asian Development Bank Institute. https://www.adb.org/publications/green-bonds-financing-renewable-energy-efficiency-southeast-asia.

Burger, J.D., F.E. Warnock, and V.C. Warnock. 2015. Bond Market Development in Developing Asia. *ADB Economics Working Papers.* No. 448. Manila: Asian Development Bank. https://www.adb.org/sites/default/files/publication/173190/ewp-448.pdf.

Deep, A., J. Kim, and M. Lee. 2019. *Overview.* In *Realizing the Potential of Public–Private Partnerships to Advance Asia's Infrastructure Development.* Manila. http://dx.doi.org/10.22617/TCS189648–2.

Ferrarini, B., J.J. Pradelli, P. Mariano, and S. Dagli. (Forthcoming). *Asia Sovereign Debt Monitor.* Manila.

Hepburn, C., B. O'Callaghan, N. Stern, J. Stiglitz, and D. Zenghelis. 2020. Will COVID-19 Fiscal Recovery Packages Accelerate or Retard Progress on Climate Change? *Oxford Review of Economic Policy.* 36. Issue Supplement 1. 2020. pp. S359–S381. https://doi.org/10.1093/oxrep/graa015.

International Energy Agency (IEA). 2020a. *Global Energy Review 2020: The Impacts of the COVID-19 crisis on Global Energy Demand and CO_2 Emissions*. Paris.

———. 2020b. *The Impact of the COVID-19 Crisis on Clean Energy Progress*. Paris.

International Monetary Fund (IMF). Fiscal Monitor Database. https://data.imf.org/?sk=4BE0C9CB-272A-4667-8892-34B582B21BA6 (accessed July 2021).

———. Investment and Capital Stock Dataset. May 2021 Update. https://infrastructuregovern.imf.org/content/dam/PIMA/Knowledge-Hub/dataset/IMFInvestmentandCapitalStockDataset2021.xlsx (accessed July 2021).

———. World Economic Outlook Database, April 2021. https://www.imf.org/en/Publications/WEO/weo-database/2021/April (accessed July 2021).

Khanna, M. 2020. COVID-19: A Cloud with a Silver Lining for Renewable Energy? *Applied Economic Perspectives and Policy*. 43 (1). pp. 73–85. https://doi.org/10.1002/aepp.13102.

Lee, M., R. Gaspar, E. Alano, and X. Han. 2019a. The Empirical Evidence and Channels for Effective Public–Private Partnerships. In *Realizing the Potential of Public–Private Partnerships to Advance Asia's Infrastructure Development,* edited by A. Deep, J. Kim, and M. Lee. Manila: Asian Development Bank. http://dx.doi.org/10.22617/TCS189648-2.

Lee, M., P. G. Quising, M. L. Villaruel, and X. Han. 2019b. Assessing Risk in Public–Private Partnerships. In *Realizing the Potential of Public–Private Partnerships to Advance Asia's Infrastructure Development,* edited by A. Deep, J. Kim, and M. Lee. Manila: Asian Development Bank. http://dx.doi.org/10.22617/TCS189648-2.

Park,C. Y., J. Villafuerte, J. Lee, and P. Rosenkranz. 2017. 20 Years after the Asian Financial Crisis: Lessons Learned and Future Challenges. *ADB Briefs*. No. 85. Manila: Asian Development Bank. http://dx.doi.org/10.22617/BRF179036-2.

Rillo, A. D. and A. Zulfiqar. 2018. Toward an Innovative Approach of Financing Infrastructure in Asia. (2) 1. pp. 87–96. https://systems.enpress-publisher.com/index.php/jipd/article/view/141.

Rowley A. H. 2020. *Foundations of The Future: The Global Battle for Infrastructure*. Singapore: World Scientific. https://doi.org/10.1142/11765.

Sawada, Y. and L. R. Sumulong. 2021. Macroeconomic Impact of COVID-19 in Developing Asia. *ADBI Working Paper*. No. 1251. Tokyo: Asian Development Bank Institute. https://www.adb.org/publications/macroeconomic-impact-covid-19-developing-asia.

Silva, A. C., B. O'Reilly Gurhy, A .F. Carvajal, C. E. Paladines, T. Jonasson, C. Cohen, Y. N. Mooi, K. Chung, and M. G. Papaioannou. 2020. Staff Note for the G20 International Financial Architecture Working Group (IFAWG): Recent Developments on Local Currency Bond Markets In Emerging Economies. Washington, DC: International Monetary Fund and the World Bank Group. https://documents.worldbank.org/en/publication/documents-reports/documentdetail/129961580334830825/staff-note-for-the-g20-international-financial-architecture-working-group-ifawg-recent-developments-on-local-currency-bond-markets-in-emerging-economies.

Susantono B., D. Park, and S. Tian. 2020. Introduction. In *Infrastructure Finance in Asia*, edited by B. Susantono, D. Park, and S. Tian. pp. i–xviii. Singapore: World Scientific. https://doi.org/10.1142/11688.

United Nations Environment Programme (UNEP). 2015. The Financial System We Need: Aligning the Financial System with Sustainable Development. *UNEP Inquiry*. Geneva. http://unepinquiry.org/wp-content/uploads/2015/11/The_Financial_System_We_Need_EN.pdf.

_____. 2016. Green Finance for Developing Countries: Needs Concerns and Innovations. *UNEP Inquiry*. Geneva. http://unepinquiry.org/wp-content/uploads/2016/08/Green_Finance_for_Developing_Countries.pdf.

Volz, U. 2018. Fostering Green Finance for Sustainable Development in Asia. *ADBI Working Paper*. No. 814. Tokyo: Asian Development Bank Institute. https://www.adb.org/publications/fostering-green-finance-sustainable-development-asia.

World Bank. 2020. *Mobilizing Private Finance for Nature*. Washington, DC. https://pubdocs.worldbank.org/en/916781601304630850/Finance-for-Nature-28-Sep-web-version.pdf.

_____. 2021a. *East Asia and Pacific Economic Update: Uneven Recovery*. Washington, DC. https://openknowledge.worldbank.org/bitstream/handle/10986/35272/9781464817021.pdf.

_____. 2021b. Debt Service Suspension and COVID-19. Factsheet. Washington DC. https://www.worldbank.org/en/news/factsheet/2020/05/11/debt-relief-and-covid-19-coronavirus.

_____. *World Development Indicators*. https://databank.worldbank.org/source/world-development-indicators (accessed July 2021).

World Federation of Exchanges. *Statistics Portal*. https://www.world-exchanges.org/our-work/statistics (accessed July 2021).

Yoshino, N. 2013. The Background of Hometown Investment Trust Funds. In *Hometown Investment Trust Funds: A Stable Way to Supply Risk Capital*, edited by N. Yoshino and S. Kaji. pp. 1–13. Tokyo: Springer. https://doi.org/10.1007/978-4-431-54309-1.

Yoshino, N. and S. Lakhia. 2020. Land Trust Method and the Evaluation of the Effect of Infrastructure Investment. *ASCI Journal of Management*, Special Issue, 49 (2). pp. 133–146. https://asci.org.in/wp-content/uploads/2021/06/AJoM-49-2-Sep-2020.pdf

Yoshino, N. and U. Abidhadjaev. 2017a. An Impact Evaluation of Investment in Infrastructure: The Case of a Railway Connection in Uzbekistan. *Journal of Asian Economics*. 49. pp. 1–11. https://doi.org/10.1016/j.asieco.2017.02.001.

_____. 2017b. Impact of Infrastructure on Tax Revenue: Case Study of High-speed Train in Japan. *Journal of Infrastructure, Policy and Development*. 1 (2). pp. 129–148. https://doi.org/10.24294/jipd.v1i2.69.

Yoshino, N., U. Abidhadjaev, and M. Nakahigashi. 2019. Inducing Private Finance to Water Supply and Inland Water Transport Using Spillover Tax Revenues. *ADBI Working Papers*. No. 996. Tokyo: Asian Development Bank Institute. https://www.adb.org/sites/default/files/publication/524011/adbi-wp996.pdf.

Yoshino N., D. Azhgaliyeva, and R. Mishra. 2020. Financing Infrastructure Using Floating-interest Rate Infrastructure Bond. *Journal of Infrastructure, Policy and Development*. 4 (2). pp. 306–315. https://doi.org/10.24294/jipd.v4i2.1236.

Yoshino, N. and V. Pontines V. 2015. The 'Highway Effect' on Public Finance: Case of the STAR Highway in the Philippines. *ADBI Working Paper*. No. 549. Tokyo: Asian Development Bank Institute. https://www.adb.org/sites/default/files/publication/175868/adbi-wp549.pdf.

Yoshino, N., F. Taghizadeh-Hesary, and M. Otsuka. 2021. COVID-19 and Optimal Portfolio Selection for Investment in Sustainable Development Goals. *Finance Research Letters*. 38 (3). https://doi.org/10.1016/j.frl.2020.101695.

Yoshino, N. and T. Yuyama. 2021. ESG/Green Investment and Allocation of Portfolio Assets. *Studies of Applied Economics*. 39 (3). https://doi.org/10.25115/eea.v39i3.4628

6 Pension Challenges in Aging Asia

Gloria Pasadilla

6.1 Introduction

Like the rest of the world, Asia is rapidly getting old. This is inevitable in a world where scientific advances have increased life expectancy and, together with changed social preferences, have reduced fertility rates and population growth. Members of the workforce behind much of Asia's rapid growth (especially in the last half of the last century) have reached, or are reaching retirement. This has implications not only for the labor force but, importantly, also for old-age income support.

This chapter discusses the impact of population aging on the macroeconomy, particularly on labor force participation, savings, growth, and productivity. Its impact on social protection, with a particular focus on the pension challenges facing countries in ASEAN+3, is also examined. In the context of regional cooperation, the chapter tackles various pension-related issues that can be discussed at the regional level, to learn practices and solutions other countries have adopted to address the aging issue. The chapter explores the link between pension systems and the financial market. It discusses how the environment of low interest rates (low-interest environment) is making pension institutions struggle to meet its future financial liabilities toward retirees and how investment in alternative assets can help. It examines the role of technology in improving the delivery of social security services and also how workers in the technology-induced gig economy could be covered adequately by existing social security schemes. Finally, it considers pension portability in the context of increasing intra-ASEAN+3 labor migration. Throughout this chapter, references are made on experiences of more developed economies that have more mature pension systems, financial markets, and that have made early strides at addressing population aging.

The next section discusses aging and its macroeconomic impact on productivity, savings, and labor force participation. Thereafter, section 6.3 dives into pension challenges of the aging population and tackles the various reform directions adopted to date, as well as the ongoing challenges to make pension systems sustainable. Section 6.4 discusses aging and pension-related issues for regional cooperation. The first subsection considers the link between pension and financial markets, highlighting the challenge of meeting pensions' fiduciary obligations in view of the persistent low-interest environment, and it examines potential portfolio diversification options, for instance investing more in "alternative" assets such as infrastructure. The second subsection considers the impact of technology, not only on pension institutions' governance and administration, but also more importantly, on the social protection of workers in the technology-induced gig economy where standard employment benefits may not apply. Finally, the third subsection discusses the portability of pension in light of the increasing mobility of workers.

6.2 Aging and the Macroeconomy

The Population Profile

ASEAN+3 is aging due to declines in population growth and longer life expectancies. Figure 6.1 shows the decline in fertility in East and Southeast Asia. From a rate of close to 6 live births per woman in the 1950s, Southeast Asia as a whole dwindled to 2.2 births per woman over 2015–2020. Among them, Singapore and Thailand have the lowest fertility rates of 1.2 and 1.5, respectively. The picture for East Asia is similar: from a relatively high fertility rate in 1950, the number has fallen below the replacement rate of 2.0. Of the three, the Republic of Korea has the lowest rate of 1.11, lower than 1.69 for the People's Republic of China (PRC). Yet, relative to other regions of the world, Asia's population is growing faster than Europe or North America, but falls far behind Africa's 4.4 fertility rate.

While fertility rates have declined everywhere, people now live longer, thanks to advances in medical technology and bioresearch. Figure 6.2 shows how life expectancies for those aged 60 have risen both in East and Southeast Asia. For example, a 60-year old person in Japan is now expected to live up to about 86 or 87; in the PRC, it will be up to 80 years old. A similar story is shown for Southeast Asia. In Singapore, old people are expected to reach 85 years. Compare this to the 1950s, when in Southeast Asia as a whole, elders were expected to live only up to 73. In general, high-income economies such as those in Europe and North America have higher life expectancies than the rest of the world.

Figure 6.1: Fertility Rate in Selected East and Southeast Asian Economies, 1950–2020

a. Southeast Asia; PRC; Hong Kong, China; Japan; Republic of Korea

b. ASEAN

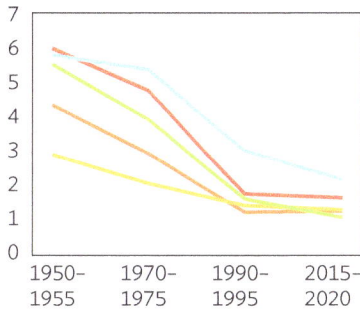
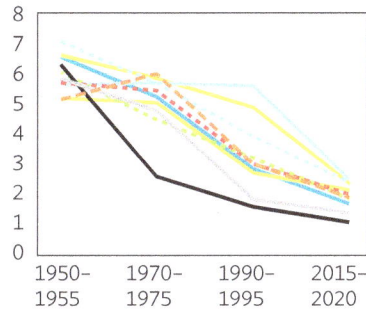

- ▬ PRC ▬ Hong Kong, China ▬ Japan
- ▬ Korea, Rep. of ▬ Southeast Asia

- ▬ Brunei Darussalam ▬ Cambodia
- Indonesia Lao PDR ⋯ Malaysia
- ▪▪ Myanmar Philippines ▬ Singapore
- Thailand ▪· Viet Nam

ASEAN = Association of Southeast Asian Nations, PRC = People's Republic of China, Lao PDR = Lao People's Democratic Republic.
Notes: Southeast Asia aggregation follows the definition of the source.
Source: UN 2019a. 2019 Revision of World Population Prospects Database (accessed August 2021).

The consequence of low fertility rates and higher life expectancies is a larger proportion of old people in national populations. Figure 6.3 shows that the median ages in the populations of East and Southeast Asia have generally increased. Japan's median age in 1950 was 22, while it is 48 in 2020; in the Republic of Korea it is 44, up from 19; and in the PRC, from 24 it rose to 38.

Compared to East Asia, Southeast Asia is still relatively young, however, with the average median age at 30 in 2020. Among its countries, Cambodia, the Lao People's Democratic Republic (Lao PDR), and the Philippines have the lowest average median age, at 25, up from 19 in 1950; and in Singapore and Thailand, median age is approaching that of the Republic of Korea—42 and 40, respectively. Indonesia and Malaysia are in the middle, with a median age of 30.

Figure 6.2: Life Expectancy at Age 60 in Selected East and Southeast Asian Economies, 1950–2020

a. Southeast Asia; PRC; Hong Kong, China; Japan; Republic of Korea

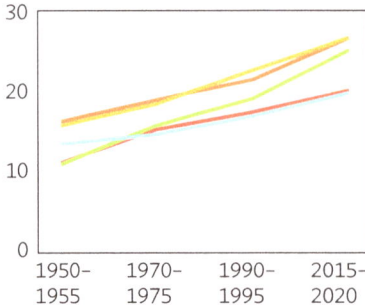

b. ASEAN

- PRC
- Hong Kong, China
- Japan
- Korea, Rep. of
- Southeast Asia
- Brunei Darussalam
- Indonesia
- Lao PDR
- Myanmar
- Philippines
- Cambodia
- Malaysia
- Singapore
- Thailand
- Viet Nam

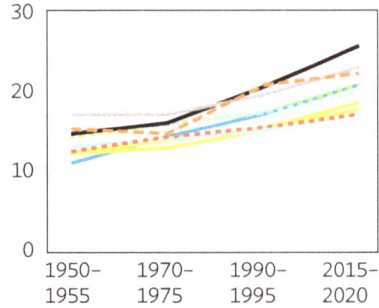

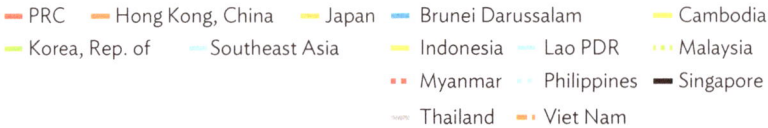

ASEAN = Association of Southeast Asian Nations, PRC = People's Republic of China, Lao PDR = Lao People's Democratic Republic.
Note: Southeast Asia aggregation follows the definition of the source.
Source: UN 2019a. 2019 Revision of World Population Prospects Database (accessed August 2021).

Another important consequence of population aging, and one that has more direct relevance to pension issues, is that the old-age dependency ratio has increased, that is, the number at retirement age of 65 years and above, divided by the working-age population (20 to 64 years old).[1] This ratio is used to estimate how many old people are supported by the working population. For example, in Figure 6.4, Japan's ratio of 52 means that roughly two workers support one old person (i.e., 65 years old and above). In contrast, in Southeast Asia, eight workers support one old person. Worldwide, all countries in the world are projected to see at least a doubling of the dependency ratio by 2050 (Lee 2016).

---

[1]   Other definition of the dependency ratio uses the population 15–64 years old as the denominator instead of 20–64 years old.

Figure 6.3: Median Age in Selected East and Southeast Asian Economies, 1950–2020

a. Southeast Asia; PRC; Hong Kong, China; Japan; Republic of Korea

b. ASEAN

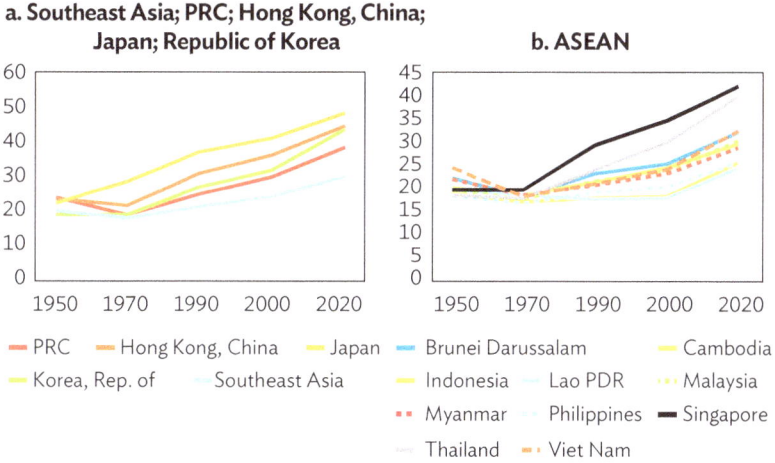

PRC — Hong Kong, China — Japan — Brunei Darussalam — Cambodia — Korea, Rep. of — Southeast Asia — Indonesia — Lao PDR — Malaysia — Myanmar — Philippines — Singapore — Thailand — Viet Nam

ASEAN = Association of Southeast Asian Nations, PRC = People's Republic of China, Lao PDR = Lao People's Democratic Republic.
Note: Southeast Asia aggregation follows the definition of the source.
Source: UN 2019a. 2019 Revision of World Population Prospects Database (accessed August 2021).

Figure 6.4: Old-Age Dependency Ratio in Selected East and Southeast Asian Economies, 1950–2020

a. Southeast Asia; PRC; Hong Kong, China; Japan; Republic of Korea

b. ASEAN

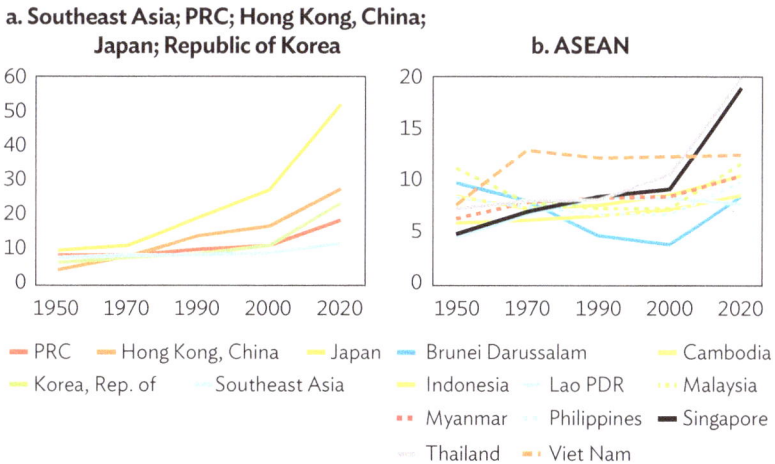

PRC — Hong Kong, China — Japan — Brunei Darussalam — Cambodia — Korea, Rep. of — Southeast Asia — Indonesia — Lao PDR — Malaysia — Myanmar — Philippines — Singapore — Thailand — Viet Nam

ASEAN = Association of Southeast Asian Nations, PRC = People's Republic of China, Lao PDR = Lao People's Democratic Republic.
Note: Southeast Asia aggregation follows the definition of the source. The data refer to the population aged 65 years and above per 100 persons aged 20–64 years old.
Source: UN 2019a. 2019 Revision of World Population Prospects Database (accessed August 2021).

How will population aging in Asia affect future growth, productivity, innovation, and the macroeconomy? Is the breakneck speed of growth in East and Southeast Asia over in light of its aging labor force (as well as the pandemic shock)? As the population ages, theory posits that labor force participation declines and economic growth drops. Furthermore, to the extent that older workers are deemed less productive than younger ones, population aging will mean a decline in productivity, which contributes to lower economic growth. Population aging also means an increase in the proportion of "dissavers" because old people tend to consume more than save, thus lowering aggregate savings in the economy. As old people cash in on their stock investments, a so-called "secular stagnation" characterized by low returns on capital due to decumulation can result. These linkages are surveyed below.

Aging and Economic Implications

Aging and labor force participation

With an aging population, labor force quantity declines but not as dramatically as the rate of aging. First, because of better health and medical services, many people remain highly functional at age 65 and above. Many who could have otherwise exited the labor force have the option to continue working, partly because many jobs are not as physically demanding as they were in the past. Second, because of policy changes by governments, for example, the removal of statutory retirement age, or anti-discriminatory policies for older workers in the workplace, older people remain employable. Open immigration policies also helped increase labor supply vitiating the dearth of labor due to the aging population. Third, technology and sociocultural values have evolved. Part-time jobs that fit older workers or work-from-home arrangements are now available, thanks to technology and the change in mindset in society that the COVID-19 pandemic accelerated. Over time, more women have also entered the work force mitigating the effect of the aging population on labor supply.

The quality of labor has, likewise, improved. Burtless (2013) notes that older workers now have higher human capital—i.e., are more educated—than the previous generation. As such, even if quantity declines, better quality workers mitigate the population aging's negative effect on the economy.

Aging, productivity, and growth

Are older workers less productive? At first brush, they may be deemed so; they may be slower to learn and to adopt new technology than younger workers. Yet, empirical evidence supporting this hypothesis is fragile. Acemoglu and Restrepo (2017), using cross-country data, find no negative relationship between aging and gross domestic product (GDP) per capita. They argue that automation technology in countries that experience demographic changes defuses the negative effect of an aging workforce. Effectively, Acemoglu and Restrepo say that labor productivity has not suffered because of the aging population; rather, projected population aging triggers a shift to new production technology, increasing labor productivity. Burtless (2013) also finds little evidence that an aging workforce lowers average productivity. He argues that productivity is a function not only of age, but also of education and experience. In this regard, many highly productive workers self-select themselves by staying longer in the workforce, while low-productivity old workers are incentivized to exit the labor force sooner. Hence, the old workers that generally remain in the labor force are the more productive ones, as shown in their wage premium relative to those of younger cohorts. The cohort in his study of 60–70 year-old retirees was productive because they were more educated than past cohorts.

On the other hand, Maestas, Mullen, and Powell (2016) find a negative correlation between population aging and growth in GDP per capita. Exploiting variability of aging across US states, they estimate that a 10% increase in the population of age 60 and above decreases state GDP per capita growth by 5.5%. Moreover, they show that, contrary to Acemoglu and Restrepo (2017), the growth slowdown results mostly from slower productivity growth (shown as slower earning growth across the age distribution) and less from slower labor force growth. The finding contrasts with Acemoglu and Restrepo's (2017) result which found no negative relationship between aging and growth across countries (instead of across US states) when the variability of technology adoption is controlled for. Hence, within an economy where states have a similar technology level, it can be surmised that aging can negatively affect growth. However, this negative effect is blunted by technology (which is productivity-enhancing) and mitigated by human capital investments.

Summing up, all else being equal, aging can lead to lower economic growth. However, since nothing is static, countries adapt new technology to augment productivity; population health improves so that even older workers remain functional for a longer time than in decades past; and productivity increases through life-long learning as well as previous work experiences. Altogether, these explain the mixed result, so far, of the effect of aging on growth and productivity.

Aging, savings, and assets

The old generally dissave, while the young save. Hence, aging can lead to a decline in private savings. This simple generalization is actually not easy to defend. In fact, the relationship between aging and aggregate saving is not straightforward. Public savings may be more directly negatively related to aging, especially if the country has a pay-as-you-go pension system and gaps between contributions and benefits are paid out of public funds. Further, if government also funds public health services, an aging population will burden public savings because health costs typically increase as the population ages.

It is a different story, however, for private savings. A negative effect of population aging on private saving is possible because of the higher proportion of net dissavers. However, with longer life expectancies and lower fertility, the working-age population will also tend to save more to provide for longer life in retirement. Moreover, with lower fertility, less is spent on child care and education, although the increase in savings may be lessened by the young consuming more to compensate for working more. The net effect on private saving is therefore ambiguous and depends on various factors. Pension systems and the generosity of payment benefits, additionally, diminish private savings especially if pension and private savings are deemed as substitute sources of old-age income (Chai and Kim 2018).

Population aging can lead to asset meltdown when retirees or baby boomers become more risk averse and start decumulating by selling stocks and buying bonds. As the price of bonds increases with a rise in demand, low returns on capital ensue. Similarly, theory posits that returns on capital fall because as labor force participation declines with population aging, higher capital intensity results. The occurrence of this scenario, however, is deemed unlikely. First, the public sector may compete for private capital to fund public expenditures, thus raising interest rates. Second, in an open economy, higher capital intensity in one country due to population aging, can lead to export of capital, mitigating the fall in rates of return. A relatively younger economy will be a net recipient of capital, while an older one becomes an exporter of capital. In this sense, an open economy context counteracts the effects of population aging on asset price movements (Lee 2016).[2]

6.3 Aging Asia's Challenging Pensions Environment

While connections between aging, growth, and productivity are ambiguous, an aging population creates clear challenges for pension systems. Add to longer life expectancies and lower population growth the fact that social and cultural shifts have frayed traditional family support, the result is that the elderly population has to rely even more on the formal pension system.

Pension systems would be panacea if it were not for the fact that they themselves face some challenges from the aging phenomenon. The main challenges are how to make the pension system sustainable, provide adequate benefits, and, at the same time, cover a large portion of the population.

Often, pension systems cover only those in formal employment, leaving the informal sector outside of its net. Some self-employed individuals or those in nonstandard employment (part-time, temporary, or contract workers, including "gig" workers) may enjoy some pension benefits but often these are less than what those with standard employment have (section 4.2). Some public pension systems have devised mechanisms for the self-employed or workers in the nonformal sector, for example through voluntary contributions. Despite this, by and large, pension coverage or membership remains low in Asia (Park and Estrada 2014, OECD 2018b).

Pension Systems Landscape

To better understand pension challenges, let us discuss the pension system landscape. Pensions are one of the pillars of social protection, which typically includes social assistance, unemployment benefits, healthcare, disability, survivorship, and other things. Often the pension system is designed such that it is so closely intertwined with other forms of social protection, especially disability and survivorship.

---

[2] At the individual level, increasing savings is not an issue for high-income earners, but is a challenge for low- and middle-income earners, whose savings have to be allocated into different baskets of needs— health, children education, daily consumption, etc.—with personal savings for retirement usually rated as last priority. Because savings, whether for pension or others, tend to be concentrated in high-income households, the aging economy can also exacerbate income inequality (Amaglobeli et al. 2019).

Pension systems have various "tiers." The so-called zero-pillar or zero-tier is usually noncontributory or non-earnings-related, with benefits assistance that is usually means-tested, usually based on residency, and funded fully out of the government budget. Mandatory defined benefit (DB) pay-as-you-go systems constitute pillar 1, while mandatory defined contribution (DC) schemes are under pillar 2. Pillar 3 accounts for voluntary contributions to private accounts that include pension plans or retirement savings plans, insurance, disability, death, and others, that usually act as supplementary savings. These can also be either DB or DC schemes, employer-sponsored or not, but are essentially flexible and discretionary. Pillar 4 is a nonfinancial pillar including informal support from family, as well as other formal social programs such as healthcare and/or housing, and other financial and nonfinancial assets such as homeownership and reverse mortgages (Holzmann, Hinz, and Dorfman 2008).[3]

Defined benefit, defined contribution, and other pension characteristics

Pension plans can differ in how they are financed (whether all from member contributions or partly from the government budget) or in what vehicles or institutions collect contributions and manage the assets. Some pension plans are occupational (usually set up by employers) while others are personal. Most importantly, some pension plans are either DB, where future benefits are promised based on some defined formula, usually a function of number of years and amount of contributions or earnings. Others are DC, where future benefits wholly depend on the amount of contributions and their investment returns. Public pensions are typically managed by a government-related institution, although it can outsource the investment of funds to external parties such as private pension funds, hedge funds, or investment banks. Contributions to the public system are usually mandatory, but some can be DB or DC schemes (pillars 1 and 2). Other pension plans are employer-sponsored, and can be voluntary and either DB or DC. Some pension plans are funded, that is, the assets (based on contributions from employers and employees as well as investments) pay for the benefits obligations. Other pension plans are unfunded in that assets do not fully cover the liabilities; many pay-as-you-go systems are of this type.[4] For government-run pensions systems, the gaps in benefits

---

[3]   More details of the World Bank's five pillars of social protection are discussed in Holzmann, Hinz, and Dorfman (2008)

[4]   Some employer-sponsored pension plans can also be either funded or unfunded. Funded ones are where both employer and employee contributions are separately placed outside the company books. They are unfunded when corporate funding share is through book reserves in the employer's accounts. The latter type of pension plan suffers when a company goes bankrupt.

become contingent liabilities that eventually have to be covered out of the national budget.[5] For employer or occupational pensions, the gaps may mean that employees would not enjoy the benefits promised under the pension plan (if under DB schemes). Increasingly, more pension plans are DC schemes which eliminate the underfunding problem but carry the possibility of low future pension benefits depending on the performance of the pension fund. Figure 6.5 provides a summary of some salient characteristics of public and private pensions.

Figure 6.5: Pension Landscape General Typology

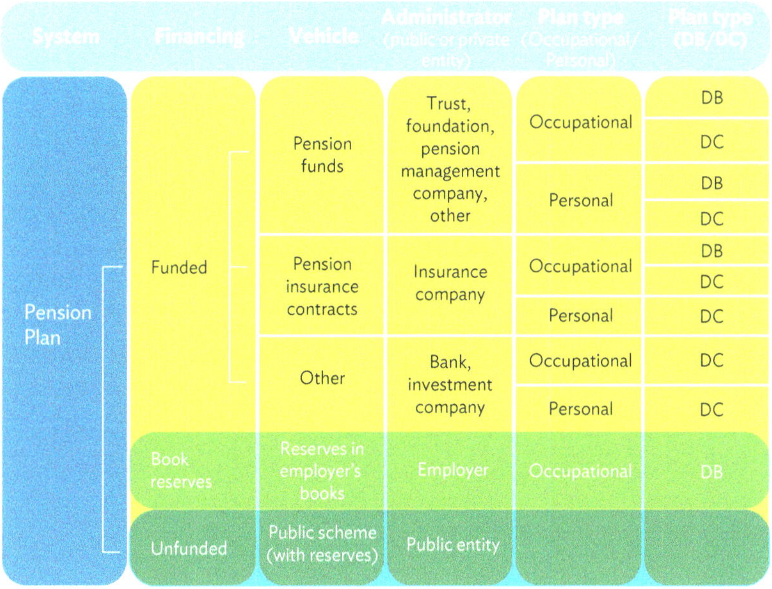

System	Financing	Vehicle	Administrator (public or private entity)	Plan type (Occupational/ Personal)	Plan type (DB/DC)
Pension Plan	Funded	Pension funds	Trust, foundation, pension management company, other	Occupational	DB
					DC
				Personal	DB
					DC
		Pension insurance contracts	Insurance company	Occupational	DB
					DC
				Personal	DC
		Other	Bank, investment company	Occupational	DC
				Personal	DC
	Book reserves	Reserves in employer's books	Employer	Occupational	DB
	Unfunded	Public scheme (with reserves)	Public entity		

DB = defined benefit, DC = defined contribution.
Source: OECD (2019a).

DB pay-as-you-go systems depend on the contribution of those in the workforce to pay retirement benefits which are computed based on number of years of contributions and earnings history. Under DB systems, an increasing proportion of retirees that the system needs to support can result in failure and bankruptcy of the pension system if contributions are insufficient and timely reforms are not undertaken. Reforms and measures can include additional government funding support, increased funding

---

[5]   The zero-pillar of pensions is social assistance that is usually funded out of the national budget as well.

through higher member contributions or a bigger number of contributors, as well as increasing the pensionable age or lowering old-age benefits. The frailty of DB systems has led some countries and some private companies that have sponsored DB retirement schemes to shift to the DC system to ensure sustainability.

Unlike DB systems, DC systems mitigate the risk of sustainability of pension institutions because the member contributions are usually reflected as individual savings accounts instead of being used to pay current retirees' benefits. Put another way, DC benefits are not predefined but depend on the amount members put in as well as its investment returns. The challenge in DC systems, however, is ensuring that the accumulated amount for retirement is adequate enough to support old-age consumption in view of longer life expectancies. This is particularly salient given recent years' low-growth/low-interest economic environment which reduces the long-term benefit of compounding investments in DC plans.[6]

Among developed economies, 58% have DB old-age pension system, 11% have DC, and 20% have both DB and DC systems. For emerging and developing economies, 64% have DB systems, 13% have DC, and 19% have both DB and DC systems.[7] Since most DB schemes are financed on a pay-as-you-go basis—i.e., current workers' contribution funds current retirees' benefits—aging's direct impact is likely to fall on public savings in case of any funding shortfall. In contrast, in DC systems, aging will not directly impact public savings but private savings (Amaglobeli et al. 2019).

Pension Systems in ASEAN+3

Table 6.1 provides an overview of the public pension systems in ASEAN+3. Almost all have DB systems, except Malaysia and Singapore, which have DC schemes. The Philippines has implemented a DC scheme starting only in January 2021, while Thailand started their mandatory provident fund in 2018. Across the region, the pensionable age ranges between 55 and 65 years. Men who reach 65 can expect to live another 14 to 24 years, which is shorter than the 18 to 29 years for women.

---

[6]   Other variations in pension schemes include notional accounts, for example, notional defined contribution plan, whereby instead of actual investment returns from the market, what is reflected in the individual pension account is the return set by the provider, e.g., the government. Singapore is, in practice, an example of a notional DC, because the rates of return on the Central Provident Fund contributions are set or guaranteed by the government.

[7]   The remaining percentage for both developed and developing economies pertain to "Other" pension systems that include only basic pension schemes (usually not based on contributions).

Table 6.1: Selected Indicators of Pension Systems in ASEAN+3

	Pension Age (years) Men (Women)	Life Expectancy at 65 (years) Men	Women	Old-Age Support Ratio (2055)	Gross Replacement Rates (%) Men	Women	Coverage (% labor force)	Type of Public Pension Plan
PRC	60 (55)	20.1	21.6	1.9	76.0	82.6	51	DB
Japan	63	23.8	29.0	1.4	34.6	34.6	95	DB
Korea, Rep. of	65	23.1	28.1	1.5	39.3	39.3	80	DB
Indonesia	55	14.5	17.7	4.5	62.1	57.8	18	DC/DB
Malaysia	55	19.9	21.6	3.4	69.4	64.1	46	DC/DB
Philippines	65	14.6	18.4	6.2	71.9	71.9	27	DB/DC
Singapore	65	24.3	27.5	1.6	53.1	47.3	61	DC
Thailand	55	20.8	23.7	2	37.5	37.5	36	DB/DC
Viet Nam	60 (55)	21.0	25.1	2.5	75.0	75.0	22	DB

PRC = People's Republic of China, DB = defined benefit, DC = defined contribution.
Note: Gross replacement rate refers to the ratio of pension benefit to individual average lifetime earnings. Support ratio refers to the ratio of working population to old-age population. Coverage refers to the ratio of the number of members to labor force. The Philippines started the DC system in January 2021
Source: Author, based on OECD (2018b, 2019c).

The number of people covered by the pension system is between 18% and 61% of the labor force in Southeast Asia, with Indonesia, the Philippines, and Viet Nam having the lowest coverage. Japan and the Republic of Korea have achieved close to total coverage, which is the ideal for inclusivity and equity. However, whether the pension amount is adequate is another story. The computed gross replacement rates by the Organisation for Economic Co-operation and Development (OECD) of pension benefits as a percentage of average lifetime earnings is low for developed countries such as Japan, the Republic of Korea, and Singapore because of higher earnings and standards of living. For the opposite reason, replacement rates are relatively high for countries such as the PRC, the Philippines, and Viet Nam (OECD 2018b, 2019c).

Table 6.2 shows the available pension pillars in the region. All economies have multi-pillar pension approach but they differ in the details. For example, Singapore and Malaysia have the most similar DC pension systems but while Singapore's is strictly only for Singaporeans and permanent residents, Malaysia allows voluntary contribution to the Employee Provident Fund by foreign workers. Contribution rates by employer and employees also vary, with Singapore having a combined maximum contribution of up to

37% of earnings while Malaysia reaches only up to 24%. Malaysia also has a separate system for certain public sector employees and the military. For private sector workers, a social insurance system (defined benefit) exists in addition to the Employee Provident Fund.

Table 6.2: Pension Systems in Selected ASEAN+3 Economies

a. People's Republic of China

Pillars	Government Workers	Workers in Formal Sector	Informal Sector/Self-Employed	Rural and Non-Salaried Urban Residents
Pillar 0	Noncontributory system: Minimum life security system			
Pillar 1	Covered separately	Social insurance (Basic pension program) through mandatory contribution by employers: Public pension fund		
Pillar 1b	Mandatory individual accounts (Basic pension program)			Individual accounts
Pillar 3	Enterprise annuities (EA) (voluntarily set up by employers)			
	Other schemes set up by employers not conforming to EA format (other occupational pension plans)			
	Other tax-deferred annuities plan for individuals (commercial insurance)			

b. Indonesia

Pillars	Government Workers	Workers in Formal Sector	Informal Sector
Pillar 0	Social assistance for poor retirees		
Pillar 1	DB social insurance scheme (*Jaminan Pensiun*) administered by BJPS Ketenagakarjaan started in 2015		
Pillar 2	Special system for public sector	Provident fund—JHT *Jaminan Hari Tua* or Old Age Security; Mandatory life insurance	Voluntary coverage in provident fund; Mandatory life insurance
Pillar 3		Occupational pension funds (either DB or DC)	
Pillar 3	Personal DC scheme		

continued on next page

Table 6.2 (continued)

c. Japan

Pillars	Government Workers	Workers in Formal Sector	Informal Sector/ Self-Employed[a]
Pillar 0	National Pension Insurance (basic income)		
Pillar 1	Mutual Aid Association (eventually subsumed under EPI)	Employee Pension Insurance (EPI)[b]	
Pillar 3		Corporate or Occupational Pension (DB/DC);	National Pension Funds Association; Small Enterprise Retirement Allowance Mutual Aid Plans
Pillar 3	Individual pension plans (DC)		

d. Republic of Korea

Pillars	Government workers	Workers in formal sector	Informal sector/ Self-employed
Pillar 0	Social assistance		
Pillar 1	Government Employees Pension Scheme; Military Personnel Pension Scheme	National Pension Service	
Pillar 1		Private school teacher pension scheme	
Pillar 3	Personal pension schemes (tax-favored) Corporate pension		

e. Malaysia

Pillars	Government workers	Workers in formal sector	Informal sector
Pillar 0	Social assistance/welfare benefits for the poor		
Pillar 1	Special system for certain public sector employees and military	Social Security Organization (DB social insurance system)	
Pillar 2	DC scheme for armed forces personnel	Employee Provident Fund (*Kumpulan Wang Simpanan Pekerja* (KWSP))	Voluntary coverage in the Employee Provident Fund
Pillar 3	Private retirement schemes (Private-sector run DC schemes)		

continued on next page

Table 6.2 (continued)

f. Philippines

Pillars	Government workers	Workers in formal sector	Informal sector
Pillar 0	Social assistance		
Pillar 1	Government Service Insurance System	Social Security System (SSS)	SSS but can be voluntary
Pillar 2	PAG-IBIG Fund; Mandatory Provident Fund		
Pillar 3	SSS P.E.S.O. Fund (Personal Equity and Savings Option) PERA (Personal Equity and Retirement Account) Private pension plans and various pre-need products (acting as supplementary savings) Occupational pension and provident funds [c]		

g. Singapore

Pillars	Government workers	Workers in formal sector	Informal sector/ Self-employed
Pillar 0	Social assistance		
Pillar 2	Central Provident Fund (CPF)		CPF (with reduced contribution rate for low-income earner)
Pillar 3	Supplementary retirement schemes; Personal pension/insurance schemes; employer-funded pension		

h. Thailand

Pillars	Government workers	Workers in formal sector	Informal sector
Pillar 0		Old-age allowance	
Pillar 1	Old civil service pension	Social security fund (sec 33) [d]	Social security fund (sec 39/40) [d]
Pillar 2	Government pension fund	National saving fund	
Pillar 3	Retirement mutual fund and pension insurance	Provident fund	

DB = defined benefit, DC = defined contribution.

Note: Pillar 0—social assistance; Pillar 1—mandatory defined benefit pay-as-you-go schemes; Pillar 2—mandatory defined contribution; Pillar 3- voluntary/ supplementary saving schemes, occupational or personal.

[a] National Pension Funds Association for self-employed and for employed but whose companies do not have corporate pension plans. Smaller Enterprise Retirement Allowance Mutual Aid plans are specifically for small businesses.

[b] Employees Pension Fund can substitute EPI (if company opts out of EPI and provides more than 50% higher benefits than EPI).

[c] A portion is mandatory lump-sum retirement benefit equal to one-half of monthly wage multiplied by number of years of service (mandatory retirement benefit is provided by employer); provident funds are voluntarily set up by companies.

[d] Social Security Fund sec 33 and 39 differ in the maximum salary on which contribution is based: B15,000 for sec 33 and B4,800 for sec 39. Sec 40 has different minimum number of years of contribution and amount.

Source: Author, based on various sources.

Indonesia, the Philippines, and Thailand have systems to cover government workers separately from the social insurance system for private sector workers. Indonesia, the Philippines, and Thailand have both DB and DC schemes. Indonesia started its DB system in 2015, and before then had a provident fund and mandatory life insurance. Thailand is the reverse: it had a DB scheme and introduced a voluntary DC scheme, the National Saving Fund, only in 2011 and a mandatory one in 2018. The Philippines also just introduced a mandatory DC system (pillar 2) in January 2021, but it has private and corporate provident funds for supplementary savings as well as tax-favored voluntary retirement savings schemes.

Japan's pension system is unique in that it allows some companies to opt out of the national insurance scheme as long as its benefits exceed that of the Employees' Pension Insurance benefits by more than 50%. Otherwise, corporate pension plans, just like in other countries, serve only as a supplementary source of retirement income. For companies that do not have corporate pension plans, its employees can join the National Pension Funds Association, which also caters to the self-employed, for supplementary savings.

Similarly, for the Republic of Korea, a separate pension scheme is designed for teachers in private schools, excluding them from the National Pension Service that serves all other workers in the formal sector. Unlike in Japan, there is no opt-out option for corporates from the National Pension Service.

The PRC's pension system is more complicated than those of the other ASEAN+3 economies. It is fragmented and organized at the provincial or municipal level, although efforts are afoot to make it more centralized. Its social insurance system in urban areas is an unfunded system with contributions from employers up to 20% of payroll. Employees contribute 8% of the previous year's average monthly earning to a separate mandatory individual account. The latter is supposed to be fully funded (akin to a provident fund) but, in reality, its assets are largely notional, because the funds have been used to pay current retirees' unfunded liabilities. The minimum vesting period is 15 years. Rural areas are covered by a separate pension system, largely noncontributory, along with individual accounts.

The pension systems in Cambodia, the Lao PDR, and Viet Nam are still nascent and are described in Box 6.1.

Box 6.1: Pension Systems in Cambodia, the Lao People's Democratic Republic, and Viet Nam

Cambodia, the Lao People's Democratic Republic (Lao PDR), and Viet Nam have very young pension systems. In all three countries, laws governing social security exist, but are only recently being implemented. In Cambodia, the National Social Security Fund, which started in 2008, appears to have provisions at the moment only for maternity and sickness, as well as for work injury, and none yet for pension and old age. The Lao PDR passed the social security law in 2013 and started implementation in 2014, while Viet Nam passed the pension law in 2009. Of the three countries, Viet Nam has the biggest contribution rate, at 22%, which bodes well for sustainability. It also mandates payment for social security in Viet Nam by all foreign employees, for as long as they have more than 1-month work contract in the country.

The challenges in these new social security systems differ from those of other ASEAN+3 economies. In particular, with respect to private sector pension liabilities, a funding gap issue does not exist as yet. Instead, the challenge is in the efficient functioning and administration of the system itself as well as collection and payment compliance by enterprises. Establishing an accurate database of workers and compensations to base projections of collections is one hurdle for the social security institution. Likewise, securing personal documents and difficulty in registration and document verification is another impediment for members. Basic institution building, digital support, and financial education, rather than strategies for sustainability and adequacy, should be priorities for capacity building in these economies (table).

continued on next page

Box 6.1 (continued)

Statutory Provisions of Social Security Schemes

Country	Pension Age	Coverage	Contribution Rate	Social Security Law
Cambodia	No provision	Private sector employees; special systems for public sector employees	2.6% of covered earnings to be paid by employer; with minimum and maximum earnings for contribution calculation	2002 (social insurance) implemented in 2008 but has no provision for old age, only maternity and sickness; work injury
Lao PDR	60 years old (men); 55 (women); at least 15 years of contributions	Employees of private and public sector; Voluntary for self-employed	5% (2.5% each for insured and employer) of gross monthly earnings. Minimum and maximum earnings exist for contribution calculation	New law in 2013; implemented in 2014
Viet Nam	60 (men); 55 (women) with at least 20 years of contributions	All employees (private and public); Voluntary for self-employed	22% (8% insured person; 14% employer) of monthly covered earnings; has minimum and maximum earnings for contribution calculation	2009 (for old age); 2014 (social insurance)

Lao PDR = Lao People's Democratic Republic.
Source: Government of the United States, Social Security Administration (2019) (accessed May 2021).

Pension expenditures

Pension expenditures in Southeast Asia range from $3 billion (Philippines) to $7 billion (Indonesia), constituting between 20% and 39% of each country's social protection expenditures. In East Asia, pension expenditures are starkly higher, from $30 billion (Republic of Korea) to $450 billion (Japan). Pension spending in Japan is 51% of social protection expenditures, while in the PRC its share is 43%, and in the Republic of Korea it is 26% (Figure 6.6).

Figure 6.6: Pension Expenditures in Selected ASEAN+3 Economies, 2015

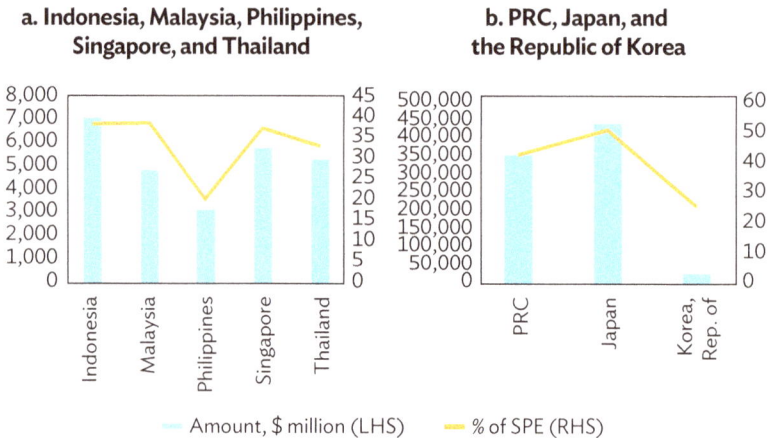

a. Indonesia, Malaysia, Philippines, Singapore, and Thailand

b. PRC, Japan, and the Republic of Korea

—— Amount, $ million (LHS)   —— % of SPE (RHS)

LHS = left-hand scale, PRC = People's Republic of China, RHS = right-hand scale, SPE = social protection expenditures.
Source: Author, based on ADB Social Protection Indicator Database (accessed March 2021).

While Table 6.2 shows that Asian countries have zero-pillar social protection or social assistance, their share in social protection expenditures is low. Social insurance, comprising pensions, health, and other social insurance, constitutes at least 60% of social protection expenditures across all countries (Figure 6.7). Among social insurance expenditures, pensions take an average of 46%. In Japan, social insurance takes close to 20% of GDP, the highest ratio among Asian economies.

Figure 6.7: Social Insurance and Social Assistance Expenditures in Selected ASEAN+3 Economies, 2015

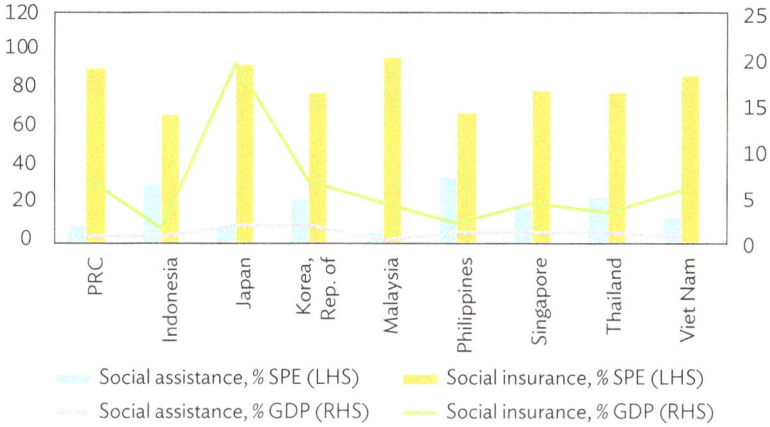

LHS = left-hand scale, PRC = People's Republic of China, RHS = right-hand scale, SPE = social protection expenditures.
Source: Author, based on ADB, Social Protection Indicator Database (accessed March 2021).

The low share of social insurance expenditures in ASEAN+3 is supported by the UN 2019 World Population Highlights Report findings that the majority of elderly consumption, especially in Indonesia, the Philippines, and Thailand, is funded out of asset reallocations (Figure 6.8). This is along with private transfers (from family and friends).[8] In these countries, public transfers are close to nil, while in the PRC, Japan, and the Republic of Korea, they remain an important source for funding for old-age consumption.

---

[8] In the PRC, anecdotal evidence shows the increasing difficulty of sourcing family support from grown-up children, first because the single-child policy makes the burden of parental support too heavy for one person; and second, the rising urban cost of living that has made sending extra money to families in the rural areas increasingly more difficult (Cai 2018). This evidence of declining family support is not unique to the PRC. In other countries too, internal migration and declining household size have reduced the ability of children to care for parents. Among developed countries, where marriage instability is more widespread and more children are born outside of marriage and stable family units, Cherlin and Seltzer (2014) see the number of Americans, for example, willing to bear the burden of family hardship support of elderly parents waning. In Japan, the emergence of people committed to living single—*ohitorisama*—is helping change social dynamics. In Canada, solo households make up 28% of the total, and 34% in the European Union. In Europe, secularism is displacing Christianity and affecting community and family ties (Ernst and Young 2020). These sociological changes add salience to the public provision of adequate retirement income for the elderly.

Figure 6.8: Financing Elderly Consumption in Selected ASEAN+3 Economies, Latest Data from 1998 to 2015
(%)

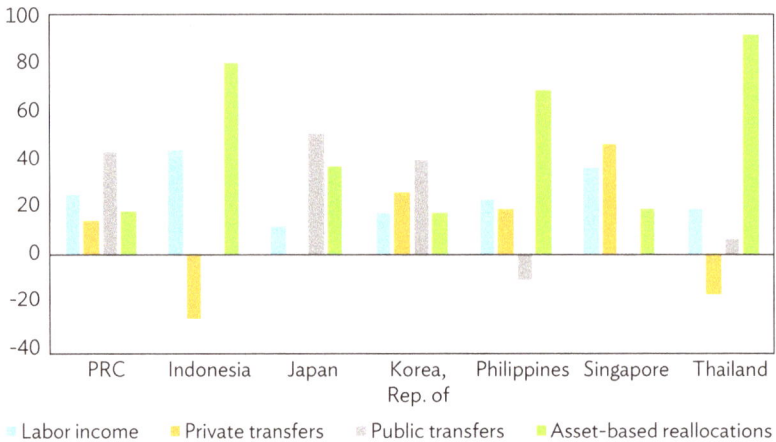

PRC = People's Republic of China.
Source: United Nations (2019b).

Pension–Savings Gap

The challenge of old-age support is an intergenerational issue if it is assumed that the old population requires transfers from the young through, for instance, their contribution in pay-as-you-go pension systems or government taxes. The problem is less stark if the old population has sufficient accumulated asset income and high private savings. Unfortunately, this is not the picture even in countries where savings rates were historically high. A World Economic Forum ('WEF') report, for example, shows a $400 trillion gap by 2050 for the eight economies in its study, with the PRC and Japan among them.[9] The calculation is based on funding from government-provided first-pillar systems and public employee systems, the funding of employer-based systems, and the levels of individual pension savings, compared with expected average annual retirement income needs and life expectancies (assuming 70% income replacement rate).

---

[9]   Refer to Figure 8 in World Economic Forum (2017a).

In the WEF computation, the PRC and Japan both have an $11 trillion retirement savings gap in 2015 which is estimated to grow by 7% and 2%, respectively. At this growth, by 2050, the PRC's pension savings gap will be $119 trillion while Japan's will be $26 trillion. WEF (2017a) also shows that 61% of Japan's pension saving shortfall is due to unfunded government pension liabilities, while 37% comes from low individual savings. For the PRC, the percentage shares are 72% from unfunded pension and 28% from low private savings.

Figure 6.9 underscores the urgency for strengthening pension institutions and undertaking reforms to bridge the public pension gaps. It also highlights the need to promote higher personal savings for retirement. Significantly, WEF (2017a) finds low financial literacy among workers, an important condition, especially for DC systems where responsibility rests heavily on individuals, who are their own investment managers, actuaries, and insurers. Another difficulty is the lack of easy access to pensions, especially in places where majority of workers are in the informal sector. For DC systems to generate decent returns on retirement, a target of 10%–15% savings rate is recommended but WEF (2017a) finds that savings rates are usually below this target. Another issue is low future investment returns (currently 5% for equities, 3% for bonds) which is currently below historic average. The section on pensions and financial markets looks closer at the problem of a low-interest environment for pension institutions.

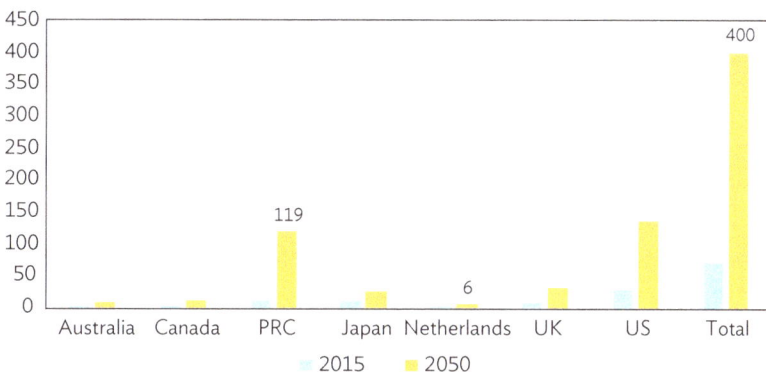

Figure 6.9: Retirement Savings Gap in Selected Economies, 2015 and 2050
($ trillion)

PRC = People's Republic of China, UK = United Kingdom, US = United States.
Note: The sum of the individual economies may not equal the total, due to rounding.
Source: World Economic Forum (2017a).

Reform Directions

To increase private savings for old age and to avoid unfunded pension systems going bankrupt, many countries have embarked on reform programs. For instance, to increase individual private savings, some countries have adopted supplementary DC pension systems on top of existing DB pension schemes (such as the Philippines and Thailand). Some DC systems are mandatory, with individual and employer contribution (pillar 2); others are voluntary (pillar 3) but are incentivized by favorable tax (only if withdrawn upon retirement and not earlier). Other countries have also tried to expand financial products that could be vehicles for retirement savings, such as life insurance or reverse mortgages on purchased properties during retirement (pillar 4). In the 1990s, some countries, especially in Latin America, privatized their systems to remove the pension burden from government.

Institutional and parametric reforms

For public pension systems, various reforms include parametric changes in the system, such as increasing contribution rates by employees and employers, expanding the number of contributors, raising the retirement age, or adjusting the benefit formulas and reducing monthly benefits payout to extend pension benefits over a longer period. Some have curtailed early retirement options and tightened eligibility rules for other benefits. Reduction of benefits, however, can worsen poverty in old age, especially in countries where pension benefits are not high to start with.

Some countries have adopted deeper institutional pension reforms by shifting from DB to DC pension systems. The shift has aimed to make systems sustainable and put most responsibility for old age on individuals instead of governments. Funding transitions from DB to DC systems, however, has proved difficult, since a generation of workers could end up paying for their own retirement needs and those of the generation ahead of them. The upfront transition cost also put significant pressure on existing public savings. Further, significant financial education is usually required in the shift to a DC system as individuals will have to manage their future income trajectories, given that many people are ignorant of financial products and their appropriateness for financing old age (WEF 2017a). In addition, costs associated with pension investments, such as commissions and fees to asset managers, can be costly and eat up workers' meager retirement savings. Fully funded DC systems are also subject to potential market risks that may leave retirees with little asset value if they retire during an economic down cycle.

Another structural reform has tried to increase coverage (defined as the ratio of pension system contributors to the size of the labor force) to expand total contribution in the pension fund.[10] This aims to help workers in nonstandard employment and those in the informal sector obtain retirement benefits through the public pension scheme. Park (2012) suggests that Asian pension systems need to improve governance and to lower operating costs to improve public trust in pension system institutions which, in turn, would help attract members, increasing pension coverage.

Flanking labor policy changes

Pension system reforms are also helped by labor policy changes. For example, flexible employment policies such as work-from-home arrangements or more part-time jobs allow more retirees to remain in the labor force. Making child care accessible and affordable also helps increase female participation in the workforce. For various reasons, women typically have lower income in retirement on average (Box 6.2). Still another useful labor policy, albeit politically sensitive, is open migration policies which support economic growth. High economic growth, in turn, makes the weight of supporting the old population easier.

Summing up, reforms adopted in many countries do not differ much, whether advanced or less advanced economies. Rather, the difference depends more on whether they have aging or young populations, and whether their social security institutions are nascent or mature. Table 6.3 summarizes examples of the reforms around the world, as discussed above.

---

[10] Sometimes working-age population, 15–64 years old, is used as denominator for coverage computation, instead of labor force.

Box 6.2: Why Women Have Less Retirement Savings?

Generally speaking, women have less retirement savings than men. The difference (as a percentage of male retirement earnings) can range between 17% (for Singapore) and 46% (for Malaysia). Several reasons explain this gap.

First, historically, women have been paid lower than men. Since retirement benefits are usually linked to earnings, the wage gap in women's working lives is reflected in retirement income.

Second, because of caring responsibilities (either for children or elderly parents), women tend to have shorter careers and years of contribution to the pension system. In some cases, because of these shortened work lives, women are unable to meet the minimum vesting period for retirement benefits.

Third, more women also work in part-time work or in the informal sector than men. Since many pension schemes do not cover informal sector workers, this affects future retirement income of women.

Fourth, women tend to be more risk averse than men. For a defined contribution scheme's accumulation phase, women tend to invest in low returns but safer assets, such as money market funds, while men invest more in stocks and mutual funds, which have higher returns but higher risk.[a]

[a] Marsh and McLennan Companies Asia Pacific Risk Center and Tsao Foundation's International Longevity Centre (2018).
Source: OECD (2019a).

Table 6.3: Summary of Pension Reforms

	Aging Population	Young Population or Nascent Institution
Advanced economy	• Shift to defined contribution (DC) from defined benefit (DB); or introduce DC pillar on top of DB • Increase retirement age • Increase contribution rates • Lower benefit formula • Restrictions on early withdrawal of benefits • Add voluntary savings tier • Digitalization • Privatization of social security to ease fiscal burden • Remove retirement age in labor force; subsidy in keeping older workers • Increase coverage (especially for gig workers) • Expansion of financial products as retirement vehicles	• Most advanced economies are aging
Less advanced	• Mostly same as above except expansion of financial instruments due to regulatory inadequacies or lack of supervisory capacity or unsophisticated financial market • Increase coverage (informal sector) • Improving trust on institution • Financial literacy education	• Improve administrative efficiencies/collection • Improving trust on institution • Financial literacy education • Policies on valid documents/identity cards

Source: Author.

Adequacy and Sustainability of Asia's Pension Systems

Adequacy and sustainability of retirement income are the most important features of pension systems. How do Asian pension systems rate on these qualities? In Asia and the Pacific, the problem of adequacy of retirement income is dire for four main reasons (OECD 2008). First, the low coverage of pension systems leaves a large sector of the population with little or no income to depend on in old age. Second, withdrawal of savings before retirement is allowed, which results in people having inadequate savings left at retirement. Third, absence of annuitization instruments[11] and a prevalence of lump-sum payments does not alleviate the risk of people outliving their savings. Fourth, although ad hoc benefits adjustments take place, some pension systems do not feature automatic adjustments of benefits to reflect changes in living cost.

---

[11] These are contracts or financial investments which pay out a fixed income stream at a later date.

The New York-based firm, Mercer, the Chartered Financial Analysts (CFA) Institute, and the Monash Centre for Financial Studies (2020) compared the sustainability and adequacy of 37 pension systems by constructing an index based on indicators deemed important for sustainability and adequacy. Eight of 37 pension systems in the sample were ASEAN+3 countries, and worthwhile to compare with those of other countries. Figure 6.10 shows that most developed economies, especially Northern European welfare economies, have the "best" pension systems in overall sustainability. Among Asian economies, Singapore and Malaysia are above the average while six other Asian countries in the study rank at the bottom, meaning that these systems have major weaknesses or lack specific features that help establish sustainability.[12,13]

The Global Pension Index study finds that, for Thailand, the weakest element is the adequacy of retirement finance, while pension sustainability is the major weakness of the PRC, Japan, and Singapore, largely because of demographic factors. Malaysia and the Republic of Korea are also relatively weak in providing adequate pensions. It is also tempting to attribute the relatively high score of Malaysia and Singapore to their DC systems, as compared to DB schemes in other countries, but this idea fails given that top-ranked Netherlands has a DB pay-as-you-go pension system.

The Melbourne–Mercer–CFA study (Mercer, Monash Centre for Financial Studies, and the State Government of Victoria, Australia 2019) is useful in comparing the systems of various countries with respect to pension adequacy and sustainability. However, it shares the weakness emblematic of indices—opacity. It is difficult to agree or disagree with this index ranking without access to the data used—a lot of them proprietary. It is also difficult to replicate and assess for a subgroup of countries such as ASEAN+3 without access to all the study's data. Instead, partly guided by the discussion in the Global Pension Index study, publicly available information that relates to either adequacy or sustainability of pension are gathered. In a limited way, these data corroborate the Global Pension index and provide details unavailable from indexed information.

---

[12] It does not measure the overall living standard of the elderly—for that, one needs to account for other factors such as health services and elderly care.

[13] Mercer's sustainability index uses 50 indicators to compare pension systems. It has three major components or subindexes: the adequacy subindex, sustainability subindex, and integrity subindex, with respective weights of 40%, 35%, and 25%. Each subindex is constructed based on the values of selected indicators or answers to specific questions on pension system characteristics that improve adequacy or sustainability or integrity.

Figure 6.10: Global Pension Overall Index, 2020

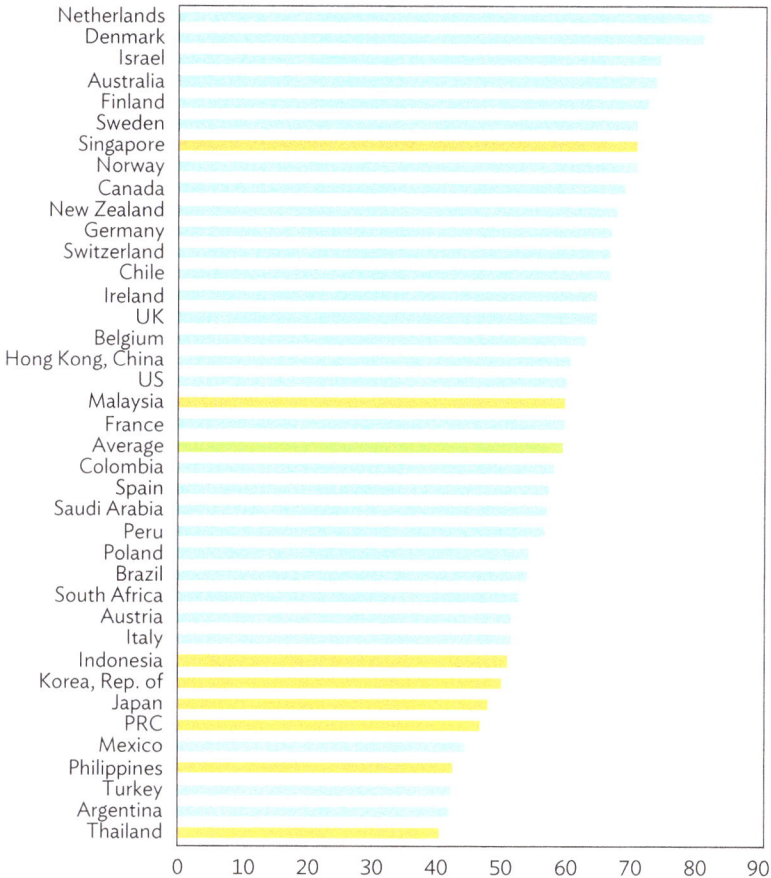

PRC = People's Republic of China, UK = United Kingdom, US = United States.
Note: The data refer to the Mercer CFA Institute Global Pension Index.
Source: Mercer, CFA Institute, and Monash Centre for Financial Studies (2020).

Factors affecting adequacy

Table 6.4, for example, shows factors that relate to the actual amount of benefit and other factors that help increase future income. Column 2 shows minimum earnings-related pension (as opposed to noncontributory or social assistance), which provides an idea of financial support for pension members in the lowest earnings bracket. It shows that, as a percentage of average wages, pension benefits in developing countries such as the PRC, Indonesia, and the Philippines are relatively higher than those in developed countries. This result is not surprising considering that average wages in less developed economies are lower.

Column 3 shows that pension benefits are adjusted to either wages or prices or both. In some countries, such as the Philippines, the adjustment is not automatic but periodic and ad hoc. Benefit adjustment is important for adequacy assessment because the value of benefits upon retirement can easily lose value over time with price and wage inflation. Computed OECD net replacement rates (column 4), defined as pension benefits over average pre-retirement earnings, are also relatively high for developing countries compared to developed economies for the similar reason that pre-retirement earnings in developed countries (the denominator) are very high relative to average retirement benefits.

Other relevant factors that contribute to increasing pension savings are incentives such as tax deductions for voluntary contributions to supplementary private pension. On this, all countries provide tax exemption either at the contribution or withdrawal phases or both. Pension benefits are not the only source of old-age savings. Other assets also contribute to financing elderly consumption. One important factor for adequacy assessment is the level of homeownership. However, Table 6.4 only provides data for Singapore at 91%, along with Japan and the Republic of Korea. Finally, how the voluntary pension assets are invested contributes to the growth of future pension benefits. The last column shows that Singapore and Japan both have relatively high shares of pension assets invested in equities and alternative assets, considered as growth assets, compared to cash, bank deposits, or even government-issued fixed-income securities.[14,15]

---

[14] Not shown in the table is the household debt-to-GDP ratio, which is another indicator for future adequacy of old-age benefits. High household debt can reduce the remaining value of future pension benefits used for consumption. Among Asian countries, the Republic of Korea has the highest household debt as a percentage of GDP at 96%, followed by Thailand (69%) and Malaysia (68%).

[15] The Mercer, CFA Institute, and Monash Centre for Financial Studies (2020) study considers other factors such as whether withdrawal of accrued benefits has a minimum age requirement or whether there are tax disincentives for early withdrawal. These factors ensure that retiree's benefits are not prematurely spent, because otherwise little might remain of the retiree's benefits when the time comes to exit the workforce. Indonesia has relatively strong measures that prevent early dissipation of retirement benefits, with limits on early withdrawals as well as incentives for annuitization. The possibility of annuitization of accrued benefits or converting part of it into a tax-favored income stream is another important factor to ensure accrued benefits can last a retiree's lifetime. Except for Indonesia and Singapore, however, all countries have no avenues for annuitization of retirement benefits.

Table 6.4: Factors That Affect the Adequacy of Pension Benefits

| | Factors Related to Received Amount | | | Other Factors That Help Increase Future Income | | |
	Minimum pension (% average wage)[a]	Adjustment of benefits	Net replacement rates (%, Male/Female)[b]	Tax deduction or exemption of voluntary pension contribution to funded plans and investment income	Home ownership (%)[c]	Proportion of private pension assets invested in growth assets[d]
Effect on adequacy	+	+	+	+	+	+
PRC	40–60	Indexed to wages and prices	83/72	yes		
Indonesia	20.6	Indexed to wages and prices	66/62	yes		26.6
Japan	12.0	Indexed to wages and prices	40/40	yes	61.7	59.7
Korea, Rep. of	5.0	Indexed to wages	45/45	yes	58	31.7
Malaysia	9.7	Index to prices	86/79	yes		
Philippines	17.8	Index to prices but only periodic	88/88	yes, specific funds		
Singapore		Index to prices	59/52	yes	91	96.8
Thailand	4.2–5.6	Index to prices	39/39	yes		18

PRC = People's Republic of China.
[a] The Mercer, CFA Institute, and Monash Centre for Financial Studies (2020) study considered the noncontributory part of pension system, while the figures in the table are the lowest pension benefit from the earnings-related system.
[b] Refers to the individual net pension benefits over average net pre-retirement earnings.
[c] Singapore's data are as of December 2018, Japan's are as of December 2013, and the Republic of Korea's are as of December 2019 (tradingeconomics.com).
[d] Share of equities and other (alternative) assets in private pension investments.
Source: OECD (2018b, 2019c); Trading Economics (accessed May 2021); and the Government of the United States, Social Security Administration (2019) (accessed March 2021).

Factors affecting sustainability

Factors relevant to the sustainability of pension income are those related to the scheme itself, such as coverage and contribution, and, more importantly, demographic factors and economic growth prospects.

On growth, developing countries can bank on higher prospects based on past GDP growth rates. Developed countries such as Japan, as well as the Republic of Korea and Singapore, project lower GDP growth because their GDP base is already large. High growth bodes well for the sustainability of pension.[16]

Japan has an almost universal pension coverage at 95%, way above the OECD average of 86%. Pension coverage in developing Asian countries are still low, ranging from 18% of the labor force in Indonesia to 46% in Malaysia (Table 6.5). The higher the coverage of the population means a bigger pool of contributors and the higher the likelihood that the retirement income system will be sustainable.

The amount of contribution and retirement age are other useful indicators for sustainability of pension systems.[17] The retirement age, especially in Indonesia, Malaysia, and Thailand, is low. These countries still have room to improve the sustainability of their pension schemes. Maximum combined mandatory contribution from both employers and employees is high in Singapore, but very low in the Republic of Korea and Thailand.

Demographic factors are critical in assessing sustainability. In this regard, Japan, the Republic of Korea, and Thailand score low in the sustainability subindex in the Global Pension Index study (Mercer; Monash Centre for Financial Studies; and the State Government of Victoria, Australia 2019) because of their low fertility rates and aging populations. For example, the dependency ratio in Japan is 58%, with the elderly making up the majority of the population. Despite its aging population, Singapore still has a high sustainability index value because of the factors related to its DC scheme such as large assets or high contribution rates and coverage.

If labor policies are sufficiently flexible to allow the older population to continue working, the sustainability problem can be alleviated. Flexible employment of the elderly and their continued contribution to the pension system, even as they start to enjoy part of their retirement benefits, help make retirement funds last longer. In Singapore, the government has

---

[16] Another factor that affects sustainability but is not shown in the table is the level of government debt to GDP. The lower it is, the greater the capacity of the government to help fund gaps in pension. In this, Japan also scores low because of its high domestic debt. In contrast, the PRC's modest public debt earns it high scores on the sustainability subindex of the Global Pension Index (Mercer, CFA Institute, and Monash Centre for Financial Studies 2020).

[17] Retirement age across Asia is shown in Table 6.1 as pension age.

provided incentives for companies to hire older workers. Other countries are following suit to allow older workers to participate in the labor force.

Finally, the longer the years after retirement up to death, the more funds need to be set aside to support the elderly. As life expectancy increases, the policy indicator that a government can adjust is the pensionable age. As discussed above, there seems to be scope for adjusting the pensionable age, especially in Indonesia, Malaysia, and Thailand.

Table 6.5: Factors That Affect Sustainability of Pension Benefits

	Factors Related to Pension Scheme			Demographic Factors			Economic Growth
	Coverage (% labor force)[a]	Maximum mandatory contribution (% of wages)[b]	Estimated years in retirement[c]	Labor participation of elderly (> 65 years old)[d]	Dependency ratio in 2030[e]	Based on past 4 years and projected growth
Effect on sustainability	+	+	–	+	–	+
PRC	51	28	16.7	21.1	27.4	High
Indonesia	18	8.7	6.5	43.7	15.4	High
Japan	95	18.3	19.5	25.3	57.7	Low
Korea, Rep. of	80	9	17.8	35.3	41	Average
Malaysia	46	27	21.1		16.4	High
Philippines	27	13	6.1	32.9	13.3	High
Singapore	61	37	18.8	28.7	36.6	Average
Thailand	36	6	21.9	24.4	32.3	High

PRC = People's Republic of China.
[a] Refers to the number of members of mandatory pension scheme over labor force.
[b] Refers to the combined employer and employee contribution to mandatory pension schemes (both social insurance and provident fund).
[c] Refers to life expectancy at birth less retirement age.
[d] Refers to 2019 data except PRC 2010.
[e] Refers to 65 years old and older population over 20–64 years old population.
Source: National social security organizations (accessed March 2021); OECD (2018b, 2019c); and the Government of the United States, Social Security Administration (2019) (accessed March 2021).

6.4 Pensions and Regional Cooperation

Although all Asian countries face aging-related challenges in their pension systems, there is little discussion about pension issues, except among academics and researchers and a few policy makers, at the regional level. In ASEAN, social protection is a topic under the Senior Officials Meeting on Social Welfare and Development.[18] Pension issues are deemed as under the banner of national initiatives and no concrete substantive pension-related regional programs have ever been launched. Only a few programs related to health cooperation or social assistance to migrants have been agreed.[19]

However, to the extent that labor mobility within ASEAN intensifies as a result of mode-4 services liberalization (movement of natural persons) under economic community building, international coordination of pension systems, such as regional pension portability, will be necessary.

In addition, in theory, if pension challenges become a future fiscal crisis because governments run deficits and accumulate debts to service their contingent retirement liabilities, a country's pension problem and its consequent macroeconomic and financial impact may have spillover effects to other Asian countries. Therefore, while pension challenges are "only" national concerns, these also have potential regional dimensions. This link, however, seems tenuous because of the lack of empirical studies globally that show a pension crisis actually graduating to a fiscal crisis.[20]

Perhaps more important for the regional significance of pension challenges is pension systems' potential role in developing the financial markets in the region. Pension funds and other institutional investors can create demand and liquidity in the regional bond markets. Thus, they can be critical players in the development of Asian regional financial markets. More regional conversations on pension issues would benefit Asian countries. Exchanging experiences and best practice policies that help solve pension challenges is always valuable.

---

[18] In turn, the Senior Officials Meeting on Social Welfare and Development is under the ASEAN Socio-Cultural Community, one of three major pillars of the ASEAN Community, the other two being political-security community and economic community.

[19] For example, see the Senior Officials Declaration of the Special ASEAN Summit on Coronavirus Disease 2019, which calls for strengthening public health cooperation measures, intensifying cooperation for adequate essential medicine provision, commitment to collective action to mitigate economic and social impacts of the pandemic, etc. Another example is the ASEAN Declaration on Strengthening Social Protection 2013, which seeks to foster minimum social protection. The declaration mentions principles on extension of coverage to migrant workers and on the availability, quality, equitability, and sustainability of social protection (ISSA 2017).

[20] While some studies trace the effects of financial and macroeconomic crisis on pensions, such as lower long-term investment returns, no research exists that empirically finds pension crisis graduating to a fiscal and cross-border macroeconomic crisis. That pension crises can become fiscal crises is only a theoretical possibility. This is perhaps because many governments made policy changes and institutional reforms precisely to prevent pension crises becoming full-blown macroeconomic crises with cross-border implications.

The rest of this section focuses on three trends and issues that have significant impact on pension policies. The link between pension and financial markets in the context of pension asset investments to fund retirement benefits is discussed. The chapter goes on to tackle issues over the growth of technology-induced nonstandard employment and its implications for pension and other social protection benefits. Finally, in the context of growing labor migration in Asia, the discussion moves to pension portability.

Pensions and Financial Markets

Pension organizations invest members' contributions and other assets to pay for future retirement benefits. Any pension institution, whether it be under DB or DC scheme or whether it is occupational or personal, private or public, needs to invest the contributions collected. Therefore, it should have an investment strategy that seeks returns that match its future liabilities.[21] In the past, it was easy to pay future benefits by investing in government-issued debts and securities. But to optimize potential returns and minimize risks through portfolio diversification, social security institutions should not only rely on government securities but also need a broad and deep financial market. This applies to whatever existing schemes, whether DB or DC schemes, because both need sufficient returns to achieve either target earnings (in DC schemes) or promised benefits (in DB systems). Thus, the financial market is important for pension institutions.

Likewise, pension institutions are critical for financial markets' growth and development and improve the depth and liquidity of the capital market. With huge assets under management (Box 6.3), pension institutions are a major source of investment funds that generate liquidity and demand for financial products, enhance competition, and promote financial innovation. For example, in the context of the Asian Bond Markets Initiative, pension organizations can be a source of demand for local currency bond issues. Since pension organizations have long-term horizons, they help in the stability of financial markets as compared to short-term speculative capital. As institutional investors, pension funds and institutions also influence good corporate governance through their vote in corporate boards, in the process, enhancing trust in the financial market (Meng and Pfau 2017).

---

[21] For DB schemes, liabilities are the fixed benefits promised to members; for DC schemes, usually a minimum return guarantee, if it exists, in the pension contract. Even without a minimum return guarantee, DC schemes still seek to maximize investment earnings for members within an acceptable level of risk.

Box 6.3: The Pension Funds Industry: A Quick Survey

Pension funds constitute the largest of total global assets under management, accounting for 37% or $57 trillion in assets, followed by mutual funds (36%) and insurance (21%) (first figure).

Total Global Assets Under Management, Share by Asset Owners
(%)

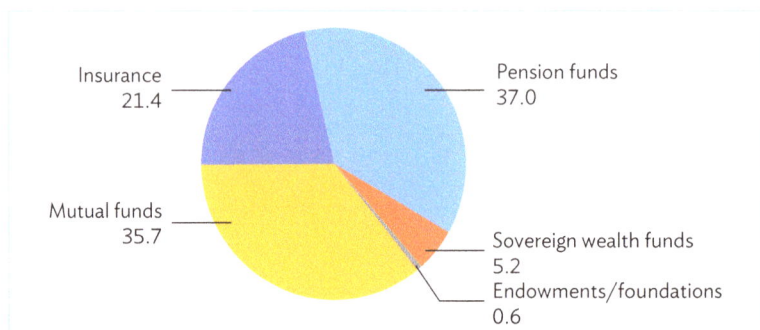

Insurance 21.4

Mutual funds 35.7

Pension funds 37.0

Sovereign wealth funds 5.2

Endowments/foundations 0.6

Source: Thinking Ahead Institute (2021).

Studies of global pension funds industry show that, in terms of assets, some pensions funds in ASEAN+3 rank among the top (table). Japan's Government Pension Investment Fund is consistently ranked first. The Republic of Korea's National Pension is third, although far in terms of absolute amount of assets. The PRC's National Social Security and Singapore's Central Provident Fund are also in the top 10, while Malaysia ranks 12th.

Top Asian Sovereign Pension Funds, 2019
($ million)

2019 Rank	Fund	Market	Total Assets[a]
1	Government Pension Investment Fund	Japan	1,555,550
3	National Pension	Korea, Rep. of	637,279
7	National Social Security	PRC	361,087
8	Central Provident Fund	Singapore	315,857
12	Employees Provident Fund	Malaysia	226,101
13	Local Government Officials	Japan	224,006

PRC = People's Republic of China.
[a] PRC's data are an estimate. Data are as of 31 December 2019.
Note: Sovereign pension funds are established by national governments to meet pension liabilities (Thinking Ahead Institute 2021).
Source: Willis Towers Watson (2020).

continued on next page

Box 6.3 (continued)

However, on pension assets' ratio to GDP, an indicator of pension system strength, ASEAN+3 shows considerable diversity. The next figure shows that while shares of pension assets in Hong Kong, China; Japan; the Republic of Korea; Malaysia; and Singapore compare relatively well with the Organisation for Economic Co-operation and Development (OECD) average of 43% in 2017, the rest of the ASEAN+3 economies do not exceed 10%. The comparison is even more stark for individual developed economies (see figure on Pension Funds Asset in Selected Economies). Australia, Canada, and the United States all have pension assets exceeding the size of their respective gross domestic products. This shows that the pension industry in the region still has large room for growth.

Pension Fund Asset in Selected ASEAN+3 Economies
(% of GDP)

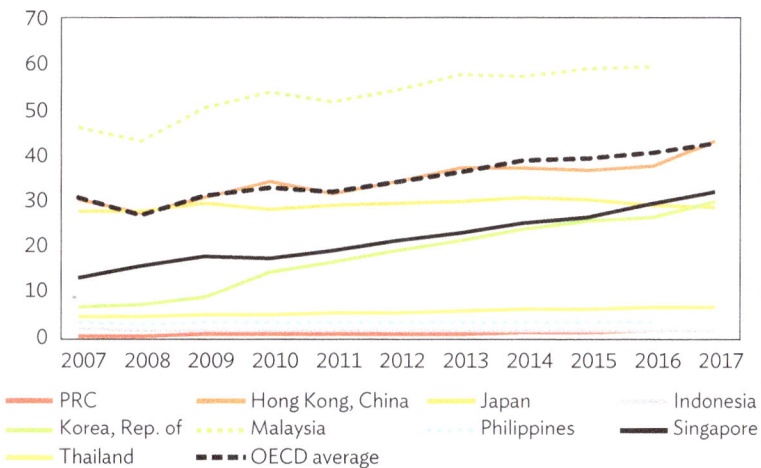

PRC = People's Republic of China, GDP = gross domestic product.
Note: The Organisation for Economic Co-operation and Development (OECD) average refers to the simple average of the 38 member economies.
Source: World Bank, Global Financial Database (accessed August 2021)

continued on next page

Box 6.3 (continued)

Pension Fund Assets in Selected Economies, 2020
(% of GDP)

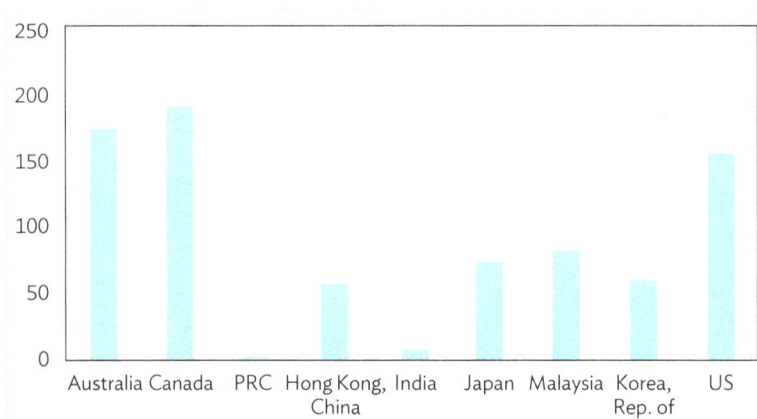

PRC = People's Republic of China, GDP = gross domestic product, US = United States.
Source: Thinking Ahead Institute (2021).

Fortunately, Asia and Pacific pension assets are growing, and posted their highest annualized growth from 2014 to 2019 (figure below). Recent research shows that the fastest-growing pension markets are in the People's Republic of China (21%); the Republic of Korea (12.3%); and Hong Kong, China (8.4%) (Thinking Ahead Institute 2021).[1] Like Japan, which has large fund assets but slow growth, North America also has the largest fund assets compared to Asia and the Pacific and Europe, constituting 44% of top pension fund assets, but growth was below 3% over the 5 years from 2014. Europe's is 26%, close to Asia and the Pacific's 27%, and its assets grew 5%.

Asset allocation of top pension funds shows a reduction in home bias in equities, falling from 67% of domestic equities in total equities in 2000 to 38.5% in 2020. Japan's share of domestic equities is below 40%, down from around 60% in 2000. The same downward trend in domestic bond holdings can be observed, but overall allocation remains high. Among the major economies (Australia, Japan, the Netherlands, Switzerland, the United Kingdom, and the United States) average allocation of domestic bonds to total bonds was 71% in 2020, down from 80% in 2000. Japan's drop was relatively more pronounced from around 80% to less than 60%.

---

[1]   This is based on a 10-year compounded annual growth rate (CAGR) from 2010 to 2020.

continued on next page

Box 6.3 (continued)

Growth of Fund Assets, 2014 and 2019
($ billion)

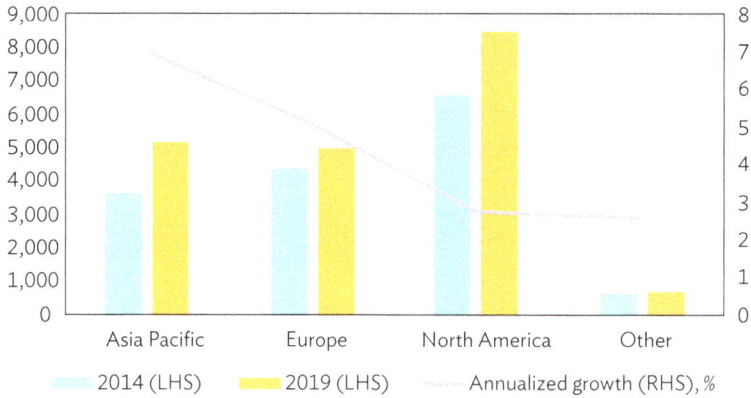

LHS = left-hand scale, RHS = right-hand scale.
Note: The country groupings are based on the definitions of the source.
Source: Thinking Ahead Institute and Pensions & Investments (2020).

Sources: Thinking Ahead Institute (2021); Thinking Ahead Institute and Pensions & Investments (2020); Willis Towers Watson (2020).

Effects of low-interest environment

Global market conditions after the global financial crisis, however, have been challenging for pension institutions. The low-interest environment has made investment in risk-free government assets inadequate for pension institutions to meet benefits obligations or provide adequate returns for members. And in reallocating more of portfolio to other financial assets such as equities or alternative assets, or alternatives such as real estate or infrastructure financing, pension organizations also face the challenge of increased portfolio risk.

A related problem is longevity risk and how a deep and vibrant market for financial instruments that accounts for longevity risk can develop. Some private pension or insurance companies put a cap on the number of years of payouts to protect themselves from this risk, but this strategy comes at the expense of retirees who risk outliving their savings and pension benefits. This section first discusses factors and issues that affect the investment returns of pension institutions, particularly highlighting the increasing role of alternative assets, such as infrastructure financing.

In the past, adequate earnings from pension assets were relatively easier to achieve with minimum risk. This was because returns from government, as well as corporate bond rates, were high enough to help meet payout obligations. Before the global financial crisis, bills and bonds took more than half of the investment portfolio of pension funds in the OECD. In a low- interest environment, such as the present US 10-year Treasury note hovering around zero percent, pension institutions can no longer depend on this low-risk strategy. With interest rates across the globe at rock-bottom, pension institutions have difficulty earning enough to meet retirement liabilities.

Various responses to low interest rates include a reduction of DB's promised benefits or increasing members' contribution rates to help pay for retirement benefits in a pay-as-you-go system. For individuals, poor returns on pension contributions discourage supplementary retirement savings. For companies, shifts from DB to DC schemes have put the burden of low future benefits on individuals rather than on company balance sheets. Some have removed employees' pension benefits altogether to avoid contingent liabilities.

A low-return environment also has disparate effects on different age cohorts (Byrne and Reilly 2017). Generations retiring in the near term have lived through previous periods of strong market returns and high interest rates during their asset-accumulating stage. Additionally, even as they face increased longevity, many of them have DB entitlements, because the shifts to DC happened more recently and affect the later generation more. In contrast, younger generations are likely to earn lower investment returns on their pension contributions than the older ones.

Investments in "alternatives"

Thanks to higher share prices, pension funds have been able to maintain reasonable returns by reshuffling their asset allocation. Because sovereign bonds can no longer give the returns necessary to meet pension promises, long-term institutional investors (insurance and pension) increased their holdings of corporate credit, equities, and structured products. In 2008, equities took 18% of OECD pension funds' portfolios. In 2018, that share increased to 24%. As long as the equity markets remain in bullish territory, meeting pension liabilities is manageable even in the low-interest environment. However, when equity markets turn bearish while interest rates remain low, the pension challenge will grow. An even more diversified portfolio beyond stocks and fixed-income securities is thus needed.

As a diversification strategy, many large pension institutions have invested in "alternatives" such as private equity,[22] real estate, and infrastructure finance (Table 6.6). Alternatives refer loosely to anything other than bonds, stocks, or cash. In theory, it can include, art, wine, precious metals, commodities, cryptocurrencies, etc. For most pension funds, alternatives refer to real estate, private equity, infrastructure finance, and hedge funds.

The average pension portfolio of the top pension funds includes a fifth of investments in alternative assets, more than 40% in equities, and the rest in bonds. North American pension funds are the most bullish, with alternatives having 35% of their investment allocation. This is in stark contrast to Asian pension funds, with only 7% going to nontraditional investments, and more than 50% of portfolios going to fixed-income securities. This investment allocation partly reflects the innate conservatism of Asian pension funds (Table 6.6).

Table 6.6: Investment Allocation of the Largest 300 Pension Funds, 2017
(% share)

Region	Equities	Bonds	Alternatives and Cash
North America	48	18	35
Asia and the Pacific	41	53	7
Europe and others	53	33	14

Note: The country groupings are based on the definitions of the source.
Source: Lynn (2018).

In Asia, Japan and the Republic of Korea have relatively more allocation in alternative assets (as shown in the "other" category in Table 6.7). The other category includes loans, real estate, insurance contracts, hedge funds, private equity funds, structured products, and other mutual funds (not invested in public equities or bills/bonds or cash/deposit). In ASEAN, alternatives investment is small, ranging between 1% (Thailand) to 10% (Indonesia). This is likely to increase as investment regulations of pension institutions become more flexible. In fact, in Thailand, investment in alternatives was only 0.1% in 2008 but increased to 1% by 2017. In contrast, the average share of investments in alternatives in the OECD in 2018 was 15%. Singapore investments recorded in the "other" column

---

[22] This refers to investment in companies not publicly traded. Some private equity funds take direct equity stakes in these private companies, new and start-up companies with significant growth potential, to gain control or influence in operations. Private equity has a longer investment horizon and benefits hugely when a company goes public.

in Table 6.7 is actually not, properly speaking, investment in alternatives. Rather, it is the allocation the Central Provident Fund (CPF) places in risk-free Special Singapore Government Securities. The government, in turn, uses the funds from the special securities' sales to invest in various types of assets, some possibly alternatives.[23]

Table 6.7: Asian Pension Funds' Allocation of Assets, 2017
(% share)

Economy	Equity	Bills and Bonds	Cash and Deposits	Collective Investment Schemes[b]	Other
Japan	8.1	31.6	8.7	...	51.6
Korea, Rep. of	2.7	42.5	18.5	7.2	29.0
Indonesia	16.9	45.9	27.5	...	9.7
Malaysia[a]	9.4	79.5	6.6	1.5	3.1
Singapore	0.2	...	3.2	...	96.7
Thailand	16.9	58.7	10.1	13.2	1.0
OECD	24.4	44.9	7.6	8.0	15.1

... = nil, OECD = Organisation for Economic Co-operation and Development.
[a] From OECD (2018a)
[b] Collective Investment Schemes are indirect investments in equities, bills and bonds, cash, and deposits.
Source: OECD (2018a, 2019a).

Judging from a 10-year performance of asset returns, alternatives yields are definitely higher than government securities and publicly traded stocks returns, which have an average yield of 5% (Table 6.8). Investment in private equity gives the highest return of 9.3%, followed by infrastructure financing at 8%.

Table 6.8: Pension Assets Returns, 2008 to 2018
(annualized, %)

Pension Asset	Annualized Return (%)
Private debt (alternative)	7.5
Infrastructure (alternative)	7.9
Private equity (alternative)	9.3
Public equities	4.8
Hedge funds (alternative)	3.7

Source: World Economic Forum (2019), citing various sources.

---

[23] Essentially, with the purchase of Singapore government securities, the CPF board gives the Singapore government flexibility to invest where it wants, while it, in turn, provides a guaranteed return. Thus, despite being a defined contribution scheme, CPF is effectively more like a notional defined benefit system (Asher 2002). This strategy allows Singaporeans to earn up to 6% return, with a guaranteed minimum interest return of 2.5% a year (Government of Singapore, Central Provident Fund n.d., accessed May 2020).

Besides having relatively higher returns, another favorable characteristic of alternatives is their low correlation with traditional financial assets. Their long-term tenure, especially with respect to alternatives such as infrastructure finance and private equity, also matches the long-term liability structure of many institutional investors, such as pension funds. The downside is that it requires very high investment expertise, which not many pension institutions have, let alone those in developing countries. The market for alternatives also has relatively little historical data of risk and return to base decisions on. Further, the market is relatively illiquid, making exit strategies difficult when investment sours.[24]

Infrastructure financing

Among alternatives, infrastructure financing is especially attractive, because of its long maturity, which matches pension funds' long-term liabilities. It also has a developmental impact: a way for pension institutions to channel funds toward developmental projects while at the same time earning sufficient returns, having predictable and stable cashflows over the long term, and delivering adequate pensions to members. In many developing countries and even in developed ones, major investments are needed in transport, energy, resource management, telecommunication, and healthcare infrastructure, to cite a few. As banks increasingly shy away from investing in these long-term projects because of capital requirement regulations, institutional investors, including pension funds, can fill the gap.

Like other alternative assets, infrastructure investment is countercyclical. While financial assets sync more with the economic cycle, infrastructure investment does less so. Once the project has matured, it provides a stable cash flow, because infrastructure projects tend to operate like natural, regulated monopolies/oligopolies. The lack of competition in markets where these infrastructure projects operate also results in stable asset values (Alonso, Arellano, and Tuesta 2016). In healthcare infrastructure, for example, while aging and longevity risks are a bane to pension funds' sustainability, they are a boon to the healthcare industry. Healthcare is a growing industry and can generate high investment returns, especially as populations age and require more care. Healthcare investment, for example in modern hospitals, is thus a natural hedge for pension funds.

---

[24] In other words, they face liquidity and market risks. Liquidity risk because the investment is tied up for several years; and market risk because, especially for private equity, many companies are unproven and can fail. For example, a new product or promising technology can easily become obsolete due to competition, leading to huge losses for private equity investors.

However, like other alternatives, perhaps especially more so, infrastructure investing is not for the unsophisticated. Infrastructure financing involves risks including political and operational risks, construction delays and cost escalation, as well as the challenge of balancing the interests of multiple stakeholders involved in a project. Usually, each project requires different expertise, because infrastructure assets are supported by physical installations that have varied characteristics.[25] Building a toll road, for example, is not the same as building a hospital or telecommunication towers. Greenfield infrastructure investments are different from maintenance and repairs. For example, pension funds can engage in direct investments to finance the infrastructure construction itself through loans or project bonds or an equity stake in infrastructure assets. It can also do so indirectly, usually through a financial vehicle such as an investment fund, or through equity stakes in companies involved in infrastructure development. Direct and indirect investments have different levels of risks and returns.

The whole range of possibilities for infrastructure investment is constrained by regulations and institutional mandates.[26] Countries that have positive pension experiences with infrastructure financing usually have a liberalized capital account and a large share of nonfinancial bonds issues to total outstanding bonds. Infrastructure investment is also positively associated with a good number of securitization deals that help spread the risk to more people (Alonso, Arellano, and Tuesta 2016). In sum, infrastructure financing needs deep financial markets and proper institutional and regulatory frameworks.

On the supply side, an important element for pension funds to invest in infrastructure is the availability of fundable and sustainable infrastructure projects. It is possible that, especially in developed countries, the more profitable infrastructure projects have already been completed, while projects that remain in need of funding and investments are riskier, with uncertain profitability. In projects with high positive externalities but low financial return, the government may need to provide a guaranteed minimum level of earning for pension funds to meet fiduciary responsibilities. What cannot and should not happen is that public

---

[25] In some countries, the institution that invests the money of pension institutions has a well-developed in-house expertise in various alternative asset investments, including infrastructure—Canada is an example of how pension contribution investments are outsourced to a pension fund and how the pension fund uses a prudent person rule instead of quantitative controls on investment managers (Box 6.4).

[26] In Mexico, to comply with investment regulations and institutional mandates, a special purpose financial vehicle was developed so that pension funds could invest in infrastructure projects.

pension institutions be coerced into funding government infrastructure projects without regard for its own fiduciary responsibilities toward its contributing members.

Investment Restrictions, Policy Changes, and Increased Risk

Among major difficulties that pension funds face are strict regulatory or investment restrictions that constrain their flexibility to place investments where they deem fit and which could generate adequate returns. Typical restrictions relate to the type of asset, geographic location, or type of project or institution. Even developed countries have restrictions on pension institutions' investments. Some have quantitative limits on portfolio allocation into different assets such as equities, real estate, corporate and government bonds, loans, and deposits. Some also place quantitative limits on investments abroad or specify that foreign investments only be in developed markets or within a specific region, such as only within the European Economic Area. Occupational pensions sometimes have specific restrictions such as quantitative limits on own employer or single-user securities, and general requirements for diversification. Among OECD countries, those without investment restrictions for their pension funds are Australia, Ireland, Japan, Luxembourg, the Netherlands, New Zealand, and the US. The UK also has no restrictions, except on related lending.

To ease investment in alternative assets, including in sustainable infrastructure, governments need to provide broader investment policy guidelines. Asset managers of pension funds have to be given flexible and broad mandates to adopt appropriate investment strategies while carrying them out with prudence. Developing countries in Asia should consider Canada's experience of flexible regulations and use of the "prudent person rule," instead of strict quantitative limits and restrictions (Box 6.4). It lays the responsibility of making risk assessment of projects on more knowledgeable asset managers themselves, while aligning compensation incentives toward a more long-term objective.

Besides greater flexibility, regulatory changes are sometimes needed to allow or increase pension fund investments in infrastructure, including "green" infrastructure, as well as alternatives such as private equity or cryptocurrency or hedge funds, which expectedly have higher risks but also higher returns. Restrictions on infrastructure investment can sometimes be surmounted by designing special financial vehicles used for infrastructure projects which satisfy pension institutions' investment criteria for risk and returns. The presence or absence of flexible investment guidelines as well as good regulations encourages or discourages investments by pension funds in infrastructure.

Box 6.4: Prudent Person Rule, Green Finance, and Investment Policies

The Canada Pension Plan Investment Board, the entity that invests the funds of the Canada Pension Plan, enjoys maximum freedom in putting funds into different investments. Its remit is simple: to maximize returns without undue risks loss. Put differently, Canada applies the "prudent person rule" in pension investments, a guideline for making financial decisions using a prudent person's common sense that does not preclude taking reasonable risks.

Canada removed strict quantitative limits on investments in different assets to give greater flexibility to managers in handling their portfolios. Its risk focus is the overall total risk over the long-term instead of short-term results. It can hold investment assets such as infrastructure for more than 20 years, or core real estate for around 18 years.

Since it changed its focus, the pension fund has become more diversified. In 2000, more than 80% of its investments were in Canada. Now, the proportion is reversed, with the majority invested outside Canada. It also has more diversified assets, with over 50% placed in "alternatives" such as private equity, infrastructure, hedge funds, natural resources, and real estate. In 2000, 95% of investments were in fixed income, but by 2016, that share was reduced to only 26.9%, with the remaining portion invested in equities and real assets.

The Canada Pension Plan Investment Board boasts of a strong internal expertise in various investments and compensation incentives that align with a long-term focus rather than short-term returns.

Similarly, the Hong Kong Mandatory Provident Fund, a fully funded privately managed pension scheme, provides investment flexibility for trustees and fund managers. They are allowed to invest globally and in different financial instruments, including financial derivatives. For supervision, it puts its accent on transparency of the fund portfolio composition, performance, fees, and others, for members to make their own choices on where to put their contributions.

continued on next page

Box 6.4 (continued)

All Mandatory Provident Fund trustees have to be approved in coordination with the Hong Kong Monetary Authority based on capital adequacy, capability, fitness and propriety of controllers, skill, knowledge, experience and qualification of directors and chief executive officers, and internal control standards. Approved investment schemes, nevertheless, have to be authorized by the Securities and Futures Commission.

Is the prudent person rule compatible with taking into consideration economic, social, and governance criteria (ESG) for investments? In particular, should pensions be tasked to help with green financing as part of "responsible" investment practice?

The most common concern in green financing and ESG investing, in general, is its impact on investment performance and thus its interaction with the fiduciary duty of pension institutions toward its members. While a few studies find that firms with "high sustainability" (accounting for issues of governance, culture, and performance) outperform "low sustainability" firms over the long term (18 years in the study) (Eccles, Ioannou, and Serafeim 2011), there are difficulties with applying ESG criteria. First, how long is the "long term"? Second, there is no standard metric to evaluate ESG and sustainability. In fact, there are concerns about falling victim to greenwashing as the global issuance of green, social, and sustainability bonds has surged. Without a common industry standard, issuers of green bonds can make false promises. The investment jargon in this area is also not so transparent. ESG can sometimes lead to exclusion of some companies from the fund portfolio, achieve lower performance than a benchmark index in the short term, or exhibit higher volatility because of a smaller number of stocks.

Some developed economies, however, have already started to require consideration of ESG issues in the management of pension assets, or to mandate disclosure of how pension funds' investment guidelines address social and environmental issues (Caplan, Griswold, and Jarvis 2013). In the United States, ESG considerations are not mandatory but can be considered part of a prudent investment plan. But if they affect estimates of value, risk, and return, then ESG is advised to form part of the investment decision-making process.

Sources: World Economic Forum (2017b); Cumbo (2021); and Caplan, Griswold, and Jarvis (2013).

Partly due to low yields on fixed securities and partly to an evolving appreciation for equities and alternative assets, pension funds and insurance, including conservative Asian funds, are increasingly venturing into alternatives, as well as into foreign investments (Table 6.9). For example, in over a decade, the Republic of Korea increased its investment limit in indirect investment in securities from 30% to 50% and increased its total for investment risk assets to 70% (such as equities, bonds, real estate investment trusts [REITs], investment funds, etc.). It also allowed investment in REITs listed in regulated markets and abolished the extra investment limit in foreign bond fund. Similarly, Indonesia permitted loans up to a maximum of 20% of the portfolio from zero previously, and allowed pension fund investment in asset-backed securities, derivatives, REITs, medium-term notes, and repurchase agreements. Permitted investment in property was increased from 15% to 20%, and up to 5% of the pension fund portfolio was allowed for direct investments abroad.

Table 6.9: Pension Investment Restrictions

Economy	Equity	Real Estate	Bonds/Bills (public)	Retail Investment Funds	Private Investment Funds	Loans	Deposits
Japan	None	None	None	None	None	None	None
Korea, Rep. of – DC	0	0	None	70% (bond fund: no restriction)	0	0	None
Korea, Rep. of – DB	70% (only listed companies)	0 (direct) but 70% for REITs	None a	70%	70%	0	None
Korea, Rep. of – personal pension trust	None	None	None	None	None	None	None
Korea, Rep. of – personal pension insurance	None	25%	None	None	None	None	None
Indonesia	None; [5%, only direct equity]	20%; [0]	None; [0]	None; [0]	15%; [5%, should be approved by OJK]	10%, medium-term notes; [0]	None; [0]
Thailand	None; [None, but with restrictions on type of securities and certification of exchange]b	0 (direct) but indirectly through REITS of infrastructure funds, no restriction	None; [None if foreign government bond has 2 highest credit rating; 35% otherwise]	None; [Permitted only in 15 countries specified]	–	0	None

DB = defined benefit, DC = defined contribution, REIT = real estate investment trust, OJK = Otoritas Jasa Keuangan (the Indonesian Financial Services Authority).

a Private corporate bonds with BBB– investment grade or higher: 70%; The combined total of investments in equity, REITs, private bonds, retail, and private investment funds should not exceed 70% of portfolio assets.

b Securities should be regulated by an International Organization of Securities Commissions (IOSCO) member regulator and listed in an exchange that is a full member of World Federation of Exchanges.

Note: None means no restrictions; figures in brackets [ ] apply to foreign assets.

Source: OECD Survey of Investment Regulations of Pension Funds and Other Pension Providers Database (accessed March 2021).

Thailand has also given its provident fund greater investment flexibility and adjusted its regulations in line with international standards. Its civil servant pension fund, together with Malaysia's provident fund, has announced more upcoming investments in foreign assets. Thailand plans to invest in private equity, such as the development of multi-family residential real estate projects in a foreign country. To eliminate many risks involved in foreign investments, it will co-invest with a local partner that will oversee the investments.[27] Thailand is also looking into investing in other ASEAN countries, especially in Malaysia and Singapore, as well as in developed markets. Malaysian pension funds are also proposing to increase foreign asset allocation in their portfolio but this is still subject to central bank approval. In Thailand, the increase in foreign investments syncs with the central bank policy of weakening the baht by allowing greater capital outflows.

Pension institutions' diversification strategies definitely carry more risk. Foreign investments, for one, need to be hedged for exchange fluctuations. They also require expertise and knowledge about the foreign market, industry, and the intricacies of various investment instruments. Even investments in publicly traded equities expose pension funds to greater market risks than investments in government bonds. Default or bust in asset prices can lead to insolvency of private pension funds.[28] Unlike banks, pension funds and insurance companies are not subject to runs on the basis of suspicions of insolvency, but they can still go bankrupt through investment errors. For DC pension funds with no guaranteed returns, all risks are passed directly to the household sector through either low or negative returns on their contributions.

With large institutional investors shifting from fixed-income instruments to other assets, there is also the risk of price bubbles. More funds flowing into property investments, for example, have historically led to higher risk-taking and large property price swings.

Annuities for the aging population

While high return-high risk assets exist, low-risk ones that give payouts throughout the lifetime of retirees are few, if not nonexistent. The argument is that few financial institutions are willing and able to offer decumulation

---

[27] See Man (2020).

[28] Besides exposure to more market risk, the pension fund also errs in promising higher guaranteed returns (or benefits) based on wrong mortality projections.

products with fixed payment promises over a very long time, because of the difficulty of hedging longevity and other price risks (inflation, interest rates) associated with long-term payment promises (Schich 2009). The obstacle lies in the supply side of financial market instruments.[29] Some argue that governments should facilitate the development and expansion of markets by helping develop financial instruments and associated infrastructure.[30] As more retirees take out pension savings to buy annuity-like products, a market for hedging longevity and other risks needs to be developed to spur supply of these financial instruments.

Annuitized products, for example, inflation-indexed and ultra-long-term fixed-income securities, are useful as payout instruments but are undersupplied or nonexistent because of difficulties in developing these products. These include entrenched advantages of more traditional financial products, the difficulty of measuring and pricing extreme longevity risk, the relative and limited depth and breadth of mortgage markets, and the limited financial sophistication of the average household (OECD 2008). Government is important in supplying or facilitating the supply of such financial products for retirees. Box 6.5 shows an example of how the public sector can facilitate.

Box 6.5: Singapore's Annuity Scheme

In 2009, Singapore introduced CPF LIFE, a national annuity scheme that stands for Central Provident Fund Lifelong Income for the Elderly. CPF members can pay for the annuity out of the retirement balance in their CPF fund. By providing them with lifelong retirement income, CPF LIFE is meant to address the problem of Singapore residents outliving their savings because of increase in life expectancy.

The lack of opportunity to convert the lump-sum savings into a lifelong stream of income is a particular challenge for the elderly in Singapore and across the world. CPF LIFE offers this opportunity. Prior to CPF LIFE, Singapore residents were expected to have pension payouts that lasted about 20 years before their

continued on next page

---

[29] For example, the policy proposal of annuitizing parts of retirement wealth so it lasts until the end of the retiree's life span requires an entity willing to take the other side of the transaction (Schich 2009).

[30] The issue of government involvement is not simple. For example, by providing guarantees on ultra-long-term fixed- income securities, the risk is brought back again to the government, which had, over the years, already pushed those risks to the individuals through shifts from DB to DC and other institutional reforms.

Box 6.5 *(continued)*

savings were exhausted. With CPF LIFE, they can receive at least the total amount of their savings as payouts and bequests (if money remains in their CPF balance when they die).

CPF LIFE has very interesting features. First, residents can choose the desired amount of payout. They can choose to have a bigger payout and leave less for beneficiaries (the Standard Plan); or have less payout to leave more as bequests (Basic Plan). They can also opt to top up their retirement account to pay for a higher CPF LIFE premium or transfer some of their CPF savings above a specific threshold to their non-working spouse. Second, members are eligible to receive pension starting age 65 but can opt to receive it later, with the government incentivizing such option through up to 7% higher payouts for every deferred year. CPF LIFE also introduced the Escalating Plan to index payouts to the rising cost of living. The plan offers benefits that increase annually by 2% in return for a lower initial amount. At the same time, the government has programs to encourage re-employment of older workers through wage subsidies and other incentives to employers.

To help those with low savings, the government invests means-tested grants, funded through the government budget, into CPF savings of low-income households for them to save enough to take advantage of the benefits of CPF LIFE. These grants are in the form of an earned income tax credit which flows into eligible member's retirement savings or medical savings account. The grants can also come as generous subsidies for homeownership. Members can also opt to unlock part of their home equity to purchase CPF LIFE. In addition, members' CPF savings returns are guaranteed by the government, unlike other defined contribution pension schemes where all risks are on individuals. For members with lower balances, the guaranteed interest rates are higher. For the first S$30,000 of a member's CPF LIFE monies, a 6% interest is earned annually, while the next S$30,000 earns 5%, and the remaining balance earns only 4%.

Sources: World Economic Forum (2017b) and Government of Singapore Central Provident Fund (n.d.) (accessed May 2021).

Summary

This subsection has discussed the symbiotic relationship between pension systems and financial markets. Both need each other: pension institutions with their huge asset holdings spur growth of financial markets, while financial markets help pension institutions earn returns to pay benefits to its members.

But the post-global financial crisis low-interest environment has put pension institutions in a precarious situation of being unable to meet future liabilities to retirees. Risk-free government fixed-income securities are no longer the dependable sources of pension earnings they once were. The situation highlights the need to deploy more of members' contribution and pension assets to alternatives, and more Asian pension funds are gearing up for these to earn more.

Infrastructure financing is one type of pension investment worth considering because of its developmental impact, particularly on Asian economies. Alternative investments, however, expose pension assets to higher risk from market volatilities as well as other types of risks such as liquidity and bankruptcy. Unfortunately, it is difficult to measure the investment volatility of alternative investments because unlike financial assets such as listed equities and securities, alternative assets have no publicly available historical prices.

Asian pension funds are conservative in their investments compared to peers in North America and Europe. This is partly because Asia follows stringent quantitative limit restrictions on pension investments, often specifying allocations of portfolio investments into specific types of assets. Asia can consider the prudent person rule for investments that is practiced in other developed economies which provide greater flexibilities to asset managers in managing their portfolio while still having control over their investment behavior. In practice, a combination of both quantitative restrictions and the prudent person rule works in many countries.

Pensions and Technology

The digital revolution is transforming many facets of life. It is also taking place at the same time as demographic aging and other social changes, such as migration and declining family ties. How does the digital transformation impact social security systems, designed as an automatic stabilizer to smooth out consumption over life's many uncertainties as well as certainties such as old age? This section discusses the many applications of new technologies in social security governance and administration. It then highlights technology's impact on employment arrangements and their effect on pension and other social security benefits.

Impact of Technologies on Social Security

Digital technologies have improved ways of doing business. They have enhanced service quality, decreased cost, and improved the integrity of business processes. Their applications in social security are likewise pervasive: from contribution collection to service delivery to financial planning, digital technologies are utilized by both public and private pension institutions, albeit in varying degrees across countries. In the past, complex registration procedures, geographical barriers, and costs of compliance were obstacles to the formalization of informal workers. With technology, informal activities are able to enter the realm of the formal economy—think Uber for example—thus increasing the coverage of social security systems, and consequently, improving the financial sustainability of pension systems (ISSA 2019b).

Uses for social security administration and governance

Digitalization improves social security administration and governance. It can simplify registration and improve contribution collection. Big-data analytics applied to social security can help predict and detect complex fraud activities and prevent error. It improves modeling, making scenario analysis and forecasting and obtaining accurate actuarial projections and analyzing risk and cost. It helps increase the overall quality of service delivery by helping monitor internal culture, behavior, and employees' compliance with customer protection processes.

The provision of timely, transparent, and efficient service through the use of platforms increases people's trust in social security institutions. Along with social media which can be utilized for financial education, platforms allow experts to answer questions on financial planning. User-friendly interfaces also improve users' compliance and lowers administrative burdens.

There are also regulatory technologies (regtech) that facilitate regulatory compliance. Embedded in regtech are "smart contracts" or computer protocols that can self-execute, self-verify, and self-constrain the performance of a contract, reducing the need for some areas of supervision (ISSA 2019b). All these potential reductions in compliance cost contribute to overall lower operational cost for both pension providers and members.

Improved customer service

Financial products, including for retirement, are made more accessible and comprehensible through financial technology (fintech). With the use of data analytics, financial product designs become more personalized. Robo-advice which is cheaper than human advice can make financial planning more accessible. These are very useful especially for DC plans where members are bombarded with a myriad of financial options. Pension dashboard and platforms make one's investments and future pension finances transparent and easy to track even if placed in multiple schemes (occupational, personal or public schemes). The new technologies also help providers manage financial risks.

Table 6.10 gives examples of the applications of digital technologies in social security system governance, administration and customer service. Although these applications have been applied mostly in more developed countries, they provide a kind of "wish list" for pension systems in developing Asian countries that would like to modernize their systems.

Risks of technology

Technology, nevertheless, has to be used with caution because despite its usefulness, there are risks and challenges. For example, data can be mismanaged or hacked resulting in huge losses from fraud and cybercrime. The unequal access to technology due, among other things, to income inequality, can also lead to exclusion of certain portions of the population, for example, the less educated or less well-paid workers.

While fintech start-ups create additional competition for financial organizations and result in lower prices for consumers, they can also complicate financial regulation. Fintech firms are nimble because they are not burdened with an infrastructure legacy that is very costly to upgrade. But if allowed to cherry-pick some aspects of pension provision, these unregulated entities can leave traditional players with less profitable businesses and create incentives for them to take on higher risks.

Table 6.10: Examples of Technology's Social Security Applications

Artificial intelligence (AI)	• Improve customer services through e-services and intelligent chatbots • AI-based image recognition automate administrative processes by recognizing documents • Together with data analytics, predict customers' debt risks and eligibility assessment for additional social security benefits
Data management and analytics	• Apply discovery and profiling techniques to detect evasion and fraud in contribution collections and benefits delivery (particularly complex fraud operations) • Help develop preventive approaches, program, and services improvements
Digital identity, biometrics, and e-government	• Development of new generation value-added personalized customer services • Validate identity and perform proofs-of-life for pensioners • Pay benefits directly to or collect contribution from biometric smart cards • Secured online transactions • E-government facilitates coordinated public services, one-stop shop for contributors and for beneficiaries, facilitating interaction with various public and private services
Blockchain	• Re-engineer paper-based information flow through secured, paperless, and traceable system • International data exchange to implement social security agreements and enforce integrity controls related to the life status of pensioners • Traceability whether information requests were responded to within agreed time periods
Fintech and regtech	• Fintech increase accessibility for paying contributions or investing in private pensions to a broad consumer base • Increase efficiency of operation of pension schemes through risk management applications, automation of investment processes and facilitation of regulatory compliance • Enhance engagement; reduce compliance costs • Robo-advice can help members with financial planning

Source: ISSA (2019b) and OECD (2017).

Technology, Labor, and Social Protection

Technology not only disrupts competition in financial organizations, but it also has profound impact on labor markets. While technology creates new jobs, it makes many current jobs and tasks redundant. Job destruction and reallocation have been part of development and growth for a long time, but their rapid pace in the age of digital technology creates challenges. The discussion below of how developed countries are grappling with "fair" determination of employment status, particularly of platform workers to improve their social protection, provides insights and useful policy options if and when similar challenges become more pervasive in Asia.

Nonstandard employment and social protection

One example of a technology-related challenge is social protection. The new work arrangements that technology has facilitated result in a fundamental rethinking of appropriate social protection designs, particularly for nonstandard employment. Social protection systems were designed around traditional forms of employment, but these may not apply, at least not to the same extent, to workers with nonstandard contracts (OECD 2019b).

Nonstandard employees are either engaged in independent work or short-duration or part-time employment.[31] They may have fixed-term contracts, voucher-based contracts, zero-hour contracts, or work with temporary labor agencies. Generally, most are self-employed and do not have the same level of social protection as employees. During an "out-of-work" spell,[32] they are 40% to 50% less likely to receive any form of income support and if they do, the benefits are lower than for standard employees (OECD 2019b). They also tend to contribute less for their retirement and can opt out of mandatory contributions. Consequently, their pension entitlements are lower. In theory, unlike the self-employed, part-time and temporary workers are still covered by mandatory social protection. In practice, they struggle to meet minimum contribution requirements or earnings thresholds, partly due to career discontinuities or periods when they are in between temporary jobs.

Some of the new forms of employment emerged because of changes in preferences, innovations in business models and work organizations, technological developments, and policy choices. Some workers do well and prefer the independent arrangement, which perhaps explains the rise in the number of people in nonstandard employment. In the OECD, they already constitute a third of employment (OECD 2019b).

---

[31] Companies prefer employees to contractors, according to the Coasian explanation, because of the high transaction cost to specify and monitor all contingencies in a service contract. However, since technology now enables companies to efficiently contract with external parties, it has also lowered the transaction costs that previously induced companies to prefer employees to contractors. This partly explains the rise in nonstandard employment with advances in digital technology.

[32] Today, especially in gray zone employment arrangement discussed below, there is also a blurred distinction between in-work and out-of-work categories. It is difficult to distinguish whether a self-employed person prefers to voluntarily not work or he/she is affected by lack of demand or price fluctuations of his/her service. Unlike for standard employees who have an employer to confirm a layoff, the self-employed has to demonstrate that his/her business is no longer operational.

The rise in self-employment, in some countries, has also been policy-induced. Often, to spur entrepreneurship, besides being given many tax incentives, the self-employed are exempt from paying most social security contributions and nontax compulsory payments. They are supposed to self-insure by purchasing private insurance, but many do not.

There is concern that some nonstandard employment may be false self-employment, arranged only to circumvent paying for legally mandated benefits for employees or to avoid regulations on taxes and unionization—in other words, a form of employment arbitrage. Others are in a legal "limbo" or a gray zone, especially those in the platform economy, because their work has characteristics of full-time employment and independent contractorship.[33]

The online "gig economy" and gray employment relationships

Prior to the digital economy, "employees" and "independent contractors" were distinct. Employees enjoy a range of legally mandated benefits and protections not available to independent contractors. These included right to organize and collectively bargain for compensation, insurance coverage, overtime pay, and others (Harris and Krueger 2015). But workers in the online gig economy can neither fit in neatly as employees nor as independent contractors. Often, gig economy work consists of paid micro tasks,[34] which means no payment between tasks (ISSA 2019a). Such an arrangement, while acceptable to some who merely use their gig work as a supplement to their main source of income (usually from standard employment), can result in inadequate income for others.

Online gig workers typically work with platforms or intermediaries that match workers to customers. A known example is the ride-hailing companies, such as Uber, Lyft, Grab, and Go-Jek. The relationship between the platform and the worker (driver, in this case) has some elements of an arms-length business relationship similar to that of an independent contractor. For example, they can choose how much and when to work, or can work simultaneously with different intermediaries, characteristics

---

[33] Netherlands gives an example of an effort to try to address possible labor arbitrage by putting the burden of declaring workers as employees or contractor on the employers (for example, the platform operator), instead of based on the self-declaration of the worker. If the employer misclassifies, it is liable for all insurance and tax payments. Adverse reaction, however, arose from various stakeholders including from those which the law purportedly wanted to protect, e.g., the gig workers themselves (OECD 2019b).

[34] Arguably, the fragmentation and individualization of work result in information and power asymmetry between platform workers and employers because the workers have few opportunities to share useful information and common concerns.

similar to the self-employed. At the same time, they also have some elements of an employee relationship. Their intermediaries have control over work performance through set fees, rating systems, or control of customer information; the worker does not set his/her own rates. The intermediary may also deactivate their accounts removing access to the platform, an action akin to firing traditional employees (Harris and Krueger 2015).

For the moment, best-practice regulation to address the gray area in employment relationship is still emerging. The State of California has passed a "gig law'" to force technology companies to provide social protection and provide the same employee benefits to platform workers. The law gives clear conditions about when to consider the arrangement a standard employment relationship. However, it was overthrown through a public referendum sponsored by platform operators, Uber, Lyft, and others. So far, the US and the European Union court decisions appear inconsistent (OECD 2019b) but are possibly converging to a similar outcome (Box 6.6). In Canada, determination of whether standard or nonstandard employment exists is decided case by case. While this approach is more flexible, it nevertheless gives large discretion to adjudicators, resulting in uncertainty and possibly inconsistent decisions.

Box 6.6: Uber and Lyft: Are Platform Drivers Employees?

Platforms such as Uber and Lyft argue that their service is to provide the infrastructure that matches workers and clients; that they are in the technology, not transport, business. Thus, drivers that use their platform cannot be their employees.

The court in California, on the basis of the newly passed "gig law," disagreed and ruled that they are in the business of "selling rides." They were therefore asked to provide drivers standard employee benefits, including paid leave.

Although the two companies lost their argument in court, they won their case in the November 2020 referendum which approved Proposition 22 exempting platform providers from providing employee benefits to gig workers, except if the company sets drivers' hours, requires acceptance of specific ride and delivery requests, or restricts working for other companies. Gig workers, considered as independent contractors, are not covered by state employment

continued on next page

Box 6.6 (continued)

laws such as minimum wage and unemployment insurance, but are entitled, under Proposition 22, to healthcare subsidies, vehicle insurance, medical coverage for on-the-job injuries, and minimum earnings.

In contrast, in the United Kingdom (UK), the Supreme Court decided unanimously to consider platform-using drivers as workers not as independent contractors, making them eligible for minimum wage, vacation leaves, pension benefits, rest breaks, and protection against unlawful discrimination. Significantly, "workers" under British law are a distinct class that falls between employees and independent contractors.

The difference between the outcomes in California and in the UK may, ultimately, be small depending on how they are applied. In both, drivers obtained some but not all benefits that standard employment provides.

Source: Author, based on Siddiqui (2020) and Hiltzik (2021).

Making social protection future-ready

How can social security be future-ready? How can social security programs be redesigned to address the needs of nonstandard workers?

For those easy to identify as self-employed, independent contractors, and part-time or temporary workers, solutions are afoot. Some countries have adjusted contributory programs to accommodate career discontinuities by lowering thresholds for eligibility.[35] Other solutions include deferral of contributions during crises or non-work, using broad income bands taking into consideration interruption in contribution periods for the determination of contribution levels. Social assistance, usually unrelated to work histories but based on residence, is also available in many countries, sometimes as zero-interest loans to bridge temporary out-of-work or low-income periods (OECD 2017).

---

[35] Earnings-related pension benefits usually have minimum vesting periods. Meeting minimum contribution requirements is often difficult for some types of nonstandard workers. A 10-year out-of-work spell combined with a late career start reduces pension entitlements by 20% on average (OECD 2019b)

Other reform options include making entitlements portable between social insurance programs intended for different labor market groups.[36] In some sectors, governments may need to intervene to curb the monopsony power of some companies in hiring labor. The power asymmetry affects not only those working in the platform economy but also own-account workers and on-call labor. Worse, antitrust regulations prohibit self-employed workers from collective bargaining, obviating the possibility of equal bargaining positions.

For those in the employment gray zone, to ensure access to labor and social protection, a step would to be clarify their classification and employment status—whether they are contractors or employees or belong to a separate employment category altogether (next subsection). This is salient because as more platforms or intermediaries arise that match different services and customer needs, this type of employment will likely increase in future.

Some countries use tests to determine worker status based on actual working relationship rather than on the employment contract per se. There is a presumption of employee status if the tests which examine the worker's financial independence plus elements of worker subordination and control from the client are met. The assessment is based on the worker's integration in the organization; the extent of worker's control of his/her condition of work, including place and time of work; who provides the tools, materials, or machines used at work; regularity of payments; extent to which the worker takes on financial or entrepreneurial risk; and whether the work must be carried out personally by the worker (OECD 2019b). Once employee status is determined, there is another question on who the employer is, especially in triangular employment arrangements, i.e., where there is an intermediary and worker used by him to provide services to a user-firm (client) within its premises. The question is important because it determines whether the intermediary or client (or both) is obliged to pay for all the taxes and social protection contributions.

"Independent worker" status

Harris and Krueger (2015) suggest a social protection compromise by defining a different employment category called "independent worker," a hybrid of independent contractor and employee. In their proposal,

---

[36] What is ordinarily preferable is to have programs to help nonstandard workers become employees if they wish to, by providing training and re-training programs. Some governments, Singapore for example, sponsor vouchers for adult learning and continued education to make the labor force adapt to new trends in the labor market.

independent workers receive some social protections and benefits, such as the right to organize, paid employer share of social security and medicare, tax withholding, and employer share for payroll taxes. However, because it is difficult to attribute work hours to any single intermediary, they would not qualify for overtime payments nor minimum wages. Moreover, since independent workers have a difficult time qualifying for unemployment insurance benefits in any case (because they have discretion over how much time to work, when and with whom), neither should they be required to contribute to unemployment programs.

Platforms/intermediaries can also help lower the cost of paying for social protection benefits. By pooling independent workers for purchasing and providing insurance and other benefits, they can negotiate more efficiently for lower fees with insurance/pension providers. This would be a win-win situation if governments were to allow intermediaries to negotiate on behalf of "independent workers" without risking that the relationship be turned into an employment relationship. In this way, most (though not all) legal benefits and protections in standard employment relationships can be extended to independent workers, preserving the social compact that has protected both workers and employers over the centuries (Harris and Krueger 2015).

Countries such as the UK and Italy that have defined an intermediate category of workers, however, show potential danger in the approach. The UK defined "worker" status, while Italy has "semi-subordinate worker" status with the intention of extending social protection to the new distinct class of workers (OECD 2019b). But when boundaries are vaguely defined because they are difficult to define in the first place, the new classification creates opportunities for employers to classify some who would have been employees as workers or semi-subordinate workers The new classification is therefore a vehicle for taking away rights and protections from those who would have had them had there been no intermediate worker category.

Paying for social protection

If employers were to pay for more social protection benefits to "independent workers," the cost would likely be partly shifted anyway to workers in the form of lower net fees or compensations, while the intermediary takes higher commissions to pay for worker benefits. However, to the extent that the intermediary may have more bargaining power with insurance/pension providers, the cost could be overall lower than if workers were left to purchase insurance on their own. The surplus could be shared between workers and employers, resulting in less than full shifting of the cost to the workers (Harris and Krueger 2015).

Through agreement with digital platforms, some private insurance companies support gig and nonstandard workers by tailoring products to their needs. For example, Axa-Uber provide drivers (in Europe) with benefits such as parental leave, sickness and injury compensation, and childbirth allowance (ISSA 2019a). Though limited in scope compared to comprehensive social protection, it nevertheless provides some of social protection needs of platform workers.

Another challenge in the gig economy is how to tax the increasing number of nonstandard workers. Some fail to report income from the gig economy partly because declaring self-employment income could often be cumbersome. By doing so, however, pension benefits are also diminished. Tripartite agreements between platforms, financial institutions, and social security or labor institution provide possible models that can facilitate tax and contribution collections as in Indonesia and Malaysia (Box 6.7).

Box 6.7: Facilitating Tax Payments

In 2017, to simplify registration of drivers and contribution collection procedures, Indonesia's National Social Security Administering Body for Employment (BJPS Ketenagakerjaan) agreed with Gojek, a ride-hailing on-demand service provider, and Bank Mandiri, to require online registration in a website developed by BJPS Employment and Gojek. Every month, drivers' contributions to cover accident and death insurance are automatically withdrawn from their Gojek accounts. With this simple procedure, more Gojek drivers have registered with social security and are able to pay contributions monthly.

Similarly, in Malaysia, the Social Security Organization (PERKESO) together with Grab, another ride-hailing company, required drivers to register and pay contribution as a condition to obtain or renew their Public Service Vehicle licenses and be authorized as Grab drivers. The amount of contribution deducted from the driver's account varies depending on the plan signed up for.

Source: ISSA (2019a).

Pension Portability

As migrant workers in Asia have increased, another important issue for ASEAN+3 is the portability of pensions. All over the world, more and more workers stay part of their working life abroad because of globalization. Some move to another country as students or interns. When they start working, they can be transferred within the firm to another country or else move across firms for career advancement. Many move to different countries as migrant labor, and eventually return to their home country or to a third country for many reasons, including possibly for tax arbitrage. Within ASEAN, greater mobility of skilled workers is also part of its economic integration objectives, which is expected to deliver more worker migration.

When workers move to another country, they usually acquire pension rights as well as other social benefits such as healthcare and others in their host country. It helps if, when they return home or move to another country to work or reside, they do not lose at least their pension rights, along with survivor and disability and other social security benefits to which they have contributed part of their earnings while in the host country.[37]

Portability of social security refers either to cross-border portability or cross-firm portability within country. In this section, portability refers more to cross-border portability understood as "a migrant's ability to preserve, maintain, and transfer both acquired social security rights and rights in the process of being acquired from one private, occupational, or public social security scheme to another, independent of nationality and country of residence" (Holzmann and Jacques 2018).

Compared to defined benefit (DB) schemes, define contribution (DC) schemes are more portable because these are like individual savings accounts that can be withdrawn and exported. Even if at times there can be a minimum holding period or tax implications, these are not major obstacles for portability of DC benefits. Portability in a DB pension system, however, is more complicated. Preserving and maintaining social security rights in the context of DB schemes means that the migrant worker does not lose his/her contribution because he/she is unable to complete the minimum number of years to qualify for benefits because of transfer to

---

[37] Noncontributory social security benefits, for example, minimum income guarantees for low-income individuals, are usually funded out of the government budget. These social protection benefits are usually, and understandably, not portable across countries.

another country. Even when the migrant worker has fulfilled the qualifying condition, exporting his/her social security benefits is also not so simple although less problematic.

There are various options for making benefits portable, but signing social security agreements is, at this time, taken as the best option, especially for public pensions (Genser and Holzmann 2019).

Labor Migration in Asia

Before discussing pension portability, it is worth taking a look at the status of migration from and into Asia. Figure 6.11 shows that among Asian countries, the PRC is the biggest labor exporter, with more than 10 million Chinese workers abroad. But its share of the working population is a minuscule 1%.[38] As a share of working population, Singapore, the Philippines, and Malaysia are the countries with the highest percentage, even though, for Singapore, its expatriate workers only number more than 300,000. The Philippines and Indonesia are the highest labor exporters among ASEAN countries.

Figure 6.11: Migrants from Selected ASEAN+3 Economies and Their Share in the Population Living Outside of Home Country, 2019

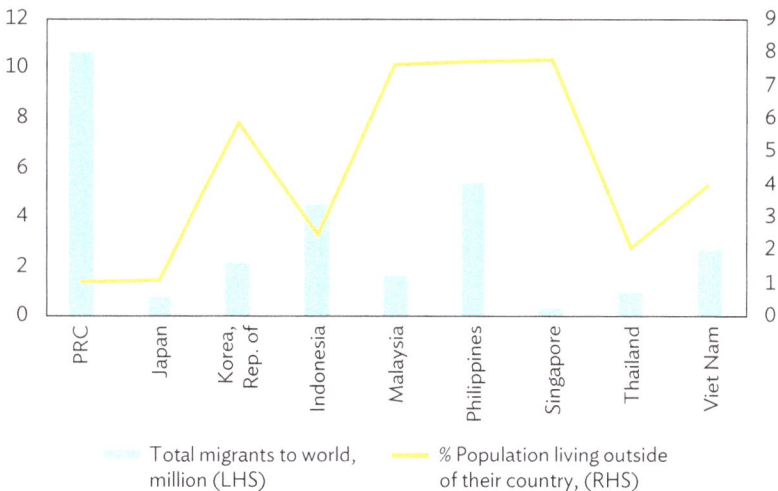

LHS = left-hand scale, PRC = People's Republic of China, RHS = right-hand scale.
Source: Author, based on UN International Migrant Stock 2019 Database (accessed March 2021).

[38] This refers to population age 15 to 64 years old.

Most Asian migrants go outside Asia. However, Malaysians go mostly to Singapore. For Indonesia and Singapore too, most of their migrants work only within ASEAN. The Philippines, which exports close to 8% of its working population, only has 2.5% of them going to ASEAN and 7% to East Asia. The Republic of Korea, Thailand, and Viet Nam have a greater proportion of migrants going to East Asia than ASEAN (Figure 6.12).

Figure 6.12: Destination of Migrants from Selected ASEAN+3 Economies by Origin, 2019
(% share)

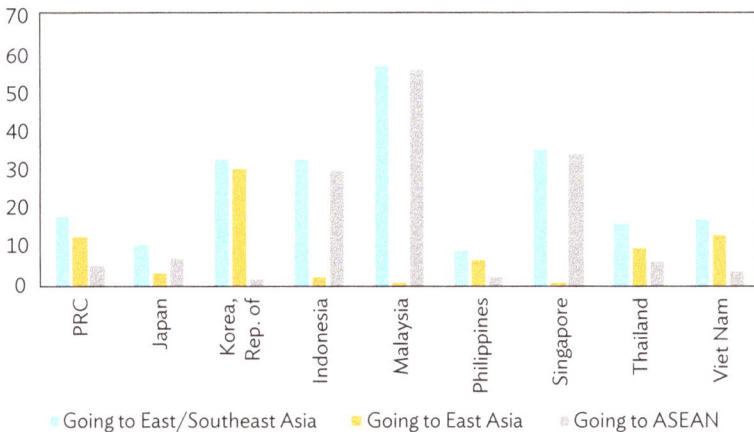

PRC = People's Republic of China.
Note: East and Southeast Asia groupings are based on the definitions of the source.
Source: Author, based on UN International Migrant Stock 2019 Database (accessed March 2021).

The growth of migrants from ASEAN+3 working within ASEAN+3 has been fast for Japan, Malaysia, and Singapore, while it is moderate for the PRC and the Republic of Korea. The number of migrants to Indonesia, the Philippines, and Viet Nam has not changed considerably over the years (Figure 6.13).

Figure 6.13: Migrants from ASEAN+3 Economies by Destination, 1990–2019
(million)

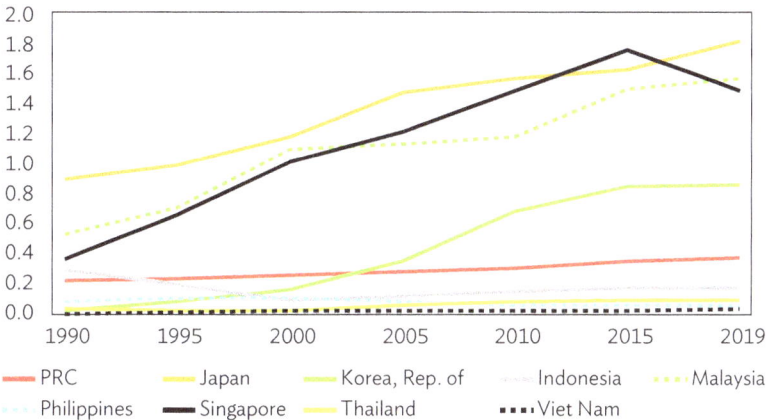

PRC = People's Republic of China.
Note: The reporting ASEAN+3 economies are the PRC, Indonesia, Japan, Malaysia, the Republic of Korea, the Philippines, Singapore, Thailand, and Viet Nam.
Source: Author, based on UN International Migrant Stock 2019 Database (accessed March 2021).

Migration and Pensions

The growing number of migrants in Asia begs the question about what happens to their social security rights if they make contributions in their host countries.[39] There are usually various issues to consider. First, if they return home or move to another country assignment, what happens to their social security contribution if they have not fulfilled the qualifying requirements (if such exist)? The same goes for any other retirement accounts including occupational pension, private pension, and other private retirement savings instruments? Second, if they have satisfied the qualifying requirements, are the benefits exportable to their home countries or to any other country where they may choose to reside? Third, what are the pension taxation issues to consider? Fourth, do international agreements such as the World Trade Organization-General Agreement on Trade in Services (WTO-GATS) carry implications for social security rules and bilateral or regional social security agreements because the GATS requires national treatment and most-favored-nation obligations?

---

[39]   Box 6.8 illustrates that the problem of portability is not only between countries but can also be within country if the social security scheme is highly fragmented, as in the case of the PRC.

Box 6.8: The People's Republic of China's Hukou System and Pension Portability

Rural migrants in the People's Republic of China (PRC), under the *hukou* system, are like foreigners in their own country. *Hukou* is the PRC's system of population registration that helps control internal migration. In particular, rural migrant workers do not enjoy the same social protection as urban residents because of the peculiarities of the PRC's social security scheme.

The PRC's mandatory pension system is composed of two parts. One is a social insurance pooling system where employers contribute up to a maximum of 20% of wages, and the other is an individual account where employees' maximum contribution of 8% is placed. The first operates on a pay-as-you-go basis, meaning that current employer contributions are used to pay current retirees. The second operates akin to a provident fund which, unlike the first, should, in theory, be highly portable.

Because social security is not centralized but managed by local/city authorities and transfer of the pooled funds is difficult, migrant workers do not get their full retirement benefits compared to their urban counterparts. While the government had changed the law to allow greater portability of social security benefits if workers transfer work or retire in another province, in practice, the administrative hoops to be able to do so make pension portability difficult.

Source: Author.

Portability of supplementary personal pensions

Migrant workers may contribute to a statutory public pension scheme, which can be either mandatory or voluntary. Aside from the statutory ones, there are also occupational pensions that are usually managed within the company, as well as other retirement savings instruments (or private pensions) sanctioned by different countries and privileged with some tax benefits. These supplementary schemes are particularly useful for self-employed people, as well as others looking to supplement their retirement savings. The complications for pensions, particularly if they are country-specific, begin when the migrant worker leaves either for another assignment, or employment, or retirement to another country.

Supplementary personal retirement savings instruments that citizens invest in are usually regulated differently according to different national rules. In some countries, there are conditions regarding transfers of such schemes to another country, some of which, legitimately so—for example, to ensure that the tax-exempted contributions in occupational or personal pensions remain only for retirement purposes. While there are bilateral or multilateral social security agreements for public pensions, arrangements are slightly complicated for supplementary schemes primarily because of tax issues.[40]

The crux of the problem is that personal pension savings instruments are designed to cater to specific country regulations to benefit from tax exemption and fiscal incentives. If there were a pension product that satisfied all features necessary to qualify for fiscal benefits in each country, and countries had bilateral social security agreements that covered supplementary retirement savings, then that product would be easily portable across these countries. Savers could then simply continue contributing to the same pension product provider even when they moved to another country without significant tax complications. In the European Union (EU), the Pan-European Personal Pension Product (PEPP), a pension product that can be marketed throughout the EU, is supposed to be, in theory, just such a "super-pension" product. It can be accessed online, transparent with respect to fees and costs, portable across the EU, consumers can easily switch PEPP product providers or investment options free of charge, has flexible payouts (whether annuities, lump sum, regular drawdowns) at the decumulation phase. In Asia, no product similar to PEPP exists. However, the PEPP's rollout success remains to be seen, as the first PEPPs will come out in late 2021 or early 2022.

At the moment, it is not certain if PEPP will receive the same tax incentives as local products by EU member states, yet it will be competing with these local pension products. It is argued that PEPP may be more relevant in EU countries with less-developed pensions systems, and less so in others with already a wide range of personal pension products. If so, in Asia where personal pension products are just emerging, PEPP-like products may hold enormous promise. Thus, this new EU experiment on PEPP will be worth

---

[40] Tax issues aside, granted that portability of personal pension product is possible, the exit fees and the cost of the transfer process can also be expensive. The reason is that pension savings are supposed to fund long-gestation, often illiquid, projects like infrastructure or private equity and, in return, receive an illiquidity premium. However, if workers are able to switch easily and freely at any time, the illiquidity premium would be difficult to justify, resulting in lower returns for savings invested in a personal pension product. A middle ground is to allow a switch between pension products and providers but with minimum years of holding period.

watching and, if successful, can be replicated in ASEAN+3 region. It will encourage an increase in supplementary pension savings especially for migrant workers in Asia by assuring them of a portable source of old-age income wherever they decide to retire in the region. It will also be attractive to self-employed individuals or gig workers who do not have occupational pension benefits. It will also help develop a regional market for capital in the ASEAN+3. However, as with most policies, success lies in the details of the regulations and their implementation. The EU's experience of PEPP's success or failure can provide some guidance in the future for Asia.

Exportability of benefits and tax issues

If the worker chooses to retire in his/her home country or another country, his/her pension benefits can be exported. The issue is whether the benefits are going to be taxed in the origin or destination country, or both. If benefits are taxed at the origin and again at destination, savers are disincentivized to move retirement locations. Some countries have double taxation treaties to deal with situations such as these, but if the origin–destination country pair do not have such treaties, the pensioner will be doubly taxed.

The issue of taxation is very complex, especially because of its diversity. Some countries tax during decumulation (or payout stage), others during accumulation and contribution phase (Genser and Holzmann 2016). Countries have different permutations and combinations of exempt (E) and tax (T). The Republic of Korea, for example, taxes the contribution, exempts the accumulation or returns, and again taxes the payout (TET), while Japan has an EET regime whereby it exempts the contribution and accumulation of returns but taxes the payout (OECD 2018c). Even within these permutations, there are variations. For example, the tax at payout may be levied only for lump-sum withdrawal above a certain threshold, while below it is tax-free; annuities are also more favorably taxed than other types of payout. In others where progressive taxation is maintained, public pension income is exempt depending on the total income of the pensioner.

Portability of public statutory schemes through bilateral social security agreements

Social security agreements between countries significantly help achieve portability. Most such agreements are bilateral, although these can also be multilateral as in the EU case. Although in theory, bilateral social security agreements (BSSAs) can cover all aspects of (usually public statutory) social protection including healthcare benefits, most BSSAs focus on long-term benefits (old age, survivor's, and disability pension).

Comprehensive BSSAs usually include agreements on definition or coverage of social benefits that will be coordinated, time-limited exemption from contribution; exportability benefit calculation, disbursement, service delivery, and administrative support and coordination. The agreements usually aim at equality of treatment, something akin to the national treatment principle in trade agreements which prohibit discrimination between domestic and foreign. An important part of the BSSA is the totalization of benefits which sums up the periods of employment in both countries for determination of the qualifying period. Without it, the worker risks not meeting the minimum vesting period requirement and loses his/her social security benefits as he/she moves from one country to another. Under the BSSAs, civil servants (those with temporary posting in embassies) are exempted from paying into the host country's social security schemes. BSSAs also avoid double coverage for a period of time because of exemption of having to pay social security taxes in both the host and home countries for the same earning.

The principles of the BSSA are largely observed across agreements but the content and implementation across countries are variable (Holzmann and Jacques 2018). It is also mostly present among developed countries with developed social security schemes. A critical element for BSSAs with developing countries is a well-functioning social security scheme (usually in the labor sending country), as well as a significant number of bilateral migrant flow. Otherwise, the resource-intensive negotiation and development of a BSSA outweigh its benefits. Some countries can also take unilateral action to make eligible benefits fully portable without need for bilateral agreement. Likewise, statutory pension schemes designed as account-based, as most DC schemes are, are usually more portable. For example, Singapore allows permanent residents who choose to retire in their home country to withdraw all their Central Provident Fund (CPF) savings lump sum.

Globally, 23.3% of worldwide migrants in 2013 live in countries that have BSSAs between home and host countries (Holzman and Jacques 2018). The majority (more than 53%) live in countries where social security benefits are not necessarily portable but are exportable and where countries have no BSSAs. The remaining 23% either live in countries where migrant workers have no access to social security (9.4%) (they neither contribute nor receive benefits from social security) or else they live as informal workers and thus get no social security benefits to take home (14%).

In Asia, 2.1 million migrant workers are in countries that have BSSAs. These are workers from East Asia moving around the region, since only Japan, the Republic of Korea, and the PRC have BSSA between each other.[41] They constitute 32.2% of the total Asian migrant workers to Asia. Another 2.9 million or 45% of Asian expatriates go to countries where migrant workers have access to social security but their countries have no BSSAs. Finally, 1.5 million from Asia (23%) go to Singapore where access is not allowed in the CPF unless they have become permanent residents (Table 6.11). Expatriate workers, however, are allowed up to S$5,000 tax-deductible annual contribution to a personal life insurance which is considered as retirement savings. If permanent residents decide to return to their home country, they can opt to bring home all their CPF savings or let it stay in Singapore while still being able to collect annuities income outside the country.

Table 6.11: Social Protection for Asian Migrant Workers

Social Protection Regime	Intra-Asia Migrant Stock (million)	% of Intra-Asia Migrants	Global Comparative Figure
I. With access to social protection and social security agreement	2.1[a]	32.2	23.3
II. With access but without social security agreement	2.9	44.8	53.3
III. Without access to social protection	1.5[b]	23	9.4
IV. Undocumented migrants	...	...	14

... = not available.
[a] Bilateral migrant worker flow between the Republic of Korea, Japan, and the People's Republic of China.
[b] Asian migrants to Singapore.
Note: The aggregation of Asian migrants is based on UN DESA's country grouping and data. The global figures were obtained from Holzmann and Jacques (2018).
Source: UN International Migrant Stock 2019 Database (accessed March 2021); and Holzmann and Jacques (2018).

---

[41] These BSSAs have limited coverage, mainly on temporary exemption from contribution to the host country's social security system in the first x years of expatriate work. They do not contain agreement on totalization and exportability.

WTO-GATS and social security agreement

As a bilateral international agreement, BSSAs grant benefits to partner countries but not to others. The question is whether benefits granted under the social security agreement, particularly the portability features, are supposed to be extended to other member countries of the World Trade Organization (WTO) under the most-favored-nation commitment that countries agreed to under the General Agreement on Trade in Services (GATS).[42]

It appears that the answer is no. The reason is that GATS exempts public social security or national pension schemes operated by a public institution, and BSSAs are mostly about public social security. Likewise, the Annex on Financial Services to GATS explicitly excludes social security from its scope on the basis that it constitutes a "service supplied in the exercise of governmental authority." The gray area, however, is when private service providers are tapped for outsourcing by the government, for example, pension funds that carry out investments on behalf of the public institution; or with respect to personal pension plans offered by the private sector. The introduction of a private element in public services may render the scheme subject to most-favored nation rule and other obligation (Olivier 2018). The consequence can be that the supply of social security services can become open to competition if committed for liberalization under the country's GATS commitments, for example the provision of personal pension products or retirement savings instruments. It is an issue that is worth looking into if ASEAN adapts personal retirement savings products for the region that are akin to the EU's PEPP.

6.5 Conclusion

Aging impacts the economy through labor participation, productivity, and savings. Its effects are still ambiguous, based on various empirical research that account for technology and human capital quality. Aging also affects pension sustainability and adequacy. The pension savings gap is getting bigger largely because of unfunded public pensions as well as low personal savings for retirement. Many countries have undertaken pension reform but more need to be done.

---

[42] The most-favored-nation provision essentially prohibits discrimination between countries, hence any favor given to one has to be given to all.

Pension issues are considered a national concern. But some pension issues can be discussed at the regional level; for example in ASEAN or ASEAN+3 processes, even for just an exchange of experiences. Pension issues link closely with the financial market, which is discussed in the regional meetings. Experiences on lifting some investment restrictions on pension funds can likewise be regionally relevant, together with knowledge sharing on investments in alternative assets such as private equity and infrastructures.

Digital technology has also entered the realm of pensions. Advances not only impact the governance and administration of pension institutions but also labor employment arrangements that have repercussions for future pension income. In particular, workers in nonstandard employment arrangements, gig workers, and platform workers will have less old-age retirement benefits if nothing is done to address the effect of technology on the world of work and social protection. Regional discussions and exchange of experiences about what countries in Asia have done to address the pensions issue for nonstandard employment workers are warranted. What is different among ASEAN+3 countries' categories of labor employment and how gig workers are classified can be added to the conversations.

Finally, considering increasing migrant labor in Asia, the issue of portability also merits discussion, especially if foreign workers contribute to pension schemes in host countries in Asia and later retire in their home countries. It is an issue that touches upon equity and fairness.

References

Acemoglu, D. and P. Restrepo. 2017. Secular Stagnation? The Effect of Aging on Economic Growth in the Age of Automation. *American Economic Review*. 107 (5). pp. 174–179. https://doi.org/10.1257/aer.p20171101.

Alonso, J., A. Arellano, and D. Tuesta. 2016. Pension Fund Investment in Infrastructure and Global Financial Regulation. In *Retirement System Risk Management: Implications of the Regulatory Order*, edited by O. Mitchell, R. Maurer, and M Orszag. Oxford Scholarship Online. https://doi.org/10.1093/acprof:oso/9780198787372.001.0001.

Amaglobeli, D., H. Chai, E. Dabla-Norris, K. Dybczak, M. Soto, and A. Tieman. 2019. The Future of Saving: The Role of Pension System Design in an Aging World. *IMF Staff Discussion Note*. No. 19/01. Washington, DC: International Monetary Fund. https://www.imf.org/-/media/Files/Publications/SDN/2019/SDN1901.ashx.

Asher, M. 2002. Pension Reform in an Affluent and Rapidly Ageing Society: The Singapore Case. *Hitotsubashi Journal of Economics*. 43 (2). pp. 105–118. Tokyo: Hitotsubashi University.

Asian Development Bank. Social Protection Indicator Database. https://spi.adb.org/spidmz/ (accessed March 2021).

Burtless, G. 2013. The Impact of Population Aging and Delayed Retirement on Workforce Productivity. *Center for Retirement and Research Working Paper*. WP 2013–11. Boston: Boston College. https://crr.bc.edu/wp-content/uploads/2013/05/wp_2013-111.pdf.

Byrne, A. and C. Reilly. 2017. Investing for Retirement in a Low Returns Environment: Making the Right Decisions to Make the Money Last. *Pension Research Council Working Paper*. PRC WP 2017. Philadelphia: Wharton School. https://pensionresearchcouncil.wharton.upenn.edu/wp-content/uploads/2017/09/WP-2017-7-Byrne-Reilly.pdf.

Cai, Y. 2018. [The People's Republic of] China's Aging Migrant Workers Are Facing a Return to Poverty. *Sixth Tone News*. 28 November. https://www.sixthtone.com/news/1003252/chinas-aging-migrant-workers-are-facing-a-return-to-poverty.

Caplan, L., J.S. Griswold, and W.F. Jarvis. 2013. *From SRI to ESG: The Changing World of Responsible Investing*. Wilton, CT: Commonfund Institute. https://files.eric.ed.gov/fulltext/ED559300.pdf.

Chai, H. and J. Kim. 2018. Demographics, Pension Systems, and the Saving-Investment Balance. *IMF Working Paper*. No. 18/265, Washington, DC: International Monetary Fund. https://www.imf.org/-/media/Files/Publications/WP/2018/wp18265.ashx.

Cherlin, A. and J. Seltzer. 2014. Family Complexity, the Family Safety Net, and Public Policy. *The Annals: The American Academy of Political and Social Science*. 654 (1). pp. 231–239. https://doi.org/10.1177/0002716214530854.

Cumbo, J. 2021. How Green Is Your Pension? *Financial Times*. 26 February. https://www.ft.com/greenpensions.

Eccles, R., I. Ioannou, and G. Serafeim. 2011. The Impact of Corporate Sustainability on Organizational Process and Performance. *Management Science*, 60 (11). pp. 2835–2857. Boston: Harvard Business School. https://www.hbs.edu/ris/Publication%20Files/SSRN-id1964011_6791edac-7daa-4603-a220-4a0c6c7a3f7a.pdf.

Ernst and Young. 2020. *Megatrends 2020 and Beyond*. London. https://assets.ey.com/content/dam/ey-sites/ey-com/en_gl/topics/megatrends/ey-megatrends-2020.pdf.

Genser, B. and R. Holzmann. 2019. Pensions in a Globalizing World: How do (N)DC and (N)DB Schemes Fare and Compare on Portability and Taxation? *World Bank Discussion Paper*. No. 1928. Washington, DC: World Bank. http://hdl.handle.net/10986/31639.

_____. 2016. The Taxation of Internationally Portable Pensions: An Introduction to Fiscal Issues and Policy Options. *CESifo DICE Report*. 14 (1). pp. 24–29. Munich: Ifo Institut-Leibniz-Institut fur Wirtschaftsforschung an der Universitat Munchen. https://www.econstor.eu/bitstream/10419/167246/1/ifo-dice-report-v14-y2016-i1-p24-29.pdf,

Government of Singapore, Central Provident Fund. n.d. Schemes. https://www.cpf.gov.sg/Members/Schemes (accessed May 2021).

Government of the United States, Social Security Administration. 2019. Country Summaries. *Social Security Programs Throughout the World: Asia and the Pacific, 2018*. Washington, DC. https://www.ssa.gov/policy/docs/progdesc/ssptw/2018-2019/asia/index.html.

Harris, S. and A. Krueger. 2015. A Proposal for Modernizing Labor Laws for Twenty-First-Century Work: The "Independent Worker". *The Hamilton Project Discussion Paper*. 2015–10. December. Washington, DC: Brookings Institution. https://www.hamiltonproject.org/assets/files/modernizing_labor_laws_for_twenty_first_century_work_krueger_harris.pdf.

Hiltzik, M. 2021. Column: In Blow to Uber, U.K. Court Reaches Obvious Conclusion that Its Drivers are Workers. *Los Angeles Times.* 19 February. https://www.latimes.com/business/story/2021-02-19/british-court-says-uber-drivers-employees.

Holzmann, R., R.P. Hinz, and M. Dorfman. 2008. Pension Systems and Reform Conceptual Framework. *World Bank SP Discussion Paper.* No. 0824. Washington, DC: World Bank. https://documents1.worldbank.org/curated/en/716871468156888545/pdf/461750NWP0Box334081B01PUBLIC10SP00824.pdf.

Holzmann, R. and W. Jacques. 2018. Status and Progress in Cross-Border Portability of Social Security Benefits. *IZA Discussion Paper.* No. 11481. Bonn: IZA—Institute of Labor Economics. http://ftp.iza.org/dp11481.pdf.

International Social Security Association (ISSA). 2017. *Megatrends and Social Security: Family and Gender.* Geneva. https://ww1.issa.int/sites/default/files/documents/publications/2-Megatrends%20Gender%20Family-Final-217637.pdf.

———. 2019a. *Social Security for the Digital Age: Addressing the New Challenges and Opportunities for Social Security Systems.* Geneva. https://ww1.issa.int/sites/default/files/documents/events/2-Digital%20economy-264063.pdf.

———. 2019b. *Applying Emerging Technologies in Social Security.* Geneva. https://assets.cdn.sap.com/sapcom/docs/2020/06/c87c28a2-9a7d-0010-87a3-c30de2ffd8ff.pdf.

Lee, R. 2016. Macroeconomics, Aging and Growth. In *Handbook of the Economics of Population Aging,* edited by J. Piggott and A. Woodland. 1. pp. 59–118. https://doi.org/10.1016/bs.hespa.2016.05.002.

Lynn, A. 2018. How the World's Largest Pension Funds Allocate their Assets. *Infrastructure Investor.* 6 September. https://www.infrastructureinvestor.com/how-the-worlds-largest-pension-funds-allocate-their-assets/.

Maestas, N., K. Mullen, and D. Powell. 2016. The Effect of Population Aging on Economic Growth, the Labor Force and Productivity. *NBER Working Paper.* No. 22452. Cambridge, MA: National Bureau of Economic Research. https://doi.org/10.3386/w22452 .

Man, J. 2020. GPF Mulls Offshore Pension Partnerships in Alts Push. *Asian Investor.* 19 February. https://www.asianinvestor.net/article/gpf-mulls-offshore-pension-partnerships-in-alts-push/458290.

Marsh and McLennan Companies Asia Pacific Risk Center and Tsao Foundation's International Longevity Centre. 2018. Gender Retirement Savings Gap of Low-Income Professionals. Singapore. https://www.mmc.com/content/dam/mmc-web/Files/APRC/Gender-Retirement-Savings%20Gap-Of-Low-Income-Professionals_digital.pdf.

Meng, C. and W. Pfau. 2017. The Role of Pension Funds in Capital Market Development. *GRIPS Policy Research Center Discussion Paper*. 10–17. National Graduate Institute for Policy Studies: Tokyo. http://www3.grips.ac.jp/~pinc/data/10-17.pdf.

Mercer, CFA Institute, and Monash Centre for Financial Studies. 2020. *Mercer CFA Institute Global Pension Index.* Melbourne. https://www.mercer.com.au/content/dam/mercer/attachments/private/asia-pacific/australia/campaigns/mcgpi-2020/MCGPI-2020-full-report-1.pdf.

Mercer, Monash Centre for Financial Studies, and the State Government of Victoria, Australia. 2019. *Melbourne Mercer Global Pension Index.* Melbourne. https://info.mercer.com/rs/521-DEV-513/images/MMGPI%202019%20Full%20Report.pdf.

Olivier, M. 2018. *Social Protection for Migrant Workers in ASEAN: Developments, Challenges, and Prospects.* Geneva: International Labour Organization. https://www.ilo.org/wcmsp5/groups/public/---asia/---ro-bangkok/documents/publication/wcms_655176.pdf.

Organisation for Economic Co-operation and Development (OECD). 2008. Pensions in Asia/Pacific: Ageing Asia Must Face Its Pension Problems. Paris. https://www.oecd.org/finance/private-pensions/46260941.pdf.

————. 2017. *Technology and Pensions: The Potential for FinTech to Transform the Way Pensions Operate and How Governments are Supporting its Development.* Paris. https://www.oecd.org/finance/Technology-and-Pensions-2017.pdf.

————. 2018a. *Pension Markets in Focus.* Paris. https://www.oecd.org/daf/fin/private-pensions/Pension-Markets-in-Focus-2018.pdf.

————. 2018b. *Pensions at a Glance: Asia/Pacific.* Paris. https://doi.org/10.1787/pension_asia-2018-en.

————. 2018c. The Tax Treatment of Retirement Savings in Private Pension Plans. *OECD Project on Financial Incentives and Retirement Savings Policy Brief.* No 1. Paris. https://www.oecd.org/daf/fin/private-pensions/Tax-treatment-of-retirement-savings-Policy-Brief-1.pdf.

_____. 2019a. *Pension Markets in Focus*. Paris. https://www.oecd.org/daf/fin/private-pensions/Pension-Markets-in-Focus-2019.pdf.

_____. 2019b. *The Future of Work: OECD Employment Outlook 2019*. Paris. https://doi.org/10.1787/9ee00155-en.

_____. 2019c. *Pension at a Glance: OECD and G20 Indicators*. Paris. https://doi.org/10.1787/b6d3dcfc-en.

_____. OECD Survey of Investment Regulations of Pension Funds and Other Pension Providers Database. https://www.oecd.org/finance/private-pensions/annualsurveyofinvestmentregulationofpensionfunds.htm (accessed March 2021).

Park, D. , ed. 2012. *Pension Systems in East and Southeast Asia: Promoting Fairness and Sustainability*. Manila: Asian Development Bank. https://www.adb.org/sites/default/files/publication/29954/pension-systems-east-southeast-asia.pdf.

Park, D. and G. Estrada. 2014. Emerging Asia's Public Pension Systems: Challenges and Reform Efforts. In B. Clements, F. Eich, and S. Gupta (eds). *Equitable and Sustainable Pensions: Challenges and Experience*. Washington, DC: International Monetary Fund. https://doi.org/10.5089/9781616359508.071.

Schich, S. 2009. Challenges for Financial Intermediaries Offering Decumulation Products. *OECD Journal: Financial Market Trends*. 2008 (2). Paris: Organisation for Economic Co-operation and Development. https://doi.org/10.1787/fmt-v2008-art15-en.

Siddiqui, F. 2020. Uber's Secret Project to Bolster its Case Against AB5, California's Gig-worker Law. *Washington Post*. 6 January. https://www.washingtonpost.com/technology/2020/01/06/ubers-secret-project-bolster-its-case-against-ab-californias-gig-worker-law/.

Thinking Ahead Institute. 2021. Global Pension Asset Study 2021. London. https://www.thinkingaheadinstitute.org/content/uploads/2021/02/GPAS__2021.pdf.

Thinking Ahead Institute and Pensions & Investments. 2020. The World's Largest Pension Funds—2020: Global Top 20 Pension Fund Assets Rebound Strongly. London. https://www.thinkingaheadinstitute.org/content/uploads/2020/11/TAI_PI300_2020.pdf.

Trading Economics. Japan Home Ownership Rate. https://tradingeconomics.com/japan/home-ownership-rate (accessed May 2021).

United Nations. 2019a. 2019 Revision of World Population Prospects Database. https://population.un.org/wpp/ (accessed August 2021).

_____. 2019b. World Population Aging 2019 Highlights. Department of Economic and Social Affairs. New York. https://www.un.org/en/development/desa/population/publications/pdf/ageing/WorldPopulationAgeing2019-Highlights.pdf.

_____. International Migrant Stock 2019 Database. https://www.un.org/en/development/desa/population/migration/data/estimates2/estimates19.asp (accessed March 2021).

Willis Towers Watson. 2020. Asia Pacific Leads Growth as Top 20 Global Pension Fund Assets Rebound Strongly. *Press Release.* 7 September. https://www.willistowerswatson.com/en-SG/News/2020/09/asia-pacific-leads-growth-as-top-20-global-pension-fund-assets-rebound-strongly (accessed August 2021).

World Bank. Global Financial Development Database. https://databank.worldbank.org/reports.aspx?source=global-financial-development (accessed August 2021).

World Economic Forum (WEF). 2017a. We'll Live to 100—How Can We Afford It? *White Paper.* Geneva. http://www3.weforum.org/docs/WEF_White_Paper_We_Will_Live_to_100.pdf.

_____. 2017b. Case Studies in Retirement System Reform. *White Paper.* Geneva. http://www3.weforum.org/docs/WEF_Retirement_Handbook_2017.pdf.

_____. 2019. Investing in (and for) Our Future. *White Paper.* Geneva. http://www3.weforum.org/docs/WEF_Investing_in_our_Future_report_2019.pdf.

7 Regional Financial Cooperation in ASEAN+3: Taking Stock and Moving Forward

Cyn-Young Park and Ramkishen S. Rajan

7.1 Introduction

Financial cooperation in the ASEAN+3 region, which was prompted by the experience of the Asian financial crisis in 1997, has deepened considerably in recent decades. Substantial progress has been made in various areas, including the set-up of regional financial safety net arrangements through the Chiang Mai Initiative Multilateralization (CMIM), the establishment of regional surveillance and monitoring frameworks through the ASEAN+3 Macroeconomic Research Office (AMRO), and the implementation of the Asian Bond Markets Initiative (ABMI) to help develop homegrown sources of funding. Over the years, the CMIM has expanded and achieved notable improvements.[1] Along with the stock of foreign exchange reserves and bilateral swap arrangements among economies in the region, the CMIM has turned into a powerful layer of the region's multi-layered financial safety net together with AMRO, a regional surveillance and monitoring system. The ABMI has also facilitated remarkable progress in local currency bond market development, with marked increases in issuance of local currency bonds by member economies, alongside improvements in regional bond market infrastructure, and stronger regulatory cooperation to promote cross-border bond trading.

---

[1] Since a strong and credible surveillance unit is a critical component of any significant CMIM reforms, the importance of AMRO cannot be overstated. As Grimes and Kring (2021, p. 436) note: "AMRO's development as a capable and independent surveillance and program design unit is a precondition for whatever future CMIM's members are moving toward, whether that future be delinking from the IMF, creating a more equal relationship with the IMF, or simply providing better and more regionally sensitive information to members as they manage their own economies or provide policy feedback to their partners."

The chapters of this volume span the period from the global financial crisis to the onset of COVID-19 and analyze selected aspects of financial cooperation and integration in the region. ASEAN+3 financial cooperation has passed substantial milestones in building regional liquidity support, promoting economic surveillance and policy dialogue, and developing local currency bond markets. However, challenges remain to support the region's growing demand for long-term capital, possibly in areas of infrastructure investment and the pension and insurance sectors to prepare for aging populations. A great deal more needs to be done to bolster regional financial cooperation and mobilize long-term finance, enhance financial resilience, and reinforce regional financial safety net arrangements.

A broad theme emerging from this volume is that while progress in regional financial development and cooperation has generally been substantial, to date it is rather patchy and remains a work in progress.

7.2 Key Insights and Policy Priorities

This chapter draws together some specific messages from other parts of this volume and summarizes their main ideas and policy recommendations. The framework for developing the capital markets in Asia covers strengthened regulatory cooperation across the finance sector and improvements to its capacity to deal with emerging issues such as funding infrastructure for climate change mitigation and navigating the implications of rapid change though technological innovation in fintech. Comparison between different aspects of financial integration and development of regional financial safety nets in Asia versus Europe are included because they offer pointers for future agenda of regional financial cooperation in a coherent manner.

Deepening Local Currency Corporate Bond Markets, Managing Risks to Capital Flow Volatility

While bank-based financial systems still play a dominant role in ASEAN+3, the size of the local currency bond markets as a share of the region's GDP has grown markedly over time. Of some concern is that the local currency bond markets in many regional economies remain largely dominated by government bonds (the Republic of Korea, Malaysia, and Singapore being exceptions), although growth of corporate bond markets has been robust.[2] To support further development of local currency corporate bond markets,

---

[2] As noted in Chapter 1, there is a clear dichotomy in the region with capital market development in Cambodia, the Lao People's Democratic Republic, and Myanmar lagging by quite a distance.

the ASEAN+3 central banks may have scope to establish a regional repo market which will provide cross-border liquidity to dealers in local currency corporate bonds. Corporate debt markets must also become more accessible to lower-rated issuers to play their appropriate economic role. Hence, the proposed regional repo market should accept lower-rated issues as collateral. To resolve conflict between what is acceptable as repo collateral and what market development requires, ASEAN governments may wish to turn to the Credit Guarantee and Investment Facility (CGIF), which was opened in 2010 by ASEAN+3 countries with ADB assistance. The CGIF offers guarantees for bonds issued by firms facing constraints in obtaining long-term funding from the local bond market. The CGIF could provide enough of a credit guarantee for lower-rated corporate bond issues to be accepted as collateral in a regional repo market. Such a repo market would in turn enhance liquidity of these corporate bonds.

While the internationalization of bond markets in the region has helped keep the cost of funding low, the notable rise in corporate debt and bank loans to firms denominated in US dollars rather than in local currency remains a source of vulnerability for ASEAN+3 economies. The scale of vulnerability depends on the abilities of firms to hedge against the foreign exchange risks using financial instruments. Besides developing foreign exchange derivative markets that allow foreign investors to better manage currency risks, it is important to broaden the domestic bond market investor base since domestic investors may be less exposed to currency valuation risks than foreign counterparts. This would go some way to reduce the "original sin redux" (Carstens and Shin 2019), which may have partly triggered sharp reversals in portfolio flows and the significant credit tightening in emerging economies in the region and elsewhere seen at the beginning of the COVID-19 pandemic and in other times of financial stress.

Nevertheless, greater sophistication in the international financing activities of regional firms tends to obscure the sources of increased external vulnerability, as was outlined in Chapter 1. Rapid financial innovation combined with strong capital flows makes it especially challenging to maintain financial stability. Keeping up with new challenges in this regard is critical for the ASEAN+3 region since it is so open to the forces of financial globalization.[3]

---

[3] Data from the Bank for International Settlements (BIS) on international debt securities finds that offshore affiliates have been especially important for nonfinancial firms from emerging economies, with firms in the PRC particularly active in using offshore affiliates (usually shell companies based in Hong Kong, China) to issue debt that is held mainly in the Cayman Islands and the British Virgin Islands.

Recognizing and Managing Banking Concentration Risks

While banking systems in regional economies were generally in good shape before the COVID-19 pandemic, concerns remain in some countries that increased nonperforming loans among banks and nonbank financial institutions could give rise to financial distress as central bank support winds down.[4] While nonbank financial institutions play an important role in the global financial system, unlike banks they are not fully supervised. As the nonbank financial sector has grown in size and its interconnectedness with banking systems, the risks related to liquidity, leverage, and market volatility need to be managed. The impact of COVID-19 on credit markets also exposes the risks to financial stability of rising nonperforming loans. The risks can be magnified through financial interconnectedness of the global financial systems and institutions, as well as by weak regulatory features.

Beyond this, the region remains vulnerable to concentration of cross-border borrowing from regional and global banks. Consequently, regional regulatory cooperation should be strengthened to guard against region-wide slow-burn contagion, sparked by a sustained international credit crunch as funding risks concentrate among large banks. One possible solution would be to treat banks involved as regional systemically important banks (R-SIBs).

The R-SIBs designation could be achieved within the ASEAN Banking Integration Framework (ABIF) with the regional subsidiaries of big banks required to hold additional capital buffers. Given the significance of R-SIBs, which hold assets and liabilities in multiple currencies across different jurisdictions, it may be pertinent to explore how cross-border collateral arrangements can be used to help regional institutions deal with liquidity issues. Regionally active banks may face liquidity and collateral pressures in foreign markets while their holdings of eligible collateral may not be sufficient in every market. Cross-border use of collateral may be effective in reducing their liquidity pressures and collateral burdens. These can be alleviated if the region's central banks are allowed to accept foreign collateral denominated in local currencies or local currency bonds. Absent a regional supervisory college, AMRO could expand its mandate to monitor regional risks that might be generated by the activities of systemically

---

[4] See Ikeda et al. (2021) for a discussion on bank resilience through the pandemic and concerns about impact of credit losses with policy unwinding.

important financial institutions, include both traditional banks and the big tech firms moving into the financial sphere.[5]

To self-protect from the concentration risk of contagion, countries may also be able to more actively use macroprudential measures. An example is the levy on banks' non-core foreign currency liabilities in place in the Republic of Korea since 2011. Such a levy, which could be limited to banks from jurisdictions in the region most likely to cause concentration risks, could be used to lengthen the maturity structure of foreign borrowing. However, given the cross-border spillover effects from the imposition of such measures, they are best conducted through some form of regional coordination.

Reducing US Dollar Dependence

Chapters in this volume highlight concerns about the continued dominance of the US dollar as an invoicing and reserve currency and in external financing. The former is referred to as the Dominant Currency Pricing (DCP) paradigm and the latter as Dominant Currency Financing (DCF) paradigm. In addition—or as a consequence of the DCF and DCP— the US dollar continues to dominate as a reserve and anchor currency, which in turn presents significant challenges to the regional economies, since exchange-rate flexibility has limited capacity to insulate economies from external shocks.[6]

While some regional economies (particularly the PRC, Japan, and Thailand) have taken important steps to internationalize their respective currencies on a *de jure* basis, they have not made significant headway on a *de facto* basis.[7] There are, however, some signs that regional (own and partner) currencies are increasingly being used for trade among ASEAN+3

---

[5] ADB (2019) goes further and suggests that the mandate of the CMIM be expanded to deal with possible resolution or recapitalization of regional systemically important financial institutions experiencing financial stress.

[6] Of course, a case could be made that limited insulating power from exchange rate flexibility is better than no insulating power by having a fixed exchange rate.

[7] The yuan shows the most potential in terms of becoming an international currency and has made noticeable progress in recent years. An important recent initiative is the creation of the Cross-Border Interbank Payment System (CIPS) which offers clearing and settlements for cross-border yuan transactions. Others have suggested that the introduction of a digital currency (the e-yuan) may offer a fillip for the yuan's internationalization. All said, the PRC faces multiple challenges in this regard given the stop-start approach toward capital account and financial market opening and deepening and rather limited adjustments in its monetary policy regime (Chapter 3 includes a discussion of the Monetary Trilemma in the case of the PRC). While reform of the foreign exchange regime seems to be firmly on the country's agenda, its pace and timing appears to have been affected by the intermittent shocks (such as the global financial crisis, sharp capital outflows in mid-2014 to mid-2016 and the COVID-19 pandemic).

economies and with the European Union. Policy actions could help nudge this trend forward.

The Local Currency Settlement Framework (LCSF), pioneered by Malaysia, Thailand, and Indonesia, is noteworthy in its aim to substitute the US dollar with local currencies for trade and investment settlements among the three countries. It essentially helps relax domestic foreign exchange rules relating to the offshore use of currencies for international trade and foreign direct investment by providing mechanisms for appointed commercial banks to trade currencies directly and offer financial services in partner currencies. As the framework is expanded to include more regional transactions (such as local currency bonds) and economies, transactions costs in direct exchanges of local currencies are expected to fall below those used to triangulate transactions involving the US dollar.

Beyond the LCSF, further liberalization and coordination of rules and regulations relating to cross-border settlement practices is needed. Scope may exist to revisit the creation of a regional exchange rate surveillance process, using a regional basket of currencies like the ASEAN+3 currency unit (ACU) as a reference indicator, which could encourage coordination on exchange-rate policies and lead to more stable intraregional exchange rates. Greater exchange-rate stability among the regional economies could make it less costly to use local currencies for trade, investment, and financial transactions.[8]

While reducing the region's US dollar dependence must remain an objective for the medium to long terms, the immediate aim should be to develop a region-specific integrated policy framework that promotes macro-financial stabilization in a US-dollar-dominated financial system. Many regional economies need the conceptual guidance. To date, they have tried to manage their economies amid large and volatile international capital flows through some combination of partial exchange rate flexibility, sterilized foreign exchange intervention, and active use of macroprudential and capital flow management measures. The massive accumulation of foreign currency reserves across economies in the region offers a strong buffer against capital flows and foreign exchange rate volatility given the dominance of the US dollar. However, it is not without significant economic cost. Besides the CMIM, use of cross-border collateralization and regional

---

[8] Some have suggested that the time may be ripe for the region to consider creating an Asian digital common currency as an electronic medium to reduce the US dollar dominance (Inui, Takahashi, and Ishida 2020). While this may be premature, the issue of central bank digital currency (CBDC) is discussed briefly in the next subsection.

currency swap arrangements with pooled reserves could reduce the risk of acute foreign liquidity shortage and cross-border funding pressure in times of financial turmoil. AMRO may be well placed to take this discussion forward.

Fintech Challenges and Opportunities

While the more conventional forms of finance (traditional banks and capital markets) remain highly relevant, the rapid rise of fintech globally and among ASEAN+3 economies cannot be ignored, given the implications for financial inclusion and financial stability.

The COVID-19 pandemic and the accompanying social distancing and lockdowns have accelerated the shift toward fintech activities, which can be broadly divided into five major categories of financial services (FSB 2017). These are (i) payments, clearing, and settlement; (ii) deposits, lending and capital raising; (iii) insurance; (iv) investment management; and (v) market support. The focus of this volume is on the first two categories. The first includes digital advances, point-of-sale technologies, mobile money, cryptoassets, and remittance services, while the second includes borrowing or capital raising though broadly alternative finance, such as crowdfunding, peer-to-peer (P2P) lending, online balance sheet lending, and invoice and supply chain finance.

Fintech can offer significant benefits in greater efficiency, transparency, convenience, and enhancing financial inclusion. That said, such benefits are not automatic, and in many cases early adopters tend to be urban, financially literate, and well educated, with the new technology producing no discernible improvement in financial access for those most in need. The expansion of fintech may therefore give rise to greater inequities between genders; urban versus rural dwellers; larger firms versus micro, small, and medium-sized enterprises; and the like. The promotion of financial literacy and using fintech to encourage financial inclusion will be imperative.

As with any type of financial liberalization and innovation, if not properly harnessed, fintech activities could be accompanied by significant risks in financial stability at both the microfinancial and macrofinancial levels. Of particular concern is the development of P2P lending as possibly damaging the banking system by reducing both deposits and loans, as well as the rise of private digital currencies which could destabilize the flow of credit domestically and reduce the effectiveness of conventional monetary policy tools. There is much scope for learning and sharing experiences across countries in the region, given that they are all impacted by these challenges.

There is also a need to balance the benefits of financial innovation with possible costs concerning financial stability, consumer protection, cybersecurity, privacy and data protection, and anti-money laundering/counterterrorist financing (AML/CFT). These areas require greater regional and international cooperation in the development of legal, regulatory, and supervisory frameworks; monitoring capital flows; harmonizing of standards; and better sharing of data. Some of these issues could be dealt with among regional institutions, including AMRO, ASEAN, and the ASEAN+3 finance ministers and central bank governors' meetings, and other finance forums and working committees within ASEAN.

Fintech innovations backed by established firms pose particular challenges. Regulators need to recalibrate their policy frameworks to better equip themselves to deal with specific types of systemic and contagion risks from the interconnected activities of bigtech firms across multiple sectors in various jurisdictions (BIS 2019; Crisanto, Ehrentraud, and Fabian 2021). The scope and definition of R-SIBs should be expanded to include bigtechs entering the finance space. In some regional economies, the role of bigtechs in financial services is expanding and they are becoming increasingly important for the broader region. In this context, it is pertinent that discussion about how bigtech firms are treated in relation to R-SIBs can pave the way for cross-border regulatory practices to manage risks related to such entities.

Given the challenges posed by private digital currencies, many economies in the region are also looking to create central bank digital currencies (CBDCs), with the PRC taking the lead. It is plausible that CBDCs may lead to an increased use of local currencies in general, though ASEAN+3 economies do not share the same degree of interest in such a project. That noted, there may be scope for regional cooperation with the focus on using CBDCs to reduce the cost of cross-border foreign exchange transactions and increase transparency. Given that development of CBDCs among most central banks in the region is still in its infancy even as it is progressing quite rapidly in some instances, cross-border considerations could promote interoperability among payments systems and so reduce transactions costs (Auer, Haene, and Holden 2021). There are positive signs in this regard. For instance, several regional economies (the PRC; Hong Kong, China; and Thailand) are taking part (along with the United Arab Emirates) in a cross-border digital currency payments project called the Multiple CBDC (m-CBDC) bridge, with support from the BIS. The aim is to explore the application of wholesale CBDCs for multicurrency cross-border payments using blockchain technology.[9]

Financing Sustainable Infrastructure Investments

Despite significant improvements in infrastructure development, the region's financing gap remains extremely wide, especially if climate mitigation and adaptation are included in needs estimates. To the extent that the COVID-19 pandemic has exacerbated fiscal sustainability concerns, innovative ways need to be developed for both the public and private sectors to contribute to overcoming the infrastructure deficit and help fund environment-friendly infrastructure.

One promising method for governments to finance infrastructure is through land value capture, i.e., raising revenues through taxes when land values rise because public infrastructure has been upgraded. While land value capture may be suited to some types of projects, even with this potential source of fiscal revenue, the public sector may not be able to close the infrastructure gap in any significant way without compromising fiscal sustainability.

It is also critical to better incentivize the private sector to support infrastructure projects. Despite much initial enthusiasm for public–private partnerships (PPPs) and related mechanisms that include the private sector in infrastructure financing, results to date have been disappointing. Part of the reason has to do with concerns relating to project riskiness (governance, macroeconomic, and political) and high capital costs. Regional and multilateral development banks could play more active roles in promoting credit enhancement products to reduce the risk gap that has prevented the takeoff of PPP projects in the region.

Floating-interest-rate infrastructure bonds may be a possible way of raising private finance in infrastructure projects through offering higher rates of return. The return on investment will be dependent on tax revenues

[9]   See BIS (2021a) for the details. In parallel to this, other countries in the region have also been actively exploring the use of wholesale CBDCs for cross-border transactions including Singapore and Canada who have already successfully tested cross-border and cross-currency payments using wholesale CBDCs (Bank of Canada, Monetary Authority of Singapore, Accenture, and J.P. Morgan 2019). In addition, the BIS is working with central banks from Australia, Malaysia, Singapore, and South Africa to test the use of CBDCs for cross-border settlements–the so called Project Dunbar (BIS 2021b).

collected through the economic activity that development of surrounding infrastructure spurs on. Regional cooperation is needed to support establishment of a regional floating-interest-rate bond in cases where the spillover effects of tax revenues from an infrastructure project extend across country borders, such as for water transport infrastructure along the Mekong River.

The rapid rise of climate change impacts and hazards requires that much greater attention is paid to the use of renewable energy and low-carbon infrastructure. However, mobilization of private finance for this remains an acute challenge in the region, the recent surge in interest in green bonds notwithstanding. There remain concerns about greenwashing (false information about environmental benefits) and lack of generally accepted standards about what constitutes environmental, social, and governance (ESG) investment. While several standard-setting bodies and international organizations have undertaken research and brainstormed policy responses to tackle the macroeconomic and financial risks emanating from climate change,[10] regional cooperation may have a role in developing standards and other measures to facilitate the development of ESG bonds in the region and particularly to help promote green finance. Scope may exist for creating regional consistency on carbon taxes to reduce any regional distortions.

Managing the Financial Sustainability of Pensions

An important structural issue for many ASEAN+3 economies is that the rapid aging of their populations carries significant implications, especially over the sustainability of pensions. Concerns are especially stark in the PRC and the higher-income economies of Japan, the Republic of Korea, Singapore, and Thailand, old-age dependency ratios are rising sharply.

Despite the scale of pension coverage and sustainability as an issue, there appears to have been little discussion about it at the regional level. This is concerning from the perspectives of social welfare and macroeconomics as unsustainable pensions and rising contingent retirement liabilities might spark fiscal crisis in one country with effects that spill over to neighbors.

---

[10] Examples of such bodies include the Network of Central Banks and Financial Supervisors for Greening the Financial System (NGFS) consisting of over 90 members; the industry-led Taskforce on Climate-related Financial Disclosures (TCFD) and Taskforce on Climate-related Financial Risks (TCFR) constituted by the Basel Committee for Banking Supervision; and the Group of 20 Sustainable Finance Working Group, recently relaunched under the joint chairmanship of the US and the PRC. See Cheng, Gupta, and Rajan (2021) for a discussion on central banks and green finance.

On a positive note, pension funds with large assets under management are a potential source of demand that could facilitate development of local currency bonds. They should be especially welcome given their long-term investment outlooks. Indeed, greater regional investments with a longer time horizon could help alleviate the "original sin redux" problem previously discussed. In a low-interest-rate environment, pensions may need to seek higher yields by investing in assets such as private equity, real estate, and infrastructure. However, regional pensions funds have remained conservative and underinvested in these areas, especially infrastructure. Even if shovel-ready regional projects were available, use of pension funds for infrastructure investment is often restricted by regulations and institutional mandates. It is therefore important that regulations be made more flexible, and mandates of asset managers of pension funds be sufficiently broadened to incentivize long-term funds to invest in infrastructure along with 'alternative assets' offering higher returns—failing which some regional pension systems may not be able to meet their liabilities to retirees. However, given the riskiness of such investments, regional asset managers and institutional investors first need more expertise and domain knowledge. Greater regional dialogue is needed on the lifting of investment restrictions and sharing of best practices on alternative assets.

Given the growing mobility of labor, regional economies should also explore bilateral social security agreements to ensure portability of pensions as a second-best option, given that a regional agreement on the issue is most likely to be complicated. Given the rise of non-standard employment, social protection systems need to be redesigned to be future-ready and meet the needs of workers in the gig economy.

7.3 Financial Integration and Regional Safety Nets: Asia and Europe Compared

Given increasing financial interconnectedness in the global and regional financial systems and institutions, it is essential that international financial cooperation is leveraged to manage risks to financial intermediation that might disrupt flows of capital from savers to investors. A clear message that resonates from this volume is the growing financial interconnectedness among regional economies and consequent financial spillover effects, either through large banks with assets and liabilities across multiple jurisdictions, or via capital markets. New challenges have emerged from the rapid rise of fintech and need to fund climate-resilient infrastructure, while ongoing structural challenges posed by rapid population aging persist. Similar issues are apparent in other regions, most notably western Europe.

It is worthwhile to compare and contrast the progress of financial integration and development of regional financial safety net arrangements in ASEAN+3 and the euro area, partly given the fact that both have comparable degrees of regional economic integration through strong intraregional trade and foreign direct investment flows over the last few decades. In 2020, more than 45% of all euro area exports were intraregional, while the corresponding share in ASEAN+3 was a similar 47% (Figure 7.1a). The intraregional share of foreign direct investment stocks is much higher in ASEAN+3, at about 66.5% compared to 57.1% in the euro area (Figure 7.1b). However, the intraregional share in bank flows and portfolio holdings is larger in the euro area than in ASEAN+3 (Figures 7.1c and 7.1d).

Figure 7.1: Intraregional Shares, 2020—ASEAN+3 versus Euro Area
(% of total)

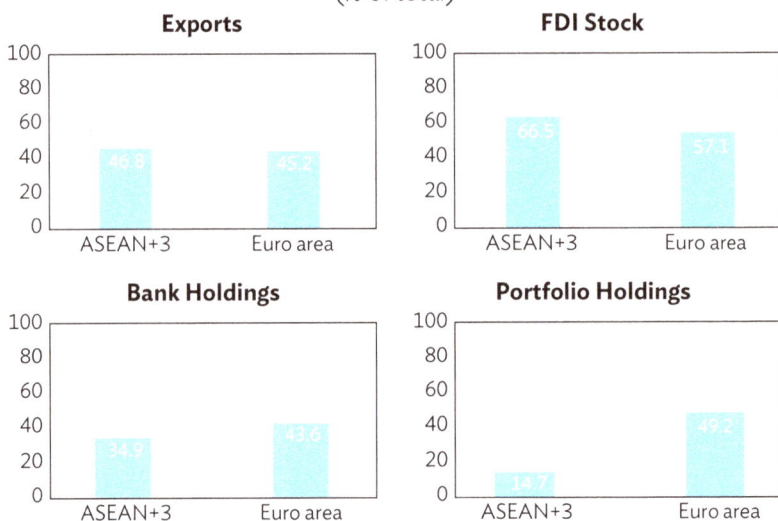

FDI = foreign direct investment
Note: The data are as of June 2020 for portfolio holdings and 2019 for FDI stock. ASEAN+3 includes Hong Kong, China.
Source: ADB calculations using data from (i) Exports: International Monetary Fund (IMF). Direction of Trade Database (accessed April 2021); (ii) FDI stock: International Monetary Fund (IMF) Coordinated Direct Investment Survey (accessed August 2021); (iii) Bank holdings: Bank for International Settlements. Locational Banking Statistics. (accessed May 2021). Asia Regional Integration Center (ARIC). Integration Indicators Database (accessed May 2021); and (iv) Portfolio Holdings: International Monetary Fund. Coordinated Portfolio Investment Survey (accessed March 2021).

Yet, the progress of financial integration, especially in the form of the institutional framework, differs substantially between the two regions. After the sharp currency devaluations of the Asian financial crisis, there was much discussion among ASEAN+3 on the feasibility of the regional economies or a subset of them adopting a common currency, largely given that the introduction of the euro in 1999 went quite smoothly (Fabella 2002). The acute difficulties faced by several countries during the European sovereign debt crisis of 2009–2012, on one hand, and Asia's relatively quick rebound from the global financial crisis, on the other, shifted the debate from the possibility of a monetary union to a comparison of regional monetary facilities.

Table 7.1 illustrates the differences between the characteristics of CMIM and the European Stability Mechanism (ESM). At a broad level, as with the ESM, while the CMIM is meant to offer financial assistance to member economies with financial difficulties, its design differs crucially in some important respects. The CMIM is not protected by international treaty and the resources at its disposal are not transferred to it by member economies unless an economy makes a financing request. However, the ESM is an independent international institution endowed with "paid-in capital" from member states and the ability to raise money from financial markets. This enables it to act swiftly and autonomously during crisis situations (Hyun and Paradise 2019). Further, while the CMIM has only two lending instruments for countries in financial distress (crisis prevention and crisis resolution facilities), the ESM also provides for bank recapitalization and capital market intervention besides loans and credit lines to member states during episodes of financial volatility and turmoil (ADB 2019).

An important area in which the CMIM can learn from Europe is the operationalization of collaboration and cooperation with international organizations during economic and financial crises. For instance, the role of the International Monetary Fund (IMF) is written into the legal provisions of the ESM, which clearly delineate respective roles and approaches in case of joint financing, from a country submitting a financing request and the subsequent disbursal of aid and conditions the recipient must meet, followed by surveillance of the country during the repayment period.[11] Under the ESM, a euro area member country that requests financial

---

[11] While the ESM has its own Early Warning System (EWS), surveillance is carried out by the European Commission in conjunction with the European Central Bank (Zoppè and Dias 2019). On the other hand, AMRO as a regional institution created to support implementation of the CMIM undertakes surveillance for the ASEAN+3 economies on its own.

assistance is generally expected to make a similar request to the IMF (Henning 2017).[12]

Table 7.1: Comparing the Main Elements of CMIM and ESM

Features	CMIM	ESM
Establishment	Established in March 2010, replacing the Chiang Mai Initiative, which was established in May 2000	Inaugurated in October 2012, following the European Financial Stability Facility, established in June 2010 as a temporary backstop in response to the European debt crisis
Members	All 13 ASEAN+3 member economies and Hong Kong, China	All euro area member countries
Objectives	(i) Address balance of payments and short-term liquidity difficulties in the ASEAN+3 region; and (ii) supplement international financing arrangements	Help euro area member countries undergoing severe financial distress
Type	Multilateral currency swap arrangement	Fund
Financial capacity	$240 billion swap arrangement	Capital: €700 billion (€80 billion paid-in, €620 billion callable capital)
Lending capacity	$240 billion (€218 billion)	€500 billion ($551 billion)
Lending instruments	(i) Crisis prevention facility (ii) Crisis resolution facility	(i) Loans within macroeconomic adjustment program (ii) Primary and secondary market purchases (iii) Precautionary credit line (iv) Loans for indirect and direct recapitalization of financial institutions (v) Pandemic crisis support
Governance and decision-making	A request for activation of swap transactions can be submitted to the CMIM Coordinating Countries (2 chairpersons—1 from ASEAN, 1 from plus-3 countries) and subject to approval of the Executive Level Decision Making Body.	Most important decisions, including those on granting financial assistance to member states, are made by mutual agreement by the ESM board of governors (19 finance ministers and EC and ECB as observers).
Conditionalities	(i) IMF de-linked portion: 40% of maximum drawable amount	For a number of support mechanisms, financial assistance is linked to policy conditions specified in a memorandum of understanding between beneficiary member state and the EC, ECB, and the IMF

continued on next page

---

[12] Also see Volume 1 for a discussion on possible reforms to CMIM and AMRO.

Table 7.1 (continued)

	(ii) Portion linked to IMF conditionalities: 60%	
Surveillance	Yes, through AMRO	Only countries with financial assistance
Usage	Never been used	(i) Loans within a macroeconomic adjustment program: Greece (EFSF, ESM), Cyprus (ESM), Portugal (EFSF), Ireland (EFSF)
		(ii) Loans for indirect bank capitalization: Spain (ESM)
		(iii) All other instruments have not been used.

AMRO = ASEAN+3 Macroeconomic Office; ASEAN+3 = Association of Southeast Asian Nations plus the People's Republic of China, Japan, and the Republic of Korea; CMIM = Chiang Mai Initiative Multilateralization; EC = European Commission; ECB = European Central Bank; EFSF = European Financial Stability Facility; ESM = European Stability Mechanism; IMF = International Monetary Fund.
Source: ADB (2019); AMRO and the CMIM (accessed September 2021); ESM Explainers (accessed September 2021); and ESM History (accessed September 2021).

Beyond exchange rate regimes and regional financing facilities, another interesting area is the contrasting approaches to financial regionalism. Conceptually, a useful starting point is the Financial Trilemma framework (Figure 7.2; Schoenmaker 2013).[13] Under the framework, a country can, at any time, only attain two of three objectives: financial integration/openness, financial stability, and national financial policies (i.e., financial autonomy). Consider a situation where a country that maintains financial openness by allowing foreign banks to freely enter chooses to tighten loan-to-value ratios to curb domestic credit. If domestic borrowers have the option of taking out cross-border loans or get funding from the domestic branch of the foreign banks, this could compromise financial stability. To maintain financial stability, the country must be prepared to either limit financial integration or forsake autonomy over national financial policies in favor of harmonized regulations. This is where Europe differs from Asia.

At one end of the spectrum, driven by the experience of the sovereign debt crisis, euro area economies have been discussing the possibility of creating a banking union since 2012. The union would be founded on three pillars: the single-supervisory mechanism, the single-resolution mechanism, and a single-deposit insurance scheme. While progress has been made on the first two pillars, the European Deposit Insurance Scheme (EDIS) remains under discussion, given political economy concerns over the complete

---

[13] This contrasts with the more well-known monetary trilemma which states that if a country maintains a fully open capital account, it must forsake either complete monetary policy autonomy or complete exchange rate fixity. Monetary trilemma for ASEAN+3 economies is discussed in Chapter 3 of this volume.

Figure 7.2: The Trilemma of Financial Stability

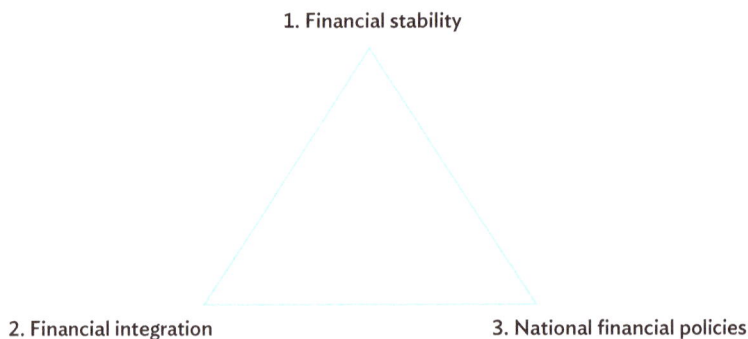

1. Financial stability

2. Financial integration

3. National financial policies

Source: Schoenmaker (2011, 2013).

mutualization of national deposit insurance schemes. While a banking union remains a work in progress, regional economies in Europe have nonetheless gone a long way in being willing to forsake autonomy over national financial oversight. Three European independent supervisory authorities have been established over the years to oversee banks, capital markets, and insurers.[14]

In sharp contrast, while the Asian financial crisis did help shape the decision to create the CMIM, the limited impact of financial crises since then has reduced the urgency of moving toward a region-wide integrated banking union. To be sure, while the ASEAN+3 economies have generally accepted the broad set of standards established by the Basel frameworks, they have chosen to maintain financial policy autonomy as a means to ensuring financial stability. This, in turn, has implied that the regional economies have forsaken a degree of financial integration in limiting foreign bank entry; for instance, through requiring foreign banks to locally incorporate as standalone domestic banks and so effectively ring-fencing the domestic banking system, or by levying macroprudential regulations on foreign borrowing (as the Republic of Korea did in 2011) or as in Singapore imposing different stamp duties to moderate foreign purchases of property (Rajan, Robinson, and Lim 2021). More broadly, such concerns have kept

---

[14] These include the European Banking Authority, the European Securities and Markets Authority, and the European Insurance and Occupational Pensions Authority. The European Union (EU) also established the European Systemic Risk Board in 2010 to oversee the EU-wide financial system and address macro-financial risks of the region.

the region's financial markets and systems fragmented and have limited private risk-sharing channels.

While an ASEAN+3-wide banking framework does not exist, governors of the 10 ASEAN central banks ratified an ASEAN Banking Integration Framework (ABIF) in December 2014.[15] While the stated aim of the framework is to facilitate the creation of an ASEAN Single Market in the regional banking sector (i.e., equal access and treatment), the ABIF's scope is rather modest, providing ASEAN countries a way to enter reciprocal bilateral arrangements that give Qualified ASEAN Banks greater market access and operational flexibilities. Countries negotiate bilaterally, with the focus being on reciprocal arrangements that boost financial stability.

Progress on banking and overall financial market integration in ASEAN and the wider East Asian region will remain limited if countries are unwilling to harmonize national regulations, let alone create a supranational regulatory body, as it compromises national financial sovereignty. Heterogeneity in development, capacities, and ambitions across countries makes the prospect of fully integrated financial markets unlikely any time soon, though it is a useful vision that can continue to guide policy priorities. That said, greater cross-border banking activity is already taking place and can be expected to grow with the emergence of regional digital banks and other fintech firms. While many central banks have taken steps to monitor and manage some of these risks, far greater pressures on the governments to harmonize financial regulations are inevitable, since without it the region might be left vulnerable to acute systemic risks. A systemic risk highlighted in Europe is the vicious feedback loop between banking and sovereign debt crises (Acharya, Drechsler, and Schnabl 2014; Brunnermeier et al. 2016). For ASEAN+3 region, this volume has highlighted risks from the rising role of regional systemically important financial institutions in cross-border banking flows. Failure of any of these institutions could undermine regional financial stability significantly, and so requires closer regional monitoring.

---

[15] This is part of a wider ASEAN Financial Integration Framework (AFIF) endorsed by ASEAN Finance Ministers in 2011, which envisages greater capital market and insurance integration, and aims to liberalize the flow of capital across the ASEAN region, harmonize payments and settlements systems, and strengthen regional financial and surveillance arrangements.

7.4 Conclusion

The COVID-19 pandemic has once again made growing interdependence, the spillover effects of actions, and the need for closer cooperation apparent in view of the high degree of economic and financial interconnectedness in the region. On the trade front, countries reaffirmed their commitment to global free trade and investment in general and vigorously negotiated the Regional Comprehensive Economic Partnership. ASEAN economies, in particular, have also remained steadfast in their support for the ASEAN Single Window to promote seamless intraregional trade, while remaining committed to the ASEAN Digital Integration Framework Action Plan.[16] While room for improvement exists for coordinated financial action, progress in nurturing regional cooperation that promotes financial stability and resilience has been significant over the past two decades.

Moving forward, ASEAN+3 regional financial cooperation should focus more on a specific agenda with vision and goals to further develop regional capital markets for long-term finance, strengthen cross-border market infrastructure, improve regulatory cooperation, and tackle emerging issues such as financing climate change mitigation and the rapid rise of fintech in general and of bigtech firms in finance. Part of this is managing cross-border risks and enhancing crisis surveillance. A clear long-term vision is essential for navigating the path of regional financial cooperation to achieve substantial results along agreed milestones of necessary reforms. More substantively, there may be scope to establish a regional forum for financial development and stability, co-hosted by ADB and AMRO, to make progress on issues raised in this volume.

---

[16] These initiatives broadly come under the umbrella of the ASEAN Economic Community Blueprint 2025 laid out in 2015 (ASEAN Secretariat 2015).

References

Acharya, V., I. Drechsler, and P. Schnabl. 2014. A Pyrrhic Victory? Bank Bailouts and Sovereign Credit Risk. *The Journal of Finance.* 69 (6). pp. 2689–739. https://doi.org/10.1111/jofi.12206.

ASEAN+3 Macroeconomics Research Office (AMRO). About AMRO: AMRO and the CMIM. https://www.amro-asia.org/about-amro/amro-and-the-cmim/#howitworks (accessed September 2021).

Association of Southeast Asian Nations (ASEAN) Secretariat. ASEANstats Data Portal. https://data.aseanstats.org/.

_____. ASEAN Economic Community Blueprint 2025. https://aseandse. org/asean-economic-community-blueprint-2025/.

Asian Development Bank (ADB). 2019. *Strengthening Asia's Financial Safety Net.* Manila. Retrieved from http://dx.doi.org/10.22617/TCS190563-2.

Asia Regional Integration Center (ARIC). Integration Indicators Database. https://aric.adb.org/database/integration (accessed May 2021).

Auer, R., P. Haene, and H. Holden. 2021. Multi-CBDC Arrangements and the Future of Cross-border Payments. Working Paper No. 115. Basel: Bank for International Settlements. https://www.bis.org/publ/bppdf/bispap115.htm.

Bank for International Settlements. 2019. *Annual Report*, Chapter III. Basel. https://www.bis.org/publ/arpdf/ar2019e3.pdf.

_____. 2021a. Multiple CBDC (mCBDC) Bridge. Themes. Basel. https://www.bis.org/about/bisih/topics/cbdc/mcbdc_bridge.htm.

_____. 2021b. BIS Innovation Hub and Central Banks of Australia, Malaysia, Singapore and South Africa will Test CBDCs for International Settlements. Press Release. 20 September. Basel. https://www.bis.org/press/p210902.htm.

_____. Consolidated Banking Statistics. Basel. https://www.bis.org/statistics/consstats.htm.

_____. Locational Banking Statistics. Basel. https://www.bis.org/statistics/bankstats.htm (accessed May 2021).

Bank of Canada, Monetary Authority of Singapore, Accenture, and J.P. Morgan. 2019. Jasper–Ubin: Design Paper Enabling Cross-Border High Value Transfer Using Distributed Ledger Technologies. https://www.mas.gov.sg/-/media/Jasper-Ubin-Design-Paper.pdf.

Brunnermeier, M.K., L. Garicano, P.R. Lane, M. Pagano, R. Reis, T. Santos, D. Thesmar, S. Van Nieuwerburgh, and D. Vayanos. 2016. The Sovereign-Bank Diabolic Loop and ESBies. *American Economic Review*. 106. pp. 508–12. https://www.aeaweb.org/articles/pdf/doi/10.1257/aer.p20161107.

Carstens, A. and H.S. Shin. 2019. Emerging Markets Aren't Out of the Woods Yet. *Foreign Affairs*. 15 March.

Cheng, R., B. Gupta, and R.S. Rajan. 2021. Why are Some Countries Greening Macroprudential Regulations Faster than Others? Unpublished. Lee Kuan Yew School of Public Poicy, National University of Singapore.

Crisanto, J.C., J. Ehrentraud, and M. Fabian. 2021. Big Techs in Finance: Regulatory Approaches and Policy Options. *BIS-FSI Briefs*. 12, March. https://www.bis.org/fsi/fsibriefs12.htm.

European Stability Mechanism (ESM). ESM Explainers. https://www.esm.europa.eu/explainers (accessed September 2021)

_____. ESM History. https://www.esm.europa.eu/about-us/history#headline-the_context (accessed September 2021).

Fabella, R. 2002. Monetary Cooperation in East Asia: A Survey. ERD Working Paper Series. No.13. Manila: Asian Development Bank. https://www.adb.org/sites/default/files/publication/28308/wp013.pdf.

Financial Stability Board (FSB). 2017. Financial Stability Implications from FinTech: Supervisory and Regulatory Issues that Merit Authorities' Attention. Basel. https://www.fsb.org/wp-content/uploads/R270617.pdf.

Grimes, W.W. and W.N. Kring. 2020. Institutionalizing Financial Cooperation in East Asia: AMRO and the Future of the Chiang Mai Initiative Multilateralization. *Global Governance*. 26 (3). pp. 428–48. https://doi.org/10.1163/19426720-02603005.

Henning, R. 2017. Avoiding Fragmentation of Global Financial Governance. *Global Policy*. 8 (1). pp. 101–06. London: London School of Economics and Political Science. https://doi.org/10.1111/1758-5899.12394.

Hyun, S., and J.F. Paradise. 2019. Why Is There No Asian Monetary Fund? *ADBI Working Paper Series*. No 1061. Tokyo: Asian Development Bank Institute. https://www.adb.org/sites/default/files/publication/546901/adbi-wp1061.pdf.

Ikeda, Y., W. Kerry, U. Lewrick, and C. Schmeider. 2021. COVID-19 and Bank Resilience: Where do we Stand? *BIS Bulletin.* 44, July. https://www. bis.org/publ/bisbull44.htm.

International Monetary Fund (IMF). 2017. Collaboration Between Regional Financing Arrangements and the IMF. *Policy Paper,* July. https:// www.imf.org/en/Publications/Policy-Papers/Issues/2017/07/31/ pp073117-collaboration-between-regional-financing-arrangements-and-the-imf#:~:text=Collaboration%20Between%20 Regional%20Financing%20Arrangements%20and%20the%20 IMF,-Publication%20Date%3A&text=Summary%3A&text=It%20 proposes%20both%20modalities%20for,Fund%20and%20the%20 various%20RFAs.

———. Coordinated Direct Investment Survey. https://data.imf. org/?sk=40313609-F037-48C1-84B1-E1F1CE54D6D5 (accessed August 2021).

———. Coordinated Portfolio Investment Survey. http://data.imf.org/cpis (accessed March 2021).

———. Direction of Trade Database. https://www.imf.org/en/Data (accessed April 2021).

Inui, T., W. Takahashi, and M. Ishida. 2021. A Proposal for Asia Digital Common Currency. *RIEB Discussion Paper Series.* No.2020-19. Kobe: Research Institute for Economics and Business Administration, Kobe University.

Rajan, R.S., E. Robinson, and R. Lim. 2021. Macroprudential Policies and Financial Stability in Singapore. Paper prepared for MAS-BIS Conference on Macro-Financial Stability Policy, 26–28 May 2021. Singapore: Monetary Authority of Singapore.

Schoenmaker, D. 2011. The Financial Trilemma. *Economics Letters.* 111. pp. 57–59.

———. 2013. *Governance of International Banking: The Financial Trilemma.* Oxford: Oxford University Press. https://doi.org/10.1093/acprof:o so/9780199971596.001.0001.

United Nations Conference on Trade and Development. *World Investment Report 2019* Statistical Annex Tables. http://unctad.org/en/Pages/ DIAE/World%20Investment%20Report/AnnexTables.aspx.

Zoppè, A. and C. Dias. 2019. *The European Stability Mechanism: Main Features, Instruments and Accountability.* Brussels: European Parliament. https://www.europarl.europa.eu/RegData/etudes/ BRIE/2014/497755/IPOL-ECON_NT(2014)497755_EN.pdf.

Index

A

ABF1 (Asian Bond Fund 1), 7–8, 8*b*
ABF2 (Asian Bond Fund 2), 8, 8*b*, 74
ABIF. *See* ASEAN Banking Integration Framework
ABMF (ASEAN+3 Bond Market Forum), 8*b*, 212, 272
ABMI. *See* Asian Bond Markets Initiative
ACCDs (appointed cross-currency dealers), 128–29, 131–32
Acemoglu, D., 286–87
Acharya, V., 54
ADB. *See* Asian Development Bank
Adler, G., 25
Adrian, T., 54
AEC (ASEAN Economic Community), 128, 129, 129n26
aging populations, 281–89. *See also* pension systems; social security systems
    annuities for, 330–31, 331–32*b*
    asset price movements and, 288–89
    economic implications of, 286–89, 353
    family support for, 301n8
    growth in GDP per capita and, 287
    labor force participation and, 286, 288
    old-age dependency ratio and, 284, 285*f*, 370
    population profile, 282–86, 283–85*f*
    productivity of, 286–87
    savings impacted by, 288
Aizenman, J., 23, 49, 94n7, 99
Aldasoro, I., 58
Allen, F., 65, 69

alternative finance
  balance-sheet lending, 206
  conventional lending compared to, 178, 179*t*
  crowdfunding, 177, 186, 198, 206–7, 209, 245
  financial inclusion and, 187
  market value and development of, 176, 177*t*
  peer-to-peer lending, 161, 176–77, 186, 197–98, 205–6, 367
  regulation of, 199, 205–7
  risks associated with, 197–98, 215
  transaction value of, 177, 178*t*
Alves, I., 65
AMRO. *See* ASEAN+3 Macroeconomic Research Office
Amstad, M., 54, 75
anchor currencies, 92–93, 98, 105, 117–18, 118*f*, 125, 365
annuities, 330–31, 331–32*b*
appointed cross-currency dealers (ACCDs), 128–29, 131–32
artificial intelligence (AI), 23, 162
ASEAN Banking Integration Framework (ABIF), 74, 131–32, 211, 364, 377
ASEAN Catalytic Green Finance Facility, 257, 264*b*, 273
ASEAN Economic Community (AEC), 128, 129, 129n25
ASEAN Working Committee on Financial Inclusion, 210–12
ASEAN+3. *See also specific countries*
  aging in. *See* aging populations
  anchor currencies for, 117–18, 118*f*, 125
  contagion in. *See* contagion
  cooperation in. *See* regional financial cooperation
  financial inclusion in. *See* financial inclusion
  financial integration in, 371–72, 373*f*
  financial systems in. *See* financial systems
  fintech in. *See* financial technology
  foreign bank presence in, 5, 5n6, 6*f*
  foreign exchange reserves in, 29–30, 29–30*f*, 120
  GDP and trade shares, 96, 96n10, 97*f*
  in global monetary system. *See* global monetary system
  infrastructure in. *See* infrastructure investment
  Local Currency Settlement Framework among, 119, 128–33, 140–41
  pensions in. *See* pension systems
  remittances and international money transfers from, 171
  trade invoicing currencies for, 25, 27*f*
  trilemma perspective on, 97–105, 100*f*, 103–4*f*
ASEAN+3 Bond Market Forum (ABMF), 8*b*, 212, 272

ASEAN+3 Macroeconomic Research Office (AMRO)
  financial distress concerns of, 22
  fintech risk assessment by, 210
  monitoring mandate of, 364–65
  regional financial cooperation and, 1, 30, 361, 378
Asian Bond Fund 1 (ABF1), 7–8, 8*b*
Asian Bond Fund 2 (ABF2), 8, 8*b*, 74
Asian Bond Markets Initiative (ABMI), 8, 8*b*, 240–42, 272, 361
Asian Development Bank (ADB)
  Asian Economic Integration Report, 341–42
  CGIF and, 9*b*, 75–76, 363
  on CMIM mandate, 365n5
  debt projection model, 266
  financial inclusion as priority of, 180
  green finance and, 256, 257, 262*b*
  on infrastructure needs, 227–28
  on local currency bond markets, 342
  on MSMEs, 184, 187
Asian digital common currency, 366n8
Asian financial crisis (1997–1998)
  banking networks in, 66
  causes of, 50, 52
  CMIM created in response to, 376
  contagion in, 50, 53, 59
  credit booms and, 52
  currency devaluations in, 372
  exchange rates in, 101
  lessons learned from, 4
  reforms following, 1, 2, 7–10
  resiliency during, 10
  sudden-stop contagion in, 54
asset price movements, 288–89
Association of Southeast Asian Nations. *See ASEAN entries; specific countries*
automation technology, 287
Avdjiev, S., 52
Ayyagari, M., 23–24

B

baht, 106, 108, 110, 121–22, 123*f*
balance-of-payments crisis. *See* sudden-stop contagion
balance-sheet lending, 206
Bali Fintech Agenda, 199, 200*t*
Bangkok International Banking Facilities (BIBF) initiative, 121–22
Bangko Sentral ng Pilipinas (BSP), 78, 128–31
Bank for International Settlements (BIS)
      Consolidated Banking Statistics, 59–60, 66, 72, 78
      credit-to-GDP gap estimates, 58
      on cyberattacks, 193
      on debt securities, 113, 363n3
      digital currencies as defined by, 172
      on DLT-based payment systems, 196
      on fintech regulation, 200
      international banking database, 111, 111n16
      Locational Banking Statistics, 60, 63–65, 91
      Multiple CBDC project and, 369
      triennial survey of, 89
Bank Indonesia (BI), 75, 78, 128–29, 131, 261*b*
Bank Negara Malaysia (BNM), 75, 78, 128–29, 131
Bank of Japan (BOJ), 75, 78, 131, 138–39, 175, 214
Bank of Korea, 75, 76, 78, 175
Bank of Thailand (BOT), 75, 78, 128–31, 136, 175, 213
banks and banking. *See also specific banks*
      assets as share of GDP, 9–10, 11*f*
      central. *See* central banks
      competition among, 3, 204
      cross-border. *See* cross-border banking
      destabilization of, 161, 208, 367
      digital, 23, 186, 188, 204, 205, 211
      financial systems based on, 1, 7, 33, 50, 362
      fintech collaboration with, 187–88, 190, 203
      foreign. *See* foreign banks
      global banking network, 65–67, 66*t*, 70–73, 71–72*f*, 71*t*
      G-SIBs, 77–78
      interconnectedness of, 22, 50, 54, 59–61, 65–67, 77
      nonperforming loans and, 22, 198, 205, 364
      QABs, 131–32, 132n28, 209, 211, 377
      regulation of, 203–5
      R-SIBs, 77–78, 364, 368
      unbanked/underbanked groups, 135, 185–86, 185n9, 186*f*, 215

Beck, T., 23–24
Belt and Road Initiative, 32n34, 128, 137
BI. *See* Bank Indonesia
BIBF (Bangkok International Banking Facilities) initiative, 121–22
big data, 162, 204, 212–13, 334
bigtech firms
        access to consumers, 167
        characteristics of, 163
        in financial sphere, 191, 193–94, 197, 204, 365, 368
        regional cooperation and, 212, 378
        regulation of, 198, 201
        as SIFIs, 199n17
bilateral social security agreements (BSSAs), 350–53, 352n42, 371
BIS. *See* Bank for International Settlements
blockchain technology, 23, 174, 213, 214, 369
BNM (Bank Negara Malaysia), 75, 78, 128–29, 131
BOJ. *See* Bank of Japan
bonds and bond markets
        corporate. *See* corporate bond markets
        cross-border trading in, 361
        ESG, 269–71, 270f, 273, 370
        floating-interest-rate infrastructure, 243–45, 245f, 254, 272, 274,
            370
        green. *See* green bonds
        infrastructure investment and, 10, 21n16, 263–65b, 370
        local currency. *See* local currency bond markets
        social, 258, 269–71, 270f, 273
        sovereign, 7–8, 21, 21t, 141, 240, 320
        sustainability, 258, 269, 270f, 327b
        transition, 257–58
Boot, A.W.A., 23
Borio, C., 58, 68b
BOT. *See* Bank of Thailand
Bretton Woods system, 98–99, 101
Brunnermeier, M:, 54
Bruno, V., 53
BSP (Bangko Sentral ng Pilipinas), 78, 128–31
BSSAs (bilateral social security agreements), 350–53, 352n42, 371
Burtless, G., 286, 287

C

Cambodia
> current-account deficit in, 57–58
> foreign bank presence in, 5n6
> median population age in, 283
> pension system in, 298–99b
> Project Bakong in, 133, 135–36, 135n28, 174

Cambridge Centre for Alternative Finance (CCAF), 176, 190

Canada Pension Plan Investment Board, 326b

capital
> allocation of, 3
> countercyclical, 76
> cross-border, 4–5, 105
> human, 286, 287, 353
> long-term, 3, 33, 132, 274, 362
> outflows, 22, 49, 53, 118, 125–26, 209, 330

capital account openness
> *de facto* vs. *de jure,* 3
> local currency bond markets and, 18
> macroeconomic performance and, 126n24
> in trilemma, 94, 97–105, 100f, 103–4f
> yen internationalization and, 120

carbon taxes, 258, 370

Carstens, A., 19, 28n29

CCAF (Cambridge Centre for Alternative Finance), 176, 190

Cecchetti, S., 54

central bank digital currencies (CBDCs)
> fundamental forces and, 139
> monetary policy and, 207–9, 216
> motivations for issuing, 135, 137, 141–42, 172–73, 215
> Project Bakong, 133, 135–36, 135n28, 174
> regional financial cooperation and, 368–69
> research and development on, 174–76, 175t
> risks associated with, 161, 212–14
> state of preparation for, 133, 133–34t, 137–39

central banks. *See also* central bank digital currencies; *specific banks*
> cooperation among, 7–8, 74–75
> currency swap arrangements with, 94, 94n6, 123, 130–31
> in emerging market economies, 28n29, 77
> financial regulation by, 201
> international reserves held by, 51, 73
> Local Currency Settlement Framework and, 128–29, 132

Central Provident Fund (CPF), 322, 322n24, 331–32b, 352
CGIF (Credit Guarantee and Investment Facility), 9b, 75–76, 363
Chan, E., 74
Chaudhuri, C., 165
Cherlin, A., 301n9
Cheung, Y.W., 50, 53, 55
Chiang Mai Initiative Multilateralization (CMIM)
        currency swaps and, 32
        ESM compared to, 372–74, 374–75t
        expansion of mandate, 365n5
        information-sharing mechanism with IMF, 31
        liquidity provided by, 73
        motivations for creation of, 376
        regional financial cooperation and, 1, 30, 361
China. See People's Republic of China
Chinn, M., 99, 108
CIPS (Cross-Border Interbank Payment System), 123, 129–30, 365n7
clearing and settlement mechanisms, 123, 130, 164, 175, 195, 199
climate change
        financing for mitigation of, 228, 378
        greenhouse gas emissions and, 229, 256, 257, 267
        infrastructure and, 231, 255, 370
        UN Framework Convention on, 255–56
cloud computing, 23, 193
CMIM. See Chiang Mai Initiative Multilateralization
common lender channel of contagion, 49–51, 59, 67, 70, 73, 78
consumer protection
        data governance and, 24
        digital currencies and, 138
        financial innovation and, 191, 368
        regulations for, 202, 206
contagion, 49–78. See also slow-burn contagion; sudden-stop contagion
        in Asian financial crisis, 50, 53, 59
        common lender channel of, 49–51, 59, 67, 70, 73, 78
        global banking network and, 65–67, 66t, 70–73, 71–72f, 71t
        in global financial crisis, 50, 53, 55, 59, 67
        literature review, 52–54
        as macrofinancial risk, 191, 198, 199
        policy recommendations, 73–78
Coppola, A., 53
coronavirus. See COVID-19 pandemic

corporate bond markets
 development of, 10, 51
 in emerging market economies, 18, 18n13
 internationalization of, 17–19, 18f
 local currency, 14, 54, 74–76, 362–63
 repo markets and, 74–76, 363
 sectoral breakdown of, 14, 16f
corporate financing, 1, 7, 20, 33, 238
COVID-19 pandemic
 credit markets impacted by, 364
 currency swap arrangements during, 94
 Debt Service Suspension Initiative and, 268–69
 digital transformation and, 23, 34
 economic impact of, 265–67, 266f
 ESG bonds and, 269–71, 270f, 370
 exchange rates during, 27, 28f, 86
 financial systems during, 2, 20–24, 33
 fintech and, 161, 183–84, 188–90, 189f, 367
 green fiscal recovery methods, 267–68
 infrastructure investment and, 231, 265–71, 274
 local currency bond markets and, 14
 sovereign bond issuance in, 21, 21t
 US dollar during, 33, 86, 86nn1–2
CPF (Central Provident Fund), 322, 322n23, 331–32b, 352
credit enhancement mechanisms, 239–40
Credit Guarantee and Investment Facility (CGIF), 9b, 75–76, 363
credit-to-GDP gaps, 58, 59f, 73
cross-border banking
 financial integration and, 5, 33
 international bank claims, 61–65, 62–64t
 liabilities in, 91–92, 91f, 111–12, 112–13f, 120, 154–55f
 regional financial cooperation in, 211, 377–78
Cross-Border Interbank Payment System (CIPS), 123, 129–30, 365n7
crowdfunding, 177, 186, 198, 206–7, 209, 245
cryptoassets, 135, 161, 171–72, 194–95, 203, 207–8, 215
currencies. See also regional currencies; specific currencies
 anchor, 92–93, 98, 105, 117–18, 118f, 125, 365
 blocs, 92–93, 93f
 digital, 133–34t, 133–39
 fiat, 135, 137, 172, 174, 195, 207
 swaps, 1, 31–33, 94, 94nn6–7, 123, 130–31, 367

current-account balances, 50, 53–58, 58f, 73
customer service, 335
cyberattacks, 190, 193, 196

D

data sharing, 212
DB pensions. *See* defined benefit pensions
DCF (Dominant Currency Financing) paradigm, 25, 27, 27n24, 365
DCP (Dominant Currency Pricing) paradigm, 25, 27, 27n24, 365
DC pensions. *See* defined contribution pensions
debt securities. *See also* bonds and bond markets
      currencies for, 91–92, 91f, 113–17, 114f, 116f, 156–59f
      domestic, 12, 13f
      international, 12, 14f
      offshore affiliates and, 363n3
Debt Service Suspension Initiative, 268–69
debt sustainability, 21, 235–37
defined benefit (DB) pensions, 290–92, 294, 304, 308, 315n22, 320, 344
defined contribution (DC) pensions, 290–94, 303–8, 306b, 312, 315n22,
      320, 344
developing economies
      current account convertibility in, 127b
      debt securities in, 117n18
      digital currencies in, 173
      financial inclusion in, 23–24, 189
      infrastructure gap in, 228, 228t
      pensions systems in, 292, 325
      trade finance gaps in, 213
Diebold, F.X., 54
difference in difference method, 247b
digital banking, 23, 186, 188, 204, 205, 211
digital commerce, 166–67, 166t, 167–68f
digital currencies. *See also* central bank digital currencies
      cryptoassets, 135, 161, 171–72, 194–95, 203, 207–8, 215
      defined, 172
      promotion of, 188–89
      regulation of, 202–3
      risks associated with, 367–68
digital financial literacy, 160–61, 184, 202
digital payments, 164–71
      banked status of consumers, 185–86, 186f

      in COVID-19 pandemic, 188–89
      defined, 164, 165
      digital commerce, 166–67, 166t, 167–68f
      in emerging market economies, 165, 165t
      e-money for, 135–36, 164, 169–71, 180–82, 182f, 202
      e-wallets for, 135, 164, 166, 169, 174, 195, 215
      international money transfers, 171
      mobile POS payments, 166–67, 166t, 167–68f
      penetration rate of users, 167, 168–69f
      regulations for, 202–3
      remittances, 171, 188, 190, 202
      risks associated with, 194–97
      share of consumers using, 167, 168f, 180–81, 181f
      transaction value of, 166–67, 166t, 167f
digital wallets. *See* e-wallets
direct exchange markets, 32n34, 129–31
distributed ledger technology (DLT), 135–38, 136n30, 163, 172–75, 186,
           195–97, 212–14
dollar. *See also* dollar dominance
      as anchor currency, 117–18, 118f, 365
      in COVID-19 pandemic, 33, 86, 86nn1–2
      in cross-border bank liabilities, 91, 91f, 111–12, 112–13f
      debt securities issued in, 91, 91f, 114–16, 114f
      in foreign exchange markets, 89, 90f
      in global financial crisis, 34, 87
      international bank claims and, 65
      as reserve currency, 90, 90f
      for trade invoicing, 25, 27f, 88, 89f
      for trade settlement, 88, 89f, 108–10
dollar dominance
      financial vulnerability from, 28
      in global monetary system, 86–96, 139, 140
      implications of, 93–94, 121
      international bank claims and, 65
      paradigms of, 25, 27, 27n24, 365
      risks and challenges of, 95–96, 118, 129
      strategies for reduction of, 32, 365–67
      supporting factors for, 95
      in trade invoicing, 25, 27f, 88, 89f
      trade settlement and, 88, 89f, 108–10
Dominant Currency Financing (DCF) paradigm, 25, 27, 27n24, 365
Dominant Currency Pricing (DCP) paradigm, 25, 27, 27n24, 365

Drehmann, M., 58
Dungey, M., 54

E
ECB (European Central Bank), 138, 139, 175, 214
economic growth
    aging populations and, 287
    analysis of prospects for, 233
    anchor currencies and, 117
    as common regional factor, 55
    fintech services and, 191
    infrastructure development and, 227
    monetary policy and, 98
    public–private partnerships and, 253
    theory and evidence on, 3
EDIS (European Deposit Insurance Scheme), 376
Eichengreen, B., 49
EMEAP (Executives' Meeting of East Asia-Pacific Central Banks), 8, 8b,
    8n8, 78
emerging market economies
    central banks in, 28n29, 77
    credit booms in, 52
    current account convertibility in, 127b
    debt composition of corporations in, 19, 20f
    digital payments in, 165, 165t
    dollar dominance as challenge for, 118
    exchange rate arrangements in, 24–25, 27
    financial stability in, 209
    local currency bond markets in, 17–19, 18n13
    macroprudential measures in, //
    nonperforming loan ratios in, 22
    pensions systems in, 292
    sudden-stop contagion in, 33
    trilemma perspective on, 99–105, 100f, 103f
e-money, 135–36, 164, 169–71, 180–82, 182f, 202
employer-sponsored pensions, 290, 291n4, 294, 302
employment
    in gig economy, 281–82, 338–39, 339–40b, 343, 371
    gray zone, 337n33, 338–39, 341
    labor force participation, 286, 288
    migrant workers, 344–48, 345–47f, 350–52, 352t
    nonstandard, 337–38, 343

        self-employment, 337–38, 340–41
        tax payments and, 343*b*
        technology and, 336
environmental, social, and governance (ESG) investment
        bonds, 269–71, 270*f*, 273, 370
        disclosure requirements, 260
        pension systems and, 262*b*, 327*b*
        standards for, 262*b*, 370
e-payments. *See* digital payments
equity crowdfunding, 206–7
equity markets, 7, 10n9, 55, 187, 273, 320–21
Erdem, M., 52
ESM (European Stability Mechanism), 372–74, 374–75*t*
euro
        in cross-border bank liabilities, 91, 91*f*, 111–12, 112–13*f*
        debt securities issued in, 91, 91*f*, 114*f*, 115–16
        digital project involving, 138
        in foreign exchange markets, 89, 90*f*
        international bank claims and, 65
        as reserve currency, 90, 90*f*
        for trade invoicing, 27*f*, 88n3
        for trade settlement, 88, 89*f*, 110
euro area
        financial integration in, 371–72, 373*f*
        GDP and trade shares, 96, 97*f*
        in global banking network, 66–67, 66*t*, 71–72*f*, 71*t*, 72–73
        international bank claims, 61–65
        sociological changes in, 301n9
        sovereign debt crisis in, 10, 53, 59, 61, 66, 372
European Central Bank (ECB), 138, 139, 175, 214
European Deposit Insurance Scheme (EDIS), 376
European Stability Mechanism (ESM), 372–74, 374–75*t*
e-wallets, 135, 164, 166, 169, 174, 195, 215
exchange rates
        anchor currencies for management of, 92–93, 98, 105, 117–18, 118*f*,
            25
        in Asian financial crisis, 101
        in COVID-19 pandemic, 27, 28*f*, 86
        fixed, 7, 25, 97–99, 102, 104
        floating, 24, 93
        IMF annual report on, 24, 26*t*
        regional financial cooperation on, 366

in trilemma, 94, 97–105, 100*f*, 103–4*f*
volatility of, 20, 25, 117, 133
Executives' Meeting of East Asia-Pacific Central Banks (EMEAP), 8, 8*b*, 8n8, 78

F
Federal Reserve (US)
currency swaps and, 31, 94, 94nn6–7
digital currency studies by, 138
global central bank proposal for, 118
international reputation of, 95
monetary policy of, 21, 94, 96, 96n9
repurchase agreements with, 31n33
fertility rates, 282, 283*f*
fiat currencies, 135, 137, 172, 174, 195, 207
financial cooperation. *See* regional financial cooperation
financial crises. *See also* Asian financial crisis; global financial crisis
credit booms and, 52
indicators for prediction of, 58
risk factors for, 3, 4
sovereign debt crisis, 10, 53, 59, 61, 66, 372
financial inclusion
barriers to, 191
definitions of, 160, 179
digital currencies and, 136, 173, 174, 176
fintech and, 23–24, 160–61, 179–89, 214–15, 367
G20 action plan for, 160
of individuals, 180–82, 181–82*f*, 186
of MSMEs, 161, 184–87, 185*f*, 185*t*
narrowing gaps in, 23–24
financial integration
benefits of, 3–4
dimensions of, 3–5
fintech and, 209
growth of, 34, 73
international comparison, 371–72, 373*f*
regional, 128, 129, 132
financial literacy
digital, 160–61, 184, 202
financial inclusion in relation to, 179
gaps in, 182, 303
promotion of, 367

financial regulation
    decision-making in, 258, 261–62*b*
    environmental risks and, 261*b*
    of fintech, 198–207, 200*t*, 215, 335
    framework for, 126
    harmonization of, 209, 377
    macroprudential, 377
    regional cooperation on, 22, 364, 377, 378
    shortcomings of, 4
    strengthening of, 2
    technology and, 335
financial stability
    capital markets and, 12
    corporate bond market and, 10
    currency internationalization and, 126
    currency swaps and, 32
    digital currencies and, 137, 138
    dollar dominance and, 95
    in emerging market economies, 209
    fintech and, 23, 24, 161, 191–98
    regional, 32–33, 363, 378
    regulations for assurance of, 198–207
Financial Stability Board (FSB)
    on fintech, 162–63, 191, 193, 198, 210
    on global systemically important banks, 78
    infrastructure investment and, 265
    membership of, 77
    SIFI framework, 199
financial systems
    bank-based, 1, 7, 33, 50, 362
    in COVID-19 pandemic, 2, 20–24, 33
    crises in. *See* financial crises
    evolution of, 7–19
    globalization of, 4, 4n4, 265, 363
    interconnectedness of, 364, 371–72
    openness of, 3–4, 33, 375
    regulation of. *See* financial regulation
    resiliency of, 10, 78, 362, 372
    safety nets in, 2, 7, 31–33, 201, 361–62, 371–78
    stability of. *See* financial stability
financial technology (fintech), 160–216
    alternative finance. *See* alternative finance

bank collaboration with, 187–88, 190, 203
banked status of consumers, 185–86, 186f
categorization of services, 162–63, 367
COVID-19 pandemic and, 161, 183–84, 188–90, 189f, 367
currency and. *See* digital currencies
customer service and, 335
financial inclusion and, 23–24, 160–61, 179–89, 214–15, 367
financial stability and, 23, 24, 161, 191–98
income and wealth distribution affected by, 182–84, 183f
monetary policy design and, 207–9, 215–16
payments and. *See* digital payments
regional cooperation and, 23, 34, 209–14, 367–69
regulation of, 198–207, 200t, 215, 335
risks associated with, 191–99, 192t, 210–14, 367–68
as share of GDP, 186–87, 187t
fixed exchange rates, 7, 25, 97–99, 102, 104
floating exchange rates, 24, 93
floating-interest-rate infrastructure bonds, 243–45, 245f, 254, 272, 274, 370
Forbes, K.J., 53
foreign banks
in currency internationalization, 121
financial services provided by, 132, 375–76
local incorporation of, 377
participation rates, 5, 6f
presence in ASEAN+3, 5, 5n6, 6f
foreign exchange markets, 89, 90f, 105–6, 106f, 133, 141
foreign exchange reserves, 29–30, 29–30f, 90, 90f, 120
Franco, L., 192–93
Frankel–Wei method, 92, 92n4, 117
Fry-McKibbin, R., 55, 67
FSB. *See* Financial Stability Board
Fu, J., 188

G
G20 (Group of Twenty)
on cryptoasset monitoring, 195, 215
on Debt Service Suspension Initiative, 268
financial inclusion as priority of, 160, 179
on infrastructure investment, 227, 265, 273
Gale, D., 65, 69
game theory, 67, 68b

General Agreement on Trade in Services (GATS), 353

gig economy, 281–82, 338–39, 339–40b, 343, 371

global banking network, 65–67, 66t, 70–73, 71–72f, 71t

global financial crisis (2007–2009)

    capital outflows during, 53

    contagion in, 50, 53, 55, 59, 67

    currency swap arrangements during, 94, 94n6

    Lehman Brothers collapse in, 87, 95, 123

    lessons learned from, 4, 268

    resiliency during, 10, 372

    US dollar during, 34, 87

global financial cycles, 50, 53, 140

globalization, 4, 4n4, 265, 363

global monetary system, 86–142. See also currencies

    cross-border bank liabilities in, 91–92, 91f, 111–12, 112–13f, 120, 154–55f

    debt securities in, 91–92, 91f, 113–17, 114f, 116f, 156–59f

    dollar dominance in, 86–96, 139, 140

    foreign exchange markets in, 89, 90f, 105–6, 106f

    foreign exchange reserves in, 90, 90f

    trilemma of international finance and, 94, 97–105

Global Pension Index, 308, 309f

Global System for Mobile Communications Association (GSMA), 169, 169n1

global systemically important banks (G-SIBs), 77–78

global warming. See climate change

Gochoco-Bautista, M.S., 74

Gopinath, G., 27n24, 88

Gourinchas, P.O., 65

gray zone employment, 337n33, 338–39, 341

Great Recession. See global financial crisis

Green, J.R., 68b

green bonds

    defined, 240, 269

    market for, 257, 263b, 270f, 370

    regional cooperation and, 272

    standards for, 258, 263–64b

green finance, 255–65

    challenges related to, 260

    debt capital market and, 263–65b

    defined, 231, 255, 256

    governance architecture for, 258–60, 260t, 261–62b

    pension systems and, 327*b*
    promotion of, 273, 370
    regional cooperation and, 273, 275
    UNEP framework for, 257–65, 259–60*t*, 261–62*b*, 264*b*
green fiscal recovery methods, 267–68
greenhouse gas emissions, 229, 256, 257, 267
green infrastructure projects
        acceleration of, 257
        capital market gaps in, 239
        examples of, 229n1
        financing for, 255, 259*t*, 263*b*
        pension systems and, 325
        promotion of, 231, 231*f*, 275
Greenspan, Alan, 51, 74
greenwashing, 258, 271, 327*b*, 370
G-SIBs (global systemically important banks), 77–78
GSMA (Global System for Mobile Communications Association), 169, 169n1
Gyntelberg, J., 54

H
Harris, S., 341
Hausmann, R., 50
home currencies. *See* regional currencies; *specific currencies*
Hong Kong, China
        as banking center, 55, 60, 63–65, 129
        pension system in, 326–27*b*
Hong Kong Monetary Authority (HKMA), 75, 78, 136, 213, 327*b*
Hsiao, C.Y-L., 55, 67
Huang, Bihong, 160, 174, 206
human capital, 286, 287, 353
Hutchison, M., 49

I
IEA (International Energy Agency), 267
IMF. *See* International Monetary Fund
income distribution, 182–84
independent contractors, 338, 339–40*b*
independent worker status, 341–42
Indonesia. *See also* Bank Indonesia
        alternative finance in, 176
        concentration risk for, 60

        current-account deficit in, 58
        digital payments in, 167, 168*f*
        foreign bank presence in, 5n6
        green bonds issuance in, 264*b*
        loans to MSMEs in, 184, 185*f*, 185*t*
        local currency bond markets in, 14
        Local Currency Settlement Framework and, 128–29, 141, 366
        median population age in, 283
        pension system in, 294, 295*t*, 300, 300*f*
        remittances and international money transfers from, 171
        sovereign bond issuance in, 21, 21*t*
        sudden-stop contagion risk in, 56
        Sustainable Finance Roadmap, 258, 262*b*
        tax payment facilitation in, 343*b*
        trilemma perspective on, 102, 104*f*
information asymmetries, 3, 162, 163, 193
infrastructure investment, 227–75
        bond markets and, 10, 21n16, 263–65*b*, 370
        conflicts of interest between users and investors, 243, 243*f*
        COVID-19 pandemic and, 231, 265–71, 274
        debt sustainability and, 235–37
        financing gaps, 227–30, 228*t*, 233, 254, 274
        fiscal space for, 233–36, 234*f*, 235*t*
        green. *See* green finance; green infrastructure projects
        international cooperation and, 265
        pension systems and, 323–25
        private sector role in. *See* private financing
        public–private partnerships, 230, 252–54, 273–74, 369
        public sector role in, 34, 229–37, 229*f*, 232–33*t*
        regional cooperation and, 272–73, 275
        risk-return profile and, 230, 230*f*
        spillover tax revenue from, 243–45, 245*f*, 246–49*b*, 274
        sustainable, 229, 269, 272–73, 324–25, 369–70
interconnectedness
        of banks, 22, 50, 54, 59–61, 65–67, 77
        of financial systems, 364, 371–72
        fintech and, 199
        investor sentiment and, 49–50
        manifestations of, 53
        measurement of, 50–52, 54–56, 67
interest rates
        deregulation of, 3

floating, 243–45, 245f, 272, 370
liberalization of, 120
negative, 173, 208
International Capital Market Association, 258, 269, 270
International Energy Agency (IEA), 267
International Monetary Fund (IMF)
    Annual Report on Exchange Arrangements and Restrictions, 24, 26t
    Assessing Reserve Adequacy Emerging Markets metric, 30
    Bali Fintech Agenda supported by, 199
    currency invoicing/settlement data, 106
    on Debt Service Suspension Initiative, 268–69
    ESM collaboration with, 373–74
    Financial Access Survey, 184
    foreign exchange reserves of member countries, 90, 90f
    information-sharing mechanism with CMIM, 31
    infrastructure investment and, 265
    Integrated Framework, 29
    on local currency bond markets, 17
    on monetary policy transmission, 207
    on reorientation of expenditures, 235
    on revenue increases, 234
    special drawing rights basket, 90, 118–19, 123, 123n22
international money transfers, 171
International Organization of Securities Commissions, 207
investor sentiment, 24, 49–50, 236
Ito, Hiro, 86, 99, 108, 116, 126n24

J
Japan. *See also* Bank of Japan
    alternative finance in, 176, 205
    currency shares in trade with partners, 149f
    digital payments in, 180, 202
    fintech adoption in, 182
    in global banking network, 66–67, 66t, 70–73, 71–72f, 71t
    international bank claims, 61–65
    Kyushu Railway Company of, 249b
    land trusts in, 250, 252
    life expectancy in, 282
    local currency bond market in, 12, 12f
    median population age in, 283
    old-age dependency ratio in, 284

pension system in, 262*b*, 294, 296*t*, 300, 300*f*, 370

retirement savings gap in, 302–3

sociological changes in, 301n9

trilemma perspective on, 100*f*, 101–2, 104*f*

on yen for international transactions, 32n34

Jinjarak, Y., 49

jobs. *See* employment

K

Kalotychou, E., 52

Kaminsky, G., 52

Kara, G., 50, 52, 67

Kawai, Masahiro, 86, 99, 108, 124n24

Kawai–Pontines method, 92, 92n4, 117

Kim, D.H., 50

Kim, S., 76

Koch, C., 50, 53, 59, 67

Korobov, G., 190

Kose, M.A., 3–4

Krueger, A., 341

Kyushu Railway Company, 249*b*

L

labor force. *See* employment

Lakhia, Saloni, 227, 250

land trusts, 250–51*f*, 250–52

land value capture, 234, 237, 369

Lao People's Democratic Republic (Lao PDR)

current-account deficit in, 57–58

loans to MSMEs in, 184, 185*t*

median population age in, 283

pension system in, 298–99*b*

LCSF (Local Currency Settlement Framework), 119, 128–33, 140–41, 366

Lee, M., 253, 254

Lehman Brothers collapse (2008), 87, 95, 123

life expectancy, 282–83, 284*f*

loans

to MSMEs, 184–87, 185*f*

nonperforming, 22, 198, 205, 364

peer-to-peer, 161, 176–77, 186, 197–98, 205–6, 367

local currency bond markets

corporate, 14, 54, 74–76, 362–63

    development of, 7–8, 10, 33, 73–76, 361

    in emerging market economies, 17–19, 18n13

    internationalization of, 14, 17–18f, 17–19

    investor profile, 14, 15f

    maturity profile, 14, 16f

    pension funds and, 371

    policy timeline for, 8–9b

    private financing and, 240–42, 241t, 242f

    size of, 10, 12, 12f, 362

    volatility of yields in, 17, 17n12

Local Currency Settlement Framework (LCSF), 119, 128–33, 140–41, 366

Loretan, M., 50

Luciani, M., 54

Lyft, 339–40b

M

Ma, G., 54, 74

macroprudential measures, 19, 74, 76–77, 365

Maestas, N., 287

Malaysia. *See also* Bank Negara Malaysia

    concentration risk for, 60

    digital payments in, 167, 168f

    foreign bank presence in, 5n6

    green bonds issuance in, 264b

    loans to MSMEs in, 184, 185f

    local currency bond markets in, 14

    Local Currency Settlement Framework and, 128–29, 131, 141, 366

    median population age in, 283

    pension system in, 292–94, 296t

    sudden-stop contagion risk in, 56

    tax payment facilitation in, 343b

    trilemma perspective on, 104f

MAS. *See* Monetary Authority of Singapore

Mas-Colell, A., 68b

Masson, P., 49–50

McCauley, R., 52

McGuire, P., 52

McKinnon, R., 3

medium-size enterprises. *See* micro, small, and medium-size enterprises

Mendoza, E.G., 49n2

micro, small, and medium-size enterprises (MSMEs), 161, 183–87, 185f, 185t, 213, 367

migrant workers, 344–48, 345–47f, 350–52, 352t
Mishra, M., 188
Mizen, P., 18, 53
mobile money. *See* e-money
mobile POS payments, 166–67, 166t, 167–68f
mobile wallets. *See* e-wallets
Monetary Authority of Singapore (MAS), 75, 78, 131, 175, 205, 211
monetary policy. *See also* currencies; exchange rates; interest rates
    economic growth and, 98
    effectiveness of, 135–37, 161, 195, 367
    of Federal Reserve, 21, 94, 96, 96n9
    fintech and design of, 207–9, 215–16
    global financial cycles and, 50, 53
    macroprudential measures and, 76
    in trilemma, 94, 97–105, 100f, 103–4f
money laundering, 135, 161, 172, 190, 205
money transfers, 171
moral hazard, 197n15, 206, 240
Morgan, Peter J., 160
Morris, S., 196
MSMEs. *See* micro, small, and medium-size enterprises
Mullen, K., 287
multilateral development banks, 229, 239, 254, 265, 273, 369

N
National Bank of Cambodia (NBC), 135–36, 135n29, 174
negative interest rates, 173, 208
Nemoto, N., 206
nonperforming loans, 22, 198, 205, 364
Nor, T. Mohd, 92, 93

O
official development assistance, 234
old-age dependency ratio, 284, 285f, 370
Organisation for Economic Co-operation and Development (OECD), 293, 310, 312, 320, 322, 325, 337
original sin redux, 18–19, 24, 50, 111, 115, 363, 371

P
pandemic. *See* COVID-19 pandemic
Pan-European Personal Pension Product (PEPP), 349–50, 353

Panizza, U., 50
Park, Cyn-Young, 1, 22, 50, 52, 53, 73, 361
Park, D., 254, 305
Pasadilla, Gloria O., 281
Pasricha, G.K., 94n7
Patel, N., 77
pay-as-you-go pensions, 288, 290–91, 302
PBOC. *See* People's Bank of China
peer-to-peer (P2P) lending, 161, 176–77, 186, 197–98, 205–6, 367
pension systems, 289–353
       adequacy of, 307–10, 310nn15–16, 311t
       alternative assets and, 320–23, 321–22t, 328
       annuities and, 330–31, 331–32b
       characteristics of, 289–92, 291f
       defined benefit, 290–92, 294, 304, 308, 315n22, 320, 344
       defined contribution, 290–94, 303–8, 306b, 312, 315n22, 320, 344
       employer-sponsored, 290, 291n4, 294, 302
       ESG considerations and, 262b, 327b
       expenditures, 300–301, 300–302f
       exportability of benefits and tax issues, 350
       financial markets and, 315, 316–19b, 354
       GATS exclusion of, 353
       Global Pension Index and, 308, 309f
       infrastructure financing and, 323–25
       investment allocation in, 320–23, 321–22t
       low-interest environment and, 319–20
       Melbourne-Mercer study of, 308, 308n14, 312
       for migrant workers, 344–48, 345–47f, 350–52, 352t
       nonstandard employment and, 337–38, 343
       overview in ASEAN+3, 292–95, 293t, 295–97t, 298–99b
       pay-as-you-go, 288, 290–91, 302
       portability of, 344–45, 347–51, 348b, 349n41
       reform programs for, 304–5, 307t
       regional cooperation and, 313–14, 370–71
       restrictions on, 325–26, 326–27b, 329t
       retirement savings gap and, 302–3, 303f, 306b
       risks associated with, 330, 330n29
       supplementary schemes, 348–50
       sustainability of, 292, 307–8, 311–13, 312n17, 313t, 370–71
       technology and, 333–43, 336t, 354

People's Bank of China (PBOC)
       CBDC development and, 174, 176, 213
       CIPS established by, 129–30
       currency swaps and, 131
       devaluation of yuan by, 125–26
       digitalization of yuan by, 136–37
       as EMEAP member, 78
       Green Finance Committee, 261–62*b*
       local currency bond markets and, 75
People's Republic of China (PRC)
       alternative finance in, 176–78, 197, 205–6
       Belt and Road Initiative, 32n34, 128, 137
       concentration risk for, 60, 72
       digital currency in, 136–37, 142, 174, 368
       digital payments in, 166, 167, 168–69*f*, 181
       family support for aging populations in, 301n9
       fertility rate in, 282
       fintech adoption in, 182–83, 183*f*
       hukou system in, 348*b*
       life expectancy in, 282
       loans to MSMEs in, 184, 185*f*
       local currency bond market in, 12, 12*f*, 19
       median population age in, 283
       pension system in, 294–95, 295*t*, 300, 300*f*, 348*b*, 370
       remittances and international money transfers from, 171
       retirement savings gap in, 302–3
       sudden-stop contagion risk in, 56–57
       trilemma perspective on, 100*f*, 101–2, 104, 104*f*
PEPP (Pan-European Personal Pension Product), 349–50, 353
permissionless systems, 196, 196n12
Philippines. *See also* Bangko Sentral ng Pilipinas
       concentration risk for, 60
       current-account deficit in, 58
       digital banking in, 211
       digital currency in, 188–89
       digital payments in, 167, 168*f*
       fintech integration in, 187
       green finance in, 257–58
       loans to MSMEs in, 184, 185*t*
       Local Currency Settlement Framework and, 128–29, 141
       median population age in, 283

    pension system in, 292–94, 297t

    remittances and international money transfers from, 171

    sovereign bond issuance in, 21, 21t

    Star Toll Highway in, 248b

    sudden-stop contagion risk in, 57

    trilemma perspective on, 104f

pound sterling

    in cross-border bank liabilities, 91, 91f

    debt securities issued in, 91–92, 91f

    in foreign exchange markets, 89, 90f

    as reserve currency, 90, 90f

    for trade settlement, 88, 89f

Powell, D., 287

PPPs (public–private partnerships), 230, 252–54, 273–74, 369

Prasad, E.S., 3–4

PRC. See People's Republic of China

principal components, 55–57, 56–57f

private financing, 237–54

    credit enhancement mechanisms and, 239–40

    engagement with, 34–35

    floating-interest-rate infrastructure bonds, 243–45, 245f, 254, 272, 274, 370

    of green infrastructure projects, 231, 239, 255–56

    land trusts, 250–51f, 250–52

    local currency bond markets and, 240–42, 241t, 242f

    mechanisms of, 229, 229f

    nature of, 237–39

    as percentage of GDP, 232, 232f

    public–private partnerships, 230, 252–54, 273–74, 369

    sources of credit, 237, 238t

    spillover tax revenue and, 243–45, 245f, 246–49b, 274

    user fees, 230, 236, 243, 274

procyclicality, 191, 191n11, 198, 199

Project Bakong, 133, 135–36, 135n28, 174

prudent person rule, 326–27b

P2P lending. See peer-to-peer lending

public debt, 233, 235–36, 265–66, 266f, 268

public–private partnerships (PPPs), 230, 252–54, 273–74, 369

Q

Qian, X., 50, 53, 55

Qualified ASEAN Banks (QABs), 131–32, 132n27, 209, 211, 377

R

Rajan, Ramkishen S., 1, 50, 52, 73, 361
regional currencies, 105–39. *See also specific currencies*
    as anchor currencies, 117–18, 118*f*, 125
    central bank digital currencies and, 133–34*t*, 133–42
    for cross-border financial transactions, 111–17, 112–14*f*, 116*f*
    for debt securities, 113–17, 114*f*, 116*f*
    direct exchange markets for, 32n34, 129–31
    in foreign exchange markets, 105–6, 106*f*
    internationalization of, 119–31, 127*b*
    Local Currency Settlement Framework, 119, 128–33, 140–41, 366
    policy recommendations for, 132–33
    for trade invoicing, 25, 106–8, 107*f*, 120, 121*f*, 124–25, 125*f*
    for trade settlement, 105–10, 106–7*f*, 109*f*, 120, 121*f*, 123–25,
        124–25*f*
regional financial cooperation, 361–78
    AMRO and, 1, 30, 361, 378
    bigtech firms and, 212
    CBDCs and, 368–69
    CMIM and, 1, 30, 361
    concentration risks and, 364–65
    in cross-border banking, 211, 377–78
    on exchange rates, 366
    fintech and, 23, 34, 209–14, 367–69
    infrastructure investment and, 272–73, 275
    international comparisons, 371–74, 373*f*
    in local currency bond markets, 73, 74
    pension systems and, 313–14, 370–71
    for reducing dollar dependence, 365–67
    on regulation, 22, 364, 377, 378
    repo markets and, 74–76, 363
    reserve accumulation and, 29–32
    on sustainable infrastructure investment, 369–70
    trilemma of financial stability and, 375–76, 376*f*
regional systemically important banks (R-SIBs), 77–78, 364, 368
regulation. *See* financial regulation
Reinhart, C., 52
remittances, 171, 188, 190, 202
Remolona, Eli, 49, 50, 52–55, 59, 64, 67, 74
renewable energy, 258, 267–68, 370
repo markets, 74–76, 363

Republic of Korea (ROK). *See also* Bank of Korea; won
     alternative finance in, 176
     concentration risk for, 60, 72
     currency shares in trade with partners, 150–51*f*
     digital payments in, 180
     fertility rate in, 282
     green finance in, 258
     levy on non-core foreign currency liabilities in, 365
     loans to MSMEs in, 184, 185*f*
     local currency bond markets in, 14, 19
     median population age in, 283
     pension system in, 262*b*, 294, 296*t*, 300, 300*f*, 370
     sudden-stop contagion risk in, 56–57
     trilemma perspective on, 101, 102, 104*f*
Restrepo, P., 286–87
retirement savings, 302–3, 303*f*, 306*b*. *See also* pension systems
Rey, H., 50, 53
risk management, 3, 204, 261*b*
Rodriguez, C., 116
ROK. *See* Republic of Korea
Rose, A.K., 49
R-SIBs (regional systemically important banks), 77–78, 364, 368

S
safety nets, 2, 7, 31–33, 201, 361–62, 371–78
savings, 288, 302–3, 303*f*, 306*b*
Schoenholtz, K., 54
Schularick, M., 52
self-employment, 337–38, 340–41
Seltzer, J., 301n9
Shapley values
     advantages of, 51, 65–67, 77–78
     calculation of, 67–69, 68*b*, 69*f*, 78, 84–85
     global banking network and, 70–73, 71–72*f*, 71*t*
     mathematical properties of, 68*b*
Shaw, E., 3
Shim, I., 64
Shin, H.S., 19, 53, 196
Shin, K., 22, 53
SIFIs. *See* systemically important financial institutions
Silva, A.C., 241
Singapore. *See also* Monetary Authority of Singapore

     as banking center, 55, 60, 63–65
     Central Provident Fund, 322, 322n24, 331–32b, 352
     digital banking in, 211
     digital payments in, 167, 168f, 180, 202
     fertility rate in, 282
     green bonds issuance in, 264b
     life expectancy in, 282
     loans to MSMEs in, 184, 185t
     median population age in, 283
     pension system in, 292–94, 292n6, 297t, 370
     regional cooperation with Canada, 214
     trilemma perspective on, 102, 104f
slow-burn contagion
     in Asian financial crisis, 50, 53
     characteristics of, 49
     common lender channel of, 50–51, 59, 70, 73
     concentration risk of, 50–51, 59–65, 74, 77–78, 364–65
     literature review, 52–54
     policy recommendations, 73–74, 364–65
small enterprises. *See* micro, small, and medium-size enterprises
social bonds, 258, 269–71, 270f, 273
social security systems
     bilateral agreements, 350–53, 352n42, 371
     financial markets and, 315
     independent worker status and, 341
     portability of, 344–45, 347, 350–51
     self-employed persons and, 338
     statutory provisions of, 298–99b
     tax payment facilitation and, 343b
     technology and, 333–35, 336t
South Korea. *See* Republic of Korea
sovereign bonds, 7–8, 21, 21t, 141, 240, 320
sovereign debt crisis, 10, 53, 59, 61, 66, 372
spillover tax revenue, 243–45, 245f, 246–49b, 274
Star Toll Highway, 248b
Stein, J., 27n24
Stiglitz, J., 3
Storey, D., 206
sudden-stop contagion
     in Asian financial crisis, 54
     common regional factors and, 50, 53, 55–57
     defined, 49, 49n2, 54

in emerging market economies, 33

literature review, 52

risk assessment for, 54–58

Susantono, B., 254

Sussangkarn, C., 132

sustainability bonds, 258, 269, 270*f*, 327*b*

Sustainable Development Goals (UN), 179, 227, 229, 255

sustainable infrastructure investment, 229, 269, 272–73, 324–25, 369–70

systemically important financial institutions (SIFIs), 54, 191, 194, 199, 199n17, 364–65

T

Taipei,China, in global banking network, 66–68, 66*t*, 70, 71*f*, 71*t*

Tang, C., 55, 67

taper tantrum (2013), 2, 29, 34, 96, 118

Tarashev, N., 68*b*

Taylor, A.D., 3–4

Taylor, A.M., 52

technology

artificial intelligence, 23, 162

automation, 287

big data, 162, 204, 212–13, 334

bigtech. *See* bigtech firms

blockchain, 23, 174, 213, 214, 369

cloud computing, 23, 193

distributed ledger, 135–38, 136n30, 163, 172–75, 186, 195–97, 212–14

employment effects, 336

financial. *See* financial technology

pension systems and, 333–43, 336*t*, 354

regulatory compliance and, 335

risks associated with, 335

social protection and, 337–38

terrorism financing, 135, 161, 172–73, 203, 216, 368

Thailand. *See also* baht; Bank of Thailand

concentration risk for, 60

currency shares in trade with partners, 152–53*f*

digital payments in, 167, 168*f*, 181, 186

fertility rate in, 282

loans to MSMEs in, 184, 185*f*, 185*t*

local currency bond markets in, 14

Local Currency Settlement Framework and, 128–29, 141, 366

        median population age in, 283
        pension system in, 293, 294, 297t, 370
        sudden-stop contagion risk in, 56
        trilemma perspective on, 104f
Tian, M., 50, 52, 67
Tian, S., 254
Tovar, C.E., 92, 93
trade finance, 213
trade invoicing
        dollar dominance in, 25, 27f, 88, 89f
        regional currencies, 25, 106–8, 107f, 120, 121f, 124–25, 125f
trade settlement
        dollar dominance in, 88, 89f, 108–10
        regional currencies for, 105–10, 106–7f, 109f, 120, 121f, 123–25,
                124–25f
transition bonds, 257–58
trilemma of financial stability, 375–76, 376f
trilemma of international finance, 97–105
        constraints of, 94
        corner solutions, 98, 102, 105
        indexes for, 99–101, 100f
        overview, 97–99, 98f
        triangle configurations, 101–5, 103–4f
Tsatsaronis, K., 68b

U
Uber, 339–40b
unbanked/underbanked groups, 135, 185–86, 185n9, 186f, 215
United Kingdom. *See also* pound sterling
        alternative finance in, 205
        in global banking network, 66–67, 66t, 71–72f, 71t, 72–73
        international bank claims, 61–65
        pension system in, 325
        platform drivers in, 340b
        worker status as defined in, 342
United Nations (UN)
        Framework Convention on Climate Change, 255–56
        Sustainable Development Goals, 179, 227, 229, 255
        World Population Highlights Report, 300–301
United Nations Environment Programme (UNEP), 257–65, 259–60t,
                261–62b, 264b

United States. *See also* Federal Reserve
    alternative finance in, 205
    family support for aging populations in, 301n9
    GDP and trade shares, 96, 96n10, 97f
    in global banking network, 66–67, 66t, 70–73, 71–72f, 71t
    international bank claims, 61–65
    local currency bond market in, 12, 12f
    pension system in, 325
    taper tantrum (2013), 2, 29, 34, 96, 118
user fees, 230, 236, 243, 274

V
Vegh, C.A., 52
Veredas, D., 54
Viet Nam
    concentration risk for, 60
    digital payments in, 167, 168f
    fintech adoption in, 182–83, 183f
    pension system in, 298–99b
    remittances and international money transfers from, 171
    sudden-stop contagion risk in, 57
Volz, U., 258, 261b

W
Warnock, F., 53
wealth distribution, 182–84
WEF (World Economic Forum), 302–3
Whinston, M.D., 68b
won, 105–6, 108, 110, 115
workers. *See* employment
World Bank
    Bali Fintech Agenda supported by, 199
    on cybersecurity risks, 190
    on Debt Service Suspension Initiative, 268–69
    financial inclusion as defined by, 179
    fintech risk assessment by, 210
    Global Findex Database, 180
    infrastructure investment and, 265
    on private financing, 256
World Economic Forum (WEF), 302–3
World Trade Organization (WTO), 353

Wu, E., 50, 52
Wyplosz, C., 49

Y
Yap, Josef T., 227
Yellen, M., 50, 52, 67
yen
        as anchor currency, 117–18, 118*f*
        in COVID-19 pandemic, 86
        in cross-border bank liabilities, 91, 91*f*, 111–12, 112–13*f*, 120
        debt securities issued in, 91, 91*f*, 115
        direct exchange markets for, 32n34, 130–31
        in foreign exchange markets, 89, 90*f*, 105
        international bank claims and, 65
        internationalization initiatives, 119–21, 128, 130–31
        as reserve currency, 90, 90*f*, 120
        for trade invoicing, 120, 121*f*
        for trade settlement, 88, 89*f*, 106, 110, 120, 121*f*
Yi Gang, 174
Yilmaz, K., 54
Yoshino, Naoyuki, 227, 250
yuan
        as anchor currency, 117–18, 118*f*, 125
        debt securities issued in, 91*f*, 92
        digitalization of, 136–37, 142
        direct exchange markets for, 129–30
        in foreign exchange markets, 89, 90*f*, 105
        internationalization initiatives, 123–26, 123n21, 128–30, 365n7
        as reserve currency, 90, 90*f*
        for trade invoicing, 124–25, 125*f*
        for trade settlement, 106, 108, 110, 123–25, 124–25*f*

www.ingramcontent.com/pod-product-compliance
Lightning Source LLC
Chambersburg PA
CBHW042312210326
41598CB00042B/7369